THE REFORM OF CLASS AND REPRESENTATIVE ACTIONS IN EUROPEAN LEGAL SYSTEMS

This book examines the principal trends and policy goals relating to collective redress mechanisms in Europe. It identifies three principal areas in which procedures and debates have emerged: within consumer protection and competition law, and from some national court systems. It identifies differing national models of public and private enforcement in consumer protection law in the Member States, and the search for more efficient and inclusive procedures that would deliver increased access to justice and enhanced compliance with desired standards (arguably through deterrence).

A sequence of case studies illustrates the pros and cons of differing models. Lessons are also drawn from the experience of class actions in the USA over the transactional costs of private law mechanisms and adverse economic consequences.

The various policy strands are unravelled and prioritised, and options for the future are recommended. The American 'private enforcement' model is contrasted with the more prevalent European public and mediated enforcement tradition. New developments involving Ombudsmen and oversight of compensation by public enforcement bodies are identified, and underlying theories of restorative justice and responsive regulation discussed. Public, private, formal, informal, ADR and voluntary methodologies are evaluated against criteria, and it is concluded that the optimal options for collective redress in Europe involve a combination of approaches, with priority given to public and voluntary solutions over private court-based mechanisms.

Volume 8: Studies of the Oxford Institute
of European and Comparative Law

Studies of the Oxford Institute of European and
Comparative Law

Editor
Professor Stefan Vogenauer

Board of Advisory Editors
Professor Mark Freedland, FBA
Professor Stephen Weatherill
Professor Derrick Wyatt, QC

The Reform of Class and Representative Actions in European Legal Systems

A New Framework for Collective Redress in Europe

Christopher Hodges

MA (Oxon), PhD (Lond), FSALS

Head of the CMS Research Programme on
Civil Justice Systems,
Centre for Socio-Legal Studies,
University of Oxford

Solicitor of the Supreme Courts of England and Wales,
and of Hong Kong

·H A R T·
PUBLISHING

OXFORD AND PORTLAND, OREGON
2008

Published in North America (US and Canada) by
Hart Publishing
c/o International Specialized Book Services
920 NE 58th Avenue, Suite 300
Portland, OR 97213-3786
USA
Tel: +1 503 287 3093 or toll-free: (1) 800 944 6190
Fax: +1 503 280 8832
E-mail: orders@isbs.com
Web Site: www.isbs.com

Hart Publishing Ltd, Worcester Place, Oxford, OX1 2JW
Telephone: +44 (0)1865 517530 Fax: +44 (0) 1865 510710
E-mail: mail@hartpub.co.uk
Website: http://www.hartpub.co.uk

British Library Cataloguing in Publication Data
Data Available

ISBN: 978-1-84113-902-9

Typeset by Compuscript Ltd
Printed and bound in Great Britain by
TJ International Ltd, Padstow, Cornwall

Acknowledgements

Many people have contributed to what is still a developing understanding of the phenomenon of collective redress in Europe. Most recently, a large number of contributors and participants have taken part in an ongoing project on 'the globalisation of class actions' led by Professor Deborah Hensler of Stanford Law School and me, and the conference on that topic in Oxford on 12–14 December 2007. I am very indebted to the 30 or so scholars who contributed national reports to that project, which can be viewed at <http://globalclassaction.stanford.edu> accessed 5 June 2008. To Deborah Hensler I owe a huge personal debt, not least for involving me in such an exciting project and sharing her enormous knowledge and wisdom, but also for our thoroughly enjoyable collaboration. She also kindly agreed that, notwithstanding the written output that we plan for the globalisation project, I could go ahead and publish a monograph on the developing situation in Europe in parallel with our extended and ongoing work on the global situation. I have consciously tried to avoid territory that we plan to include in our global work.

Warm thanks are also owed to numerous colleagues at the Centre for Socio-Legal Studies. I single out for particular thanks Dr Magdalena Tulibacka, my ever patient and supportive colleague, who has researched various aspects and critically analysed all output. Professor Denis Galligan, Director of the Centre for Socio-Legal Studies, has advised and encouraged our research on civil justice systems throughout the past four years. I must also thank the other members of the Academic Advisory Board that oversees our research for their support and encouragement: Sir Ross Cranston, Professor Mark Mildred and Professor Steven Weatherill.

Professor Stefan Vogenauer, Director of our sister Institute for European and Comparative Law at Oxford, has also been an indefatigable collaborator on a related project on European civil justice and contract law, and kindly agreed to publish this volume in the Institute's research series.

I would also like to thank various officials, particularly in the European Commission, the Ministry of Justice and Department for Business, Enterprise and Regulatory Reform in London, and various colleagues from the consumer, business and legal worlds for verifying facts and for a series of stimulating discussions, during which ideas about the way forward have been tested and evolved. I spare their blushes by not naming names here, although they are acknowledged in footnotes where relevant, but am most grateful to them all. This has been a fascinating voyage of discovery, with a sound course for the future hopefully now successfully charted.

No research would be possible without funding, and thanks go to those who have sponsored our research programme on civil justice systems at the Centre, notably Malcolm Carlisle OBE and colleagues at the European Justice Forum, Linda Willett and colleagues at Bristol-Myers Squibb Inc, and David Marks and colleagues at CMS Cameron McKenna. I particularly thank them for scrupulously observing arm's length relationships in relation to all aspects of our research, notably as to its scope, performance and conclusions, such that, as should go without saying, but I wish to state clearly, the work, findings and views presented are mine alone.

I would also like to thank Richard Hart for agreeing to publish this book particularly quickly and his very efficient team for their expert and professional support.

Finally, I owe a huge debt to my wife Fiona for putting up with a preoccupied and distracted spouse during the gestation of yet another book. I dedicate this book to the citizens of Europe.

Oxford
June 2008

Contents

TABLES

FIGURES

CASE STUDIES

Glossary

ADR	Alternative dispute resolution, i.e. alternative to resolution through judgment in the public courts.
BEUC	The European association of consumers' associations.
BUSINESSEUROPE	The Confederation of European Employers' associations.
CA	Consumer association.
CAT	Competition Appeal Tribunal.
CFA	Conditional fee arrangement.
Class action	A procedure for combination of multiple individual claims in which a single claim stands as representative of the class, the typical example being under Rule 23 of the US Federal Rules of Procedure.
Collective action	A procedure for resolution of multiple individual claims on a collective basis.
Community law	The law of the EU.
CPC Regulation	Regulation (EC) 2006/2004 on consumer protection cooperation.
CPR	Civil Procedure Rules of England and Wales.
DECO	The consumers' association of Portugal.
DG COMP	The Directorate-General for Competition of the European Commission.
DG SANCO	The Directorate-General for Health and Consumer Affairs of the European Commission.
ECJ	European Court of Justice.
European Commission	The Commission of the EU.
ECHR	European Convention on Human Rights.
EU	European Union.
FOS	Financial Ombudsman Service.
FSA	Financial Services Authority.
FS&MA	Financial Services and Markets Act 2000.
GAR	Guaranteed annuity rates.
Globalisation Project	The project on globalisation of class actions led by Professor Deborah Hensler of Stanford Law School and Dr Christopher Hodges of the Centre for Socio-Legal Studies, University of Oxford, see <http://globalclassaction.stanford.edu> accessed 5 June 2008.

GLO	Group Litigation Order, as defined in the Civil Procedure Rules of England and Wales.
HSE	Health and Safety Executive.
KapMuG	*KapitalanlegerMusterverfahrensGesetz*, the German Capital Investors' Model Proceeding Law.
KVI	*Verein für Konsumenteninformationen*, The Austrian consumers' association.
Member State	A Member State of the EU.
MHRA	Medicines and Healthcare products Regulatory Agency.
NCA	National competent authority.
NGO	A non-governmental organisation.
OECD	Organisation for Economic Co-operation and Development.
OFT	The UK Office of Fair Trading.
Opt-in	The approach in a multi-party action in which all individual claimants have to take a positive step in order to participate.
Opt-out	The approach in a multi-party action in which all individual claimants who fall within the definition of the class will be deemed to be bound by the result of the representative case(s) without being required to take any positive step, save that any individual may leave the class and not be bound if she or he takes a positive step to indicate this.
Representative action	A procedure for combination of multiple individual claims in which a single claim or entity represents the group. A US class action and a claim brought by a European representative organisation are both examples, albeit different ones.
SME	Small and medium-sized enterprise, defined in Commission Recommendation 2003/361/EC of 6 May 2003 as having between 50 and 249 employees.
TSD	Trading standards department of a local authority.
USA	United States of America.
VZBV	*Verbraucherzentrale Bundesverbands*, the German national consumers' association.
Which?	The consumers' association of the UK.

Table of Cases

EUROPEAN CASES (ECJ AND ECHR)

NATIONAL CASES

Australia

Austria

Belgium

France

Germany

Netherlands

Portugal

Spain

United Kingdom

United States

Table of Legislation

NATIONAL LEGISLATION

Australia

Austria

Germany

Hungary

Israel

Italy

Netherlands

Norway

Poland

Portugal

Slovakia

Slovenia

Spain

Sweden

UK (England and Wales)

United States

1

Introduction

THIS BOOK EXAMINES the phenomenon of collective mechanisms for redress in Europe. Collective redress is currently a hot topic. However, rather too many questions arise in the current debate. How much change is enough or too much? How do you avoid producing excessive litigation? Where does the balance lie between providing compensation for legitimate claims and preventing unmeritorious claims? If the system encourages the vast majority of claims to be settled, how do you avoid the 'blackmail effect' that it will be cheaper for defendants to settle unmeritorious claims than fight them? How do you identify which individual claims are more or less meritorious in a group? How do you avoid excessive transactional costs? How do you maintain a balance without undermining respect for the rule of law?

How do you fill a possible gap in delivery of regulation and compensation where multiple claimants can suffer small levels of loss, but infringers may escape with large illicit gains, thereby undermining economic performance and confidence in the rule of law? If this situation exists to a significant degree, how can more compensation be delivered (presumably through an increase in litigation) without encouraging excessive undesirable consequences? Or at what point should people not expect compensation as long as they are assured that illicit gains have been removed from crooks and they have been punished and others deterred?

The key question that is facing European legislators is how to enable collective redress without producing the undesirable consequences that are associated with the most obvious historical model, namely the US class action. The issue is complicated by the fact that discussion of collective redress has evolved beyond its traditional scope of provision of compensation and taken on aspects of regulatory enforcement and control of behaviour. The literature in the United States is considerable, although it is not widely understood that the law plays a function there, in combining compensatory goals with 'private enforcement', which is fundamentally different from that which it performs in Europe. The growing European literature on collective redress is largely dominated by doctrinal or even political analyses, and can be confusing.

Much analysis of collective redress is bound by assumptions that what is being considered is a US-style court-based mechanism. Some recent debate has, in contrast, adopted a much wider scope. The wider perspective is necessary because it is realised that the subject matter in fact encompasses litigation, compensation, regulation, enforcement, behaviour modification, behavioural psychology and several substantive areas of both public and private law. This book is an initial attempt to grapple with this extremely wide context. It should immediately be said that the book does not aim to be anything like comprehensive in addressing the relevant areas. Instead, it attempts to define and analyse the scope of the areas that deserve consideration in the current debate in order to identify areas for further more detailed research, but also to assist those who may be tempted to take political or policy decisions within the near future.

It is not intended that this work should be an encyclopaedia or exhaustive commentary on all of the many mechanisms and rules that might provide collective redress. Instead, it is concerned with identification of the major trends and developments, including recent developments and likely future evolution. To this end, key points are illustrated by reference to particular examples taken from national or Community instruments, but this is done on a deliberately selective basis so as to illustrate the issues.

Terminology in relation to aggregated litigation and redress can be confusing. What is meant by the terms 'class action', 'collective action' and 'representative action'? Such a dry approach tends to obscure the real point—what are the aims and objectives of these procedures and are they achieved? It is those questions with which this book is primarily concerned. It is merely useful to bear in mind that there are two broad mechanistic models for court-based aggregated procedures, one in which a single claim represents a group of others, and a second in which a number of individual claims are brought and grouped together because of their similarity. The boundaries between these two approaches are in practice somewhat blurred and, as will be seen below, there are several variations, which it can be challenging to place within simple categorisations.

Broadly speaking, leading examples of the former representative mechanism are, first, the US class action (one individual claim is asserted to represent a class of others, whose owners are bound by the result of the single claim unless they opt-out of the class and procedure) and, secondly, the European collective procedure in which a consumer association brings a claim in defence of general consumer interests, or the interests of a defined group of consumers who have opted-in to the procedure and are bound by it. The leading example of the second type of procedure is the English Group Litigation Order, in which a number of similar individual claims are mandatorily grouped together by the Court for the purpose of orderly management in their processing, and the result will bind all in the group (but in practice the court might not permit other claims to proceed if they are not brought so as to be able to be processed within the group). However, the latter procedure will usually involve selection of one or some test or lead cases, which are representative of the group.

Different terminology has been applied to these mechanisms in inconsistent ways. For present purposes, and without wishing to engage in extended but ultimately sterile debate, it might be said that the US class action and the European consumer association action are essentially 'representative' mechanisms, although they are fundamentally different. All of these mechanisms involve a class or group of claimants, but the term 'class action' is best used to refer to its most well-known historical manifestation, the US class action—this is particularly so since that procedure should not be confused with the US Multi District Litigation procedure, which is more akin to the English GLO.

The debate in this area in Europe has mostly involved the term 'collective action' and, although that term has been primarily applied to the consumer association type of procedure, it is proposed here to adopt this term as a generic one covering *all* aggregated types of mechanisms. There is another reason for this. The European debate has also begun to use the term 'collective redress'. That term encompasses wider mechanisms than court-based aggregation procedures, and includes other means of delivering redress, such as through the involvement of public authorities, no-fault compensation schemes, business schemes and codes of conduct, mediation and other forms of alternative dispute resolution and voluntary action. The concept of collective redress is ultimately concerned more with outcomes than mechanisms, although it necessarily takes as wide a view of mechanisms as possible.

It is taken as axiomatic that *redress* is a worthy goal. Obtaining redress encompasses broad ideas of setting things right. This may involve preventing problems that have arisen in the past from continuing, and restoring things to where they should be, but also trying to make sure that in future things go right and do not go wrong again. The collective aspect arises because what is being dealt with are things that affect many people, rather than a few individuals. The primary aim of this book is to work out what works best in delivering collective redress. In order to achieve this, it may be necessary to start by looking at what mechanisms exist (and there is a bewildering explosion of experimental, innovative mechanisms to look at), but the more important inquiry is to examine what types of problem arise and what approaches deliver the best results in solving them.

This task is a big challenge. It needs a great deal of information and assimilation of several different streams of analysis, which are rarely looked at together. The leading streams include legal philosophy (what mechanisms are morally appropriate, such as in observing fundamental rights, and deliver the most just result), law and economics (which procedures are the most efficient, or best deliver deterrence), psychology (which mechanisms best promote behavioural compliance), logic (which procedures work satisfactorily) and socio-legal studies (which mechanisms in practice work best and deliver the best outcomes). It may be too ambitious to attempt to combine this heady mixture of approaches, expertise and knowledge, but consideration of the literature shows that many of these individual disciplines have developed silos of approaches that are disconnected from reality, and the real answers for real life can only be found by attempting to take a holistic overview. It should immediately be said that this book is only a first, and far from complete, attempt to take such an overview. However, the analysis undertaken here shows at least that the attempt is worth undertaking, since it can point to some conclusions that should be useful in real life in delivering more and better collective redress, and therefore being worthy of underpinning ongoing policy decisions.

The book, therefore, essentially comprises three parts. The first part, chapters two to four, examines the factual position of the state of development of collective redress mechanisms. It gives an indication of the history of the introduction of mechanisms at national and European level, and notes the divergent models, some relating to general court rules and others to specific sectoral instruments. It reveals an almost bewildering flowering of different but interesting approaches. However, the development of concern over collective redress at European level in relation to competition and consumer protection emerges as an important lever for change.

Three phases are identifiable in the development of collective actions in Europe. The first phase was the spread of national legislation to seek *injunctive* relief from courts in order to defend general consumer interests by means of a single collective procedure, in which the right of action was often that of a consumer organisation. This approach began in the 1960s and coincided with the rise of Western consumerism. The process was significantly enhanced and solidified by the advent of a series of European measures aimed at harmonising consumer protection law, which provided for consumer organisations to adopt the mechanism of seeking collective injunctive relief as one means of enforcement of the substantive rules. This solidification could not have taken place without the structure, goals and mechanisms of the EU. This EU-inspired momentum gathered particular pace during the 1990s, and led to pressure for phase three.

The second phase started from the mid-1980s, and is possibly still continuing. This phase comprised the development in some jurisdictions of court rules for the management of multiple similar cases. The trigger for this development was that the courts in some Member States began to be confronted by multiple similar cases and they simply needed to develop a mechanism in order to be able to process the cases efficiently without becoming swamped by them. The development of court rules was formally unconnected with phase one, but the coincidental occurrence of both phenomena was linked, in that the emergence of mass similar individual claims would clearly not have occurred in the absence of mass production and consumerism. The rules in some of the jurisdictions are horizontal (ie apply to any type of claim, such as the English GLO, the Swedish Class Action law and Dutch settlement law), whereas others are specific to particular sectors (such as capital investors in Germany). However, all of these mechanisms apply generally to any type of legal relief, and therefore permit collective damages claims. Further, all of these mechanisms are essentially of the opt-in type. This development has as yet only occurred in a small number of jurisdictions, but has set the scene for the third phase.

The third phase is currently in progress and its eventual outcome is unresolved. This is the debate over the wider introduction of collective actions for *damages* in all European jurisdictions, particularly led by EU measures, on a representative or collective basis. After simmering for some years in the consumer protection area, it has emerged from 2005 with particular heat in relation to enforcement of EU competition law.

The three types of mechanisms identified here will be examined in greater detail. Before proceeding further, however, one should note that we are not here concerned with the standard procedural techniques of joinder of parties to an existing suit, or aggregation or consolidation by the court of identical or similar individual actions. These traditional mechanisms are widespread and unremarkable, and will not be analysed further here. The traditional principle that a person may bring an individual suit based on express assignment (or, in some states, authorisation[1]) of a right of action by another is also universal and not analysed further. However, this right of assignment does play a significant part in the story, since we are essentially concerned here with the ability of a party to bring an action on behalf of others without express assignment, or at least with less formality than is traditional. As will be discussed, the traditional approach to rights, expressed in France as *nul ne plaid par procureur*,[2] is at the heart of the debate of whether considerations of efficiency may overcome a Kantian system based on the supremacy and inalienability of individual rights.

A considerable amount of comparative analysis can be undertaken on the technical aspects of the national laws on collective redress. It is not proposed, however, to undertake such analysis in this work, but to do so in the context of the output of the Globalisation Project.[3] Instead, we continue on a path of examining the more fundamental European trends and policies.

The second section of the book, chapters five to seven, analyses the issues that have arisen in the European debate, the policy rationales and goals of the main types of mechanisms or proposals, and the strength of the evidence and arguments for each. It notes the emergence of goals as diverse

---

[1] For example, as in Belgium: see T Bourgoignie, D Trubek, L Trubek and D Stingl, 'Consumer Law, Common Markets and Federalism in Europe and the United States' in M Cappelletti, M Seccombe and J Weiler (eds), *Integration Through Law, Europe and American Federal Experience* (Berlin, Walter de Gruiter, 1987) vol 3.

[2] See ch 5.

[3] See glossary.

as encouragement of business compliance with regulatory requirements, maintenance of an orderly and level market, behaviour modification and delivery of effective compensation. It continues by considering the adverse effects that are associated with class or collective actions, notably capture by intermediaries in pursuit of personal rent maximisation and the debate on how these might be avoided. This leads to a summary of the challenges that are faced in designing balanced mechanisms that provide effective regulation and compensation. There is an attempt to summarise some of the important theories and findings from scholarship in areas that are, as said above, not always brought together in discussing collective redress, notably theory and policy on economics, regulation and enforcement, behavioural psychology, sentencing and dispute resolution.

In the final section, chapters 8 to 10 outline the policy choices that need to be made, and analyses the range of alternative options that have been put forward as solutions. A series of policy benchmarks are put forward against which mechanisms for delivering collective redress can be measured, and an evaluation is then undertaken in which the broad differing mechanisms are applied against such criteria. The analysis concludes with a proposed approach that offers a principled policy towards regulation and compensation in a modern industrial-consumer state. The proposed solution constitutes an integral approach to dispute resolution and regulatory enforcement, combining both public and private mechanisms, in a 'real world' context.

The book attempts to go beyond theoretical approaches and ask the simple pragmatic socio-legal question: which mechanisms work best? Given that many mechanisms are relatively new, it is too early to answer this question with empirical data. However, it is becoming clear that it is possible to give an answer based on an overview of theory and policy of both regulation and compensation, plus an analysis of what has happened in practice in the existing mechanisms. Accordingly, an important part of this book is the series of case studies of significant cases. The case studies are far from comprehensive, but have been selected to illustrate the issues that arise and some of the different mechanisms that have so far been applied, so as to illuminate the relative effectiveness of different approaches and what problems remain with them. Importantly, it is possible from the case studies to make some general evaluation of outcomes. It will be seen that the experience of certain jurisdictions has been evolving towards ways in which the compensatory and behavioural compliance goals can be combined in new and efficient ways, avoiding the undesired consequences. These new holistic approaches are happily underpinned by developments in theoretical scholarship. The result of the analysis set out in this book is that Europe may be able to introduce a new and attractive approach towards collective redress, which builds on previous knowledge by fusing different approaches and provides benefits to behaviour, consumers, competitors, business and the economy, without the harmful risks.

The primary purposes of scholarly endeavour are to analyse and illuminate. It is inherent in objective analysis of the evidence that one may challenge previously received opinion. I suspect that some aspects of this work may do so. However, in analysing the policy options in relation to collective redress, I have been at pains to go beyond criticism and analysis and to identify ways forward that offer sensible solutions. I hope that the findings of this endeavour may be useful for the 500 million citizens of Europe in their endeavours not only to find effective and speedy redress, but also to live and work together in greater harmony and to succeed economically.

2

Consumer Collective Redress Mechanisms

INITIAL CONSUMERIST MODELS

M ECHANISMS FOR COLLECTIVE redress spread quickly across many continental European Member States from the 1960s, as part of the rise in importance of consumer rights and protection.[1] The phenomenon started with mechanisms to protect general consumer interests, often as an adjunct to enforcement of the new national consumer protection legislation.[2] The available remedies would typically be limited to orders related to the defendant's conduct, such as injunctive relief, rather than monetary claims.[3] An injunction might be granted against traders for allegedly breaching consumer protection, fair trading, environmental or competition laws.[4]

It is clear that, although there was a general trend over the 30 years from the 1960s to the 1990s, the individual national mechanisms could differ considerably. It is, indeed, somewhat difficult to identify and generalise about the original national mechanisms.[5] This is because the national systems have both developed over time, and have now been overlaid by various EU mechanisms.

---

[1] T Bourgoignie, D Trubek, L Trubek and D Stingl, 'Consumer Law, Common Markets and Federalism in Europe and the United States' in M Cappelletti, M Seccombe and J Weiler (eds), *Integration Through Law, Europe and American Federal Experience* (Berlin, Walter de Gruiter, 1987) vol 3; G Woodroffe, *Consumer Law in the EEC* (London, Sweet & Maxwell, 1984); K Mortelmans and S Watson, 'The Notion of Consumer in Community Law: A Lottery?' in J Lonbay, *Enhancing the Legal Position of the European Consumer* (London, British Institute of International and Comparative Law, 1996); and G Howells and S Weatherill, *Consumer Protection Law* (2nd edn, Aldershot, Ashgate, 2005).

[2] The Commission's Green Paper: Access of Consumers to Justice and the Settlement of Consumer Disputes in the Single Market COM(93) 576, 16 November 1993. For the international picture, see: OECD, 'Background Report: OECD Workshop on Consumer Dispute Resolution and Redress in the Global Marketplace, 19–20 April 2005, Washington, DC' (Paris, 2005) 31.

[3] See: OECD, 'Background Report: OECD Workshop on Consumer Dispute Resolution and Redress in the Global Marketplace, 19–20 April 2005, Washington, DC' (Paris, 2005) 31.

[4] In the United Kingdom, see the Enterprise Act 2002.

[5] For sources, see National Reports in the Stanford-Oxford Global Class Actions Project— <http://globalclassaction.stanford.edu>; the 'Europa' website—'Consumer Scene Country by Country' <http://ec.europa.eu/consumers/strategy/scene_en.htm>; the Consumer Law Compendium—<http://ec.europa.eu/consumers/cons_int/safe_shop/acquis/comp_analysis_en.pdf>; and the Leuven Study—<http://ec.europa.eu/consumers/redress/reports_studies/comparative_ report_en.pdf>, all accessed 5 June 2008.

It is a mistake to imagine that the EU measures, notably Directive 98/27 on injunctions,[6] harmonise much of the pre-existing national collective mechanisms. It may even be said that the effect of that Directive is to obscure rather than harmonise or simplify the overall position. It can, however, be said that a number of different models developed at national level, and these will be examined below.

For present purposes, there are three important observations: that the Western European nations introduced instruments for the collective redress of consumer protection law; that these measures all involved seeking injunctive relief from the courts (and not damages); and that they often (but not in all Member States) permitted consumer organisations to institute such collective actions on behalf of all consumers. The general position across the EU Member States as it currently stands is summarised in Table 1.

Table 1—National Laws for Collective Consumer Protection

Country	Representative Action Involving a Consumer Association	General Class Action for Damages
Austria	Collective actions can be brought only by organisations, not by individuals or a group of consumers. Consumer organisations (the Consumer Protection Organisation VKI) may bring injunction actions, test cases of group actions, funded by the Federal Ministry of Social Affairs and Consumer Protection. Draft law 2008.	
Belgium	1991 Act. Consumer Ombudsman can bring injunction actions in the name of consumers.	
Bulgaria	Law on Consumer Protection of 2005. Consumer organisation can bring: a) injunction action to protect collective consumer interests; b) compensation action to protect collective consumer interests; c) compensation action in the name of a group of identified consumers, who must be identified and mandated in writing by at least two consumers.	

(continued)

---

[6] Discussed at ch 4 below.

Table 1—(continued)

Country	Representative Action Involving a Consumer Association	General Class Action for Damages
Cyprus	98/27. Injunction actions by consumer associations to protect interests of consumers, not damages actions. No limitation to collective interest—thus individual interests can also be protected.	
Czech Republic	1992. Injunctive actions by consumer organisations to protect collective interests of consumers, no damages actions.	
Denmark	Injunctive actions, no damage actions.	2008—class actions allowed for Consumer Ombudsman.
Estonia	Consumer Protection Act, in force since 2004. Association can bring injunction action to protect collective interests of consumers. Consumer Protection Board may represent consumer(s) in court actions with their consent.	Joint claim.
Finland	1978 Consumer Law Act—Consumer Ombudsman can initiate action before Market Court. If he or she refuses, consumer association may bring action.	2007—Consumer Ombudsman.
France	1973 (1988, 2001), 1992, 2004.	2008?
Germany	Injunction actions by consumer organisations.	2005 Investors.
Greece	1994 + moral damages.	
Hungary	1997 Consumer Protection Act. Consumer Organisation can initiate injunction action, not damages action, to protect consumer interests, even if individual consumers cannot be identified.	Joint claim.
Ireland	1986 Consumer associations do *not* have powers to bring injunctions proceedings.	Proposed 2005.
Italy	1998, 2005, 2006. Consumer associations.	2008.

(continued)

Table 1—(continued)

Country	Representative Action Involving a Consumer Association	General Class Action for Damages
Latvia	Injunction actions, no limitation to collective interests.	
Lithuania	1994 Consumer associations.	Merge cases.
Luxembourg	1983, 2005 + damages.	
Malta	1996 Director of Consumer Affairs—injunction action implementing the Injunctions Directive. Orders issued by the Director, not a court. Malta Consumers' Association, the only consumer association, does not appear to have powers to commence injunctions proceedings. No limitation to collective interests.	
Netherlands	1994. 2006 Consumer Agency.	2005 (settlements).
Norway	1914. Civil Procedure Act: Consumer Council can bring actions in its own name, in the name of individual consumers or a group of consumers. Injunction actions and damages actions.	2005.
Poland	Consumer ombudsmen, consumer associations, and NGOs + damages.	Cumulate claims. 2009?
Portugal	1983/1995 consumer associations + damages.	Test case.
Romania	Injunction actions can be brought by consumer associations to protect individual and collective consumer interests.	Yes if power of attorney.
Slovakia	1992 Consumer Protection Act—consumer associations can bring injunction actions.	
Slovenia	Consumer Protection Act: Consumer associations can bring injunction actions.	
Spain	1984, 2000 Consumer associations + damages.	
Sweden	Consumer Ombudsman.	2002.
Switzerland	Yes.	Cumulate claims.
UK: England	Consumer association (if approved) can bring injunction action.	GLO 1999.

(continued)

Table 1—(continued)

Country	Representative Action Involving a Consumer Association	General Class Action for Damages
	CA can also bring a collective follow-on claim in the Competition Appeal Tribunal (CAT) 2002. New consumer mechanism for damages in 2008?	
UK: Scotland	CAT 2002.	

France

A classic example of the broad approach to consumerist collective mechanisms is found in France, where several different mechanisms have been introduced since the Royer Act of 1973. The following is a non-exhaustive summary of some of the French mechanisms.[7]

a) When a criminal offence has been committed, a consumer association that has been approved for this purpose may exercise the rights of a party to the prosecution in respect of events directly or indirectly harming the collective interest of consumers.[8]

b) Approved consumer associations may also bring an action in either a civil or criminal court that deals with civil actions, to stop illegal behaviour or to remove illegal clauses from a particular contract or a standard contract offered to consumers, under pain of a fine.[9] This type of action, being preventative in nature, tends to be brought together with a compensation action of type a) above.[10]

c) Where no criminal offence has been committed, approved consumer organisations may join (intervene in) proceedings in civil courts and request the same relief as under b).[11]

d) Approved associations, or entities approved under Directive 98/27/EC, may bring an action before a civil court to stop or prohibit any illegal behaviour proscribed under national legislation implementing that Directive.[12]

---

[7] See V Magnier, *National Report: France* in the Stanford Law School-Centre for Socio-Legal Studies, Oxford Globalisation of Class Actions Project (see <http://www.law.stanford.edu/classactionconf> accessed 5 June 2008). Translations of the texts by Professor Magnier are at app 1.

[8] Art L. 421-1 of the Consumer Code.

[9] Art L. 421-2 of the Consumer Code.

[10] V Magnier, 'National Report: France' in the Stanford Law School-Centre for Socio-Legal Studies, Oxford Globalisation of Class Actions Project (see <http://www.law.stanford.edu/classactionconf> accessed 5 June 2008).

[11] Art L. 421-7 of the Consumer Code.

[12] Art L. 421-6 of the Consumer Code. These EU provisions are examined at ch 4 below.

e) Where several individual identified consumers have suffered personal prejudice having a common origin through the actions of the same person, any approved association recognised as being a nationwide representative may, if instructed to do so by at least two of the consumers concerned, sue for damages in any court on behalf of those consumers. This action *en representation conjointe* is taken in the individual interest of each of the individual consumers.[13]

f) Where several identified investors have suffered personal prejudice having a common origin through the actions of the same person, any approved association of investors may, if instructed to do so by at least two of the investors concerned, sue for damages on behalf of those investors before any court.[14]

Various points should be noted about these French provisions. First, there are in this jurisdiction several possible mechanisms. Secondly, there is some fusion and overlap between the criminal and private law mechanisms. Thirdly, the right to initiate these forms of collective redress is given to private organisations, usually consumer associations. Fourthly, only approved consumer associations are so empowered. The association must be properly constituted, with the express aim of protection of consumer interests.[15] Fifthly, it is often a requirement that, once the collective mechanism has been triggered, each individual who wishes to take part in it must provide personal signed authorisation to the collective agent. In other words, every claimant must opt-in to the procedure. The implications of this traditional rule will be considered below.

In Germany and Austria, actions by interest groups of associations (*Verbandsklagen*) similarly have a long history, originating as early as the Act against Unfair Competition of 1896[16] and established for modern consumer organisations in 1964.[17] The consumer associations in these states have been extremely active in policing unfair standard contract terms and unfair competition. Indeed, the associations have traditionally constituted the primary enforcement mechanism for infringements in such areas of law.

One might set out an exhaustive catalogue of similar national collective mechanisms at this point, but it is unnecessary for present purposes, and would confuse rather than assist the search for the important fundamental

---

[13] Art L. 422-1 of the Consumer Code.

[14] Art L. 452-2, al. 1er, of the Monetary and Financial Code.

[15] Art L. 421-1 of the Consumer Code.

[16] The historical development of association complaints in Germany is described in Ellen Schaumburg, *Die Verbandsklage im Verbraucherschutz- und Wettbewerbsrecht* (2006) 24–33.

[17] H-W Micklitz, 'Collective Private Enforcement of Consumer Law: The Key Questions' in W van Boom and M Loos, *Collective Enforcement of Consumer Law: Securing Compliance in Europe through Private Group Action and Public Authority Intervention* (Europa Law Publishing, 2007).

issues. As can be seen from Table 1, the point is that almost every EU Member State has either an indigenous form of collective action in the consumer protection area or has introduced or reformed one during the decade since 2000 in order to implement the EU consumer protection measures (discussed later at chapter four), and that such mechanisms usually involve a pre-existing private entity as representative of the individual claimants in the group and coordinator of the claims. However, the subject matter over which the private entity, a consumer association, can take action has traditionally been limited to injunctive relief to protect the *general* consumer interest, rather than to pursue *individual* interests or losses.

Differentiation between Public and Private Models in National Enforcement Systems

The Member States had from an early stage adopted differing approaches towards the enforcement of consumer protection provisions, in that they differed over whether the primary or only enforcement should be by means of public or private entities. Some states protected collective interests through an independent administrative authority, notably the Office of Fair Trading in the UK, the Consumer Ombudsman in the Nordic states, and the Director of Consumer Affairs in Ireland. However, by 1993, 8 of the then 12 Member States had introduced a right for consumer organisations to bring claims for the protection of the collective interest of consumers, with one (Belgium) permitting such actions to be undertaken by both consumer organisations and by an administrative authority.[18] The position has developed further since then, along what might be regarded as parallel tracks that constitute inherently opposing approaches.

Thus, two broad models for enforcement of consumer protection can be identified, with some hybrids. The first is a public model, in which the sole or primary enforcement role is taken by a public authority. The opposing model is where a private organisation, often one or more consumer or trade associations, takes the primary role. Reasons why a private sector entity might be involved might be due to the absence of a relevant effective public authority, a wish to conserve public funds or a politically motivated desire to involve consumers in market control. These two models will be considered in greater depth. The particular position of former socialist states and new Member States also needs to be understood.

Adopting a similar approach, Cafaggi and Micklitz have recently analysed the collective enforcement of consumer law into administrative and

---

[18] Green Paper: Access of Consumers to Justice and the Settlement of Consumer Disputes in the Single Market COM(93) 576, 16 November 1993, 64.

judicial mechanisms.[19] They note that administrative enforcement through a government or agency applies in 18 of 26 Member States studied (and exclusively only in Latvia and Lithuania), and judicial enforcement through consumer or business organisations occurs in 22 of the 25. It will, however, be argued here that it is necessary to enquire more deeply into the precise national arrangements in order to observe greater structural differences than are revealed by the juxtaposition of the two variable categories of administrative and judicial mechanisms.

MODEL A: PRIMACY OF PUBLIC BODIES

Two distinct seams of tradition are discernible here. On the one hand, there is the British and Irish approach resting on public authorities that have horizontal jurisdiction (such as the Office of Fair Trading, which covers all competition enforcement) plus sectoral authorities (such as for all trading activities of utilities or transport). On the other hand is the Nordic model, in which consumer ombudsmen take centre stage in covering consumer protection and competition enforcement. The two models are not so far apart in their general approach, and perhaps the most significant differences lie in the names and scope of the particular authorities. In all of the relevant states, systems are also found that provide compensation without the need to go to court, whether based on particular schemes or business codes.

The UK

In England and Wales there are various national regulatory authorities and a network of local authorities. The primary national enforcement authority for both competition law and consumer protection is the Office of Fair Trading (OFT). Various sectors have dedicated regulators, such as telecommunications, broadcasting, electricity and gas, rail and postal services.[20] In addition, every local authority has Trading Standards departments, which enforce consumer protection law.

The UK Government has adopted a 'Better Regulation' policy,[21] which seeks to enhance competitiveness through reducing burdens on business[22] and

---

[19] F Cafaggi and H-W Micklitz, 'Administrative and Judicial Collective Enforcement of Consumer Law in the US and the European Community', European University Institute Working papers, Law 2007/22.

[20] Respectively: Oftel, Ofcom, Ofgem, Ofrail, Postwatch.

[21] See CJS Hodges, 'Encouraging Enterprise and Rebalancing Risk: Implications of Economic Policy for Regulation, Enforcement and Compensation' (2007) *European Business Law Review* 1231.

[22] It has been estimated that UK small businesses spend 9.5% of their total working time ensuring compliance with regulations, excluding regulations on tax, employment relations, health and

a risk-based approach to enforcement.[23] Specified enforcers[24] are required[25] to prioritise their enforcement activities based on the five principles of good enforcement,[26] namely proportionality, consistency, targeting, transparency and accountability. These principles are now established in UK law through a Statutory Code of Practice for Regulators.[27]

An influential report found in 2005 that regulators lack effective tools to punish persistent offenders and reward compliant behaviour by business.[28] In the 2005 Consumer White Paper, the government set out 'a strategy to empower consumers and support business success' for the next 5 to 10 years, which contained the following statements:[29]

> We have rejected the old-fashioned idea that businesses need to be routinely regulated and inspected to keep them in line. The vast majority of businesses want to act responsibly. The pressure to attract and retain customers is a far more powerful and effective incentive on business to act with integrity and responsibility than anything Central or Local Government can do.

> Our consumer regime will be based on the principle of proportionate, risk-assessed and evidence-based intervention. Instead of regulating and inspecting on a routine all-inclusive basis, we want to see more effort targeted on rogue traders, and a lighter touch for mainstream responsible businesses.

Following the Consumer White Paper, Consumers Direct was established as a national first point of contact for consumers, which refers consumers to high quality specialist advice and redress services.[30] Significant effort has

---

safety and environment issues: F Chittenden, S Kauser and P Poutziouris, *Regulatory Burdens of Small Business: A Literature Review* (Small Business Research Trust). That study also found that for businesses with less than 20 employees, the compliance costs were at least 35% higher than for firms with more than 500 staff. It further found that governments had yet to discover how to reduce this relatively higher burden, which led to the small business sector and the economies of the countries studied being smaller than they otherwise would be: see also G Bannock and A Peacock, *Governments and Small Businesses* (London, Paul Chapman Publishing, 1989) 17.

[23] P Hampton, *Reducing administrative burdens: effective inspection and enforcement* (HM Treasury, 2005). See also Better Regulation Task Force, *Less is More: Reducing Burdens, Improving Outcomes* (2006). *Moving Towards The Local Better Regulation Office: The way ahead* (Department for Trade and Industry, 2005).

[24] See The Legislative and Regulatory Reform (Regulatory Functions) Order 2007, SI 2007/3544.

[25] Legislative and Regulatory Reform Act 2006: <http://www.opsi.gov.uk/acts/acts2006/pdf/ukpga_20060051_en.pdf> accessed 1 July 2008.

[26] <http://bre.berr.gov.uk/regulation/documents/pst/pdf/concord.pdf> accessed 5 June 2008.

[27] Published by the Department for Business, Enterprise and Regulatory Reform on 17 December 2007: <http://www.berr.gov.uk/files/file45019.pdf> accessed 5 June 2008.

[28] Hampton, n 23 above, para 7.

[29] Department of Trade and Industry, *A Fair Deal for All. Extending Competitive Markets: Empowered Consumers, Successful Business* (2005). See also Department of Trade and Industry, 'Extending Competitive Markets: Empowered Consumers, Successful Business', Consultation Document (2004); and Department of Trade and Industry, 'Empowering Consumers in the Enterprise economy: The Enterprise Bill Consumer Measures' (2002).

[30] <http://www.consumerdirect.gov.uk> accessed 5 June 2008.

been put into consumer education, particularly access to information on rights, responsibilities and options on redress.[31]

In accordance with the above government policy, the OFT regards its mission as to make markets work well for consumers through supporting economic progress, making markets work well and delivering significant benefits to consumers, businesses and the economy.[32] The OFT's approach to compliance and enforcement[33] is built on the belief that most businesses want to treat their customers fairly and to comply with the law. Accordingly, the OFT encourages business compliance through providing guidance and liaison, empowers consumers through providing advice and information campaigns, and seeks improved trading practices through encouraging effective self-regulation and positive incentive schemes though its Consumer Codes Approval Scheme.[34] Under the latter, business codes may be formally approved by the OFT.[35] Similarly, suppliers in the energy and postal services sectors are statutorily required to belong to redress schemes that provide for complaint resolution and awards of compensation when warranted, and estate agents are required to belong to an independent approved ombudsman scheme.[36]

Self-regulation is a notable feature of the UK's approach to regulation and enforcement.[37] This is similar to the emphasis on ADR that is found in relation to private law claims. The policy is based on academic regulatory theory and experience that self-regulatory structures are particularly effective when subject to public oversight based on systems control, transparency and accountability.[38]

---

[31]   Office of Fair Trading, 'Consumer education: A strategy and framework' (2004).

[32]   OFT Annual Plan 2007–08: <http://www.oft.gov.uk/shared_oft/about_oft/349517/ap08.pdf> accessed 5 June 2008.

[33]   Statement of consumer protection enforcement principles, <http://www.oft.gov.uk/shared_oft/reports/consumer_protection/oft964.pdf> accessed 1 July 2008.

[34]   OFT, 'Consumer Codes Approval Scheme: Core Criteria and Guidance' (2004). See <http://www.oft.gov.uk/advice_and_resources/small_businesses/codes/> accessed 5 June 2008.

[35]   Enterprise Act 2002 s 8. The British Association of Removers is a recent example of an approved code, which includes financial protection such as money back guarantees of up to 150% if a member cancels a removal at short notice or ceases to trade, plus an obligation on all members to use fair terms and conditions, and formal procedures for dealing with consumer complaints and a conciliation service: see <http://www.oft.gov.uk/news/press/2008/26-08> accessed 5 June 2008. Other approved codes are those of the Society for Motor manufacturers and Traders, the Vehicle Builders and Repairers Association Ltd, the Direct Selling Association and the Carpet Foundation.

[36]   The Consumers, Estate Agents and Redress Act, 2007.

[37]   OECD, 'United Kingdom, Challenges at the Cutting Edge' (Paris, 2002). I Bartle and P Vass, *Self-Regulation and the Regulatory State—A Survey of Policy and Practice* (University of Bath School of Management, Centre for the Study of Regulated Industries, 2005). The government's Better Regulation Task Force published a sequence of reports pressing the advantages of self-regulation between 1999 and 2005.

[38]   AI Ogus, 'Rethinking Self-Regulation' (1995) 15 *Oxford Journal of Legal Studies* 97–108; J Black, 'Constitutionalising Self-regulation' (1996) 59 *Modern Law Review* 24–55; and I Bartle, n 37 above.

Many ombudsmen,[39] specialist tribunals and business codes of conduct exist.[40] It is beyond the scope of this work to delve further into this rich dispute resolution matrix, but merely because such mechanisms were historically established to resolve individual claims does not mean that they do or can play any role in multiple situations.

An example of a combined approach, in which a regulatory authority and an ombudsman work alongside each other and sometimes together, can be found in the financial services sector. There is a strong regulatory authority, the Financial Services Authority and also a Financial Services Ombudsman (FOS). The scope and operation of the FOS are described in Appendix 2. The FOS has no formal collective redress mechanisms, but has the flexibility to have developed various strategies to address multiple claims. Strategies include: first, grouping similar cases so as to identify a lead case that can be resolved and leads to formal resolution or voluntary settlement of the other cases; secondly, where cases turn on a point of law, referral of a test case to the court for its binding resolution; and thirdly a 'wider implications' procedure where issues may be resolved by a regulator or through some ADR-style procedure.

UK Consumer Protection Law

As outlined above, the OFT has a pivotal role in enforcement of consumer protection law, assisted by other local authorities, whether under domestic or EU measures (notably the Injunctions Directive and Consumer Protection Cooperation Regulation, which are discussed in chapter four below). The role of non-public authorities in enforcement is limited in scope and constrained in effect. Given the power and effectiveness of the public authorities, the national consumers' association, which remains the only body to have any formal enforcement power, chooses not to use it, and has not sought an extended role. Private entities have only been involved in the UK enforcement system in roles required under EU consumer protection legislation (discussed below at chapter four), so as not to undermine the primacy of the public authorities in policing the markets. Indeed, the UK was initially reluctant even to devolve power to private entities under the EU legislation.[41]

---

[39] A recent list of public sector ombudsmen included 24 UK ombudsmen, 30 other public complaint handling bodies and 50 public sector tribunals.

[40] OECD, 'United Kingdom, Challenges at the Cutting Edge' (Paris, 2002); and J Stuyck *et al*, 'Commission Study on alternative means of consumer redress other than redress through ordinary judicial proceedings' (Catholic University of Leuven, 17 January 2007, issued April 2007).

[41] The consumers' association was only approved under Directive 93/13/EEC on unfair contract terms after bringing a judicial review against the government for failure to implement the Directive correctly, and the government caved in: see Case C-82/96 *R v Secretary of State for Trade and Industry, ex p Consumers' Association and Which? Ltd*. It remains the only designated body under the Unfair Terms in Consumer Contracts Regulations 1999, SI 1999/2083 sch 1, pt II.

Enforcers are divided into three categories: general enforcers (the OFT and local authorities),[42] enforcers designated by the Secretary of State[43] and Community enforcers.[44] Some of the designated enforcers have general designation (can bring cases in all matters), whilst others have limited designation (can bring cases within the scope of this designation). All enforcers of consumer protection law are given powers to apply to the courts for enforcement orders against businesses infringing any of a wide range of consumer protection laws.[45] However, no enforcer may apply to the court for an enforcement order unless it has consulted the OFT, save where the OFT thinks that the application should be made without delay.[46] The OFT may direct that if an application to the court in respect of a particular infringement is to be made, it must be made only by the OFT or such other enforcer as the OFT directs,[47] although this does not prevent an application for an enforcement order being made by a Community enforcer.[48]

Thus, various public enforcement bodies are empowered to take action against infringements under the Unfair Terms in Consumer Contracts legislation, but a private organisation must apply and satisfy criteria designated by the Secretary of State.[49] Only one private entity, the Consumers' Association, has been designated. The OFT retains overall control over policy and enforcement on unfair contract terms, and all of the sectoral public regulatory authorities and any consumer bodies that are empowered to act under the legislation are required to notify the OFT before any action is taken and of the outcome of any proceedings.[50] The OFT has been particularly active in attacking unfair contract terms[51] and the Consumers'

---

[42] Enterprise Act 2002 s 213(1).

[43] *Ibid* s 213(2). The Secretary of State may designate bodies that have protection of the collective interests of consumers as one of their purposes. As at 2007 the following had been designated: the Civil Aviation Authority; the Director General of Electricity Supply for Northern Ireland; the Director General of Gas for Northern Ireland; Ofcom; the Water Services Regulation Authority; the Gas and Electricity Markets Authority; the Information Commissioner; the Office of Rail Regulation; the Financial Services Authority; and the consumers' association (Which?). A public body will only be granted designated enforcement powers if it is independent: see the DTI guidance at <http://www.dti.gov.uk/files/file11976.pdf> accessed 5 June 2008.

[44] Enterprise Act 2002 s 213(5). Community enforcers are qualified entities for the purposes of the Directive 98/27 on cross-border injunctions (based in other EEA states) and specified in the list published in the *Official Journal of the European Communities*.

[45] The principal statute is the Enterprise Act 2002 pt 8, which implements the Injunctions Directive and the Consumer Protection Cooperation Regulation (CPCR).

[46] Enterprise Act 2002 s 215.

[47] Enterprise Act 2002 s 216.

[48] *Ibid* s 216(6).

[49] The Unfair Terms in Consumer Contracts Regulations 1999, SI 1999/2083 sch 1, pt II.

[50] The Unfair Terms in Consumer Contracts Regulations 1999, SI 1999/2083 regs 10–14.

[51] See Bulletins on many enforcement actions taken and Guidance issued at <http://www.oft.gov.uk/advice_and_resources/publications/guidance/unfair-terms-consumer/> accessed 1 July 2008. A recent leading example is a test case between the OFT and the consumer banks over whether charges for unauthorised overdrafts are subject to the Unfair Terms in Consumer Contract Regulations, and hence unfair: OFT press release, 31 August 2007.

Association has referred cases to the OFT, but not taken enforcement proceedings itself.[52]

A further Better Regulation approach is also apparent in the specified enforcement procedures, which encourage a responsive approach[53] between enforcers and business. It is an important feature that consultation with the business concerned is required unless urgent action is necessary, and consultation should normally last at least 14 days.[54] An enforcement order must also indicate the nature of the conduct objected to and direct the person to comply, by not continuing or repeating the conduct, not engaging in such conduct in the course of any business, or not consenting to or conniving in the carrying out of such conduct by a company.[55] Breach of an enforcement order is a contempt of court and can incur a fine or imprisonment. An enforcer or the court has power to accept an undertaking from a person to comply, in the former case simplifying the compliance process by avoiding the need to go to court.[56]

Compensation Orders

Powers have long existed in the UK for any criminal court to make a compensation order in criminal proceedings in favour of private parties,[57] and, more recently, for an enforcement authority to bring civil (non-criminal) proceedings for recovery of any property obtained through unlawful conduct.[58] The Financial Services Authority has extended powers to apply for a compensation order and investigate and seize infringers' assets.[59] The Australian Competition and Consumer Commission[60] also has similar powers; and this model is close to the continental *partie civile* mechanism in which a private party 'piggy backs' on a criminal action, without extra cost but with the ability to benefit from the evidence and conclusions in a follow-on damages award.[61]

In a significant extension of the responsibilities of regulatory authorities, many such general and sectoral bodies are from 2008 to have a new armoury of civil powers that will include compensation orders[62] and will also be subject

---

[52] See eg estate agents in 2007, <http://www.which.co.uk/reports_and_campaigns/house_and_home/Reports/utilities_and_services/Estate_agents_contracts_news_article_557_89603.jsp> accessed 5 June 2008.

[53] Discussed further at ch 8.

[54] Enterprise Act 2002 s 214.

[55] Enterprise Act 2002 s 217.

[56] Enterprise Act 2002 ss 219 and 217(9).

[57] Powers of Criminal Courts (Sentencing) Act 2000 s 130, traceable to s 35 of the Powers of Criminal Courts Act 1973.

[58] Proceeds of Crime Act 2002 s 240.

[59] Financial Services and Markets Act 2000 ss 382 and 383.

[60] See <http://www.accc.gov.au/content/index.phtml/itemId/142> accessed 5 June 2008.

[61] See the provisions discussed above in France and case study below from Spain on colza oil.

[62] See Regulatory Enforcement and Sanctions Act at <http://www.opsi.gov.uk/acts/acts2008/pdf/ukpga_20080013_en.pdf> accessed 25 July 2008.

to a requirement that in pursuing enforcement they should aim to eliminate any financial gain or benefit from non-compliance.[63] This latter requirement is likely to entail a significant evolution and extension in the role of public enforcement authorities, through requiring oversight of private compensation. The policy background is explained further in chapter eight below.

UK Competition Law

The OFT is also the primary public enforcement body under UK competition law. It or the government may refer certain matters to the Competition Commission, and proceedings occur before a special court—the Competition Appeal Tribunal (CAT). Since 2002, designated private bodies can also be granted certain specific functions that contribute to enforcement.

First, a designated consumer body may make a 'super-complaint' to the regulator, the OFT, that any feature, or combination of features, of a market in the UK for goods or services is or appears to be significantly harming the interests of consumers.[64] It is the relevant public authority,[65] rather than the consumer body, which is empowered to take any subsequent action, but the OFT must publish a response explaining its position.[66] The power to designate a consumer body for these purposes rests with the Secretary of State, who may do so only if it appears to him or her to represent the interests of consumers of any description, and only subject to any other criteria that he or she has published.[67]

---

[63] Regulators' Compliance Code, Department for Business Enterprise and Regulatory Reform, 2007, at <http://www.berr.gov.uk/files/file45019.pdf> accessed 5 June 2008, para 8.3. The Code is made under s 22 of the Legislative and Regulatory Reform Act 2007.

[64] Enterprise Act 2002 s 11: <http://www.oft.gov.uk/advice_and_resources/publications/guidance/enterprise_act/oft514> accessed 1 July 2008.

[65] The authorities that have a duty to respond to super-complaints are: OFT (general authority); the Civil Aviation Authority (responsibility for traffic services under the Transport Act 2000); the Office of Gas and Electricity Markets (OFGEM, responsibility for gas and electricity services under the Gas Act 1986 and Electricity Act 1989 amended by Utilities Act 2000); the Office of Telecommunications (OFTEL, responsibility for telecommunications industry under the Telecommunications Act 1984—role now taken over by the Office of Communications (OFCOM)); the Northern Ireland Authority for Energy Regulation (OFREG-NI); the Office of Water Services (OFWAT); and the Office of the Rail Regulator (ORR).

[66] The response must be published within 90 days of the super-complaint being received. Possible consequences include enforcement action, a market study or a market investigation by the authorities, or a finding that the complaint requires no action, is unfounded or frivolous.

[67] Enterprise Act 2002 s 11. Guidance for bodies wishing to apply for such designated status is at <http://www.oft.gov.uk/NR/rdonlyres/98D1E0AD-11C1-4997-BA27-26C9D93F7487/0/oft514.pdf>. So far the organisations designated are: the Consumers' Association, National Consumer Council and Citizens Advice (designated in July 2004); Energywatch and Watervoice (both designated in January 2005); Postwatch, CAMRA and the General Consumer Council of Northern Ireland (all designated in October 2005).

A super-complaint must be accompanied by facts and evidence.[68] Super-complaints have been made in relation to private dentistry, doorstep selling, consolidation of postal services, care homes, home collected credit and payment protection insurance.[69] Several of these cases have led to market studies being carried out by the authorities.

This mechanism does not grant consumer organisations the power to institute proceedings against traders. The role is to alert regulators and provide information to them. It is the regulatory authorities that have been entrusted with the powers to initiate proceedings and take other steps. As a result, consumers are involved in the system as a watchdog and may bark but not bite: biting is reserved to the public authority. Providing evidence may be quite problematic for consumer organisations—it requires time and resources that consumer bodies do not have in abundance.

The second mechanism arises in the context that any person who has suffered loss as a result of an infringement of competition law may institute a *claim for damages* before the CAT.[70] Multiple individual claims that all relate to the same infringement may also be brought in a representative capacity by a 'specified body', provided each individual has consented to the claim being brought. A typical example of such a claim is said to be where consumers have bought goods for personal use where the price has been inflated by a price-fixing agreement. Any body may apply to the Secretary of State to be 'specified', on the basis of published criteria,[71] although only one body has to date been approved, Which?, the consumers' association.[72] However, no damages claim may be brought until it has been established (by either the OFT or the European Commission) that an infringement of competition law has occurred.[73] Thus, there is a two-stage process, which separates the functions of infringement enforcement from the consequential issue of compensation, the latter being a 'follow on' to the former. Further, responsibility for enforcement remains with an independent regulator, not with a consumer organisation.

The conditions that the specified body must meet before bringing proceedings are that the claims must relate to the same infringement, each consumer must give consent, and complaints must relate to goods or services received

---

[68] OFT Guidance, 'Super-complaints: Guidance for designated consumer bodies' specifies. The facts and evidence do not need to be comprehensive enough for the regulators to immediately start proceedings. They are only to help the OFT or other regulator decide whether and what action is appropriate. They must, however, provide a reasoned case—frivolous complaints will be rejected. An annex to the guidance provides an indicative list of evidence to be.

[69] <http://www.oft.gov.uk/Business/Super-complaints/cases.htm> accessed 5 June 2008.

[70] Competition Act 1998 ss 47A and B.

[71] Guidance for prospective specified bodies is available at <http://www.dti.gov.uk/files/file11957.pdf> accessed 10 June 2008.

[72] The Specified Body (Consumer Claims) Order 2005, SI 2005/2365.

[73] This is known as a 'follow on' claim, as opposed to a 'stand alone' claim.

by consumers. If these conditions are met, the specified body can also take over individual claims brought by consumers. An award is normally to be paid to individual consumers; although there is a possibility for CAT to arrange for the award to be paid to the specified body that will then enforce the award (the latter is possible if all individual consumers and the specified body are in agreement). A specified body may be liable to an adverse costs order if it loses, as would any other litigant, although the risk in a 'follow on' case is minimal. Any award of costs or expenses against a specified body in any proceedings under section 47B may not be enforced against any individual on whose behalf a claim was made or continued in those proceedings.[74]

Which? has brought one collective damages claim after a finding by the CAT that various companies were involved in a cartel to fix the prices of replica football T-shirts.[75] The popular perception of this case was that it involved a clear case of liability following a binding finding of infringement, and that the association was frustrated by the opt-in requirement in not being able to facilitate compensation for more consumers. On investigation, the facts and issues turn out to be more complex.

Case Study: Replica Football Shirts[76]

On 1 August 2003, the Office of Fair Trading fined nine companies for unlawfully fixing the prices of a range of replica football shirts between 2000 and 2001.[77] In the case of JJB Sports Plc, the OFT based its fine on two per cent of the UK turnover infringements affected,[78] which was £659 million in the year ended 31 January 2001.[79] The Competition Appeal Tribunal (CAT) reduced the penalty to £6.7 million, noting that it represented approximately one per cent of the company's UK turnover. However, neither body identified the amount of illicit gain nor the extent of any overcharge to consumers.

After extensive publicity of the OFT action, the company had issued an offer for anyone who came to its shops with the shirts concerned to

(continued)

---

[74] Enterprise Act 2002 Sch 4, cl l 7.

[75] See <http://www.which.co.uk/reports_and_campaigns/consumer_rights/campaigns/Football%20shirts/index.jsp> accessed 10 June 2008.

[76] Certain information kindly supplied by Deborah Prince of Which? and Martin Rees and Kate Vernon of DLA Piper LLP, which acted for JJB Sports Plc.

[77] Oft decision dated 1 August 2003 No CA98/06/2003; appealed as *Allsports Ltd, JJB Sports Plc v Office of Fair Trading* [2004] CAT 17; *Umbro Holdings Ltd, Manchester United Plc, Allsports Ltd v Office of Fair Trading* [2005] CAT 22; *JJB Sports Plc v Office of Fair Trading* [2006] Court of Appeal EWCA Civ 1318. The fines initially totalled £18.57 million, but were reduced on appeal to £15.49 million.

[78] Judgment on Penalty, 19 May 2005, para 58.

[79] Judgment, 1 October 2004, para 28.

exchange them for a current England shirt and mug, with retail value £25, irrespective of whether the shirts had been bought in its shops or from other retailers. This voluntary goodwill offer, made in the light of adverse publicity, was advertised in football magazines and some 16,000 people availed themselves of the deal.

The UK consumers' association *Which?* believed that around 2 million consumers had purchased shirts and that prices had been inflated by £15–£20 per shirt. In March 2007, it instituted the first collective claim for damages under Schedule 4 of the Enterprise Act in the CAT,[80] but for jurisdictional reasons in relation to the date of introduction of the new powers, could only claim against one company that had been involved in the cartel, JJB Sports Plc. The damages claim included a claim for exemplary damages for disregard of consumer detriment, on the basis that that head of claim had not been included in the OFT's fine.[81]

Which? faced various problems. First, the opt-in procedure meant that individual consumers had to be attracted to sign up. *Which?* launched a media campaign, including a page on its website that included details of how to register, but only some 130 consumers signed up and were named in the initial complaint. Secondly, all essential documents were required to be annexed to the claim form, and claimants faced problems in producing proof of purchase, many having no available receipt. Thirdly, gaining access to evidence from OFT and the defendant was a considerable and expensive task. Fourthly, the issue of funding lawyers was solved by holding a competition for lawyers to act on behalf of claimants on a conditional fee agreement that provided for a 100 per cent success fee.

JJB Sports Plc argued that it had not in fact been involved in any collusion, that consumers had suffered no overcharge, but that the products had in fact been sold at a loss (although it was found to have broken the law). It asserted that it had pursued a publicly stated policy of holding prices of replica shirts below £40 and it was the manufacturers who had colluded to raise the price, in which JJB Sports Plc had become involved merely because of communications on the issue, but without intent to fix prices to consumers' detriment.

In January 2008, a settlement was reached that JJB Sports Plc would pay £20 per shirt bought to those consumers who signed up to the action and could produce their shirts or other proof of purchase, and sign a statement of truth. *Which?* had been contacted by around 600 people

(continued)

---

[80] The Notice of a Claim for Damages is at <http://www.catribunal.org.uk/archive/casedet.asp?id=127> accessed 10 June 2008.

[81] See the 'OFT's guidance as to the appropriate amount of a penalty', at <http://www.oft.gov.uk/shared_oft/business_leaflets/ca98_guidelines/oft423.pdf> accessed 10 June 2008.

(involving around 1,000 shirts), although it did not have full details for all of them, so the total amount involved would be a maximum of £18,000. The company would also pay the reasonable costs of *Which?*, but there was a dispute over whether this would include the whole of the success fee.[82] Further, anyone who had previously accepted JJB Sports' earlier exchange offer could claim a further £5, and anyone else could bring in an unmarked shirt or receipt and be paid £10, these two offers remaining open to the end of the limitation period in 2009.[83]

The JJB Sports case illustrates various issues. On the consumers side, the association aimed at representing all consumers, but had problems. It was argued that an opt-out procedure would have been more appropriate than the opt-in rule, since the result would automatically cover all consumers and would avoid the time and expense in publicising the case and having everyone sign up. Questions arose of how any overall settlement could be structured in relation to the (possibly large number of) purchasers on whose behalf a judgement or settlement might have been agreed, but who had no interest in claiming anything: it might possibly have involved payment to a football charity. On the company's side, there was concern over the injustice of the situation, given no evidence of intended wrongdoing or of consumer detriment. On an overall balance of benefits and costs, a majority of consumers received nothing (whether through personal choice, inability to prove their claim, or ignorance of the situation), whereas some consumers received extra low value benefits, so an issue of inequality of outcome arose, and the company would end up paying a large fine and large legal costs of both sides. Control over costs was clearly an important lesson: the court was unable to exercise cost control since it was essentially not involved in the process, which was stayed whilst the parties negotiated to settle the case.

The question therefore arises, in cases where small or no detriment is established, whether a goal of restoring market balance is achievable or relevant. Both the consumers' association and the company wished to find a resolution to an issue that satisfied the reputational and commercial interests of them both. Perhaps these factors were more important than overall justice. If other cases were to involve clearer consumer detriment, there would remain problems if the mechanism were to be either opt-in or opt-out. If it were opt-out, there would be no guarantee that all consumers affected would be paid any restitutionary amount, since they might simply not come forward, whereas others may gain a windfall, and this would not satisfy a requirement for access to or delivery of individual restorative justice or fairness. The situation would be far easier to resolve and litigation might

[82] See *The Lawyer*, 9 January 2008.
[83] Details at: <http://www.which.co.uk/reports_and_campaigns/consumer_rights/campaigns/Football%20shirts/index.jsp> accessed 10 June 2008.

have been avoided if the authorities' initial investigation had identified, even roughly, the extent of any detriment.

A recent example of strong enforcement by the OFT against a cartel, followed by successful settlement of private claims, was the airline fuel surcharges case. It represents a bifurcated approach, in which private compensation was achieved as a classic 'follow on' to regulatory enforcement.

Case Study: Airline Fuel Surcharges

In August 2007, the UK and US authorities imposed fines on British Airways for infringements under a cartel with Virgin Atlantic involving fuel surcharges on flights between August 2004 and March 2006.[84] Virgin Atlantic escaped a fine as it had confessed the cartel to the OFT, and was excused under the leniency programme.[85]

A US-based law firm subsequently brought damages claims in a class action in a US federal court, which was settled in February 2008. The surcharges involved between £5 and £60, and applied to 5.6 million passengers. The two airlines agreed to repay a total of $200 million ($59 million to US passengers and £73.5 million to UK passengers), representing up to £20, which was around one-third of the fuel surcharge levied per long-haul ticket, and could be claimed until 2012. Around 40,000 individual travelers and 300 businesses registered via a website.[86]

Michael Hausfeld, the senior partner of Cohen Milstein Hausfeld & Toll, who brought the class action, said that '[t]his is the first time that there has been a trans-jurisdictional recovery on a parity basis'[87] with 'non-US citizens [being] rewarded on an equal footing to US citizens before the US courts'.[88] The firm's fees have yet to be approved by the court, but would be expected to be around $60 million.

The Nordic Model

The Nordic model[89] traditionally gives the primary responsibility for enforcement of consumer protection to a Consumer Ombudsman, a public

---

[84] Office of Fair Trading, Press release, 1 August 2007. British Airways was fined £121.5 million by the British authorities, and $300 million by the US Federal Trade Commission.

[85] See 'OFT's Guidance as to the appropriate amount of a penalty' (2004).

[86] *Financial Times* (23 February 2008).

[87] C Ruckin, 'Cohen Milstein lands $200m BA-Virgin settlement' *Legal Week* (15 February 2008).

[88] D Fortson, 'UK businesses braced for class action suits after BA and Virgin pay out $200m' *The Independent* (16 February 2008).

[89] K Viitanen, 'Enforcement of Consumers' Collective Interests by Regulatory Agencies in the Nordic Countries' in W van Boom and M Loos, *Collective Enforcement of Consumer Law: Securing Compliance in Europe through Private Group Action and Public Authority Intervention* (Europa Law Publishing, 2007).

authority, who usually takes action through a special tribunal, usually called a Market Court.[90] State authorities other than the Consumer Ombudsman have limited competence in enforcement of consumer protection issues, and criminal powers and courts are rarely used. Consumer ombudsmen were established in the Nordic states between 1973 and 1978, and supervise marketing and standard contract terms.

Where the Market Court[91] considers a marketing practice unfair, it may impose an injunction, an order to issue corrective advertising, or criminal sanctions. In Sweden, since 1996, more traditional criminal sanctions have been replaced by a power to impose a market disruption fee, not exceeding SEK 5 million (around €500,000) or 10 per cent of the trader's annual turnover.

A methodology frequently employed by the consumer ombudsmen is that of taking preventive measures, notably issuing advance opinions, or marketing guidelines and negotiating with trade associations agreed positions on standard contract terms. There is, therefore, a strong emphasis on soft law techniques. The existence of statutory powers under which the ombudsmen may institute proceedings before the Market Court that may lead to imposition of significant sanctions (or for the ombudsman to impose penalties directly in lower value situations) frequently leads in practice to the ombudsman and the trader reaching agreed solutions without the need for formal court action.[92] This result is encouraged by the adoption of a no-cost rule in the Market Court, in other words that both sides bear their own legal costs. The practical operation of the ombudsman system therefore achieves negotiated solutions through dialogue and avoids the costs and longer durations that would be involved in court proceedings.

The Nordic authorities have traditionally been concerned primarily to be able to take ex ante action to prevent or stop undesirable market behaviour, in the belief that precautionary action is more effective than ex post prosecution. Accordingly, the primary court power has been to impose an injunction against specified behaviour. During the decade from 2000, however, the

---

[90] Finnish Consumer Protection Act 34/1978; Danish Class Actions Act 2007; Finland (2007).

[91] The Nordic states also have boards that issue recommendations on compensation, but these can be slow as well as unenforceable. Since 1991, the Swedish Consumer Ombudsman and organisations may bring matters before the Swedish Public Complaints Board, which has existed since 1977. The Finnish Public Consumer Dispute Board has also existed for many years, and the Consumer Ombudsman has been empowered to initiate group complaints before it since March 2007. The Danish Consumer Complaints Board has a threshold of €100 (and many consumer problems are below that), it takes too long and is not binding. The other option is the Consumer Ombudsman, who can make an administrative order.

[92] Resolution of issues through test cases is also useful. In Finland, the Consumer Ombudsman can assist a claimant in a pilot case, and can also decide that the national Consumer Agency will pay all the consumer's legal costs and indemnify any costs liability to an opponent: Consumer Agency Act (1056/1998), art 9. Between two and six such decisions are made a year: see K Viitanen's 'Finnish Report in the Globalisation Project' at <http://globalclassaction.stanford.edu> accessed 10 June 2008.

Nordic states have extended the powers so as to provide a mechanism for the court to award compensatory damages. As with the exercise of the pre-existing powers by consumer ombudsmen, it may be anticipated that the availability of this power will lead to the ombudsmen being able to agree compensation arrangements with traders as part of a package of measures that conclude a matter, in order to avoid the time and expense of going to court.[93]

Hence, collective action mechanisms for compensation of groups have been introduced in Sweden, Finland, Norway and Denmark. The main features of these systems are summarised in Table 2. The texts of the relevant laws for the first three states are in Appendices three to five.

Three points can be made about these systems, covering the types of permitted claimants, the inclusion of features intended to protect against abuse and the continued reliance in practice on the Consumer Ombudsman as facilitator of much collective redress.

On the first issue, the Swedish, Danish and Norwegian laws all permit a collective claim to be brought by three types of claimants, whereas the Finnish approach restricts the right to the Consumer Ombudsman.[94] The approach of the Finnish Government's proposal was explained as 'in order to diminish suspicions concerning the possible misuse of the new act' and 'to ensure the actions could not be taken in purpose too blackmail or damage'.[95]

Perhaps, however, a more relevant way of analysing the position is that *all four* Nordic states allow their consumer ombudsmen the right of bringing a collective action for damages, whereas three states also permit two more categories of coordinators. The other two categories of permitted claimants in Sweden, Denmark and Norway are, first, any individual member of the group of claimants that has a claim and seeks damages both for him- or herself and for the group and, secondly, a private organisation that seeks damages for its members in relation to a matter that falls within the legitimate specified purposes of the organisation.[96]

The second notable point is the inclusion of features designed to diminish opportunities for abuse of the class action procedure. The introduction of these collective mechanisms for damages was preceded in every state by considerable and often heated national debate over the extent to which the new mechanism might bring potential for abuse through the importation

---

[93] This has indeed been the experience of the Danish Consumer Ombudsman even in advance of his having the power to seek damages. At the conference on 'The Globalisation of Class Actions' held at Oxford University on 13/14 December 2007, Mr Henrik Saugmandsgaard Øe, the Danish Consumer Ombudsman, said that before the introduction of the compensation powers, he had been concluding a number of agreements with traders involving payment of compensation, based on traders' wish to avoid being subject to the new powers.

[94] Act on Class Actions 444/2007. See comments of the Consumer Ombudsman at <http://www.kuluttajavirasto.fi/> accessed 10 June 2008.

[95] HE 154/2006 p 16. Information kindly supplied by K Viitanen.

[96] Commentators have analysed the three types of claims as, respectively, a public action, a class action and an action by an organisation.

Table 2—Nordic Laws on Collective Damages Actions: Selected Features

	Sweden	Denmark	Norway	Finland
Legislation	Group Proceedings Act 2002[1]	Administration of Justice Act Pt 23[2]	Dispute Act 2005, ch. 35[3]	Act on Class Actions 444/2007[4]
Date in force	1 January 2003	1 January 2008	1 January 2008	1 October 2007
Permitted claimants	1. Any member of the group. 2. An organisation whose regulations safeguard consumers' or employees' interests. 3. A public authority which is suited to represent the group members.	1. Any member of the group. 2. An association, private institution or other organisation where the proceedings are within the framework of the object of the organisation. 3. A public authority with statutory authority to act.	1. Any member of the group. 2. An organisation or association charged with promoting specific interests, provided the action falls within its purpose and normal scope. 3. A public authority charged with promoting specific interests, provided the action falls within its purpose and normal scope.	The Consumer Ombudsman only.
Approval of class representative	Not explicitly required, but the court may replace a class claimant who is judged no longer suitable to represent the group. The court may appoint a representative of a sub-group.	By the court—not parties.	Nominated by the court.	—

Notification	Required information specified in the law.	The court decides manner of notification. The court may order notification wholly or partly through publication. Costs initially paid by class representative.	The court writes and decides how notice is to be given and who pays for it.	The court gives postal or electronic notice, containing information specified in the law.
Opt-in or opt-out	Opt-in only. The court pays cost of notification of members of the group.	Opt-in (and the court may decide that only those who have provided security for costs may opt in) unless the court decides opt-out is preferable, for claims for which it is evident that due to their small size it may normally not be expewcted that they may be furthered in individual proceedings and it is assumed that a class action with	Opt-in, unless the court decides opt-out if the claims involve amounts or interests thatw are so small that it must be assumed that a considerable majority of them would not be brought as individual actions, and are not deemed to raise issues that need to be heard individually.	Opt-in only: signed written letter.

(continued)

Table 2—(continued)

	Sweden	Denmark	Norway	Finland
Funding and costs	Loser pays. A conditional fee (risk agreement) is permitted if approved by the court (if reasonable). It must not be based solely on a share of the value of the object in dispute. Group members are not parties, so *not* liable for costs, save in exceptional cases. If defendant is unable to pay legal costs or reimburse the state for claimants' legal aid, a group member is liable for his or her share, but	members opting in will not be a beneficial way to handle the claims. Loser pays. The court may order the claimant to provide security for costs. A group member opting in can be ordered to provide security, unless has insurance, etc or free legal aid. Member can be ordered to pay winner's costs up to the level of security required when registering, and in addition to pay costs up to an amount paid to him or her as damages in the proceedings.	Loser pays. Class representative is liable, but the court may order class members to reimburse him or her for remuneration, expenses and liability for opponents' costs.	Loser pays. Class members not liable.

	is not obliged to pay more than he or she has gained in the action.	A member in an opt-out class can only be ordered to pay costs up to the limit of an amount that becomes payable to him or her in the proceedings.	—
Settlement approved by Court	Required. The settlement must not discriminate against certain group members or be otherwise apparently unreasonable.	Required.	Required.

[1] Lagen (2002:599) om grupprättegång.
[2] Amended by Act No. 181 of 28 February 2007.
[3] Act of 17 June 2005 no. 90 relating to mediation and procedure in civil disputes.
[4] Ryhmäkannelaki (444/2007).

of what was perceived by some as highly undesirable US practice.[97] The arguments here will be considered at chapter six below, but revolve around the view that class actions lead to excessive and costly claims and unnecessarily large transactional costs. For present purposes, it is relevant to note various features that were included into the Nordic legislation, which were designed to prevent abuse.

Leading examples of such techniques are: the requirement of court supervision of collective actions, such as in appointment of the class representative and in approval of any settlement; a condition that the group claim is the best mechanism to deal with the claims;[98] restriction of the type of claimants permitted (including that private organisations, and even public authorities, may only pursue claims that are within their normal specified objects[99]); restriction to the opt-in approach (Sweden[100] and Finland, but with some experimentation in Denmark and Norway); and maintenance of the traditional loser pays rule.

The experimentation in relation to moving away from an opt-in approach is interesting. The issues will be considered more generally below, but one should note here the following novel approaches. In Norway, the basic approach is opt-in, unless the court decides to permit an opt-out approach, on satisfaction of the conditions that the claims involve amounts or interests that are so small that it must be assumed that a considerable majority of them would not be brought as individual actions, and are not deemed to raise issues that need to be heard individually.

In Denmark, the normal rule is that the opt-in approach will apply (and the court may decide that only those who have provided security for costs may opt-in), unless the court decides, on application by the class representative, that the action relates to claims for which it is evident that—due to their small size—it may normally not be expected that they may be furthered in individual proceedings, and it is assumed that a class action with members opting in will not be a beneficial way to handle the claims, in which case an opt-out approach will apply. The explanatory notes to the Danish legislation go further, and emphasise the exceptional nature of the opt-out approach.[101] The opt-out approach is only available to the ombudsman (ie only the ombudsman will be appointed as class representative). The notes indicate that

---

[97] See H Aagaard and J Røn, 'Nye regeler om gruppesøgsmål i dansk ret' (2007) *Juristen* 141.

[98] Danish Act s 254b(5). The Swedish Act requires, inter alia, that (§8) a class action must not appear unsuitable because the grounds of certain group members' claims differ considerably from other claims, and that the majority of claims concerned cannot be equally well processed by individual actions.

[99] In Sweden, only associations that deal with consumer or employment affairs are empowered to bring collective claims.

[100] The Swedish Act (§9) requires that the representative plaintiff shall state in the complaint the name and address of all members of the group, but such information may be omitted if they are not required for the handling of the case.

[101] See Ministry of Justice note <http://www.justitsministeriet.dk> accessed 10 June 2008.

the size of the small threshold sum over which the opt-out is not available is DKK 2,000 (roughly €264). The opt-in model will be deemed to be inappropriate if the case involves a very large number of persons, such that the practical administration of opt-in notices would require a disproportionate amount of resources.

Denmark has added various features intended to avoid abuse of the system that it concluded was produced by class actions in the United States. These include identification of members (the ombudsman can demand a list of customers from companies which simplifies things considerably), requirements for notification of class members (although this remains a difficult issue), and that the group representative may be required to provide security for costs.

The third notable feature is that even though, in three of these four states, collective claims are permitted by group members and by representative organisations, there can be a strong presumption that in practice most collective damages cases will involve claims raised by the Consumer Ombudsman. The Nordic ombudsman mechanism has several obvious advantages for individual claimants over the option of instituting a class action themselves. Notably, the former involves no cost to an individual, and provides the significant persuasive power of a public official, who has the ability to deploy expertise and investigative powers to gain access to evidence, and to exercise strong persuasion to agree payment of compensation as part of a package in order to achieve closure on a public investigation that may otherwise escalate into administrative or criminal sanctions being imposed.[102]

In this context, Finland's omission of a right of collective action for individuals or associations does not look strange. Indeed, it will be interesting to see to what extent the ability for individuals or associations to bring collective actions in the other three states, which is clearly intended to be a long-stop mechanism, turns out to be used, and in what sorts of cases. Public officials have limited budgets and must prioritise their enforcement activities, so the existence of a long-stop mechanism has some rationale. However, there is scope for empirical research into what sort of cases are dealt with under which options, and why.

Nordic Compensation Schemes: Medical and Drug Injuries and Road Traffic Accidents

One other notable feature that is common to the Nordic states, and is important in order to understand the Nordic approach to dispute resolution as a

---

[102] At the conference on 'The Globalisation of Class Actions' held at Oxford University on 13/14 December 2007, Henrik Saugmandsgaard Øe, the Danish Consumer Ombudsman, said that his experience of the new system, even before it was formally in force, was that '[o]verall it is a very effective system, for example for getting repayment of unlawful fees'.

whole, is that each of these states has no fault schemes that cover payment of compensation for injuries caused by either medical treatment or taking medicinal products, and collective insurance arrangements and claims handling arrangements for motor accident claims. As a result, there are effectively *no* claims that are pursued through the courts for damages for medical negligence or drug product liability in these states, and very few for motor accidents.[103] This is an important result, given that such injuries can give rise to significant levels of litigation in other jurisdictions.

The details of the no fault compensation schemes differ between the four Nordic states, but the basic architecture is essentially similar.[104] There are separate schemes for medical and drug injuries. All of the schemes involve an inquisitorial, document-based, investigation and determination by an expert panel on whether or not the injury was caused by the medical or pharmaceutical intervention. Compensation payments are based on set scales, the amounts of which are modest but are favoured in view of the speed and reliability of determination, and avoidance of any transactional cost for a claimant. The amounts awarded are linked to what a court would award as damages in a similar situation, but the scales involved have remained modest. The schemes are administered by a public or private agency or insurance company. They are economically viable because they are not required to reimburse any of the (usually several) other sources of financial support that make payments to injured people in the Nordic systems. This absence of cross-indemnity between different support funds is crucial to the economic stability of the Nordic schemes: various social security or insurance funds may make payments to an individual (for example for income replacement, mortgage, basic healthcare costs) and the no fault medical or drug injury funds may provide what are in effect top-up payments, but none of the funds cross-claim against each other. The finance for the no fault schemes is provided by levies on, as the case may be, doctors or pharmaceutical companies, save for Denmark, where the state pays.

It is interesting to note the introduction of no fault compensation schemes in other states. Recent innovations in France and England cover primarily medical injury schemes. France's medical injury scheme, introduced in 2004, also covers injuries caused by medicines and medical devices.[105] It

---

[103] For the Finnish motor arrangements, which paid claims totalling €467 million in 2006, see <http://www.liikennevakuutuskeskus.fi/asp/system/empty.asp?P=796&VID=default&SID=644309459570198&S=1&C=25468> accessed 10 June 2008. For uninsured claims, see the Swedish Motor Insurers Bureau, Trafikförsäkringsföreningen, at <http://www.tff.se/templates/LandingPage.aspx?id=135> accessed 10 June 2008 and the Danish Motor Insurers' Bureau at <http://www.dfim.dk/Engelsk/Tekster/Hvad_er_DFIM.htm> accessed 10 June 2008.

[104] C Hodges, 'Nordic compensation schemes for drug injuries' (2006) J. Consum. Policy 29:143–175.

[105] Titre IV du Livre Ier de la Première Partie du Code de la Santé Public, tel qu'il result de la loi n° 2002-303 du 4 mars 2002 relative aux droits des maladies et à la qualité du système de santé et de la loi n° 2002-1577 du 30 décembre 2002 relative à la responsabilité civile médicale: <http://www.oniam.fr/> accessed 10 June 2008.

involves determination on causeation by regional expert panels, after which insurers are effectively required to make an acceptable offer of compensation. The NHS Redress scheme in England only covers medical injuries, but is yet to be brought into effect.[106] The proposed new approach might cap compensation at £20,000,[107] but offer a quick resolution, after an inquiry by the authorities, and an apology and offer of a package of care plus monetary award (equivalent to the amount of damages which a court would award).[108] The basic aim would be to cut administrative and especially legal costs, and to cut delay and disruption.[109]

The Netherlands

An image of the Nordic ombudsman system has recently been created in the Netherlands. The Consumer Authority, which was established from 1 January 2007,[110] includes amongst its powers authority to enter into an agreement with a party that has violated one of the consumer protection laws which are enforced by that Authority, under which the infringing party undertakes to pay compensation for the loss arising from the violation.[111] However, the Authority has stated that it intends to deploy this power with restraint, on the basis that the market (eg consumer organisations) should take the lead in such initiatives.[112]

MODEL B: EMPHASIS ON PRIVATE SECTOR BODIES

In contrast to the model discussed above, in Austria and Germany no federal public authority has existed for regulation of consumer protection law until

---

[106] NHS Redress Act 2006. See 'Making Amends', Report by the Chief Medical Officer (2003). A-M Farrell and S Devaney, 'Making amends or making things worse? Clinical negligence reform and patient redress in England' *Legal Studies* vol 27, No 4, December 2007, pp 630–48.

[107] Except for babies who suffer brain damage; birth-related brain damage cases accounted for 5% of medical litigation in 2003/04, but 60% of annual expenditure.

[108] *Making Amends*, Report by the Chief Medical Officer (2003). 'Explanatory Notes to the NHS Redress Bill' <http://www.publications.parliament.uk/pa/ld200506/ldbills/022/en/06022x--.htm> accessed 10 June 2008.

[109] The scheme originated as a response to spiralling annual expenditure on clinical negligence, which grew from £1 million in 1974 to £446 million in 2002. By 2004, legal and administrative costs exceeded compensation paid in the majority of claims under £45,000. In 2005/06, the NHS paid £592 million on negligence claims, of which one-third (£166 million) went on legal fees.

[110] S Ammerlaan and D Janssen, 'The Dutch Consumer Authority: an introduction' in W van Boom and M Loos, *Collective Enforcement of Consumer law: Securing Compliance in Europe through Private Group Action and Public Authority Intervention* (Europa Law Publishing, 2007).

[111] Wet handhaving consumentenbescherming (Consumer Protection Enforcement Act, 2007) art 2.6.

[112] Memorie van Toelichting (Explanatory Memorandum on the Act).

2006,[113] so the primary mechanism for enforcement of unfair terms in consumer contracts and of unfair competition[114] has been that of private actions through the courts. Indeed, the German tradition is described as private enforcement.[115] This tradition produces many injunction applications annually, brought by competitor companies on their own behalf and by consumer or trade organisations on behalf of those whom they represent.

The primary German umbrella consumer association, VZBV, which comprises 16 consumer centres and 25 organisations, commenced 7,215 injunction proceedings in 2002–2006. Of these, 50 per cent were settled, 25 per cent were taken to court, 25 per cent were deferred or stopped, and five per cent were cross-border. The cases resulted in 1,200 warnings. The losses of individual consumers in these cases are small, and individuals refrain from taking action themselves in view of the unfavourable cost-benefit equation of individual court actions. However, VZBV is required to establish standing in each case, and to prove that the trader acted deliberately and that its conduct caused the loss. The last two aspects can be difficult. Since 2002, VZBV has been able to file damages claims where the right has been assigned by individual consumers. This is viewed as a valuable mechanism even if only a single claim is assigned, but a drawback is the need to claim for payment through a declaratory judgment.

Similarly, the Austrian consumer association, VKI, brings many test cases. Its financial support is from the Ministry.[116] There can be consolidation of individual proceedings and individual test cases bundled as a single class action. Recently, litigation financing has been possible from a German financing company and others.

Case Studies: Austrian Cases[117]

The water supply system at a club was contaminated and led to cases of illness. VKI represented 110 claimants, with a total of €170,000 in controversy, and reached a settlement for €130,000.

(continued)

---

[113] When a national contact point for enforcement of cross-border consumer protection issues was required under Regulation 2004/2006 on consumer protection cooperation.

[114] The term 'unfair competition' covers unfair or misleading advertising or commercial practices.

[115] This and the following information was presented by Ms Helke Heideman-Peuser of VZBV at the Portuguese Presidency Conference on Collective Redress for Consumers, Lisbon, 9 and 10 November 2007.

[116] This and the following information was presented by Ulrike Docekal of VKI at the Portuguese Presidency Conference on Collective Redress for Consumers, Lisbon, 9 and 10 November 2007.

[117] Information kindly provided by Ulrike Docekal of VKI. For further details, see <http://www.verbraucherrecht.at> accessed 10 June 2008.

The 'WEB' case. A real estate investment scam led to the conviction of several bank managers. Several cases were brought by groups of individuals represented by lawyers, and VKI brought a case representing 3,200 claimants in recovering compensation of €54 million. Legal fees to all sides ran at €400,000 a day and the case would have continued until 2011 if it had not been settled. It was not possible to obtain agreement to proceed on the basis of one or two test cases, which would have reduced costs, since the defendant did not agree to waive a limitation argument, so all cases had to be pursued. The case was difficult to settle since VKI, the Ministry that finances VKI, the process financing company, and all represented consumers and their lawyers had to agree. Settlement was agreed after one year, at €19.7 million including costs. One consumer voted against the agreement, and it was concluded. Opting out is not provided for under the law; that individual would have had to bring his own case if he had wished. The procedure would now be easier under the law *Verbandsverantwortlichkeitsgesetz.*

Austrian consumers who had food poisoning on holiday were able to recover compensation if they booked the holiday through an Austrian company, but if not, through its Swiss company. VKI started a group action, but the court rejected the claims of those who had booked in Switzerland in view of the requirement that an action should have been brought in Switzerland under the Brussels I Regulation on jurisdiction.

In the Netherlands, the Civil Code permits representative actions by consumer organisations to protect the interests of others, which are sufficiently similar and include common questions of law or fact.[118]

In Italy, consumer organisations have a notably prominent role and negotiate with businesses on behalf of consumers in relation to business practices, often concluding contractual agreements on agreed conduct. An important reason why this function has developed is that the Italian court system is so slow as to have effectively broken down as a dispute resolution mechanism, so consumer organisations have filled the gap.

A new Consumer Code introduced in Italy in 2005 enhances the legal standing of consumer organisations, by creating a registry of the largest associations and permitting those that are so registered to take legal actions against businesses for an injunction for the protection of the collective interests of consumers and end users.[119] Before taking action, the organisation must send a letter to the proposed defendant requiring the latter to desist from the allegedly unlawful conduct; either party may activate a conciliation procedure before the Chamber of Commerce or similar body.

---

[118] Art 3:305a.
[119] Legislative Decree 206/2005, especially art 139.

Portugal

In Portugal, the Portuguese consumer association, DECO, regards itself as the principal enforcement agency in relation to collective consumer redress and operates under a procedure introduced in 1995.[120] Both the public prosecutor and DECO have standing. The law is opt-out and people are notified by adverts in newspapers. The public prosecutor can control the legality of a case. They have wide flexibility in the solutions reachable (eg with a telecom operator, free calls rather than repayments). The judge can use his or her own initiative on calling for evidence.

Since 1995, Portugal permits two proceedings (a right to participate in administrative proceedings and a right of group action for the prevention, interruption or judicial prosecution of defined infringements) that are exercisable by citizens and qualifying associations. [121]

It is somewhat surprising that only three cases have been pursued by DECO since 1995 (although one involved three actions). These cases demonstrate the low value of the amounts which individual consumers typically lose in similar situations, but also the fact that the infringing trader may benefit by a significant total sum. The cost-benefit ratio is clearly unfavourable for any individual consumer to pursue a unitary claim through the courts.

Case Study : Portugal Telecom Charges

DECO brought three actions in 1998 and 1999 alleging that Portugal Telecom had over-charged almost 2 million customers a total of around €120 million. Thus, the average was around €60 each. A settlement agreement allowed, which covered various situations, including the following:

a) every consumer who had his or her telecom receipts for the relevant years could present them to Portugal Telecom and would be reimbursed of the total amount overpaid;
b) since most of consumers did not have their telecom receipts, they could be reimbursed by making free calls on 13 Sundays (beginning in March and ending in June) and on the World Consumer's Day.

The public prosecutor oversees the conduct of the body in prosecuting the case, so can intervene if there is bias between some groups: he or she can hold the association accountable.

---

[120] This and the following information was presented by Luis Silveira Rodrigues of DECO at the Portuguese Presidency Conference on Collective Redress for Consumers, Lisbon, 9 and 10 November 2007, and in communications with the author.
[121] Law 83/95, of 31 August.

Spain[122]

The first relevant judgment that acknowledged collective redress in Spain is the so-called '*Sentencia de la colza*', awarded by the Supreme Court on 26 September 1997, on a criminal proceeding arising from a negligence offence that caused serious personal injuries among a large number of people. The Spanish procedure law allows anyone who has suffered damage arising from a criminal action to aggregate his or her petition of being compensated by the tortfeasor to the criminal prosecution (ie civil liability can be sought within the criminal proceedings). Therefore, criminal courts are given general competence to order a person convicted of an offence to pay compensation for any personal injury, loss or damage that results from the offence. This procedure is widely used, including in situations involving loss to multiple persons.

The leading example was the colza oil case. In this case, a national association of consumers (*Organización de Consumidores y Usuarios*) appeared before the criminal court and stood for each and all of the more than 20,000 people who had been officially listed as affected by the colza oil adulteration.

Case Study: Colza Oil

Administrative authorities authorised imports into Spain of colza oil. In order to protect national production of edible oils and fat, it was stipulated that the colza oil could not be used for human nourishment, but only for industrial activities that, eventually, turned out to be almost exclusively in iron and steel works. With the objective of ensuring that the oil would not be used for human consumption once in Spain, it was ordered that the imported oil had to be denatured from its organoleptic character by being treated with certain authorised products, one of which was the potentially dangerous product, aniline. However, some of the oil was in fact used for human consumption by some importers. Consumers were poisoned (suffering what was called 'toxic syndrome'), their health was seriously affected, and some died.

A Supreme Court judgment in 1992[123] had carefully determined the causal relationship between the consumption of colza oil and the reported injuries, and established the criminal liability of some of the oil distributors. In 1997, in a second criminal proceeding, the Supreme Court declared various public authorities criminally liable. In addition, the representatives of a national consumer association, standing procedurally

(continued)

---

[122] See P Gutiérrez de Cabiedes Hidalgo, 'National Report for Spain in the Globalisation Project'. Further information supplied by A Fererres Comella of Uría Menéndez.
[123] 23 April, 1992—RJ 6783.

for all those consumers who had been affected, asked for the compensation of all damages caused by the criminal action, and successfully demanded declaration of the subsidiary civil liability of the Spanish state. The affected consumers who were represented by the association had been previously officially identified and listed by the central government's forensic services. The criminal court awarded compensation to victims totalling €3,000 million.

The Spanish state's subsidiary liability was relevant because the oil distributors were insolvent, so, until very recently, the central government has been budgeting periodical payments to the affected through the annual State General Budget.

As a consequence of this and other cases, the General Law for Protection of Consumers and Users was passed in 1984 and gave associations of consumers and users standing to file actions to defend their members and the general interests of consumers and users.[124] This mechanism was adopted in the implementation of the EU consumer protection measures discussed in chapter four and other national provisions. The mechanism was reproduced in a general reform of civil procedure under the Civil Procedure Act of 2000, which also extended the right to bring an aggregated claim for damages to groups of individuals who have been harmed.[125]

Two types of people have standing to bring a representative or collective action: first, an association of consumers or users, which must be a legal entity whose social purpose is the defence or protection of consumers or users; and, secondly, a group of the individual consumers affected.[126] In the second case, the individuals in the group will be ascertained, since they will have formed themselves into an opt-in group, and there is no provision for further publicity and their individual claims are processed as normal without any specific provisions such as for selection of test cases or other efficient management practices (the individual claims are, therefore, collective but not representative). However, where the persons affected are indefinite or difficult to determine, a representative claim may be brought by an association.[127]

Where the claim is brought by an association, the association is required to publicise the proceedings in the media, and this constitutes notice of summons to all individuals who may then opt-in.[128] Where the people affected are

[124] Law 26/1984 of 19 July, see art 20.
[125] Law 1/2000 of 7 January; see arts 6, 11, 15, 221, 222.3, 256 and 519. These are at Appendix 6.
[126] Law 1/2000 of 7 January art 11.
[127] Law 1/2000 of 7 January art 11.3.
[128] Law 1/2000 of 7 January art 15.1.

determined or easy to determine, anyone who has responded to the publicity may subsequently participate in the collective proceedings, although they will be bound by any previous acts.[129] Where the people affected are hard to identify, the summoning procedure suspends the claim for a period determined by the court not exceeding two months, and then continues with the participation of all those who have opted in: subsequent joiners are not allowed.[130] A judgment is to determine which consumers and users must benefit under it, save that where this is impossible, it shall specify the details, characteristics and requirements necessary to demand payment and, where appropriate, to apply for or take part in the enforcement of the judgment if requested by the claimant association.[131]

Spain adopts a notably wide solution to the issue of who is bound by a judgment. First, where a judgment declares that conduct was illegal, it is to determine whether it will apply to non-parties and so be sued on by them.[132] Secondly, although the meaning is not fully clear, the law provides that:

[J]udgments shall affect all the parties to the proceedings, including their heirs, as well as non-litigants whose rights underpin the procedural standing of the parties [to the claim].[133]

It is worth noting that few multiple cases in Spain have been resolved through settlement.[134] A loser will pay the winner's costs, on the basis of an official fee scale relating to the value of the matter, but not exceeding one-third of the amount of the claim payable. Consumers and users associations are eligible for legal aid in litigation.[135]

THE CEE SITUATION

The particular historical development of the former socialist states raises idiosyncratic issues. Whilst the Western European states made cumulative efforts to strengthen their market economies and introduce consumer protection, the socialist, and now 'post-socialist', approach paid little attention to consumer law enforcement and, at least on the theoretical level, placed strong support on public enforcement. It was only with the introduction

[129] Law 1/2000 of 7 January art 15.2.
[130] Law 1/2000 of 7 January art 15.3.
[131] Law 1/2000 of 7 January, art. 221.1.
[132] Law 1/2000 of 7 January art. 221.2.
[133] Law 1/2000 of 7 January art 222.3. This provision is assumed to bind non-litigants, and it is interesting that the law provides no opt-out mechanism: see LJ Mieres Mieres, 'On the constitutionality of the new regulations about collective actions followed by associations of consumers and users' (unpublished, Barcelona, 2000).
[134] P Gutiérrez de Cabiedes Hidalgo, 'National Report for Spain in the Globalisation Project'.
[135] Law 1/1996 of 10 January on Legal Aid, as amended by Law 16/2005 of 18 July and Law 27/2006.

of market economy mechanisms—in Hungary and Poland since the early 1980s—that powers of consumer organisations grew.[136]

Until introduction of the EU *acquis*, the Czech Republic, Latvia, Lithuania, Malta, Slovakia and Romania did not have any powers for representative or consumer organisations to bring injunctions or other actions on behalf of consumers or their collective interests. In general, therefore, enforcement powers involving consumer organisations were not common in former socialist countries. There were some exceptions to this rule, such as in: Hungary, where the General Inspectorate of Consumer Protection and social organisations representing common interests of consumers and even qualified foreign entities could bring injunction proceedings;[137] Poland, where social organisations representing consumer interests could bring actions on behalf of named consumers;[138] and Estonia, where the Consumer Protection Board could take injunction actions in the name of an unspecified number of consumers.[139] The position across the new Member States since implementation of the Injunctions Directive and the consumer *acquis* has been towards involvement of consumer organisations, as an inevitable consequence of copying the references in the *acquis* to such organisations.

ISSUES WITH THE INVOLVEMENT OF CIVIL SOCIETY ORGANISATIONS

Consideration of the mechanisms outlined above reveals a rich amalgam of inter-locking public, private, formal and informal dispute resolution mechanisms across the European states.[140] It has been noted above that Member States have evolved in quite different ways in relation to the involvement of private sector organisations[141] in their collective redress mechanisms. The two models that have been identified are, indeed, opposed over whether the primary enforcement mechanism for consumer protection law should be through public authorities or private entities. It has been suggested that the reason why these two different models developed can be understood to a significant extent in terms of national historical development, in the level of confidence in such national authorities as may have existed and in

---

[136] See M Tulibacka, *Product Liability in Poland, Hungary and the Czech Republic—Law in Transition* (Ashgate, 2008).

[137] Art 39 of the Consumer Protection Act 1996.

[138] Art 61 of the Code of Civil Procedure 1964.

[139] Art 12(3) Consumer Protection Act 1994.

[140] J Stuyck *et al*, 'Commission Study on alternative means of consumer redress other than redress through ordinary judicial proceedings' (Catholic University of Leuven, 17 January 2007, issued April 2007). This important study includes reports from every EU Member State plus the United States, Canada and Australia on the range of existing mechanisms.

[141] Chapter notes the involvement of trade associations as coordinating bodies in founding certain types of collective actions.

the courts. Whatever the historical explanation, the existence of two such opposed models raises issues of which model might be more appropriate or more effective.

Classic tests of regulatory legitimacy are legislative mandate, democratic accountability, expertise, due process and efficiency.[142] The current author's analysis in 2006 was:[143]

> The involvement of consumer organisations in enforcing regulation does not score highly if measured against standard criteria for regulatory legitimacy. Assuming that there is legislative mandate, the criteria of expertise and accountability for the exercise of coercive investigative powers and sanctions, are presumably unfavourable: would consumer organisations possess sufficient technical or legal expertise, and be effectively accountable to a sufficiently wide-ranging body of the population? The study on implementation of Directive 98/27 on injunctions for the protection of consumers' interests concluded that consumer organisations could only claim to be integrated into the enforcement of consumer law if they are professionalised, but that this situation does not currently exist.[144] It would be unclear whether the criteria of due process or efficiency would be favourable. Individual organisations may or may not act fairly and even-handedly, or in an efficient manner or take economically efficient actions. Expansion of the number of regulators raises obvious problems of inconsistency between decisions of different regulators, as well as between individual regulators and courts.

Against that view, there is the evidence of widespread activity from the national consumer associations in Germany, Austria, Portugal and Italy referred to above, mostly acting in slightly different national circumstances. The consumer associations in Germany and Austria have been very active in pursuing unfair contract terms and unfair competition, and—crucially— have been funded by government. However, the introduction of the CPC Regulation[145] is based on the premise that single national public agencies are required in each Member State as being the appropriate mechanism for providing effective means of addressing cross-border enforcement.

It may be argued that the issues of democratic accountability and impartiality that are raised in relation to the exercise of any public function by a private body are less significant in relation to the exercise of some powers than others. For example, seeking injunctions in relation to unfair contract terms might be viewed as less significant than seeking possibly large sums of money on behalf of many individuals. The argument has been made in the

---

[142] R Baldwin, *Rules and Government* (Oxford, Clarendon Press, 1995).

[143] C Hodges, 'Collectivism: Evaluating the effectiveness of public and private models for regulating consumer protection' in M Loos and W van Boom (eds), *Collective Enforcement of Consumer Law* (Groningen, Europa Law Publishing, 2007).

[144] MU Docekal, P Kolba, H-W Micklitz and P Rott, *The Implementation of Directive 98/27/EC in the Member States* (Bamberg/Vienna, 2005).

[145] Discussed in ch 4 below.

US context that the involvement of properly constituted, responsible civil society bodies in a representative capacity is preferable to representation by professional investors.[146] Some consumer organisations take the view that assuming a role in the enforcement of legislation may bring too great a conflict of role for a body that is intended to exercise a representative role for consumers' interests with the government and the media.[147] Involvement in financial claims may also bring uncomfortable conflicts of interest, since the interests of the organisation may significantly diverge from those of members, or between groups of members.

It is striking that in those states that maintain the primacy of the public enforcement model, constraints are placed on consumer organisations in relation to their ability to act as regulatory enforcers.[148] Various limiting features have been noted above in France, the Nordic states and the UK (and exist elsewhere), designed to restrict the exercise of enforcement powers to a small number of bona fide permanent consumer organisations, to prevent arbitrary and inappropriate action and to promote consistent and balanced enforcement policy. Such restriction accords with principle, in strengthening the accountability and consistency of a body through it being more permanent, through being constrained by its constitution and powers, and through being answerable to its members.

This reluctance to devolve public powers raises the issue of whether consumer organisations are ineffective and, indeed, appropriate in exercising enforcement powers. The study on implementation of Directive 98/27 on injunctions for the protection of consumers' interests found that the legal and practical significance of injunctive actions is rather low, and described the picture across Member States as showing 'no coherent system'. The number of cross-border cases brought currently appears to be low. It may be significant that the first case was brought by a governmental agency rather than a consumer organisation.[149] If the mechanism of empowering private bodies is to be effective in Europe, serious issues of quality and consistency of practice across Member States need to be dealt with.[150]

The perennial issue of funding is often said to be an impediment to effective action, whether by public or private entities. Given the universal European rule on liability for litigation costs, that the loser pays, private associations may face considerable challenges in having sufficient funds to cover the legal costs of an

---

[146] S Issacharoff, 'Governance and legitimacy in the law of class actions' [1999] S. Ct. Rev. 337.

[147] Personal communication with D Prince of Which?

[148] C Hodges, 'Collectivism: Evaluating the effectiveness of public and private models for regulating consumer protection' in M Loos and W van Boom (eds), *Collective Enforcement of Consumer Law* (Groningen, Europa Law Publishing, 2007).

[149] See the Duchesne SA case study at ch 4 below.

[150] Exactly the same issues have arisen in the involvement of private sector bodies in a regulatory capacity, namely notified bodies in the New Approach product regulatory system: see C Hodges, *European Regulation of Consumer Product Safety* (Oxford, 2005) 65–7.

action, or accepting the risk of costs of losing. However, comparative research by the UK Government showed that provision of funding to consumer groups to take legal action generally results in only marginal involvement by such bodies, since they are wary of the potential legal costs of launching litigation.[151] The 'loser pays' rule is, therefore, the key impediment to further action by private entities. However, the 'loser pays' rule is firmly entrenched in the psyche and architecture of European civil justice systems, and its removal is unthinkable. It is, however, applied differently in different states.

It is significant that the Austrian and German consumer associations receive significant public funds from their governments, without which they could not operate as they have. In contrast, the ability of the Portuguese consumer association DECO to operate solely on the basis of finance from private members is striking. Part of DECO's annual budget has been allocated to collective redress since the introduction of the 2005 law, with considerable success.[152] However, DECO is exempt from legal costs except if it totally loses, in which case it has to pay between one-tenth and one-half of normal costs, but it considers the risk to be sufficiently dissuasive in relation to its budget that it will only back cases with merit.

Public funding is not, of course, the only source of funding for private organisations, but there is a significant variation in the level of funding provided by Member States to consumer organisations, whether for projects or operations.[153] In 2006, France provided over €7 million to national, regional and local consumer bodies, far more than any other Member State, whereas Bulgaria spent €30,000 on consumer organisations: see Figure I.

It would be plausible to address the funding gap, for example either by providing consumer organisations with public funds to initiate legal claims or to pay opponents' costs if they lose, or by permitting the courts to excuse the organisations from having to pay opponents' costs if they lose. However, either of these suggestions raises difficulties. Governments may be reluctant in the current economic climate to fully fund public regulators, so why should they provide funds to non-governmental bodies? Is it fair and just that certain litigants should be excused from the normal 'loser pays' rule, especially where the rule applies to prosecutions or civil claims brought by public authorities? What about distributive and corrective justice for defendants who are improperly sued?

---

[151] Department of Trade and Industry, 'Comparative Report on Consumer Policy Regimes' (October 2003).

[152] This and the following information was presented by Luis Silveira Rodrigues of DECO at the Portuguese Presidency Conference on Collective Redress for Consumers, Lisbon, 9 and 10 November 2007.

[153] Commission Staff Working Document, First Consumer Markets Scoreboard, COM(2008) 31, 29 January 2008 68 at <http://ec.europa.eu/consumers/strategy/sec_2008_87_en.pdf> accessed 10 June 2008.

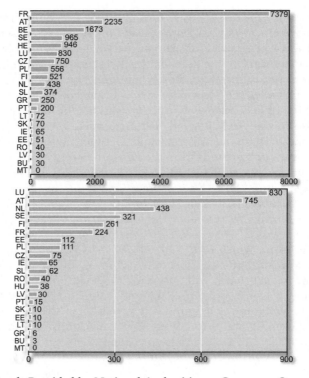

Figure I—Funds Provided by National Authorities to Consumer Organisations, Total and Average Respectively: in €'000[154]

EXPERIMENTATION AND REFORM

It is important to note that the national collective redress mechanisms outlined above are not static. In those Member States where they have existed for some years, the mechanisms are often undergoing reform and development. In other Member States, the mechanisms are by definition new and experimental. The introduction of collective mechanisms for claiming *damages* is a recent development in some states and particularly tentative.

An illustration of this careful approach can be seen in the UK, where the government has three times announced proposals to introduce general 'representative claims' for damages, first in 2001[155] and then revived

---

[154] Source, Commission Staff Working Document, First Consumer Markets Scoreboard, above, Figure 68, from data provided by national authorities to the European Commission, 2006.

[155] Lord Chancellor's Department, 'Representative Claims: Proposed New Procedures, A Consultation Paper' (2001). The proposal for a horizontal new mechanism was dropped in view of concerns about engendering excessive litigation, on the basis that certain vertical, and therefore more limited, measures, would be considered: Lord Chancellor's Department, 'Consultation Response: Representative Claims: Proposed New Procedures' (2002).

separately in 2006 in relation to consumer claims and also competition claims.[156] On the first occasion, the initiative was effectively dropped and the recent initiatives are still under consideration, but have given rise to heated opposition and debate. The rationale for the proposals was simply the assertion that:

[M]any consumers feel unable to bring a court case on their own, while those who do may consider the size of their losses are outweighed by the potentially high legal costs.

Concerns were an absence of evidence of the extent of any need,[157] plus the risk of encouraging lawyer-led and excessive litigation. The government is highly sensitive to any move that would tend to encourage a 'compensation culture', since there has been extensive media assertion that the country has been in the grip of such a culture. Despite both official[158] and academic[159] analysis finding that there has been no statistical increase in general litigation (in fact, rather the reverse since the Woolf civil procedure reforms), there remains a public perception of a problem and political sensitivity of any measure that might inflame the position.

CONCLUSIONS

The national approaches to collective redress are well established in relation to obtaining injunctive relief against infringement of consumer protection legislation. The mechanisms of enforcement differ significantly, within two broad models, depending on whether the national policy for enforcement is primary to involve public authorities or private entities. In contrast, only

---

[156] Department of Trade and Industry, 'Representative Actions in Consumer Protection Legislation: Consultation' (2006): <http://www.dti.gov.uk/consultations/page30259.html> accessed 10 June 2008; Office of Fair Trading, 'Private actions in competition law: effective redress for consumers and business', Discussion Paper (April 2007); and Office of Fair Trading, 'Private actions in competition law: effective redress for consumers and business Recommendations' (November 2007) <http://www.oft.gov.uk/shared_oft/reports/comp_policy/oft916resp.pdf> accessed 10 June 2008.

[157] See ch 7 below.

[158] Better Regulation Task Force, 'Better Routes to Redress' (2004); and Department for Constitutional Affairs, 'Tackling the "Compensation Culture": Government Response to the Better Regulation Task Force Report "Better Routes to Redress"' (2005). The Compensation Act 2006 s 1 was an attempt to clarify that a duty of care should not prevent desirable activities: the government stated that the provision did not alter the standard of care, although this statement was controversial. The Business Plan 2005/06 of the Legal and Judicial Services Group of the Department for Constitutional Affairs included a section headed 'Tackling perceptions of a compensation culture and improving the compensation system'.

[159] K Williams, 'State of fear: Britain's "compensation culture" reviewed' [2005] *Legal Studies* 499. A Morris, 'Spiralling or Stabilising? The "Compensation Culture" and our Propensity to Claim Damages for Personal Injury' (2007) 70(3) *Modern Law Review* 349–78.

national agencies enforce competition law. In both the consumer protection and competition fields, some Member States have introduced experimental mechanisms aimed at providing damages for individuals following breach by one or a small number of traders where multiple consumers or competitors suffer damage.

A diversity of such models for collective damages has emerged and is continuing to emerge. The payment of damages to a large group raises legal and administrative difficulties, especially when the individual sums may be small and difficult to prove. The historical involvement of consumer organisations in playing some role, sometimes very limited, in enforcement of consumer protection, is a feature idiosyncratic to Europe and not found in the United States or many other global jurisdictions, and has led some European jurisdictions to involve consumer associations in coordinating mass claims. Such an approach raises issues of conflicts of interest and of provision of funding. The position is further complicated by the need to address both private compensation and public enforcement issues. Different jurisdictions approach this tension in different ways. Individual states are still introducing new mechanisms or experimenting with existing mechanisms.

All of these issues reinforce the conclusion that no individual model can yet be identified that can be said to be the best solution. It is, therefore, logical to measure the performance and outcomes of all models against objective criteria. Before doing that, however, it is necessary to consider a further family of collective redress models, which has emerged in some states in order to facilitate or manage damages claims brought in the courts.

Importantly, it can be observed that even where the national or EU legislation permits a private entity to take action, this will not occur if there is another mechanism that is more advantageous, such as where a public authority is available and functions effectively, without cost to consumers. Thus, although it is technically possible for private organisations to institute collective action in the Nordic states and the UK, this is in practice unlikely where there are funding constraints and effective alternative public authority mechanisms exist.

3

Court Rules for Multiple Claims

INTRODUCTION

IN AN AGE of mass use of products and services, it is perhaps surprising that instances in which multiple individual litigation claims that relate to the same underlying issues did not arise as an issue for European national courts to confront sooner than they did. The problem has, moreover, seemingly only arisen in a limited number of jurisdictions. The principal examples of where this occurred are England and Wales (1980s onwards, culminating in the Group Litigation Order procedure in 1999),[1] Spain (the adulterated rape seed oil case, leading to the group procedure in the Civil Procedure Act of 2000),[2] the Netherlands (the DES case, requiring a settlement law in 2005)[3] and Germany (the Deutsche Telekom case, requiring the Capital Investors' Model Proceeding Law of 2005).[4] The exceptional case was that of Sweden (2003),[5] where the law was inspired by academic and judicial individuals rather than as a reaction to specific demand and, at least initially, was broadly based on the US Federal Rule 23, although the enacted version was modified so as to adopt an opt-in approach rather than the US opt-out model.

The basic requirements of collective court procedures are to provide for more speedy and efficient processing of claims than would be possible if all individual similar claims were to proceed individually, and to reach a solution that is binding on as many individual as possible. The approach often involves selection of test cases, which will have binding or persuasive effect in resolving the other individual claims in the group. The cases have tended to be claims for damages, such as for personal injuries arising out of cases on product liability (England, Spain, Netherlands) or investment (Germany). The legal mechanism that has been adopted is either a rule of court that enables a court to manage a multiplicity of individual claims

---

[1] Civil Procedure Rules (CPR) 19.III. See C Hodges, *Multi-Party Actions* (Oxford, 2001).

[2] Law 1/2000 of 7 January; see chapter two.

[3] The Act on Collective Settlement of Mass Damages, in force from 27 July 2005.

[4] The German Capital Investors' Model Proceeding Law (KapitalanlegerMusterverfahrens-Gesetz, KapMuG), 2005.

[5] Group Proceedings Act 2002.

more effectively (England), or a general law granting a representative wider rights to represent multiple consumers (civil law jurisdictions). As has been noted above, the recent extension of the Nordic model places the Consumer Ombudsman at the heart of the representative role, whereas in some other states the representative may be an individual member of the group and/or a consumer organisation.

Some of these developments took place in the context of reform of the national rules of civil procedure, against a background of increasing scrutiny on their efficiency and important collaboration on benchmarking carried out by the Council of Europe.[6] There has been a clear trend towards trying to make procedural systems faster, more efficient, and involve lower and more proportionate transactional costs.[7] Countries that have introduced reforms along these lines include Spain,[8] Germany,[9] the UK,[10] the Netherlands,[11] Denmark[12] and Norway.[13] Sweden and Switzerland are reviewing their rules. However, procedures remain very slow in some states,[14] such as Italy and Greece, where there is considerable scope for reducing complexity, cost and delay.[15]

There are, in any event, major divergences between the civil procedure rules of European Member States and the efficiency of their operation.[16] Perhaps surprisingly, these divergences are currently less marked than a simplistic divide between civil law and common law traditions. Indeed, the Commission has concluded that the divergences between national procedures 'are the product of country-specific traditions: rules of procedure as a whole represent a delicate balance and can only be harmonised gradually and with the utmost caution'.[17]

---

[6] European Commission for the Efficiency of justice (CEPEJ), 'European Judicial Systems, Edition 2006 (2004 data)' (2006), at <http://www.coe.int/CEPEJ> accessed 10 June 2008.

[7] CH van Rhee (ed), *European Traditions in Civil Procedure* (Intersentia, 2005).

[8] Law 1/2000 of 7 January 2000 on civil procedure.

[9] Zivilprozessrechtsreformordnung 2001. See P Gottwald, 'Civil Procedure in Germany after the Reform Act of 2001' [2004] 23 CJQ 338–53.

[10] Civil Procedure Rules, 1999.

[11] Wetboek van Burgerlijke Rechtsvordering (Code on Civil Procedure), amended on 1 January 2002.

[12] Administration of Justice Act, 8 June 2006.

[13] Civil Procedure Code of 2005, in force from January 2008.

[14] Green Paper: Access of consumers to justice and the settlement of consumer disputes in the single market, COM(93) 576, 16 November 1993, p 57.

[15] Note comments on lengthy delays in the survey of companies reported in S Vogenauer and S Weatherill, 'The European Community's competence for a comprehensive harmonisation of contract law—an empirical analysis' (2005) 30 EL Rev. Dec, 821–37, 832.

[16] 'Cost-effective measures taken by States to increase the Efficiency of Justice: Report prepared by the European Committee on Legal Cooperation (CDCJ) in consultation with the European Committee on Crime Problems (CDPC)', 23rd Conference of European Ministers of Justice, 8–9 June 2000.

[17] Green Paper: Access of consumers to justice and the settlement of consumer disputes in the single market, COM(93) 576, 16 November 1993, p 56.

As noted in the previous chapter, there has traditionally been strong suspicion of class actions within Europe, on the basis of a general perception that the US experience is that such a mechanism produces undesirable consequences, such as excessive litigation and economic harm (see chapter six). However, in the mechanisms considered in this chapter, the traditional suspicion of class action claims has had to give some way to the requirements of efficiency in the administration of justice. This can be illustrated by the experience in England and Wales in the 1990s[18] and more recently in Germany. The national mechanisms and their origins and experiences will now be examined in greater detail.

THE ENGLISH GLO

A series of multi-party cases arose in England and Wales from the mid-1980s and involved unprecedented high numbers of claimants seeking damages from the same defendants arising out of broadly the same issues, usually injuries allegedly caused by taking medicinal products.[19] When the large number of individual cases was brought to the High Court, lead counsel and solicitors for the parties and the judges involved realised that a new procedural mechanism would have to be invented if the situation was not to become unmanageable and descend into chaos. Accordingly, the judges involved in the successive cases invoked their inherent powers to manage cases and constructed a new approach, which was subsequently enshrined in the Rules of Civil Procedure (CPR), as the Group Litigation Order (GLO: reproduced at Appendix 7).[20]

The GLO procedure provides that all claims that fall within a definition of the group are included and will be managed together, in the same court by the same judge. The emphasis is on *managerial efficiency*. A court can make a GLO when there are a number of similar claims that 'give rise to common or related issues of fact or law'.[21] A single judge will be appointed to manage the case and will make directions as the procedure continues, usually at periodic case management conferences. Claimants who wish to join the group must join a register kept either by the court or by one of the lawyers (hence avoiding the need to issue individual proceedings).[22] The court may order that general statements of case and defence are produced

---

[18] Faced with the practical challenge of managing a sequence of dauntingly large multi-party product liability cases with no explicit rule of court, the judges and lawyers involved developed a standardised approach that was ultimately incorporated as a rule of court: see C Hodges, *Multi-Party Actions* (Oxford, 2001).

[19] See the case histories in C Hodges, *Multi-Party Actions* (Oxford, 2001).

[20] CPR 19.III. See C Hodges, *Multi-Party Actions* (Oxford, 2001).

[21] CPR 19.10.

[22] CPR 19.11(2)(a); Practice Direction—Group Litigation, cl 6.

on issues that are common. The court may appoint lead solicitors, control any advertising of the case and set a cut-off date for people to join the procedure, which is based on the opt-in approach.

The GLO rule is deliberately brief.[23] This is for two reasons. First, the general approach of the court is set out elsewhere, in the general principles that govern civil procedure,[24] and is based on the court having managerial control of all cases and an overriding objective of dealing with cases justly.[25] This approach emphasises the importance of settling cases. Settlement is promoted through pre-action protocols,[26] the approach of judges and the availability of alternative dispute resolution mechanisms. Various non-court compensation schemes operate.[27] Secondly, the approach empowers the managing judge to exercise his or her powers with considerable flexibility, depending on the needs of the specific case. However, this flexibility cannot be exercised capriciously, and it is recognised that the lawyers and parties must have a high a degree of predictability. It is recognised that managing GLOs requires special training and expertise for judges and practitioners, so few judges would be permitted to be involved.

It is particularly important to note the requirement of proportionality in relation to costs, which is a fundamental feature of the CPR. The new approach was influenced by the finding that the most common outcome is that the vast majority of cases are settled by agreement between the parties, not by any final decision of the court. Accordingly, the CPR is based on

---

[23] The Rule is supplemented by Practice Direction, and textbooks record the principles, practice and experience so as to form a practical resource for practitioners and judges. C Hodges, *Multi-Party Actions* (Oxford, 2001), 2nd edn in preparation; M Mildred, 'Group Actions' in G Howells (ed), *The Law of Product Liability* (2nd edn, Butterworths, 2007).

[24] The revolutionary approach adopted in the Civil Procedure rules 1999 was based on reports by Lord Woolf, 'Access to Justice: Interim Report' (1995) and 'Access to Justice: Final Report' (1996).

[25] CPR 1.1(2) specifies the following aspects of what this means:

Dealing with a case justly includes, so far as is practicable—
  a) ensuring that the parties are on an equal footing;
  b) saving expense;
  c) dealing with the case in ways which are proportionate—
    i) to the amount of money involved;
    ii) to the importance of the case;
    iii) to the complexity of the issues; and
    iv) to the financial position of each party;
  d) ensuring that it is dealt with expeditiously and fairly; and
  e) allotting to it an appropriate share of the court's resources, while taking into account the need to allot resources to other cases.

[26] In which claimants give full disclosure of their cases and evidence before instituting proceedings, and defendants then give full responses within a time limit.

[27] Notably in the health sector, such as very large personal injury compensation schemes for lung diseases due to inhaling coal dust and for hand injuries due to operating vibrating machinery. The government has been working on a compensation scheme for medical injuries suffered by patients of the National Health Service: NHS Redress Act 2005.

the premise that the primary objective of procedure should be to put the parties in a position where they can settle the litigation swiftly and cheaply by agreement, whilst of course enabling the court to be in a position to decide the case expeditiously if it should need to do so. Accordingly, parties are expected to undertake standard actions[28] in advance of commencing proceedings so as to facilitate verification of the facts and evidence, establishment of the nature of a case and defence, and encouragement of early settlement such as through mediation.

Any party to a claim (claimant or defendant) may apply to the court for a GLO, or the court may itself start the procedure.[29] This broad approach gives the court and the parties the ability to start the management process at an early opportunity, if this is thought appropriate. An application to the court for a GLO should include:[30]

a) a summary of the nature of the litigation;
b) the number and nature of claims already issued;
c) the number of parties likely to be involved;
d) the common issues of fact or law (the 'GLO issues') that are likely to arise in the litigation; and
e) whether there are any matters that distinguish smaller groups of claims within the wider group.

The criteria for making an Order that cases will be managed under the GLO process are deliberately simple, namely that there are a number of similar claims that 'give rise to common or related issues of fact or law'.[31] The court will examine the facts alleged, and will wish to satisfy itself that the case has substance, and is not hypothetical. There are two further important points. First, the Court of Appeal is known to be very unlikely to interfere with an order making or refusing to make a GLO. Secondly, if the court decides not to make a GLO, the individual cases will still be managed on similar principles of case management. It may be that the judge decides that it is too early for individual cases to be coordinated formally within a GLO, but coordination may be ordered later.

The absence of formal criteria in the English GLO system contrasts with a number of other jurisdictions, which have defined criteria. The other systems may wish to provide clarity and transparency, but they may only end up encouraging what may be a considerable amount of satellite litigation (hearings and appeals) over whether the criteria have or have not been

---

[28] Set out for some types of cases in 'Pre-Action Protocols' <http://www.justice.gov.uk/civil/procrules_fin/contents/practice_directions/pd_protocol.htm> accessed 10 June 2008. No pre-action protocol has yet been established for the GLO situation, since the circumstances of case types can vary.

[29] Practice Direction—Group Litigation cl 4.

[30] Practice Direction—Group Litigation cl 3.2.

[31] CPR 19.10.

satisfied. Such extra litigation has been a feature of the US and Canadian class action systems. All of this is avoided in the English system, where the GLO is regarded simply as one of the court's management tools. The English approach has received some academic criticism, but there have been no calls from practitioners or judges for any alteration in the approach.

The reason for the simplicity of the English approach is that a GLO is a court's tool for managing cases that have been commenced, even if they may be subsequently extended, on an opt-in basis. This approach contrasts with a classical 'class action' mechanism in which a single individual seeks to represent many allegedly similar claims. The English system does not assume that all the individual cases are necessarily the same or that the common issues that arise will predominate over individual issues (as is a certification requirement in rules such as are found in the United States). Since the GLO is a broadly conceived managerial tool, the 'certification requirements' are deliberately relaxed and the court has wide discretion over how to handle the cases in the group.

The English experience of some types of cases, notably product liability, is that individual issues may not predominate and hence, since the Norplant case, there has been a huge presumption that trying to select generic issues from the (differing) individual cases will not be the most effective approach. In other words, the experience of these cases has been that individual cases cannot be taken to be representative of the group, so a de facto 'predominance' test has been applied. There has been some tension here between the Legal Services Commission, which prefers only to spend its limited budget on resolving generic issues, and the courts, which may feel that a generic approach is simply inappropriate in a given case.[32]

It is necessary for the Order to define the group, so that it is clear which individual claims are, or are not, inside the coordinated arrangements. This will usually be a generalised description, but it is important to get it right. An example might be 'any claims against AB Limited in relation to [alleged effects of autism arising from] use of the drug X'.

The broad principles of case management in a GLO are that the managing judge has considerable discretion and is entitled to make robust orders so as to ensure that the litigation makes 'orderly progress'.[33] This means that the judge has to proceed in whatever way seems to him or her will resolve the litigation as efficiently, swiftly and fairly as possible. The aim is to avoid becoming 'bogged down' in dealing in an orderly sequence with every issue that may arise, especially if there are some issues that only affect a minority of cases in the group. It may be that, if the case goes the full distance in court, all relevant issues might theoretically have to be dealt with at some

---

[32] *Hobson v Ashton Morton Slack Solicitors* [2006] EWHC 1134.
[33] *AB v Wyeth & Brother Ltd and Another* [1991] 2 Med LR 341.

stage, but the principal aim is to decide what issues will be really important in leading to the effective early disposition of the totality of the disputes, so that these are decided as swiftly and decisively as possible. In practice, many group cases settle (this is consistent experience from the United States, Canada and now the UK), so if the court can assist in resolving one or more principal issues, then this will assist in achieving settlement. It also needs to be remembered that a group is composed merely of individual cases, and that the overriding purpose is to resolve each of the individual cases, by taking sensible short-cuts that will assist as many as possible as quickly as possible. The courts are providing a dispute resolution service to private parties, albeit within the context of the definitive power of the state, and need to be accountable for the level of service that is provided.

The judge will hold case management conferences at periodic intervals, at which the parties will tell him or her what has been going on and what they would propose to do next, and the judge will make orders on what is to happen next and set time limits. The judge may also give 'indications', which are non-binding statements of what he or she is thinking on subjects that are likely to be the subject matter of orders at a future conference. This approach can act as an early-warning system for the parties, who may nevertheless seek to persuade the judge at the next hearing that the view expressed in the indication should be altered and a different order made.

The managerial approach to civil procedure requires the judge to clarify the issues that arise in the individual cases, and those that are common to all or some of them. There are various options that may be adopted for progressing the cases. It may be decided to have a single Master Statement of Case, which sets out all of the generic issues that are common to all (or most) of the claims, so that any matters in that document do not need to be repeated in every individual claimant's statement of case.[34] If individual statements of case are ordered to be produced, they might therefore only include aspects that concern each individual claimant (eg individual facts or causation or quantification of damage). Alternatively, it might be decided that individual statements of case are unnecessary, or should be delayed, or that a Master Statement of Case is inappropriate or premature.

It may be decided that all cases should be stayed except for one, or a small number of, test case(s), in which a ruling may be made on a point of law that arises in other cases. Alternatively, it may be necessary to proceed for some time with pleading and investigation of all individual claims, and then select one or more as 'lead cases' to be tried first, on the basis that they may illustrate aspects that appear in many cases (but not necessarily all cases), and their resolution will assist resolution of those others, at least by

---

[34] Practice Direction—Group Litigation cl 14.

analogy or indication. The management court has a general power to direct trial of common issues and/or of individual issues.[35]

The practice that has emerged, at least in the product liability GLOs, has overwhelmingly been that of test cases. Thus, as in the most recent cases (Seroxat and foetal anti-convulsant medication), the court has ordered some individual cases to be pleaded fully so that a view could be taken of the issues that are common to most cases and resolved, on the basis that that would be the most effective way of resolving the greatest number of individual cases in the group. Trial of preliminary issues on hypothetical facts in a product liability case has explicitly been held to be inappropriate.[36]

The evidence from England, which mirrors that of the United States, is that certain types of case may be appropriate for certain management approaches, but not others. Thus, in product liability cases, especially alleging damage caused by pharmaceuticals or tobacco, individual issues usually predominate over generic issues. For example, there may be issues in all individual cases over whether the product caused the type of damage, or the actual damage alleged, or whether a carcinoma found in the claimant is one type or another type and whether it is capable of being caused by the product, or whether the claimant was personally aware of the risks, or whether the claim is barred by limitation. In contrast, where it is clear that there are few issues that need to be verified, and that most issues are generic, there is little problem: thus, the claimants injured in a transport disaster may need few formal hurdles to qualify to join, and the only issue may be individual liability or quantification of damage.

This explains the general managerial approach. It may be dangerous to attempt to codify a single approach to all cases. This would squeeze all types of case into the same procedural straightjacket, and the current evidence is that this would not be suitable for all cases. As and when sufficient evidence is available, it may be possible to identify that certain types of approach are most suitable for certain types of case. Hence, some sort of standard approach may evolve, which could be set out in guidelines or codified. However, it currently seems premature to undertake such a classification exercise.

The effective management of a group of cases can involve making some difficult decisions and compromises. In some types of case, decisions that are made on some management issues can make the difference between the success or failure of a case, or a defence. Accordingly, a judge should be aware of the tactical position of the parties, and anticipate that strong views will be put by those whose commercial interests are affected—especially

[35] Practice Direction—Group Litigation cl 15.
[36] *Multiple Claimants v Sanofi-Synthelabo Ltd* [2007] EWCA 1860 (QB).

claimant lawyers and defendant companies. The judge, of course, needs to remain strictly impartial and adopt a balanced approach that seeks to resolve and progress the dispute fairly.

It must be remembered that defendant companies usually need to know the extent of the financial risk of liability that is being claimed against them, in order to comply with accounting and company law requirements. They may need to set aside financial reserves and to notify insurers. It may be difficult for them to confirm insurance cover or to adequately manage the company unless they know how many claims are being made against them and what the sizes of those claims are, and whether the claims are essentially sound or of poor quality. These considerations support a managerial strategy in group litigation of requiring claims to be clarified, rather than remain shadowy.

Equally, it may be important for claimants to be able to assess the scale of their individual costs' liability and risk. The financial viability of the group enterprise is as equally important as the financial situation of each individual.

In order to be able to make orderly progress, the court and the parties need to know how many claims are in the group. There are managerial and financial reasons for this (and it is true of both opt-in and opt-out approaches, although the GLO is an opt-in procedure). The court will assess whether sufficient notice has been given to the existence of a group, and may order the claimants to pay for or arrange further publicity. Any such notice or publicity will normally include a date by which a claimant needs to have joined the group or to have taken other steps, such as applied for legal aid, or served pleadings or evidence (a cut-off date).[37] Failure to meet these deadlines will mean that the court may refuse to admit any claimant who is in default.[38] The court tries to avoid setting cut-off dates that give claimants too short a time to investigate their claims, since this can produce a rush of bad claims that have to be weeded out later and give a false impression of the viability of the group as a whole. There can sometimes be good reasons for *not* imposing a cut-off date, such as where there are difficulties over bringing the case to the attention of people who may be affected.

The court similarly has the power to strike out a group, or individual claims, where the case does not satisfy the normal requirements, such as that it is oppressive, vexatious, bound to fail, involves inordinate and

---

[37] Practice Direction—Group Litigation, cl 13.

[38] The court has found in one case that being too liberal in admitting claimants may only lead to difficulties. In *Nash and Others v Eli Lilly & Co and Others* [1991] 2 Med LR 169 and subsequent hearings, the court extended cut-off dates several times, with the result that four groups of claimants were formed. Most of these claims were subsequently held to be out of time on limitation grounds. The psychological effect on the claimants was unfortunate.

inexcusable delay, and is unjust to the defendants. In a group case, these criteria take on added significance, and an additional criterion of 'viability' has evolved: a case will be struck out if it appears that it is unviable on a cost-benefit basis. The early decisions on application of a viability test in group cases have been strengthened by a general amendment to the Rules applicable in all cases that courts are required to consider 'whether the likely benefits of taking a particular step justify the cost of taking it'.[39] In the group situation, the viability criterion can be regarded as one which is necessary to counter-balance the power that a large group of claimants can have in bringing cases: where many cases may be of limited merit, or would involve excessive costs for limited benefits, the courts will not wish to be used as providing a mechanism for the 'blackmail' of defendants to settle cases of little net worth. This is an important contrast to the general perception of class actions in the United States, where 'blackmail settlements' are said to exist.

In accordance with normal case management principles, the court may decide to order that certain evidence is, or is not, required, either at all or at certain stages of a case. This would apply to either factual or expert evidence. There is no difference of approach here between a normal unitary case and a group of cases, except that the scale of the circumstances and consequences may be larger.

The normal principles of civil litigation apply in a group setting, especially the 'loser pays winner's costs' rule. The arrangements in a group situation can, however, be complex. It is important that the rules and arrangements are clear as early as possible, since lawyers need to be able to advise clients on the financial implications, which can be significant. By joining a group, claimants have the considerable advantage of being able to share the financial costs and risks. However, the costs of a large enterprise can still be huge, and the liability of an individual in investing in the enterprise may therefore be considerable.

Costs are usually divided into 'generic' costs and 'individual' costs: the former are any aspects that relate to all claims generically (and can be large), and the latter relate to any aspects that relate only to each claimant's individual case (and are usually small). Claimants are always subject to an agreement that generic costs will be divided up and shared between them (whether under a contract or under the court's order at the start). The arrangements usually provide that people who join the group late accept liability for the generic costs that have been incurred before they join, but that people who leave the group have their liability for costs frozen or limited or continued, depending on the circumstances: this is a complex area. The court usually orders that the costs of a test or lead case shall be treated

---

[39] CPR 1.4(h).

as generic costs, since they are for the purpose of advancing the whole group's cases. It is not thought fair that a single claimant (who would be in a test or lead case) should be liable for the entirety of the defendants' costs if he or she should lose his or her case: that liability should be shared with the others in the group. The issue of liability for defendants' costs if the enterprise is lost has been contentious, but the normal principles of liability have generally been applied.

Issues on costs are complex in group cases and can have a significant impact. It may be, for example, that a generic case may succeed, but one or more individual claimants may fail on their individual issues. The resultant reduction in what the defendant has to pay may have a significant effect on the overall result.

Case Study: Benzodiazepine Tranquillisers[40]

Various products have been used to treat anxiety. Opiates and hypnotics were used for some 2,000 years. Barbiturates became available in the twentieth century, but were dangerous and lethal in overdose and used for suicide. Benzodiazepines produced from the 1960s were found to have a much improved risk-benefit balance. Benzodiazepines were found to be safe in overdose, but after some 20 years of use, there were reports of dependency and withdrawal symptoms on cessation of therapy.

Following media publicity, legal claims were made from 1987 alleging negligence against the two manufacturers, sometimes joining prescribing doctors. By 1990, over 15,000 claimants had approached solicitors and intimated claims, of which 5,500 issued proceedings, represented by around 3,000 firms of solicitors.

A single judge was appointed to manage the litigation, and adopted an approach that was consistent with, although pre-dated, the case management philosophy of Lord Woolf that was subsequently enshrined in the Civil Procedure Rules 1998. The courts held that they had inherent power to devise such rules as may be necessary to control mass litigation fairly, untrammeled by the normal adversarial system. Important techniques deployed were the voluntary transfer of cases to the appointed judge by courts around the country, the imposition of cut-off dates for claims to be brought within the coordinated management arrangements, the making of orders that cases would be struck out unless they were

(continued)

---

[40] See G Hickinbottom, 'Benzodiazepine litigation' in C Hodges, *Multi-Party Actions* (Oxford, 2001).

brought by the cut-off date, requiring pleadings to be made in the form of a master, against which individual claimants could identify in schedules which points applied to them—thereby avoiding lengthy repetition, and striking out cases that were economically unviable. The judge also indicated concerns over the merits of individual cases.

Nearly all claimants were funded from state Legal Aid. The Legal Aid Board suspected that many individual claims had not been sufficiently investigated, and required legal teams to audit claims, which resulted in many discontinuing and ultimately in the withdrawal of public funding from the entire litigation. The doctors and later the manufacturers applied to the court to strike out individual claims, which the court did on the grounds that the expert medical reports did not substantiate the injuries alleged or that the claimant had no reasonable chance of success. The remaining claims were struck out as an abuse of process, taking into account factors such as limitation defences and considerable problems in proving causation, plus the fact that delay had prejudiced the defendants' right to a fair trial.

After the case collapsed, the Legal Aid Board said that £40 million of public money had been spent on lawyers and medical experts. The defendants had presumably also spent significant sums. No claimants received any money.

Case Study: MMR Vaccines[41]

In February 1988, the *Lancet* published an Early Report on 12 children, eight of whose parents had linked the onset of behavioural symptoms to the triple vaccine given for immunisation against measles, mumps and rubella (MMR). Dr Andrew Wakefield of the Royal Free Hospital in London, a former surgeon with an interest in adult gastroenterology who was known to be interested in whether the measles virus might have a causal role in Crohn's disease, suggested that there was a causal association between MMR and autism.

A solicitor, Richard Barr, helped facilitate the referral to Dr Wakefield of children whose parents thought the vaccine might have caused an inflammatory bowel disorder as well as autism. In August 1996, the Legal Aid Board granted £55,000 for Dr Wakefield's research on a possible link between the MMR vaccine and autism.

(continued)

---

[41] Information kindly supplied by J Meltzer of Lovells LLP, and also J Stuart-Smith QC at a conference at the Centre for Socio-Legal Studies, Oxford University in December 2006.

Considerable media publicity was given to Dr Wakefield's assertion that the MMR vaccine could cause autism, and this led to a major public health scare. Thus, in broad terms, the research which led to the public health scare came about because the Legal Aid Board was prepared to grant funding for exploratory scientific research to support otherwise speculative litigation.

In 1998, the first claims were issued against three pharmaceutical companies; two manufacturers, SmithKline Beecham and Merck Co Inc, and a marketing authorisation holder, Aventis Pasteur MSD. The claims were brought under Part 1 of the Consumer Protection Act (CPA), which implements the 1985 EU Product Liability Directive. The CPA came into effect in 1988, the same year as the MMR vaccination was first routinely administered to children in the UK.

The claimants in the MMR litigation were almost all children whose claims alleged that the vaccine caused autism and other disorders. It was said that the claimants were developing normally until usually their second year, when they were given the MMR vaccination and within a few weeks or months they became ill and/or their development regressed leaving them with continuing serious disorders. The claimants said that this was not a coincidence, but attributable to the MMR vaccine.

The group of claimants was constituted in July 1999, under a practice direction from the Lord Chief Justice. Although this was before GLOs came into effect, for all practical purposes the litigation was conducted under the GLO procedures in Part 19 of the Civil Procedure Rules. The claimants were funded by the Legal Aid Board (later known as the Legal Services Commission (LSC)).

The defendants said that there was no medical or scientific evidence that the vaccine caused such disorders in any group of children so as to render it defective within the meaning of the CPA, nor was there any evidence that it had caused such a disorder in any of the claimants. It was well established that autism commonly manifested itself during the second year of an affected child's life at a time shortly after most children in this country received their routine MMR immunisation. This timing was the same prior to the introduction of MMR in 1988.

The case proceeded with eight illustrative lead cases, four chosen by the claimants and four by the defendants from a cohort of over 1,000 cases. The trial of these lead cases, which was due to have started in April 2004, was to have been restricted to the issue of whether the vaccines were defective and if so whether the defects caused the conditions complained of by the eight lead claimants.

The litigation effectively collapsed in the summer of 2003 when the LSC withdrew funding. This was a direct consequence of the LSC having

(*continued*)

assessed the experts' reports served by the parties (28 from the claimants and 32 from the defendants) from which it became apparent that the claimants' case was not supported by the scientific evidence.

One of the reasons that the litigation was so drawn out was because from an evidential point of view it was started before the claimants' lawyers were able to establish if they had a viable case. The CPA imposes a ten-year 'long stop' cut-off period for claims, which required that children immunised with vaccine put into circulation in 1988 had to bring their claims by the relevant date in 1998.

The difficulty for the claimants was that they were not really ready to proceed, having at that stage, as they admitted, inadequate evidence of causation to succeed at trial. At the first Case Management Conference in September 1999, in asking the court for the opportunity to gather further evidence, the claimants' counsel made the somewhat unusual admission that the claimants would not succeed if there was a trial in the near future because of inadequate evidence of causation.

The search for evidence of causation, which had, as it were, been licensed by public funding, had a pervasive impact on the management of the litigation. The claimants were repeatedly given time to conduct research and carry out a range of tests on the claimants and others which they hoped would provide supportive evidence. The pursuit of such evidence was one of the main reasons for the length of the pre-trial period.

When the LSC finally withdrew funding for the litigation, which had cost it at least £15 million, it candidly acknowledged that the ten-year time limit under the CPA meant that 'it was necessary to start court proceedings before the medical research had concluded' and that 'this was the first case in which research had been funded by legal aid. In retrospect, it was not effective or appropriate for the LSC to fund research. The court is not the place to prove new medical truths.

EXPERIENCE WITH ENGLISH GROUP ACTIONS

Following the introduction of the Access to Justice Act in 2000, the volume of multi-party actions recorded by the LSC has been as shown in Table 3:[42]

---

[42] Legal Services Commission, Freedom of Information disclosure to the author, September 2007.

Table 3—Number of Multi-party Actions Recorded by the Legal Services Commission in England and Wales

Year	Number of actions
2000/01	133
2001/02	67
2002/03	45
2003/04	16
2004/05	20
2005/06	8
2006/07	4

The year-on-year reduction is primarily due to the decrease in the number of child abuse actions being brought. There were substantial police investigations in the 1980s and 1990s following the identification of abuse in children's homes. These police investigations and criminal prosecutions resulted in claims. The peak in these actions has now passed.

The published data reveal a wide range of subject matter for cases brought under the GLO procedure or its previously developing arrangements. It has tended to be the case that types have 'spiked' at different times. During the 1980s and 1990s, the claims involving the largest number of claimants related to medicinal products, which were mostly lost. Of the 293 actions from 2000 to 2007, the main categories of action are shown in Table 4.

Table 4—Main Categories of Group Litigation Orders in England and Wales, 2000–07

Category	Number
Child abuse	156
Health, medical and pharmacological	34
Prisoner actions	27

An example of where efficient coordination of mass individual small claims has not worked is the recent bank charges litigation.

Case Study: Bank Charges

In March 2006, Which?, the consumers' association, launched a campaign that retail banks' charges were unfair in various circumstances, such as charges for overdrawn accounts when there was no overdraft

(continued)

facility, or for exceeding an agreed limit, or where there were insufficient funds in an account to honour a cheque or other payment.[43]

Many thousands complained to the Financial Services Ombudsman, which involved no cost to the complainant. The campaign received wide publicity, and there was a significant amount of advertising by private companies offering claims management services for bringing individual court actions. Between March 2006 and August 2007, some 53,000 customers filed claims in the county courts,[44] which significantly overloaded the system. Banks usually filed standard defences and frequently settled cases shortly before the hearing.

On 26 July 2007, the OFT commenced a test case in the Commercial Court against seven banks for determination of whether the Unfair Terms in Consumer Contracts Regulations applied to unauthorised overdrafts, and whether the prevalent terms were unfair under such Regulations.[45] The banks then applied in the county courts for claims there to be stayed pending the outcome of the Commercial Court process, and district judges listed cases in blocks, so as to afford claimants an opportunity to object to a stay, with around 30 per cent objecting.

On 27 July 2007, the Ministry of Justice took the unusual step of issuing guidance that the Financial Ombudsman Service had put its activities on hold pending the outcome of the Commercial Court test case, that the county courts were anticipated to do the same, and that claims management companies were reminded to do the same.[46]

In October 2007, it was reported that, if the test case were to be decided against the banks, the Financial Services Authority would consider using its power[47] to order them to repay amounts unfairly charged.[48] In April 2008, the High Court decided that the banks' terms were subject to the unfair terms legislation,[49] but the point is likely to be appealed and a further determination is necessary on whether each of the terms was unfair, so final resolution may take some years.

---

[43] <http://www.which.co.uk/reports_and_campaigns/money/campaigns/Banking%20and%20credit/Bank%20charges/banl_charges_campaign_559_74996.jsp> accessed 30 January 2008.

[44] See figures quoted in RP Mulheron, *Reform of Collective Redress in England and Wales: A Perspective of Need* (Civil Justice Council, 2008) table 16.

[45] See <http://www.oft.gov.uk/advice_and_resources/resource_base/market-studies/personal2> accessed 10 June 2008.

[46] Claims Management Services Regulation: Claims in Respect of Bank Charges: Guidance Note 2007.

[47] Financial Services and Markets Act 2000 ss 382 and 383.

[48] M Hickman, 'FSA could "force banks to return penalty charges"' *The Independent* (20 October 2007).

[49] *The Office of Fair Trading v Abbey National Plc and 7 others* [2008] EWHC 875.

This case illustrates that serious issues can arise over the scope for inconsistent decisions and delay if different procedures (here regulatory, ombudsmen and courts) are pursued at once.[50] The initial issue was a duplication of redress processes: the FOS and the courts. The FOS is free to claimants, but private claims need funding, and claims management companies sought opportunities to make money and successfully advertised their services, in which their commercial advantage was in bringing multiple individual cases. They had no interest in seeking coordination of claims through the GLO process. This is a salutary lesson for jurisdictions in which funding of litigation is increasingly to be provided by intermediaries. The case also highlights the fact that a historical principle of 'party autonomy' over controlling litigation is clearly outmoded, and that some issues would be resolved more efficiently if strategic control were exercised by governments, regulators and the courts.

IRELAND

In Ireland, the Law Reform Commission first proposed in 2003 a mechanism that was closely modeled on US-style class actions,[51] but this was widely criticised, not least by the Minister of Justice, who said that people could simply be expected to bring increased claims against the state. However, their final report adopted the different approach of recommending the English GLO model, on the basis that it was more suited to achieving a balanced and flexible solution.[52] The Irish Rules Committee has yet to adopt the recommended approach.

SWEDEN

Unlike the other states considered in this section, Sweden introduced its Act on Class Actions spontaneously, not in response to a need that had crystallised in particular court cases, but as a result of an initiative by Professor Per Henrik Lindblom of Uppsala University. Professor Lindblom became convinced that it would be necessary for a modern state to have a class action law and based his proposals on the model of US Federal Rule 23. In particular, the proposals were based on the opt-out class actions approach and provided for contingency fees. The introduction of the initial proposals led to a period of intense debate in Sweden, in which industry mounted a fierce opposition on the basis of the risk of encouraging a significant increase in litigation, particularly unnecessary litigation that would harm

---

[50] RP Mulheron, *Reform of Collective Redress in England and Wales: A Perspective of Need* (Civil Justice Council, 2008) 126 *ff*.

[51] The Law Reform Commission, 'Consultation Paper: Multi-Party Litigation (Class Actions)' (July 2003) LRC CP 25-2003.

[52] The Law Reform Commission, 'Report: Multi-Party Litigation' (2005) LRC 76-2005.

industry and the economy, as was argued to be the case in the United States. When the Act was eventually passed in 2002, the opt-out was reversed to being an opt-in, and the contingency fee proposal was modified.[53]

The Swedish Act, effective as of 1 January 2003, permits an individual or organisation to bring a claim on behalf of itself or others. The law defines a class action as an action that a plaintiff brings as the representative of several persons with legal effects for them, although they are not parties to the case.[54] A group action may be instituted as one of three types (a private group action, an organisation action or a public group action), depending on whether the representative plaintiff is an individual, an association or a public authority. An individual representative must have a personal claim that is subject to the action;[55] an association must be not-for-profit that, according to its rules, protects consumer or wage-earner interests in disputes between consumers and a business operator regarding any goods, services or other utility that the business operator offers to consumers;[56] and an authority must have been approved by the government as suitable to represent the members of a group that has a dispute of a given subject.[57]

There are the following special preconditions for permitting group action proceedings:[58]

a) the action is founded on circumstances that are common or of a similar nature for the claims of the members of the group;
b) group proceedings do not appear to be inappropriate owing to some claims of the members of the group, as regards grounds, differing substantially from other claims;
c) the larger part of the claims to which the action relates cannot equally well be pursued by personal actions by the members of the group;
d) the group, taking into consideration its size, ambit and otherwise is appropriately defined; and
e) the plaintiff, taking into consideration the plaintiff's interest in the substantive matter, the plaintiff's financial capacity to bring a group action and the circumstances generally, is appropriate to represent the members of the group in the case.

The originator applies to the court giving specified details[59] and, unless he or she is a public authority, must be represented by a lawyer.[60] If the court approves the group procedure, individual members of the group must then

---

[53] Act on Class Actions issued on 30 May 2002, SFS 2002:599. Text at Appendix 3.
[54] s 1.
[55] s 4.
[56] s 5.
[57] s 7.
[58] s 8.
[59] s 9.
[60] s 11.

be notified of specified information.[61] A member who does not then give specific notice to be included shall be deemed to have withdrawn (an opt-in procedure).[62] Further notification is required of settlement, a final judgment, or in various other circumstances.[63]

In order to respond to the perceived threat of importing a significant increase in US-style litigation, various filters were included in the Swedish Act. First, the special preconditions for qualifying as a class action have been noted above. Secondly, the categories of who is allowed to be a class representative adopt the familiar national (and Nordic) mechanism of empowering a public authority (see above) and the pre-existing European mechanism of a private organisation. Further safeguards included in the legislation are as follows. The plaintiff is required to protect the interests of the group members, and must afford members an opportunity to express their views on important issues if this can be done without great inconvenience.[64] The court may assign someone, besides the plaintiff or instead of the plaintiff, to conduct the action on a particular issue or a part of the substantive matter that only applies to the rights of particular members of the group if this promotes an appropriate processing. Such an assignment may be given to a member of the group or, if this is not possible, someone else.[65] If the plaintiff is no longer considered to be appropriate to represent the members of the group in the case, the court shall appoint someone else to conduct the group's action as plaintiff. If no new plaintiff can be appointed in accordance with the first paragraph, the group action shall be dismissed.[66] The court may proceed to deal with particular issues as between some of the group if that is appropriate.[67] The court is required to approve settlements concluded between the parties. The settlement must be confirmed provided it is not discriminatory against particular members of the group or in another way manifestly unfair.[68]

The normal 'loser pays' rule applies in class actions as in single cases, save for small claims. It is the group plaintiff who is responsible for the costs risk. An individual member of the group will only assume the costs risk if he or she has intervened and become a party to the proceedings.

As mentioned above, the initial legislative proposal provided for a US-style contingency fee system. The Act does not go so far, but permits a written fee agreement with a lawyer that fees shall be determined having regard to the extent to which the claims of the members of the group is successful (a risk agreement). Such an agreement may only be asserted against the members of

---

[61] s 13.
[62] s 14.
[63] s 49.
[64] s 17.
[65] s 20.
[66] s 22.
[67] s 22.
[68] s 27.

the group if a court has approved it.[69] A risk agreement may only be approved if the agreement is reasonable having regard to the nature of the substantive matter. The agreement shall indicate the way in which it is intended that the fees will deviate from normal fees if the claims of the members of the group were to be granted or rejected completely. The agreement may not be approved if the fees are based solely on the value of the subject of dispute.[70]

In the first five years' experience with the Class Action Act, there has been one claim brought by the Consumer Ombudsman and eight private claims, of which three were dismissed by the District Court.[71] The cases have involved failure to supply electricity to 7,000 people under a fixed-price contract (the Ombudsman claim), and issues such as stranded airline passengers, loss of investment value, illegal seizure by the authorities of privately imported alcoholic beverages, and aviation noise from an airport. Private organisations have backed various collective actions, but not yet brought one as representative claimant. There have been reports of other potential cases. The experience is being reviewed by the government, and a report prepared by an appeal judge.

THE NETHERLANDS

The Netherlands is unusual, in that its procedure deals only with the *settlement* of a multi-party situation, rather than with the commencement and processing of a collective action. This arose out of the specific need to provide a mechanism to resolve a specific and unusual case by providing for a settlement that had been reached between some parties to be binding on as many people with similar claims as possible. The case was the DES case.

Case Study: DES[72]

Between 1947 and 1976, many women took the medicinal product diethylstilboestrol (DES) during pregnancy to prevent premature birth and miscarriage. It was later found that the drug was associated with cervical cancer and other injuries. In 1986, six daughters of women who had taken the drug initiated proceedings against 13 manufacturers. The plaintiffs could not establish which manufacturer's product was responsible for their individual harm, but the Dutch Supreme Court

(continued)

---

[69] s 38.

[70] s 39.

[71] See PH Lindblom, 'National Report for Sweden' (Globalisation Project).

[72] See D Lunsing Scheurleer and I Tzankova, 'Way of the future', IFLR, October 2007 2. Undated Note by the Ministry of Justice. JM Newland *et al*, 'A Touch of Dutch: Group Actions in the Netherlands' (2006) 5 *Class Action* 394.

held in a controversial decision that a theory of alternative causation could apply.[73] The decision also required that DES-users should register in order to preserve their rights. After publication of this decision, a DES Centre was established. Within six weeks, over 18,000 mothers, daughters and sons had registered. Some estimates were that 440,000 people might have been affected.

The pharmaceutical industry and its insurers initiated negotiations and seven years later, in 1999, a settlement was reached that a DES fund would be established of €35 million, funded almost equally by manufacturers and insurers, on condition that the settlement would be final. Under the pre-existing law on collective actions,[74] it was required that all defendants should opt-in, which the defendants believed was unworkable, so they persuaded the Ministry of Justice to propose urgently an Act that adopted an opt-out procedure, which came into force on 27 July 2005 and enabled the litigation to be settled.[75]

Thus, the Act on Collective Settlement of Mass Damages provides that where a settlement has been agreed between a party and a foundation or association with full legal competence, at their joint request it may be submitted to the Amsterdam Court of Appeal for approval. The effect of approval by that court will be that each of the persons entitled to compensation will be regarded as a party to it, and the terms will be binding on all affected persons except those who have chosen to opt out by sending written notification to a specified person within three months after the announcement of the court's decision.[76] A person who could not have known of his or her loss at the time of the announcement may similarly opt out later by sending notification on becoming aware of the loss.[77]

The agreement must include the following:[78]

a) a description of the group or groups of persons on whose behalf the agreement was concluded, according to the nature and the seriousness of their loss;

[73] The rule on alternative causation is that where the actions of each initiator of multiple activities would have been sufficient to cause the damage, but it remains uncertain which one in fact caused an individual's damage, each activity is regarded as a cause, and the victim is entitled to claim the whole amount of damage from any one defendant: HR 9 October 1992, NJ 1994/535 (DES).

[74] Civil Code, art 3:305a–c, which came into force on 1 July 1994, permits public interest and general collective actions, but does not permit damages claims.

[75] One DES daughter opted out and compensation has been paid to many in accordance with the agreement: see <http://www.descentrum.nl> and <http://www.desfonds.nl>, both accessed 10 June 2008.

[76] Civil Code art 908 of Book 7.

[77] Civil Code art 908.3 of Book 7.

[78] Civil Code art 907.2 of Book 7.

b) the most accurate possible indication of the number of persons belonging to the group or groups;
c) the compensation that will be awarded to these persons;
d) the conditions that these persons must meet to qualify for the compensation;
e) the procedure that these persons must meet to qualify for the compensation;
f) the name and place of residence of the person to whom the written notifications relating to the opt-out should be sent.

The making of the request interrupts the limitation period for any legal action for compensation between the parties.[79] Notice of the agreement and the hearing must be mailed to the last known addresses of all persons known to the petitioners, and through one or more newspapers designed by the court.[80] The court may give the parties the opportunity to add further provisions to the agreement or to amend it.[81] The court may order that one or more experts shall make a report on points relevant to the request.[82]

The court is required to reject the request if:[83]

a) the agreement does not comply with the requirements as to its content, noted above;
b) the amount of the compensation awarded is not reasonable having regard, inter alia, to the extent of the damage, the ease and speed with which the compensation can be obtained and the possible causes of the damage;
c) insufficient security is provided for the payment of the claims of persons on whose behalf the agreement was concluded;
d) the agreement does not provide for the independent determination of the compensation to be paid pursuant to the agreement;
e) the interests of the persons on whose behalf the agreement was concluded are otherwise not adequately safeguarded;
f) the foundation or association representing the claimants is not sufficiently representative of the interests of persons on whose behalf the agreement was concluded;
g) the group of persons on whose behalf the agreement was concluded is not large enough to justify a declaration that the agreement is binding;
h) there is a legal entity that will provide the compensation pursuant to the agreement and it is not a party to the agreement.

---

[79] Civil Code art 907.5 of Book 7.
[80] Code of Civil Procedure Title 14, art 1013.
[81] Civil Code art 907.4 of Book 7.
[82] Code of Civil Procedure Title 14, art 1016.1.
[83] Civil Code art 907.3 of Book 7.

The court may decide that the costs shall be borne by one or more of the petitioners.[84] A copy of the decision shall be sent by ordinary post to the persons known to be entitled to compensation and to the relevant legal entities, containing specified details, including how to opt out.[85] A defendant may opt out during the period of not longer than six months after the expiry of the opt-out period for claimants. The purpose of this is to enable a defendant to escape from a deal in which too few claimants have opted in. It places some pressure on claimants to opt in, but also on defendants to agree reasonable settlements.

The essence of the procedure is therefore to make a reasonable settlement binding on as many possible claimants as possible and on the defendants. Most of the individual claimants may not, of course, have taken part in the claim or the settlement negotiations, and they may have limited appreciation of the relevant factors. The procedure recognises the reality that some responsible independent representation of claimants' interests is a practical approach, but also a necessary requirement. Such a system places a considerable burden to ensure fairness on the representative organisation(s) and on the court. Indeed, the judiciary was initially critical of the Act on the basis that it jeopardises their impartiality, but has since become more comfortable with the role.[86] In addition to the issue of whether the terms of a settlement are reasonable, issues may arise of conflict of interest between representatives and claimants, or between different groups of claimants. It is inevitable that a heavy responsibility is placed on the court to ensure fairness.

Useful experience has been gained with the Act since the DES case in the Dexia Bank and Shell hydrocarbon reserves cases.

Case Study: Dexia Bank[87]

A company offered various types of equity lease agreements to customers from 1992, which involved the investment of loans in shares. A total of 713,450 agreements were concluded with 395,000 customers. After the share index (AEX) fell from 700 to 270 points between September 2000 and May 2003, the loan debts significantly exceeded the share values. Various collective actions were commenced alleging that the sellers had

(continued)

---

[84] Code of Civil Procedure Title 14, art 1016.2.

[85] Code of Civil Procedure Title 14, art 1017.3.

[86] See D Lunsing Scheurleer and I Tzankova, 'Way of the future', IFLR October 2007 2; I Tzankova, 'The Netherlands Report' in the Globalisation Project.

[87] See Undated Note by the Ministry of Justice and presentations by Ben Knüppe, CEO of Dexia Bank Nederland, at the European Commission conferences at Leuven on 29 June 2007 and Lisbon on 9 and 10 November 2007.

not alerted customers of the risk that share values could go down as well as up. Dexia Bank Nederland had acquired the loan company without knowledge of the exposure, the company having been merged into Dexia rather bought as a subsidiary.

A mediation in 2005 between Dexia and various representative associations led to agreement that consumers would be paid all or part of their residual claims at the end of their contracts' duration, and the bank wrote off €1 billion. The Amsterdam Court of Appeal approved the agreement in January 2007.[88] The settlement was therefore binding an all borrowers except those who opted out: 90 per cent of consumers accepted the terms, but 23,000 opted out. At the time of writing, a number of these opt-out cases are being pursued individually and remain unresolved, but many, usually represented by claims management intermediaries working on a 'no cure no pay' fee basis,[89] have as yet not initiated individual proceedings. The court established a team of 30 people (including 10 judges) to deal with the individual claims of those who opted out. Discussions have proceeded between the court and the lawyers for the bank and the individuals about which of several options might be agreed for proceeding to resolve these individual opt-out claims.[90]

In reviewing the performance of the Dutch procedure, Mr Ben Knüppe, the CEO of the defendant bank, commented as follows: [91]

> The encouragement that the Law places on parties to use ADR was very useful. But there was perceived still to be a need for a court solution in order to resolve the issues that remained unresolved through the ADR and approved settlement mechanism. It is in the business interest to resolve things quickly. What worries me is that lawyers are regulated but aggressive consumer groups are not, and do not offer quality. Legal uncertainty led to a problem and the system was not able to resolve it properly.

The importance of a settlement mechanism that can be initiated by a defendant was shown in the Shell hydrocarbon reserves case study. In that case, the settlement was initiated by the defendant. Moreover, it was a worldwide settlement that provided compensation for *all* shareholders except for those resident in the United States.

---

[88] See <http://www.dexialease.nl> and <http://www.eegalease.nl>, both accessed 10 June 2008.

[89] These claims management companies are able to agree 'no cure no pay' fees, which are illegal for lawyers.

[90] Information kindly supplied by I Tsankova, April 2008.

[91] At the European Presidency conference at Lisbon on 9 and 10 November 2007.

Case Study: Shell Hydrocarbon Reserves[92]

On 9 January 2004, following an internal review, Shell (Royal Dutch and Shell Transport, the two former parent companies of the 'Shell Group') announced that it would re-categorise approximately 3.9 billion barrels of oil equivalent ('boe') out of its reported proved reserves. The re-categorisations were based on a determination that the reserves did not strictly comply with the definition of 'proved' reserves established[93] by the US Securities and Exchange Commission ('the SEC').[94] On 24 August 2004, the UK Financial Services Authority and the SEC announced final settlements of their investigations with respect to Shell. As a result of the settlement, Shell, without admitting or denying the SEC's findings or conclusions, entered into a consent agreement with the SEC and paid a civil penalty of $120 million.

A number of putative class actions were filed in the United States against Shell in relation to the re-categorisation. One class action was commenced in the US District Court for the District of New Jersey. A non-US shareholder, Mr Peter M Wood, was recruited into that action through an appeal on the website (<http://www.royaldutchshellplc.com> accessed 10 June 2008). The US District Court for New Jersey initially ruled that Mr Wood could represent all non-US shareholders, but a new judge reversed the ruling on the issue of 'subject matter jurisdiction'.

After the announcement of the re-categorisations, the price of Shell's shares fell. Shell made an offer to compensate certain non-US shareholders for losses alleged as a result of the price fall, without any admission of wrongdoing, illegal conduct or causation of loss. Shell entered into an agreement with a foundation (the Shell Reserves Compensation Foundation) and various associations that represent the interests of retail shareholders and the institutional investors, including the Dutch Equity Holders' Association and others, under which non-US Shell shareholders would receive $352 million. The agreement called on the SEC to distribute $96 million of the $120 million fine to the non-US investors, an amount that corresponded to their share of investor base.[95] The non-US arrangement would benefit both the shareholders who were parties to the agreement and other shareholders who fell within the definition of participating shareholders. That agreement was contingent on the US District Court of New Jersey declining jurisdiction over the non-US

(continued)

---

[92] See Undated Note by the Ministry of Justice.
[93] Rule 10-4 of Regulation S-X and interpretations of the definition published by the SEC.
[94] See <http://www.shellvergoeding.nl> accessed 10 June 2008.
[95] See <http://www.shellsettlement.com> accessed 10 June 2008 .

investors, which it did on 13 November 2007, and on approval by the Amsterdam Court of Appeal, which is expected to rule in early 2009. An agreement approved in this way would be expected to be enforceable throughout the EU.

In March 2008, Shell announced settlement in principle of the US shareholder class action claims for an additional $79.9 million plus $2.95 million, being proportional to the amounts payable under the proposed Dutch settlement, plus legal costs, subject to approval by the US Court.[96] If the Dutch and US settlements are achieved, the combined cost would be around $600 million, including the $90 million paid in 2005 to the US employee shareholders. The US legal fees would be approved by the court as a percentage of the total recovery paid.[97]

In practice, it should be understood that the Netherlands has two systems for collective claims. In addition to the Settlement Law discussed above, the litigation system permits a foundation or association to bring a collective claim without an individual lead plaintiff. Under that mechanism, there is no court supervision over appointment of lead counsel and it is only possible to bundle claims if there are no individual issues. No damages are claimable, but it has instead been the practice to request a declaration that there has been a breach.[98] *Res judicata* only applies between the parties, and this is problematic for defendants, who want to avoid more cases.

GERMANY

The traditional prevailing view amongst German lawyers was that there was no need for a class action mechanism, and that all claims could be resolved individually.[99] Indeed, even assignment of consumer claims so as to enable a representative action to be brought was held to be permissible in exceptional cases only.[100] However, the traditional approach was seriously

---

[96] Rivalry between competing US claimant law firms has been cited as playing a significant part in the structuring of the deal so as to split the European and US shareholders: see RA Nagareda, 'Aggregate Litigation across the Atlantic and the Future of American Exceptionalism', Vanderbilt University Law School Working Paper No 08-05, accessible at <http://ssrn.com/abstract=1114858> accessed 10 June 2008.

[97] A request for fees of $47 million has been reported: J Jones, 'Bad Blood over Royal Dutch Fees' *Am. Lawyer*, June 2007 58.

[98] An example of such a case involved people who visited a fair and caught Legionnaires Disease from sprayed jacuzzi water: mentioned by D Lunsingh Scheurleer at the European Commission conference at Lisbon on 9 and 10 November 2007.

[99] H-W Micklitz, 'Collective private enforcement of consumer Law: the key questions' in W van Boom and M Loos (eds), *Collective Enforcement of Consumer Law* (Europa, 2007).

[100] OLD Düsseldorf, 17 October 2003, case no 16 U 197/02.

undermined by expediency as a result of the need for the courts to be able to manage litigation brought by 15,000 individual claimants against Deutsche Telekom.

Case Study: Deutsche Telekom

Deutsche Telekom made a public offering of American Depository Shares valued at €13 billion on 17 June 2000, which were also traded in the secondary market.[101] On 24 July 2000, the company announced its planned $50.7 billion takeover of VoiceStream, and the share price declined almost seven points. On 28 July 2000, it announced a 26 per cent fall in profits for the half year.

Investors claimed that the company violated ss 11, 12(a)(2) and 15 of the Securities Act 1933 in that the Registration and Prospectus contained material misrepresentations and/or omissions in failing to disclose that the company was in the advanced stage of merger negotiations with VoiceStream and that profits had been significantly negatively affected by increased business costs, and as a result the assets were significantly overvalued, and this had contributed to a drop in share value of 86 per cent.

Attorneys commenced a class action on behalf of the US investors in the US District Court for the Southern District of New York. On 29 January 2005, an agreement was announced for settlement of the class action under which the company would pay investors $120 million, a significant part being believed to be covered by D&O insurance policies, subject to the court's approval. The company did not concede any wrongdoing.

The position of German investors was adversely compared with the fact that a class claim by investors in the United States was settled there for $120 million. Lawyers argued that many elderly investors had lost their savings, but the company rejected any wrongdoing and said that its US settlement had been undertaken because of the uncertainties of the US court system, including jury trials.

15,000 individuals brought claims against Deutsche Telekom in the Frankfurt regional court. The German Procedural Code did not permit these similar claims to be managed in some coordinated fashion, and the judges who were in charge of the many individual claims recognised that they needed some new powers, such as to try specimen 'lead claims'

(continued)

---

[101] See generally: Stanford Law School Securities Class Action Clearinghouse in cooperation with Cornerstone Research, <http://securities.stanford.edu/1016/USD00/> accessed 10 June 2008.

and in the meanwhile stay the majority of other claims.[102] It took the court clerk some three months to register the 2,100 claims filed by 754 law firms. Deutsche Telekom denied liability and delivered eight tons of paperwork evidence to the court.[103] The cases were suspended until the German legislator passed the Capital Investors' Model Proceeding Law in 2005. After settlement negotiations failed, the trial started in April 2008 and some expect the case to last 10 to 15 years.[104]

The Capital Investors' Model Proceeding Law (KapMuG)[105] provides for a test case to be brought in relation to a claim for damages for false, misleading or omitted information, or for specific performance, by investors or shareholders in takeover offer situations. The basic scheme is that where ten applications are made in similar cases, the first court will decide which questions are common, and the questions will then be decided by the Higher Regional Court, with no opt-out provision in relation to any of the individual cases, which remain stayed pending resolution of the selected common questions.

The procedure is commenced by an application in an individual case for the establishment of a model case. Such an application will be considered against admissibility criteria, and the court will announce publicly that an admissible application has been made, giving specified details in the Complaint Registry of the electronic *Federal Gazette*.[106] If nine further similar applications occur within four months, whether at the same or in other courts, the first court shall issue a model case, order that it be dealt with by the Higher Regional Court and issue publicity of this order in the Complaint Registry. The order shall contain:[107]

a) the establishment objective;
b) all points of dispute being raised, to the extent that they are relevant to the decision;
c) the evidence described; and
d) a brief summary of the essential content of the rights being claimed and the measures availed of in contesting or defending the matter.

---

[102] It is interesting that the English courts considered that they had jurisdiction to introduce a procedure to manage group claims, whereas the impasse in Germany had to be resolved by new legislation. Is this an advantage of the common law system, or merely fortuitous?

[103] C Budras, 'Deutsche Telekom case's 15,000 Claims swamp Court' *Bloomberg* (23 November 2004).

[104] *Reuters* (8 April 2008).

[105] KapitalanlegerMusterverfahrensGesetz (KapMuG): English translation at Appendix 8.

[106] KapMuG ss 1 and 2. This internet litigation register is monitored systematically by law firms who use the register to solicit claimants: *Are 'class actions' on the way in Europe?* (Clifford Chance, 2005).

[107] KapMuG s 4(2).

The Higher Regional Court shall also publicise the proceedings in the Complaint Registry,[108] at which point the lower court shall suspend all pending proceedings.[109] Parties to the model case proceedings shall be the model case plaintiff, the model case defendant and interested parties summoned, which shall include the plaintiffs and defendants of the remaining suspended proceedings. The Higher Regional Court designates a person to be model case plaintiff from amongst those who obtained the model case ruling, and the selection is not contestable.[110] In exercising this discretion, the court is required to consider the amount of the claim and any agreement amongst several plaintiffs that designates a single model case plaintiff.[111] Parties may seek the establishment of additional points of dispute up until the conclusion of the model case proceedings if the court considers them relevant.[112] The Higher Regional Court shall issue its ruling on the model case after an oral hearing, which shall be served on the parties or be publicly announced.[113] The model case ruling may be appealed on points of law.[114] It is binding on the first instance courts and all interested parties, including those who did not intervene.[115] The costs of the model case proceedings remain a matter for the first instance courts.[116] The share of the parties' costs shall be determined according to the ratio of the amount of the claim made by the respective plaintiff to the total amount of the claims made. The costs of the model case proceedings remain a matter for the first instance courts.[117]

Various comments may be made on this procedure. It will immediately be seen that the scope of the KapMuG is limited, being restricted to specific types of claim in relation to corporate transactions. The involvement of the Higher Regional Court is simply a mechanism to increase the level of confidence in the decision and avoid the need for an appeal, bearing in mind that appeal of a decision is almost inevitable in a civil justice system that comprises less experienced judges at first instance, automatic rights of appeal, and where an appeal is a full re-hearing. Selection of the model case plaintiff by the Higher Regional Court is intended to avoid a US-style 'rush for certification'.

The KapMuG was introduced quickly in order to address a problem that had arisen in a specific case. It was intended to be experimental and

---

[108] KapMuG s 6.
[109] KapMuG s 7.
[110] KapMuG s 8(2).
[111] KapMuG s 8(2).
[112] KapMuG s 13.
[113] KapMuG s 14.
[114] KapMuG s 15.
[115] KapMuG s 16.
[116] KapMuG ss 8(3) and 14(2).
[117] KapMuG s 17.

to be reviewed after five years in 2010. It has, however, already been criticised.[118] Given the administrative imperative of seeking a single decision that binds as many people as possible, there will inevitably be some claimants who cannot be fully represented in the model case procedure. This denial of rights is partly addressed by permitting third parties to take part in the model procedure, but this compromise makes some commentators uneasy. Further, the model is based on the premise that admitted third parties will remain largely passive, and this approach may not cater for all circumstances, such as where there may be a number of individual views clamouring to be heard. The balance between, on the one hand, individual autonomy and rights and, on the other hand, procedural efficiency and expediency is, indeed, a key issue with any class or collective mechanism.

ITALY

The procedural position in Italy has been characterised as involving a proliferation of special proceedings in specific legal fields in recent years.[119] Italy has had a succession of financial problems: Parmalat, Cirio, Giacometti and Argentine bonds, which have included perhaps 1,000 civil suits brought in courts across the country, in addition to a constellation of bankruptcy proceedings, criminal prosecutions, class actions in the United States and negotiations. Conciliation procedures have produced commercial solutions in some of these cases. The fundamental constitutional right for an individual to be represented by a lawyer has raised a problem. Professor Guido Alpa, Chair of the Italian Bar, has expressed concern about the impact of introducing class actions on traditional machinery and equal treatment of those damaged.[120]

In 2004, the Italian Chamber of Deputies approved a bill on 'Provisions for the introduction of class actions for the protection of consumers' rights', which did not proceed further. In July 2006, the government announced that a Bill permitting an expansion of collective actions would be introduced, after which several Bills were proposed by different parliamentarians. In a separate measure announced at the same time, contingency fees were permitted. On 21 December 2007, a revised Bill was passed, taking effect from 1 July 2008, which introduced a collective

---

[118] H-W Micklitz, 'Collective Private Enforcement of Consumer law: The Key Questions' in W van Boom and M Loos, *Collective Enforcement of Consumer Law: Securing Compliance in Europe through Private Group Action and Public Authority Intervention* (Europa Law Publishing, 2007).

[119] See E Silvestri, 'National Report for Italy' (Globalisation Project).

[120] Portuguese Presidency Conference on Collective Redress for Consumers, Lisbon, 9 and 10 November 2007.

action procedure.[121] The procedure is divided into two phases: an initial judicial phase, containing certification by the court, which is intended to act as a filter, the giving of notice of the collective proceedings and opt-in by consumers, and determination by the court of general liability issues, followed by a 'non-contentious' phase, in which the parties are expected to settle individual issues covering the payment of damages.

Two sorts of consumer association have standing to bring this type of representative claim: one of the authorised consumer associations registered under the Consumer Code[122] and 'associations and councils which are duly representative of the collective rights claimed'. The latter phrase is not defined further and can be expected to provoke argument. The collective procedure may be invoked in order to protect the collective interests of consumers and users,[123] at the court of the area where the company has its offices. The claim may be for damages or return of sums due to individual consumers or users, relating to commercial agreements, tort liability, unfair commercial practice or anti-competitive behaviour, provided that such unlawful acts damage the rights of a plurality of consumers and users.

After a collective action is filed, the court will hear the parties and rule whether or not the claim is admissible. A claim will not be admissible if it is 'groundless', if it gives rise to 'a conflict of interest' between the promoting association and class members, or if the judge does not 'ascertain the existence of any collective interest deserving protection'. Several of those terms are not defined in the law and may be expected to give rise to questions of interpretation. If the claim is approved, the consumer association must notify consumers through advertising as instructed by the court, and individuals must then notify the association in writing of their desire to join the proceedings (opt in). Individuals may so notify in writing at any stage of the action, and may also intervene as parties.

How the case is then to be progressed is not stated in article 140-*bis*, so it is assumed that normal procedures in the Code of Civil Procedure or company law, as may be relevant, are to apply. The court is, however, required

[121] Art 2, para 446 of Law of 12 December 2007 No 224 (the Financial Act) inserted art 140-*bis* into the Consumer Code (Legislative Decree no 206 dated 6 September 2005). The Act was passed under the Prodi government, and, at the time of writing, there is a rumour that the coming into force of the Act may be delayed, or its substance amended, by the new Berlusconi government.

[122] Under art 137 of the Consumer Code, in order to be listed pursuant to art 139, an association must have existed for at least three years with non-profit status, have a membership of at least 5% of the national population, represent members in at least five of the country's autonomous regions, and be independent of any manufacturing or service companies in the same sectors as it operates. Sixteen associations were listed in January 2008: see <http://213.175.14.65/organigramma/documento.php?id=1996&sezione=organigramma&gruppo=0&tema_dir=tema2>.

[123] It is unclear whether this includes investors: perhaps consumer investors may be included, but not institutional ones—the distinction may be objected to.

to set the criteria to be used in order to calculate the amount to be paid or given back to those individual consumers and users who have adhered to or joined in the proceedings. If the court has sufficient information, it is to declare the minimum amount to be paid to each consumer. The defendant then has 60 days in which to make an offer to any entitled party. Any proposal accepted by an individual consumer or user shall be enforceable. If there is no agreement, the court will establish a conciliation committee, which will consist of one lawyer from each side and an independent lawyer. The conciliation committee shall establish the terms, methods and amounts to be paid to consumers, its decisions being enforceable, and will administer the process, unless private settlements are reached.

A judicial decision on the merits or a court-approved settlement will bar any future claim on the same issues between the parties. However, individuals who do not opt in to the group or otherwise intervene will not be bound. If there is a judgment on the merits, but no settlement emerges within a reasonable time, it is unclear whether individuals may sue to recover any quantified or unquantified amounts. It appears that any individual who is not bound may bring individual proceedings, or any other association that has standing may bring a further representative action. Accordingly, questions arise over the extent to which this procedure may produce binding results.

This procedure is somewhat optimistic in assuming that all types of case can be disposed of effectively through the prescribed procedure, and contains various elements of uncertainty and instability. One such element is the assumption that the judge is able to make a generic decision on liability and also, at the same time, establish the parameters for compensation of each individual claimant. It may be that individual aspects of reliance or extent of personal damage will defeat such general approach. In its favour, the model can be seen as pragmatic in observing the requirements of the state of Italian civil procedure generally in channelling the parties towards settlement, although the assumption that settlement or court-based resolution will effectively be reached is again questionable. A conciliation committee may simply be unable to reach agreement, or one that is swift and cheap. The financial incentive would be for the lawyers to prolong disagreement.

Professor Elisabetta Silvestri has described this procedure as of Baroque complexity, which does not provide for efficient management of cases.[124] First, individuals are not entitled to instigate this procedure. The system

---

[124] See E Silvestri, 'Consumers' Collective Actions: An Update on Italian Draft legislation' (Globalisation Project). She also wonders what the fate of such a convoluted procedure may be in a country in which proceedings take so long to reach a final decision. For example, what happens if the certification decision is overturned on appeal or subsequent cassation: huge amounts of time and money may be wasted. It may also be argued that the imposition of a mandatory conciliation procedure is inconsistent with constitutional principles on due process.

treats the association or the public body granted the right of action as an individual plaintiff. At this stage, no opting-in or opting-out mechanisms are necessary, since in the eyes of the law individual consumers and users have no part to play in the suit. That fact gives rise to an unsolved problem of whether they are bound by the outcome of the proceedings, and, if so, to what extent they should or can bring individual actions for damages against the same defendant who loses the case commenced by the association. Secondly, consumers may remain unaware of either the proceedings or of a judgment or settlement. In failing to adequately address the issue of how to grant consumers adequate representation, this procedure does not seem to offer viable solutions to several problems.

POSSIBLE INTRODUCTION OF PROCEDURES IN OTHER MEMBER STATES

The introduction of new procedures on collective mechanisms has been under consideration in other states, notably in France and in CEE states.

France

As mentioned in chapter two, France has had a long history of certain types of general consumer representative action mechanisms. However, discussions on the possible introduction of more extensive collective actions have been carried on since around 1990.[125] Two high-profile cases were brought by UFC Que Choisir? to highlight the problems with the pre-existing consumer protection legislation.

Case Study: French Mobile Phones[126]

(1) In 2001, the French consumers association, UFC Que Choisir?, brought an action in the consumer collective interest (article L 421-7) against SFR (a mobile phone company) for an illegal increase of its subscription rate. UFC Que Choisir? believed that the company had benefited by €7,320,000, being €18.30 over-paid by each of 400,000 subscribers. Two consumers brought the case with the association and won. The court declared that the increase was illegal and awarded the two consumers €100 each as reparation. The association obtained €1,524 for reparation of the consumer collective interest.[127]

(continued)

---

[125] V Magnier, 'National Report for France' (Globalisation Project).
[126] Information from G Patetta, UFC Que Choisir?
[127] TGI Nanterre 15 octobre 2001—CA Versailles 16 mai 2002.

(2) On 30 November 2005, the French competition court found that the three mobile phone operators had colluded in a cartel involving mobile phone market sharing, and imposed a penalty of €534 million.

UFC Que Choisir? calculated that prices were higher in France than abroad as a result of the collusion, and that some 20 million subscribers had been affected. Consumer organisations can intervene in proceedings initiated by a consumer seeking individual damages, in order to obtain 'damages in the collective interest' based on article L 421-1 of the Consumer Code, in the context of an action relating to article L 421-7 of the Consumer Code (*action en intervention*). The damages claimed in the collective interest do not, however, allow compensation for the individual harm suffered.

UFC Que Choisir?, which had brought the initial infringement actions against the three phone companies before the competition court in 2001, decided to bring a further case to demonstrate the limitations of the system, which required individual claimants to give written consent to a case being brought on their behalf. The association commenced a follow-on action and created a website for consumers to join and calculate their damages (<http://www.cartelmobile.org> accessed 10 June 2008). The cost was considerable: the case involved 21 employees (20 per cent of staff) for six months and large financial resources of €500,000. Three cubic metres of files were required. Only 12,521 consumers joined, i.e. less than one per cent who could have done so.

A total amount of €800,000 was claimed for the 12,521 consumers as reparation (average of €60 per consumer). At the time of writing, the cases are still pending.

The mobile phone operators objected that UFC Que Choisir? had brought an '*action en representation conjointe*' (article L 422-1) and not an action in the consumer collective interest (article L 421-7). They asserted that the actions were not admissible because the association had made an appeal for the consumers to join its case, which is not allowed in the '*action en representation conjointe*'. On 6 December 2007, the commercial court decided, in the case against Bouygues Telecom, that the action was a disguised 'action en representation conjointe' and that all of the interventions were not admissible. The judge did not, therefore, address the issue of liability or reparation available for the consumers, but only these exceptions on the admissibility of the action. UFC Que Choisir? has appealed against this judgment.

President Chirac kicked the issue of collective redress into prominence with an unanticipated announcement in January 2005 that the government would consider legislation on collective actions. A Working Group delivered a Working Document in December 2005 that analysed options for introducing collective actions into French law.[128] This reached no overall conclusions, and revealed the customary split in views between consumer organisations and business interests, although it did note heavy criticism of the US class action phenomenon and associated contingency fees. Interestingly, it was commented that there was no justification for making an exception to the normal principles on costs, under which parties should finance their own proceedings, and there was no justification for creation of a financial fund to assist claimants in collective action claims, on the basis that legal costs were said to be low in France. Various competing Bills on collective actions were introduced into the legislature during 2006.

Poland[129]

In 2006, the government instructed the Civil Law Codification Commission to consider introduction of a class action law as part of its ongoing reform of the Code of Civil Procedure. Views on the advisability of such a move have been widely polarised. The debate has taken place against the background of multiple individual claims after a retail building collapsed on many people. One legal issue is whether a procedure for a representative claim would be consistent with the fundamental principles of individual rights. A practical issue is to what extent a class action system would fit into a civil law system in which first instance judges can be young professionals who have little experience and from whose decisions parties may automatically appeal by way of full rehearing.

The debate was also influenced by a desire to avoid giving judges increased discretion in view of the experiences of the previous Communist system in which judges were mistrusted and sometimes corrupt, and a current desire to prescribe procedure as fully as possible. This raises an interesting question over whether a move towards prescription is consistent with the need for judicial managerial discretion, which has been the experience of collective actions from common law jurisdictions.

A draft Act was produced in April 2008, which attempted to balance the various problems. The proposed mechanism would be generic, opt-in and involve a significant measure of managerial control by judges, restricted to those in higher courts sitting in threes. Settlements would be subject to court approval. The claimant group should comprise at least 10 people and must be represented by a lawyer, whose remuneration could be a percentage of the amount awarded to the group.

---

[128] Groupe de travail présidé par Guillaume Cerutti, Directeur General de la Concurrence, de la Consommation et de la Repression des Fraudes et Marc Guillaume, Directeur des Affairs Civiles et du Sceau, 'Rapport sur L'Action de Groupe' (16 December 2005).

[129] See M Tulibacka, 'National Report for Poland' (Globalisation Project).

CONCLUSIONS ON THE NEW DAMAGES MECHANISMS

Principles: Rights versus Efficiency?

What are the findings from the above review? A number of European states have introduced generalised collective mechanisms for claims for damages. The number of states who have so far taken this step is limited, albeit growing, and the model adopted has been different in each case. There is no absolute uniformity or harmonisation of approach, although some similarities exist. An overview of the mechanisms is at Table 5.

An immediate conclusion is that any EU enthusiast bent on furthering harmonisation of national civil procedure rules or introducing a harmonised approach to collective damages claims would currently face what appears to be an insurmountable challenge in proposing a maximum harmonisation model. A 'one size fits all' approach is simply not possible in relation to these collective mechanisms.

One point is clear—European policy-makers have consciously rejected the US model in which a single claimant may be 'first past the post' and claim to represent a class of other virtually identical claimants. The European jurisdictions are instead striving to find a new model for collective redress. Exactly how the different individual experiments may evolve, and whether further national models may strike out in new directions, is as yet unclear, as is whether the different models may cohere into a unified approach.

The origin of the introduction of these new European collective rules has usually been one of practical expediency. Judges have needed these mechanisms in order to be able to *manage* a large number of similar cases efficiently and without the judicial administrative system becoming overwhelmed. The essential features of all of the court-based models are that cases that raise similar issues are grouped together so that one, or a small number, of decisions can be taken that will be binding, and hence dispositive, on a large number of the rest of the individual cases in the group. However, within this broad concept, significant differences in philosophy and approach can be seen.

Some models assume that all cases in a group are identical, or virtually so. (This is the assumption made in the classic US class action model, and also permeates the Swedish and Germany systems.) Other models (notably the English GLO) take a less rigidly prescriptive and rights-based approach, and merely assume that the individual cases have sufficient points of similarity to enable them to be *managed* efficiently together. In this model, considerations of managerial efficiency are given greater prominence than traditional considerations of individual rights. The latter model can only operate within the background of a legal system that has a high degree of confidence in its judges and ability to deliver fair and just outcomes.

Table 5—General Court-based Collective Mechanisms

Country	General Method	Criteria	Opt-in or Opt-out	Anti-abuse Control	Costs	Achilles Heels and Overview Conclusions
England GLO 1999	Group management, with the exact technique (eg lead case(s)) at discretion of judge.	Common or related issues of fact or law.	In. Simple registration.	Judicial control and broad discretion.	Loser pays. Shared between all group members.	Claimants need finance: complex cost-sharing arrangements. Flexible.
Sweden 2002	Initiated by single claimant: individual, association or authority representing a class of others.	Common or similar circumstances.	In. Simple notice.	Approval criteria. Judicial control. Court approves settlements.	Loser pays. The group claimant is responsible, not group members (unless they have intervened).	Claimant needs finance. Effective where public authority funds.
Germany KapMuG 2005	Binding model case decided by Appeal Court.	10 similar cases. Investors only.	N/A.	Criteria.	Decided by the court depending on final outcome.	Limited subject matter of cases. Requires similar individual cases to have been brought.
Netherlands 2005	Judicial approval of negotiated settlement.	Provisional settlement agreed between a party and a foundation or association.	Out.	Court approval of settlement. Criteria for rejection. Defendant may reject if not enough claimants have accepted.	Court discretion, usually defendant pays.	Encourages settlement. Provides no mechanism for initiation or management of claims.
Italy 2008	Authorised consumer association as representative.	Unclear? Inadmissible if groundless or a conflict of interest arises.	In. Simple notification.	Court rules on admissibility. Court approves settlement.	Loser pays.	Entry criteria unclear. Assumes court can decide on criteria for individual awards, and that conciliation committee will work.

The latter model is more flexible, whereas the former may run the risk of attempting to force square pegs into round holes, or of being unable to fit a peg of whatever shape into any useful hole. This mirrors the lesson from the United States, where the assumption that a single representative case is effectively the same as all other cases in a class (a typical 'class action') has given way to a more flexible bundling of generally similar cases (Multi-District Litigation).

The principle of efficient management of multiple individual claims dictates that a two-stage process is required. The objective is to avoid having to resolve all cases individually. First, it needs to be identified whether all individual cases can be grouped in such a way that a common issue or issues can be defined that can then be resolved. Secondly, it may be necessary to resolve each individual case, by applying the generic decision to the facts in each case and also resolving any further individual issues that remain. There may be some situations in which all individual claims are identical, in which case the second stage is not required. However, history shows that such situations can be rare. Indeed, there are some situations in which a mass of individual claims may appear similar at first sight, but on closer inspection it appears that each contains individual issues that cannot effectively be resolved by deciding a generic question. This would be so where the cases turn on individual issues of causation, assumption of risk, reliance or limitation. Examples might be claims arising out of use of a medicinal product, or allegations of mis-selling of a financial product. For these reasons, the US CFR 23 includes a requirement of 'predominance' of common issues over individual issues, and drug class actions are not infrequently refused in the United States. These issues do not appear to have been understood in several of the European models. The conclusion is that a requirement for flexibility is important. Models that assume that all cases are the same and common issues can always be identified, and cases resolved through a decision on a generic basis will be inherently flawed.

European legal systems have been based on the paradigm that the disputes that are to be resolved arise between individuals. If a mechanism is introduced into such a system that individual cases are not to be permitted to proceed, but will be resolved, at least in part, by deciding an issue which the court selects, and (more importantly) in which all individuals cannot be represented, an issue of individual rights and representation will obviously arise. Such an approach necessarily involves the court and the parties making *compromises* in traditional principles, in order that the group can make the orderly progress that is required.[130] In commenting on the English GLO, Lord Woolf said that 'the effective and economic handling of group actions necessarily requires a diminution, compromise or adjustment

---

[130] *AB and Others v John Wyeth & Brother Ltd* [1996] 7 Med LR 267 at 273.

of the rights of individual litigants for the greater good of the action as a whole'.[131] Some new accommodation or trade off is required. There must be some surrender of individual rights and control in return for improved access to justice. The balance that is struck must be just.

An example of this tension, evident in Germany and elsewhere, has been an unresolved debate on whether an opt-out procedure is consistent with fundamental and constitutional rights on due process and justice. This issue is examined further at chapter five. For the present, the observation is that there is a conflict between such *rights* and criteria of *efficiency* in the desire for a collective mechanism to produce a more efficient result for the courts, public finances and the majority of individual claimants than would be possible if claims were required to be pursued individually. A modern view is clearly emerging that access to justice and the achievement of proportionality of costs are important requirements, and can to some extent override the traditional rights-based approach. Different jurisdictions currently treat these matters differently, or are at a different stage in their evolution of thinking on the issue. One senses that this issue has not reached a consensus or equilibrium in European legal systems as yet. Further change can be anticipated.

Criteria

It is disappointing from a socio-legal point of view that few states collect data on their general civil justice mechanisms, let alone collective mechanisms, and measure them against criteria. Indeed, data that would enable a transparent judgment to be made of most of the criteria are lacking. It has been a feature of the debates during introduction of all of the laws discussed here that arguments have been based on issues of principle rather than evidence of effectiveness.

By what criteria should these mechanisms be judged? This issue is discussed at chapter nine below, but for present purposes perhaps one may take requirements of accessibility, speed, efficiency, proportionate cost, fairness of procedure and outcomes, effectiveness of outcomes and avoidance of abuse. Even viewed from the perspective of a limited number of the above criteria, it is nevertheless clear that there are problems with each of the national models. The obvious issues relate to comprehensiveness and methods of operation. For example: the Dutch law does not cover initiation or management of collective claims; the German law does not provide for initiation of a collective claim, but only with resolution of a single test case selected from a group of already ongoing court cases on the assumption that that will resolve all others (and there may be others that have different

---

[131] Lord Woolf, 'Access to Justice Inquiry: Issues Paper (Multi-Party Actions)' (1996).

individual features); and the Italian law is unclear on various aspects, such as who is bound, whether the court will be able to determine individual liabilities and damages (which is highly unlikely without a mechanism for investigating some or all individual facts) and what happens if the conciliation committee fails to agree.

Only the English and Swedish mechanisms are comprehensive in being able to regulate all aspects of individual and collective aspects throughout the litigation process. Yet they adopt strikingly different approaches. The Swedish procedure is a modified US class action model, but with the crucial differences of being opt-in and imposing the 'loser pays' principle. Some would argue that the opt-in nature in particular emasculates its effectiveness, but others would see this as a necessary protection against abuse and as recognition that the class action procedure is itself inflexible, as the multi-district litigation (MDL) procedure has shown.

When viewed from the perspective of efficiency and flexibility, there is much to be said for the English approach of enabling judicial management through wide discretion. The main objection to this approach is that parties require predictability and certainty. The potential for arbitrariness and abuse by judges may be a concern in some states, as the reports from Poland demonstrate. As will be seen from the series of case studies in this book, and as appears from the US recognition of a need for both a representative class action and MDL procedures, flexibility of approach seems an important requirement. One could go further.

All of these national models (apart from the Dutch model, which does not cover the bringing of claims) adopt an opt-in approach for creation of the class. The debate between opt-in and opt-out mechanisms, and why one or other approach may be important in particular circumstances, is discussed further below at chapter five. The objection to mechanisms such as those of Germany, England and Sweden is that all individual claimants are required to initiate their individual claims, although it is possible to reduce the bureaucratic element of doing this by, for example, providing that people should simply join a register (perhaps online), thereby reducing cost and delay. However, an interesting European innovation is recently identifiable. The Danish class action law[132] specifies that although the normal approach will be opt-in, it will be open to the court, but on the application only of the Consumer Ombudsman and not of any other representative claimant, to adopt an opt-out rule. Similarly, the Norwegian class actions law gives the court the power to decide whether the procedure will be opt-in or, if the individual claims are likely to be so small that it must be assumed that a majority of them will not be pursued as individual actions and if issues are not raised that need to be heard individually, opt-out.[133]

---

[132] See ch 2 above.
[133] Act of 17 June 2005 no 90, ss 35-6 and 35-7.

Settlement

The advantage of the Dutch approach is that it encourages the parties to settle. However, the Dutch model is not alone in this: settlement is a key explicit aim of the Italian law and the English CPR, and every collective procedure will encourage settlement through clarifying the main essential issues. A disadvantage of the Dutch model is that one cannot force any party to settle. Accordingly, if a party refuses to agree, the procedure is irrelevant and inoperable. The failure to provide a procedure that enables collective cases to be both brought and managed is a clear weakness, both as a general collective procedure and in encouraging settlement.

The Dutch situation does prompt the question: is the absence of a court-based mechanism for bringing multiple damages claims necessary? It would be logical for a legal system to provide a positive mechanism for bringing mass claims, in order to provide a civilised means of accessing justice for resolution of such claims within civil society. If claims are not settled, the finding from the experience of the United States, Canada, Australia, England and Wales, Germany and Spain is that courts do need a procedure under which they and the parties may progress multiple cases efficiently to resolution.

The absence of such a mechanism in the Netherlands is, of course, arguably merely historical accident, since they needed to legislate in a hurry so as to provide specifically for a mechanism that would implement an already agreed settlement and thereby provide resolution for all parties. Without such a mechanism, the courts and the state would have seemed entirely inept. However, it is also the case that the existence of the Dutch settlement procedure positively encourages parties to settle, and this may tend to avoid the expense and delay of legal proceedings. The case studies so far, in the DES, Dexia Bank and Shell hydrocarbon reserves cases, show that private organisations stepped into the breach of representing claimants. Such organisations might be either pre-existing, perhaps permanent consumer associations, official Ombudsmen, or might be specially created ad hoc organisations.

A feature of the Dutch law that will be developed further in subsequent chapters is the importance of a mechanism in which the state provides some level of assurance to the multiple individual claimants that a proposed settlement is reasonable, especially if they have taken little or no part in the proceedings or have little understanding of the issues at stake. The aim is to ensure that the level of compensation offered to all claimants is reasonable, and also that sub-groups of claimants are not disadvantaged. These can be onerous and difficult issues for judges to pronounce on. Nevertheless, it is important that the state should provide a mechanism for controlling against abuse and conflicts of interest in collective mechanisms and in settlements. Court approval of settlements is a requirement in the Netherlands, Sweden and Italy, but not in England.

The class action law in Israel provides some interesting features on approval of settlements. The Israeli law was inspired by the US opt-out class action model, in which actions are led by lawyers, who have significant financial interests that may diverge from those of all or some sub-groups of claimants, giving rise to conflicts of interest that can be critical in relation to settlements. The drafters of the Israeli law have therefore included a series of anti-abuse controls, including a requirement that the court must approve any settlement and must first obtain the written views of an independent responsible expert on the issues of fairness and non-discrimination.[134]

Some anti-abuse mechanisms have been included in the existing European laws, but not many. If certain features were introduced, it would be more important to provide anti-abuse controls. For example, the risk of abuse would increase under an opt-out mechanism or increase in the financial incentives for claimants and especially intermediaries. At present, European states clearly adhere to the 'loser pays' rule and the opt-in rule. The issue of abuse will be discussed further at chapter six.

An Issue of Evolution

Some competition between jurisdictions is now becoming evident. Dutch lawyers have promoted the unique approach of the Dutch facility to settle multi-party cases as offering parties an efficient forum to resolve multiple cases. Further competition may be predicted not only within Europe, but also between Europe and the United States. Hitherto, European claimants have often sought to join US class actions, taking advantage of the no cost and high reward opportunities.

US courts have decided objections by defendants inconsistently, but theoretically on the same legal principles of *forum non conveniens*, the essence of which is to decide which is the most appropriate forum for resolving the case (revolving around access to evidence), whether the foreign nationals may adequately obtain justice in their home jurisdiction and whether the US system might be overburdened by an open-door policy. It would follow that as European jurisdictions introduce collective litigation mechanisms or more attractive litigation funding systems, US courts should tend to exclude Europeans from US class actions more frequently. Such an occurrence might lead to increased scrutiny on the extent and liberality of European mechanisms, and whether they satisfy the required criteria. European claimants may demand good reasons why US citizens obtain high settlements, but Europeans cannot obtain similar results in their own jurisdictions.

---

[134] Class Actions Law 2006 s 19(B)(2). See A Magen and P Segal, 'National Report for Israel' (Globalisation Project)

4

Collective Redress at European Level: Existing Mechanisms

THE EU LEGISLATIVE BACKGROUND

I T IS IMPORTANT to note the legal context in which both the Member
States and the European institutions are operating in relation to civil
justice systems. The basic point is that the Member States have considerable freedom to experiment within their national systems because they
retain almost complete sovereign authority over their systems. Community
law affords very restricted powers for legislative provisions at EU level.

The objectives of the European Union relate to the establishment of a single,
integrated market. Thus, two types of issue tend to arise in relation to realising
the essential aim: cross-border barriers between Member States and harmonisation of substantive provisions across the entire community. The power to legislate at EU level is not a sovereign power,[1] and is contained in treaties entered
into by the Member States, sovereignty being reserved to individual Member
States. Thus, all Community legislation must have a valid legal basis in the EC
Treaty, and may otherwise be annulled.[2] Further, the principle of subsidiarity
provides that measures should be taken at EU level only if and in so far as the
objectives cannot be sufficiently achieved by the Member States[3] and the principle of proportionality provides that measures at EU level must not go beyond
what is necessary to achieve the objects at which they are directed.[4]

Against this broad background, although a huge corpus of substantive measures has been created at EU level, attention to civil justice issues is relatively
recent and still circumscribed by limited Treaty powers, and the principles of
subsidiarity, proportionality and the procedural autonomy of the Member
States in relation to the mechanisms for implementation and enforcement of

---

[1] EC Treaty art 253; S Weatherill *Cases and Materials on EU Law* (6th edn, Oxford,
2006).
[2] Case C-376/98 *Germany v European Parliament and Council of the European Union*
[2000] ECR I-08419, judgment of 5 October 2000; Case C-491/01 *R v Secretary of State
for Health, ex parte British American Tobacco (Investments) Ltd and Imperial Tobacco Ltd*
[2002] ECR I-11453, judgment of 10 December 2002.
[3] EC Treaty art 5.2.
[4] EC Treaty art 5.3.

Community measures. The limitations in Community level powers constitute some impediment in relation to tackling the widely accepted problem that considerable variation exists in the effectiveness of national systems.

LEGAL COMPETENCE

The European Union's legal competence to legislate on civil justice generally or on collective procedures is somewhat circumscribed. It is well accepted that Community measures require a valid legal basis,[5] must effectively contribute to achieving a specified aim,[6] and observe the principles of subsidiarity and proportionality[7] and of national procedural autonomy.[8] Article 65(c) empowers measures taken in the field of judicial cooperation in civil matters having cross-border implications in so far as necessary for the proper functioning of the internal market, to eliminate obstacles to the good functioning of civil proceedings, if necessary by promoting the compatibility of the rules on civil procedure applicable in the Member States. This would require evidence of cross-border barriers and might, on the face of it, justify only cross-border measures. It is arguable to what extent it would justify significant incursion into domestic legal systems.

Specific provisions provide competence for measures limited to specific sectors, such as competition, consumer protection or environmental law. Thus, article 83 empowers certain measures in relation to the functioning of articles 81 and 82 on competition;[9] article 94 authorises directives for

---

[5] EC Treaty arts 5.1 and 253.

[6] Thus, a mere finding of differences in national rules is insufficient to found competence under art 95 EC: Case C-233/94 *Germany v European Parliament and Council of the European Union* [1997] ECR I-2405.

[7] Respectively, arts 5.2 and 5.3 EC.

[8] This is the fundamental principle of the European legal system that substantive laws enacted by the Community rely for enforcement on national procedural rules and national institutional and judicial enforcement networks, although its force has been eroded. See Case C-33/75 *Rewe-Zentralfinanz eG et Rewe-Zentral AG v Landwirtschaftskammer für das Saarland* [1976] ECR I-1989, 16 December 1976; and Case C-45/76 *Comet BV v Produktschap voor Siergewassen* [1976] ECR I-2043, 16 December 1976. Also, W Van Gerven 'Of Rights, Remedies and Procedures' (2000) 37 CMLR 501–36.

[9] Article 83 authorises measures that give effect to the principles set out in arts 81 and 82, being designed to:

   a) ensure compliance with the prohibitions laid down in art 81(1) and art 82 by making provision for fines and periodic penalty payments;
   b) lay down detailed rules for the application of art 81(3), taking into account the need to ensure effective supervision on the one hand, and to simplify administration to the greatest possible extent on the other;
   c) define, if need be, in the various branches of the economy, the scope of the provisions of arts 81 and 82;
   d) define the respective functions of the Commission and of the Court of Justice in applying the provisions laid down in this paragraph;
   e) determine the relationship between national laws and the provisions contained in this section or adopted pursuant to this article.

the approximation of laws, regulations or administrative provisions of the Member States as *directly affect the establishment or functioning* of the common market; and article 95 covers measures for the approximation of the provisions laid down by law, regulation or administrative action in Member States which have as their object the *establishment and functioning* of the internal market. In the consumer protection area, article 153 authorises measures which support, supplement and monitor the policy of contributing to protecting the health, safety and economic interests of consumers, as well as promoting their right to information, education and to organise themselves in order to safeguard their interests (it refers to article 95 as legal basis). There is a residual power in article 308 for appropriate measures if action by the Community should prove necessary to attain, in the course of the *operation of the common market*, one of the objectives of the Community, and the Treaty has not otherwise provided the necessary powers.

It can be seen that these powers, written primarily with the establishment of commercial laws in mind, would be stretched, in some cases to breaking point, if applied to national rules of civil procedure. Certain arguments could be made that the sectoral articles could found the introduction of collective procedures, but the issue remains debatable. Article 81 of the Lisbon Treaty on the Functioning of the European Union,[10] as and when it applies, would ease the position by empowering, inter alia:

a) effective access to justice;
b) the elimination of obstacles to the proper functioning of civil proceedings, if necessary by promoting the compatibility of the rules on civil procedure applicable in the Member States; and
e) the development of alternative methods of dispute settlement.

Taken together, however, the general and sectoral provisions appear to be founding a series of individual measures which form a slowly growing body of Community provisions on civil justice. One possible future development may be the formation of individual measures into a coherent corpus of Community procedures, whether binding or non-binding: the precedents of the US Restatements and the Common Frame of Reference on European contract law are relevant.[11]

EU POLICY ON CIVIL JUSTICE SYSTEMS

The EU's limited jurisdiction in civil justice explains why EU legislation in the field has been largely restricted to three issues: first, rules of

---

[10] Treaty of Lisbon amending the Treaty on European Union and the Treaty establishing the European Community, 13 December 2007, [2007] OJ C306.

[11] See Communication from the Commission to the European Parliament and the Council: A More Coherent European Contract Law: An Action Plan, COM(2003) 68, 12 February 2003.

public international law on jurisdictional issues; secondly, enforcement of Community legislation, such as the consumer protection measures discussed above; and thirdly, alternative dispute resolution mechanisms, especially in the cross-border matters, which encourage self-help (mediation, ADR). Consideration of remedies may also, of course, be relevant under the huge project on contract law.[12]

Extension of the competence of the European Community into the area of civil justice systems began in 1999, when the objective of establishing 'an area of freedom, security and justice' was included in the Treaty of Amsterdam and a related agreement made within the Council.[13] In 2004, the European Council adopted the Hague Programme on strengthening freedom, security and justice, although much of this relates to criminal rather than civil law aspects.[14]

Activity in this area is linked to European policy on competitiveness, as the Commission has noted: 'The prime object of the European judicial area, indeed, is to simplify the legal context within the Union.'[15] Simplification would reduce costs and hence enhance the economy. A further key objective of this rather generalised political policy has been said to be the achievement of better access to justice, explained as 'where individuals and businesses should not be prevented or discouraged from exercising their rights by the incompatibility or complexity of legal and administrative systems in the Member States'. This rather coy statement disguises the reality, which is an unstated positive policy of harmonising the Member State's rules of civil procedure.[16] The evidence from other areas of the development of harmonising legislation is that the Commission often proceeds cautiously and in a piecemeal fashion towards full harmonisation. The process may take many years. Progress can be slow and sometimes opportunistic, but often inexorable.[17]

---

[12] Green Paper on the review of the Consumer Acquis, COM(2006) 744, 8 February 2007. Second Progress Report on the Common Frame of Reference, COM(2007) 447, 25 July 2007.

[13] Tampere European Council. For a related measure in the criminal field, see Directive 2004/80/EC on compensation of victims on violent intentional crime.

[14] [2005] OJ C53/1 para 3.2.

[15] Explanatory Statement, Report on the prospects for approximating civil procedural law in the European Union COM(2002)746 + COM(2002) 654—C5-0201/2003—2003/2087(INI), Committee on Legal Affairs and the Internal Market, A5-0041/2004, 30 January 2004.

[16] This was expressly called for in the European Parliament resolution on the prospects for approximating civil procedural law in the European Union COM(2002) 654 + COM(2002) 746—C5-0201/2003—2003/2087(INI), A5-0041/2004.

[17] There are various instances where Directives have dealt with different aspects of an area in piecemeal fashion, and the Commission has finally been able to propose framework harmonisation, which often introduces what would have been thought of as unacceptably radical reform at the start of the process. One example concerns the regulation of medicinal products, for which many individual Directives were passed, on a regular basis, from 1965, until a complete Code was created by Directive 2001/83/EC and a centralised system based on a European Agency in Regulation (EC) 726/2004.

The first formal steps[18] towards harmonisation of European rules of civil procedure now follow an Action Plan.[19] Measures have been taken both within and outside the court systems. Within litigation systems, developments have taken place in the context of a European Judicial Network in civil and commercial matters (EJ-NET)[20] and a Community framework of activities to facilitate the implementation of judicial cooperation in civil matters.[21] A Green Paper on minimum standards for some aspects of procedural law is due in 2008. Individual measures include rules on the service of judicial and extra-judicial documents in civil or commercial matters,[22] on cooperation between Member State courts in the taking of evidence in civil or commercial matters[23] and a European Enforcement Order for uncontested claims.[24] A European Order for Payment procedure applies from

A recent example would be Directive 2005/29/EC on unfair commercial practices. A further example is the current work on production of a Common Frame of Reference on EU contract law, which will, despite Commission protestations to the contrary, provide the basis of an EU code of contract law when draft codes for other related areas of law have been produced: see Communication from the Commission to the European Parliament and the Council: A More Coherent European Contract Law: An Action Plan, COM(2003) 68, 12 February 2003. The European Parliament's Committee on the Internal Market and Consumer Protection noted that the project is widely considered to have the ultimate long-term outcome of a European code of obligations or a European Civil Code: Opinion on European contract law and the revision of the *acquis*: the way forward; 2005/2022(INI), 25 January 2006.

[18] Encouragement by the Community's Court of Justice towards a general procedural perspective of enforcement of EC law by national courts, as compensation for the lack of Community-wide uniform civil procedure, can be seen in the development of the doctrine of 'effectiveness and non-discrimination' in the well-known sequences of cases that includes *Brasserie du Pêcheur & Factortame III* [1996] 1 CMLR 889.

[19] Council and Commission Action Plan of 3 December 1998 on how best to implement the provisions of the Treaty of Amsterdam on the creation of an area of freedom, security and justice; text adopted by the Justice and Home Affairs Council of 3 December 1998 (known as the Vienna Action Plan); [2001] OJ C19 of 23 January 1999 <http://eur-lex.europa.eu/LexUriServ/LexUriServ.do?uri=OJ:C:1999:019:0001:0015:EN:PDF> accessed 3 July 2008.

[20] Council Decision of 28 May 2001 establishing a European Judicial Network in civil and commercial matters, [2001] OJ L174/25.

[21] Council Regulation (EC) 743/2002 of 25 April 2002 establishing a Community framework of activities to facilitate the implementation of judicial cooperation in civil matters, [2002] OJ L115/1.

[22] Council Regulation (EC) 1348/2000 on the service in the Member States of judicial and extrajudicial documents in civil or commercial matters; Proposal for amendment COM(2005) 305 final/2, 11 July 2005.

[23] Council Regulation (EC) 1206/2001 of 28 May 2001, <http://ec.europa.eu/justice_home/judicialatlascivil/html/pdf/oj_l174_20010627_en.pdf> accessed 3 July 2008. See Report COM(2007) 769, 5 December 2007, <http://eur-lex.europa.eu/LexUriServ/site/en/com/2007/com2007_0769en01.pdf> accessed 11 June 2008: Council Regulation (EC) 1346/2000 of 29 May 2000 on insolvency proceedings, <http://eur-lex.europa.eu/LexUriServ/LexUriServ.do?uri=OJ:L:2000:160:0001:0018:EN:PDF> accessed 11 June 2008.

[24] Regulation (EC) 805/2004 creating a European Enforcement Order for uncontested claims. See C Crifò, 'First Steps towards the Harmonisation of Civil Procedure: the Regulation Creating a European Enforcement Order for Uncontested Claims' [2005] 24 CJQ 200–23.

12 December 2008[25] and a European Small Claims Procedure (which does not require representation by a lawyer, but in which the loser must pay costs) for claims under €2,000 from January 2009.[26]

Important measures in relation to proper law are the Regulation on jurisdiction and the recognition and enforcement of judgments,[27] the Regulation on the law applicable to non-contractual obligations (Rome II)[28] and the proposal on contractual obligations (Rome I).[29] A report has recently been published on enforcement of civil judgments and a Green Paper on this topic is planned.[30]

The European Parliament has passed a resolution recommending the Commission to legislate to harmonise limitation periods.[31] This was initiated in the Legal Affairs Committee via a report by Diana Wallis MEP. The report[32] pointed to the considerable divergences in national rules on limitation of claims, which gives rise to cross-border issues, notably where some states give no special protection to minors and persona under disability, whereas others do. The resolution recommends that the limitation period should be standardised at four years, save where the

[25] Regulation (EC) 1896/2006 of 12 December 2006, [2006] OJ L399/1. <http://eur-lex. europa.eu/LexUriServ/site/en/oj/2006/l_399/l_39920061230en00010032.pdf> accessed 11 June 2008. For the preliminary Green Paper on a European order for payment procedure and measures to simplify and speed up small claims litigation, see COM(2002) 746. The aim is to expedite the transmission of documents, which is to be made directly between local bodies designated by the Member States. A wide variation exists between Member States in the time for transmission (between one and six months in 2005), and the costs and their transparency.

[26] Regulation (EC) 861/2007; see art 7 at <http://eur-lex.europa.eu/LexUriServ/LexUriServ. do?uri=OJ:L:2007:199:0001:0022:EN:PDF> accessed 11 June 2008. The legal basis under art 61 EC for coverage of domestic disputes as well as cross-border ones was a matter of debate. Art 16 provides that the court shall not award costs to the extent that they were unnecessarily incurred or are disproportionate to the claim.

[27] Regulation (EC) 44/2001.

[28] Regulation (EC) 864/2007 of the European Parliament and the Council on the law applicable to contractual obligations of 11 July 2007 (Rome II), which will apply from 11 January 2009 (<http://eur-lex.europa.eu/LexUriServ/site/en/oj/2007/l_199/l_19920070731en00400049.pdf> accessed 11 June 2008), [2007] OJ L199/40.

[29] Proposal for a Regulation of the European Parliament and the Council on the law applicable to contractual obligations (Rome I), COM(2005) 650, 15 December 2005 at <http://eur-lex.europa.eu/LexUriServ/site/en/com/2005/com2005_0650en01.pdf> accessed 11 June 2008. European Parliament legislative resolution of 29 November 2007 on the proposal for a regulation of the European Parliament and of the Council on the law applicable to contractual obligations (Rome I) (COM(2005)0650—C6-0441/2005—2005/0261(COD)) at <http://www.europarl.europa.eu/sides/getDoc.do?pubRef=-//EP//TEXT+TA+P6-TA-2007-0560+0+DOC+XML+V0//EN> accessed 11 June 2008.

[30] M Andenas, B Hess and P Oberhammer (eds), 'Special Issue: Enforcement Agency Practice in Europe' (2006) 17 EBLR 515–888, No 3.

[31] <http://www.europarl.europa.eu/sides/getDoc.do?pubRef=-//EP//NONSGML+TA+P6-TA-2007-0020+0+DOC+PDF+V0//EN&language=EN> accessed 11 June 2008.

[32] <http://www.europarl.europa.eu/sides/getDoc.do?pubRef=-//EP//NONSGML+REPORT+A6-2006-0405+0+DOC+WORD+V0//EN&language=EN> accessed 11 June 2008.

proper law of the claim provides for a longer period. The period should be suspended:

a) where the defendant has deliberately, dishonestly, unreasonably or as a result of a mistake concealed the existence of facts or matters giving rise to liability; or
b) during criminal proceedings.

A judgment should be enforceable for 10 years.

'E-Justice' is a concept that is now being discussed at European level.[33] Consideration is being given to improving the exchange of information in cross-border civil and commercial matters and in criminal matters. The issue was one of the main points discussed at the informal meeting of Justice and Home Affairs Ministers on 1–2 October.[34] The main focus of the initiative is the creation of an 'E-Justice portal', which will be a user-friendly system, allowing access by citizens and companies to services in other Member States. It aims to establish conditions for the networking of various judicial registers, including criminal records, insolvency, commercial and land registers. The European Commission acknowledges the potential use of this tool for the establishment of a joint electronic platform for a European Payment Order.

Community Policy in establishment of 'an Area of Freedom, Security and Justice' was confirmed by the Commission in a Communication and Note of 28 June 2006, which evaluated progress in the so-called 'Hague scoreboard plus' agenda.[35] Much of the current focus is on tackling organised crime and terrorism, but civil and criminal laws are listed as coming within the scope of interest. The Commission concludes that areas of the justice agenda that have been 'communautarised', especially cooperation in civil justice, have worked well, in contrast to poor progress in police and criminal justice areas.

The Commission, therefore, seems to indicate a future ambition to attempt to harmonise national provisions of procedural law, albeit not immediately. For the present, the Commission states that the principle of mutual recognition will continue to be the cornerstone for the Union's policies in civil and criminal law, such as in pre-trial and post-trial phases. However, the Commission indicates that it proposes to examine the efficiency of justice systems and will, in the medium term, give consideration to 'a gradual process of consolidation in single mutual recognition instruments of current mutual assistance mechanisms ... and the establishment of a single area of justice in civil matters—essential for businesses as well as

---

[33] See discussion document at <http://www.eu2007.pt/NR/rdonlyres/825565BC-C0EF-4887-9FB2-8C8B623513ED/0/20070924EJusticeJHAinformal.pdf> accessed 11 June 2008.

[34] <http://www.eu2007.pt/UE/vEN/Noticias_Documentos/20071001ConclusoesE-Justice.htm> accessed 11 June 2008.

[35] See <http://ec.europa.eu/justice_home/news/information_dossiers/the_hague_2006/index_en.htm> accessed 11 June 2008.

citizens—providing a new political impetus to the civil mutual recognition programme 2000'. Thus, the implication is that the Commission is quietly signalling an ambition to harmonise civil justice matters in a few years.

The Consumer Law Enforcement Forum[36] has been created to enhance the role that consumer organisations can play in making the EU consumer protection rules fully and equally effective throughout the Community, in particular in the new Member States. Its central function is to ensure that consumer organisations are aware of the enforcement possibilities that are available, allowing consumer organisations to learn from the experiences of others. Its publicity states:

> The project deals with the involvement and the possible roles of consumer organisations in both public enforcement i.e. getting public authorities to more fully engage with consumer problems and in private enforcement i.e. bringing case to courts via collective action (litigation).

ALTERNATIVE DISPUTE RESOLUTION

There has also been particular emphasis on alternative dispute resolution at Community level.[37] ADR is attractive because it avoids or short-circuits legal processes, involves increased informality and saves time and money.[38] In addition, ADR has attracted early attention as a Community policy since it avoids issues of whether the EU has jurisdiction to address areas of substantive civil procedure and associated resistance by governments in their internal systems. Yet, once a certain point has been reached in 'Europeanisation', national legal and governmental opinion may be prepared to accept the imposition of harmonisation. The 2008 Directive on certain aspects of mediation in civil and commercial matters continues emphasis on mediation and establishes requirements for it in cross-border disputes.[39] The preceding Green Paper highlighted some policy points that

---

[36] <http://www.clef-project.eu> accessed 11 June 2008.

[37] J Stuyck *et al*, 'Study on alternative means of consumer redress other than redress through ordinary judicial proceedings' (Catholic University of Leuven, 17 January 2007, issued April 2007).

[38] Commission Recommendation of 30 March 1998 on the principles applicable to the bodies responsible for out-of-court settlement of consumer disputes, 98/257/EC, [1998] OJ L115/31, fifth recital. Green Paper on alternative dispute resolution in civil and commercial law, COM(2002) 196, 19 April 2002.

[39] Directive 2008/52/EC of 21 May 2008 at <http://eur-lex.europa.eu/LexUriServ/LexUriServ. do?uri=OJ:L:2008:136:0003:0008:EN:PDF> accessed 11 June 2008. This Directive took several years to progress through the legislative system from the above Green Paper of 2002: one contentious issue was whether it should apply, as originally proposed, to mediation within Member States, but this was ultimately rejected and it applies only to cross-border situations from 2011. These points illustrate the Member States' protectiveness towards their national civil justice systems. See also B Knötzl and E Zach, 'Taking the Best from

are important in the discussion that follows, namely the importance of ADR as a means of achieving social harmony, by which the parties do not engage in a process of confrontation, but rather in a process of rapprochement, thereby themselves achieving a consensual solution that maintains their commercial or other relations.[40]

Various pan-European extra-judicial networks have been established and offer significantly useful cross-border dispute resolution services, although they are not as yet widely known. An Extra-Judicial Network (EEJ-NET) was launched in 2001[41] and a consumer claim form promulgated.[42] EEJ-NET is a consumer support and information structure which consists of national contact points ('clearing houses') located in each Member State. Each of the contact points relays information to the 400 or so bodies which the Member States consider as having met the Commission's requirements concerning the principles applicable to bodies responsible for the out-of-court resolution of consumer disputes.[43] A European Consumer Centre Network was created from 2007, with branches in every Member State, specifically to assist consumers in resolving their cross-border disputes within the EU.[44]

Similarly, FIN-NET (FINancial Services Complaints NETwork)[45] is a network of the competent national ADR bodies which meet the requirements of the applicable Commission recommendation.[46] It handles out-of-court cross-border complaints in relation to financial service companies. Complaints can be lodged with the FIN-NET member in the complainant's country, but will be handled by the relevant body in the country where the financial services provider

Mediation Regulations. The EC Mediation Directive and the Austrian Mediation Act' (2007) 23 *Arbitration International* 4 663. A voluntary European Code of Conduct for Mediators was launched in July 2004: <http://ec.europa.eu/civiljustice/adr/adr_ec_code_conduct_en.pdf> accessed 3 July 2008.

[40] Green Paper on alternative dispute resolution in civil and commercial law, COM(2002) 196, 19 April 2002, para 10.

[41] Council Resolution of 25 May 2000 on a Community-wide network of national bodies for the extra-judicial settlement of consumer disputes, [2000] OJ C155/1. <http://europa. eu/scadplus/leg/en/lvb/l32043.htm> accessed 11 June 2008.

[42] <http://www.eejnet.org/filing_complaint> accessed 11 June 2008.

[43] Commission Recommendation 98/257/EC of 30 March 1998 on the principles applicable to the bodies responsible for out-of-court settlement of consumer disputes, [1998] OJ L155/31; and Commission recommendation 2001/31/EC of 4 April 2001 on the principles for out-of-court bodies involved in the consensual resolution of consumer disputes, [2001] OJ L109/56.

[44] <http://ec.europa.eu/consumers/redress_cons/index_en.htm> accessed 11 June 2008. For example, the UK ECC is hosted by the Trading Standards Institute, and is co-funded by the European Commission and the UK Department for Business, Enterprise and Regulatory Reform. The centre opened in August 2007 taking enquiries from consumers and handling cross-border cases referred from other Member States. The centre is fully operational and staged an official launch on 14 November to raise awareness with consumers and stakeholders. <http://www.ukecc.net/default.asp> accessed 11 June 2008.

[45] <http://ec.europa.eu/internal_market/fin-net/index_en.htm> accessed 11 June 2008.

[46] Commission Recommendation 98/257/EC, above.

is located, and can be made in the language of the financial contract or the language in which the complainant has normally dealt with the provider.

SOLVIT[47] is a free-of-charge online problem-solving network in which EU Member States work together to solve—without legal proceedings—problems caused by the misapplication of internal market law by public authorities. There is a SOLVIT centre in every European Union Member State (as well as in Norway, Iceland and Liechtenstein). SOLVIT Centres can help with handling complaints from both citizens and businesses. They are part of the national administration and are committed to providing real solutions to problems within 10 weeks.

The network was created in July 2002 and up until the end of 2007 has resolved more than 1,300 problems encountered by citizens and businesses due to incorrect application of EU rules by national authorities. SOLVIT now accepts around 60 new cases per month. Around 80 per cent of these problems are resolved, most of them within the deadline of 10 weeks. The members of staff of the national SOLVIT centres and European Commission SOLVIT team are committed to continue providing a first-class service to Europe's citizens and businesses. Its recent successes include ensuring that a British anaesthetist, who was entitled to work in Spain under EU law, had his qualifications recognised when permission was refused by the Spanish authorities; and helping a Norwegian company to sell its bottled water in Malta without having to meet any additional labelling requirements.

EVOLUTION OF CONSUMER COLLECTIVE REDRESS

The possibility of consumer collective or class actions was first raised in the EU context in a Commission paper of 1984.[48] The paper noted the common legal tradition of the then Member States, irrespective of whether they came from civil law or common law traditions, that no individual is entitled to institute legal proceedings unless he or she establishes a direct personal interest. The interests of a number of consumers, or of consumers generally, were entrusted to the public prosecutor's office or an authorised public body,[49] or some form of action brought by an individual on behalf of other individuals.[50]

---

[47] <http://ec.europa.eu/solvit/site/index_en.htm> accessed 11 June 2008.

[48] Memorandum from the Commission: Consumer Redress COM(84) 692, 12 December 1984.

[49] In that memorandum, only two examples were noted: the UK Office of Fair Trading and the Danish *Forbrugerombudsman* (Consumer Ombudsman).

[50] The Commission's Memorandum noted very few examples of this category as at 1984: in common-law jurisdictions, a 'relator action' (brought with the approval of the Attorney General) or a 'representative action' (very rarely used since every claimant must have exactly the same interest), and in civil law jurisdictions the '*action civile*' (based on criminal proceedings) or the 'action for cessation' (for an injunction, an example being under the Belgian Law of 14 July 1971, art 55).

Alternatively, the defence of the collective interests of consumers was sometimes entrusted to associations that satisfied certain criteria.[51] The Commission concluded in 1984 that it was not possible to propose binding harmonisation of national mechanisms on collective actions, since there was too much complexity and diversity amongst the national systems.[52]

However, since then various Community measures, primarily related to consumer protection, have included a collective mechanism as one of their required provisions for enforcement. In the consumer protection field, the EU legislation specifies that Member States are required to take 'adequate and effective means' to ensure that the substantive provisions are enforced in national systems.[53] Thus, the choice of enforcement mechanism is left, as a matter of subsidiarity, to each Member State. This also recognises the practical fact that, as discussed earlier, Member States have different internal regimes and traditions in relation to their enforcement systems. In the implementation and enforcement of consumer protection measures, an important consideration therefore lies in whether the primary mechanism involves public authorities or a significant reliance on private bodies, especially consumer organisations. One can easily misunderstand, in reading the EU legislation involved, that the use of consumer organisations as an enforcement mechanism is the primary or only approach in all Member States, whereas in fact the inclusion of such an approach is a mandatory, but not necessarily exclusive or primary, mechanism.

The EU consumer protection measures specify the mechanism of empowering consumer organisations to take enforcement action. The measures involved are:

a) Directive 84/450/EEC on misleading advertising;[54]
b) Directive 93/13/EEC on unfair contract terms;[55]
c) Directive 98/27/EC on cross-border injunctions for breach of specified consumer protection Directives;[56]
d) Regulation 2006/2004 on consumer protection cooperation;[57] and
e) Directive 2005/29/EC on unfair business-to-consumer commercial practices ('UCP').[58]

Some of these measures have included the requirement that Member States are obliged to provide in their implementing legislation a mechanism for

---

[51] *Ibid.* However, the Commission noted that the conditions to be satisfied by a consumer organisation varied considerably between states.
[52] *Ibid.*
[53] See, for example, Directive 93/13/EEC art 7.1 and Directive 2005/29/EC art 11.1.
[54] art 4.1.
[55] art 7.
[56] arts 1–3.
[57] arts 4.2 and 8.3.
[58] art 4.

collective action to be taken by consumer representative bodies to defend the collective rights of consumers in specified circumstances. The available remedies would typically be limited to orders related to the defendant's conduct, such as injunctive relief, rather than monetary claims.[59]

The mechanism of relying on consumer organisations pre-existed in some Member States and, as has been seen, was a, or the, principal mechanism in some Member States. In addition to this practical issue, however, was a political motivation. No specific mechanism need have been mentioned in the EU legislation. However, the involvement of consumer organisations in the enforcement of consumer protection legislation in *all* Member States was a means of involving consumers not only in relevant legislation, but particularly in EU (and national) legislation. The EU authorities were aware that they were perceived by many voters as being remote and of little value.[60] Politicians and the EU institutions were keen to adopt measures that could be presented as being consumer friendly.

The test for consumer organisations to qualify to exercise autonomous cross-border enforcement powers is where the body has a 'legitimate expectation'.[61] However, it may be questioned whether the legitimate expectation test affords sufficient certainty and whether the test is too wide. The formulation is imprecise and affords scope for significant variations in interpretation of which bodies may have a legitimate interest in bringing individual cases. It was noted in chapter two above that there are arguments that the involvement of private sector bodies in exercising powers of enforcement of public norms gives rise to issues of democratic accountability, consistency and the adequacy of resources. The EU legislation does not attempt to address these issues, such as by providing mechanisms and requirements for accreditation, supervision and oversight, such as apply to notified bodies under the EU New Approach product regulatory legislation. Notified bodies are, similarly, private entities which are empowered with certain regulatory powers if they satisfy published criteria. They are subject to oversight by public competent authorities, and their approval may be withdrawn if performance falls.[62]

Given that the delegation of certain powers to private bodies is optional in some of these EU measures, a further issue is whether it should be a requirement to specify a basis under which Member States could decide the

---

[59] See OECD, 'Background Report: OECD Workshop on Consumer Dispute Resolution and Redress in the Global Marketplace, 19–20 April 2005, Washington, DC' (Paris, 2005) 31.

[60] Note rejection of the draft EU Constitution by voters in France and the Netherlands in 2005.

[61] Directives 84/450 art 4.1; 93/13 art 7.2; 98/27 arts 1–3; 2005/29 art 4; and Regulation 2006/2004 arts 4.2 and 8.3.

[62] See Council Resolution of 7 May 1985 on a New Approach to Technical Harmonisation and Standards, [1985] OJ C136/1; CJS Hodges, *European Regulation of Consumer Product Safety* (Oxford, 2005) ch 5.

circumstances in which such delegation could take place. However, as will be seen, such issues may be overtaken by developments. The EU measures will now be examined in greater detail.

Misleading Advertising

As part of Member States' obligation to ensure that adequate and effective means exist for the control of misleading advertising, specified legal powers to take actions must be available to persons or organisations regarded under national law as having a legitimate interest in prohibiting misleading advertising.[63] Most Member States have accorded consumer associations the right to bring actions under this provision.[64]

Unfair Terms in Consumer Contracts

Member States are required to ensure that adequate and effective means exist to prevent the continued use of unfair terms in contracts with consumers by sellers or suppliers.[65] Such means shall include provisions whereby 'persons or organisations, having a legitimate interest under national law in protecting consumers', may take actions according to national law before the courts or administrative tribunals for a decision on whether contractual terms drawn up for general use are unfair, so that appropriate and effective means to prevent the continued use of such terms can be applied.[66]

As at 2000, Member States had implemented the above provision in different ways. In some states, only consumer associations were entitled to seek injunctions, whereas in others the initiative could be taken by a regulator responsible for upholding the public interest, such as the Office of Fair Trading (OFT) in the UK, the Director of Consumer Affairs in Ireland,[67] the consumer ombudsman in the Nordic states, the *Verbraucherschutzvereine* in Germany, and the relevant Ministry in Spain and in Portugal.[68] In its 2002

---

[63] Directive 84/450/EEC art 4.1.

[64] See Green Paper: Access of consumers to Justice and the settlement of consumer disputes in the single market, COM(93) 576, 16 November 1993 10.

[65] Directive 93/13/EEC art 7.1.

[66] *Ibid*, art 7.

[67] The European Communities (Unfair Terms in Consumer Contracts) Regulations 1995, Regulation 8(1).

[68] Report from the Commission on the Implementation of Council Directive 93/13/EEC of 5 April 1993 on Unfair Terms in Consumer Contracts, COM(2000) 248, 27 April 2000. France and Belgium have created collegiate bodies whose main mission is to recommend the elimination of unfair terms, and the courts are reported to refer to the recommendations of these bodies in their judgments. Data showed a difference in approach, with Germany, Austria, France and the UK predominantly adopting preventative actions, which were rarer in Belgium and Spain, and unknown in Ireland and Luxembourg, where the approach was on individual actions.

Green Paper, the Commission noted that the UK system, in which the OFT was pivotally involved, was notably effective in reaching compliance, in both qualitative and quantitative terms, including through direct negotiation that might avoid the necessity for court action and costs.[69]

The 'Injunctions Directive'

Directive 98/27 on injunctions for the protection of consumers' interests (the 'Injunctions Directive') permits qualified entities in one Member State to apply to the courts or administrative authorities in other Member States for measures that include an order requiring the cessation or prohibition of any infringement of the collective interests of consumers in the first Member States[70] under specific European consumer protection measures.[71] A 'qualified entity' is any body or organisation which, being properly constituted according to the law of a Member State, has a legitimate interest in ensuring that the provisions of the Member States relating to actions for a cross-border injunction are aimed at the protection of the 'collective interests of consumers' under listed consumer protection Directives.[72] Thus, the Directive does not specify whether a 'qualified entity' must be a public or private body. The procedure grants no rights to individual consumers, but empowers qualified entities to act as enforcement agents. The 'collective interests of consumers' does not include the culmination of the interests of individual consumers harmed by an infringement.[73]

The Injunctions Directive was imposed onto pre-existing national mechanisms for collective redress, which differed significantly between themselves, as discussed in chapter two.[74] The Directive does not attempt to harmonise the national internal arrangements, nor the powers or modes

---

[69] The report said that the OFT had moved from a situation of no prior regulatory control in the area of unfair terms to examining over 800 cases annually.

[70] Directive 98/27/EC.

[71] The measures covered are: Directive 84/450 on misleading advertising; Directive 85/577 on contracts negotiated away from business premises; Directive 87/102 on consumer credit; Directive 89/522 on television broadcasting; Directive 90/314 on package travel, package holidays and package tours; Directive 92/28 on advertising of medicinal products for human use; Directive 93/13 on unfair terms in consumer contracts; Directive 94/47 on the protection of purchasers in respect of property timeshare contracts; Directive 97/7 on the protection of consumers in respect of distance contracts: some of these provisions have since been amended or incorporated into other legislation, and the Injunctions Directive has been overtaken by the Consumer Protection Regulation and the UCP Directive, discussed below.

[72] *Ibid*, arts 1–3.

[73] Directive 98/27, recital 2.

[74] An impression of the picture of national mechanisms before the Injunctions Directive can be seen from the Consumer Law Compendium at <http://ec.europa.eu/consumers/cons_int/safe_shop/acquis/comp_analysis_en.pdf> accessed 11 June 2008.

of operation of national systems. It should therefore be no surprise that Member States have adopted differing approaches to the nomination of qualified entities under the Directive, ranging from a single entity in seven states (such as the governmental regulator in Ireland, and the Consumer Ombudsman in Sweden and the Netherlands) to 73 predominantly private bodies in Germany and 71 in Greece.[75] The official number of qualified entities across 28 Member States was 276 in 2007, of which over one-half are accounted for by Germany and Greece alone, but the total rises to 468 if the 204 individual local weights and measures authorities are included. The 2007 study for the Commission found that there is a wide variation in national law determining criteria for recognising consumer associations as qualified entities.

The 2005 study for the European Commission on implementation of the Injunctions Directive found that the legal and practical significance of injunctive actions is rather low, and described the picture across Member States as showing 'no coherent system'.[76] The 2007 Leuven study found that injunction procedures falling within the scope of the Directive are popular and widely applied in Austria, Belgium, Finland, Germany, Hungary and Sweden, but the procedure is not popular in 10 other states.[77] As noted above, the tradition of enforcement by public bodies is strong in Scandinavia, Ireland and the UK, but the Directive has resulted in public bodies taking an important role in enforcement in many Member States.[78] However, for some years only one cross-border injunction was sought or obtained,[79] and this action was instituted by the UK regulator (the OFT) rather than by a consumer organisation.

---

[75] H Schulte-Nölke, C Twigg-Flesner and M Elbers, *EC Consumer Law Compendium—Comparative Analysis* (2007) at <http://ec.europa.eu/consumers/cons_int/safe_shop/acquis/comp_analysis_en.pdf>. See earlier Commission communication at [2003] OJ C321/26; the list in Germany includes local tenants' associations.

[76] MU Docekal, P Kolba, H-W Micklitz and P Rott, *The Implementation of Directive 98/27/EC in the Member States* (Bamberg/Vienna, 2005).

[77] J Stuyck *et al*, 'Study on alternative means of consumer redress other than redress through ordinary judicial proceedings' (Catholic University of Leuven, 17 January 2007, issued April 2007) para 477.

[78] J Stuyck *et al, ibid*, para 454. Individual consumers are entitled to bring injunction proceedings in Belgium, the Czech Republic, Denmark, Slovakia and Slovenia, but this 'is not a general trend among Member States'. Member States are entitled to examine whether the purpose of the qualified entity justifies its bringing an action in a specific case (art 4(1)) and to require parties only to start proceedings after having consulted with the defendant or both the defendant and a relevant public body (art 5(1)), but there is no general trend to implement this (Finland and the UK have). Actions for damages in injunction proceedings are only available in Sweden, although moral damages may be awarded in Greece.

[79] Although anecdotal reports refer to communications about infringers between the authorities of different Member States, which may have resulted in domestic enforcement action that would have avoided the more cumbersome and costly cross-border mechanism.

Case Study: Duchesne SA[80]

A trader domiciled in Belgium sent unsolicited mail order catalogues to UK residents together with notification of a prize win, usually £10,000. The OFT instituted proceedings for an injunction in Belgium under national legislation implementing the Injunctions Directive. The Belgian court issued an order banning the practice as constituting a breach of the Misleading Advertising Directive, on the basis that consumers believed that they had only to make a purchase in order to secure a prize, whereas winners were pre-selected and few recipients would receive a prize. The company was reported to have received about 4,000 orders per day from its catalogues, and many consumers complained. On appeal, the injunction was upheld, with a penalty of €2,500 per mailing issued in breach up to a maximum of €1 million. The Court of First Instance and Court of Appeal in Belgium reached different conclusions as to whether Belgian or English law applied, but the activity would have been a breach of both.

The Injunctions Directive covers only cross-border infringements. The mechanism that it adopted, of permitting Member States to decide whether to choose public and/or private 'qualified entities', was clearly designed to build on the existing non-uniform national situations. In implementing this Directive and the Consumer Protection Cooperation Regulation discussed below, some Member States have chosen to reform their internal mechanisms, if only by applying the same regime to injunction proceedings for internal infringements as for cross-border infringements. The pan-EU picture, therefore, remains somewhat confused, with differing models existing in different states.

The 2007 Leuven study reached various conclusions about the Injunctions Directive. First, it considered the mechanism to be important because of pursuing matters of public interest, given the inability of individuals to take action to correct infringements of collective consumer interest.[81] However, it voiced criticism of certain shortcomings. The scope of an injunction is limited to the territory of one Member State, with the result that businesses can defy enforcement by changing one aspect of violation or changing their corporate identity, and individuals can escape.[82] Costs issues are not covered in the

---

[80] *Cour d'appel de Bruxelles*, 8 December 2005; and *Duchesne SA v L'Office of Fair Trading*, unreported, RG: 2005/KR/38. See OFT Press Releases AR0012585, 208/04, 63/04 at <http://www.oft.gov.uk/news/press/2004/208-04> accessed 3 July 2008, referred to in *TS Today* (February 2006); and 'Justice 4 you' <http://www.oft.gov.uk> accessed 11 June 2008. See also Report from the Commission: First Annual Progress Report on European Contract Law and the Acquis Review, COM(2005) 456, 23 September 2005.

[81] J Stuyck *et al*, 'Study on alternative means of consumer redress other than redress through ordinary judicial proceedings' (Catholic University of Leuven, 17 January 2007, issued April 2007) para 443.

[82] J Stuyck *et al*, *ibid*, para 478.

Directive, and most states apply the 'loser pays' rule,[83] so the costs may be too high and deter consumer associations. The procedures are subject to the delays inherent in normal court procedures.

The Consumer Protection Cooperation Regulation

The Consumer Protection Cooperation Regulation (the CPC Regulation)[84] provides for cross-border enforcement of 15 designated measures comprising the corpus of EU consumer legislation. Unlike the other Directives mentioned here, the CPC Regulation does not give rise to substantive rights, but provides enhanced mechanisms for enforcement collaboration between Member States.

It should be remembered that the primary purpose of the CPC Regulation is to create a pan-EU network of national *public* authorities responsible for enforcing EU consumer law and to oblige them to work together in a mutual assistance model and with the Commission.[85] The rationale for the Regulation is to address a gap in effective cross-border enforcement and assistance. Purely internal situations remain domestic matters. The introduction of the mutual recognition scheme required Germany, Austria and the Netherlands to create federal consumer enforcement authorities for the first time, so as to be able to collaborate with those pre-existing authorities in the UK (OFT) and Nordic states. This would prove to be an important development, and one on which further developments could be built. The involvement of private organisations is included as a purely secondary enforcement tool.

Thus, in addition to collaboration between the normal national enforcement authorities, Member States have an option to designate 'bodies having a legitimate interest in the cessation or prohibition of intra-Community infringements',[86] and such a body may take all necessary enforcement measures available to it under national law.[87] A recital to the Regulation sets out a formal statement of the rationale for empowering consumer organisations to assume such a regulatory role:

> Consumer organisations play an essential role in terms of consumer information and education and in the protection of consumer interests, including in the

---

[83] Each party pays its own costs in Finland, Poland and Latvia, and the party who brings the case bears the costs in Greece: para 473.

[84] Regulation (EC) 2006/2004 on cooperation between national authorities responsible for the enforcement of consumer protection laws. This is in force from 29 December 2005, and the provisions on mutual assistance from 29 December 2006.

[85] G Betlem, 'Public and Private Transnational Enforcement of EU Consumer Law' in W van Boom and M Loos, *Collective Enforcement of Consumer Law: Securing Compliance in Europe through Private Group Action and Public Authority Intervention* (Europa Law Publishing, 2007).

[86] Regulation (EC) 2006/2004 art 4.2.

[87] *Ibid*, art 8.3.

settlement of consumer disputes, and should be encouraged to cooperate with competent authorities to enhance the application of this Regulation.

The network of national authorities provides a new opportunity for both bilateral and cross-Community cooperation in enforcement. This opportunity has already been seized through adoption of the 'EU Sweep', advertised as 'a new kind of enforcement action'. The Member State authorities, coordinated by the Commission, have undertaken a simultaneous systematic check on similar activities, in the first instance relating to websites selling airline tickets. The initial sweep in September 2007 found that over 50 per cent of websites showed irregularities. In a second, enforcement phase, authorities contacted companies and asked them to correct their sites or clarify their position. In June 2008, it was announced that more than half of the sites that had been found to have had irregularities had been corrected.[88]

The Unfair Commercial Practices Directive

Directive 2005/29/EC prohibits unfair commercial practices, including misleading actions and omissions and aggressive commercial practices.[89] Member States must ensure that adequate and effective means exist to enforce compliance.[90] Although the Directive states that such means shall include persons and organisations that are regarded under national laws as 'having a legitimate interest in combating unfair commercial practices' being permitted to take action before the courts and/or administrative authorities to enforce unfair commercial practices within the EU, it is for each Member State to decide which facilities are to be available.[91] Thus, a Member State is not required to introduce the possibility for direct legal action by 'interested persons' if it has a system of centralised public enforcement.

The facilities shall be available regardless of whether the consumers affected are in the territory of the Member State where the trader is located or in another Member State.[92] The purpose of this rule is so that infringements that are initiated by a trader in one state but have effect in another can be dealt with. Thus, the Member States must ensure that powers are

---

[88] Commission announcement at <http://ec.europa.eu/consumers/enforcement/sweep/index_en.htm> accessed 2 July 2008.

[89] An unfair commercial practice is a commercial practice which is contrary to the requirements of professional diligence, and materially distorts, or is likely to distort, the economic behaviour with regards to the product of the average consumer whom it reaches or to whom it is addressed, or of the average member of the group when a commercial practice is directed to a particular group of consumers; Directive 2005/29/EC art 5.2. Misleading or aggressive commercial practices are deemed to be unfair; *ibid*, arts 5–9.

[90] Directive 2005/29/EC art 11.

[91] *Ibid*.

[92] *Ibid*.

available either to order cessation of an unfair commercial practice or to order its pre-emptive prohibition.[93]

OTHER EU COLLECTIVE MECHANISMS

In addition to the above measures in the consumer protection field, two other EU measures include collective mechanisms. In these, there is provision for collective action to be taken by a representative body that is likely to be a trade association, so as to provide an efficient means of attacking counterfeiters or other infringers that harm the interests of a business sector, especially one that involves small and medium-sized enterprises.[94]

Intellectual Property Enforcement

A collective claim for damages for breach of intellectual property rights can be brought by a representative trade organisation, such as a trade association, under article 4 of Directive 2004/48/EC. This requires Member States to recognise, as persons entitled to seek redress, a list that includes, in addition to intellectual property right holders:

a) intellectual property collective rights-management bodies (inter alia); and
b) professional defence bodies which are regularly recognised as having a right to represent holders of intellectual property rights, in so far as permitted by and in accordance with the provisions of the applicable law.

The aim of these provisions is to deploy strong and effective measures against the threat of intellectual piracy, counterfeiters and organised crime. However, the mechanism may be applicable in a wider context. The above wording has caused some confusion in the intellectual property and government world.

Late Payments

A similar mechanism is included in Directive 2003/35/EC on combating late payment in commercial transactions.[95] This was to be implemented by Member States from August 2002.[96] The primary enforcement obligation is on Member States to ensure that adequate and effective means

---

[93] *Ibid*, art 11.2.
[94] Commission Recommendation 2003/361/EC of 6 May 2003 defines micro, small and medium-sized (SME) companies, with SMEs as having between 50 and 249 employees.
[95] [2000] OJ L200/35.
[96] *Ibid*, art 6.

exist to enforce the provisions of the Directive, for example in relation to preventing the continued use of terms which are grossly unfair.[97] In addition, it is specified that such means:

> ... shall include provisions whereby organisations officially recognised as, or having a legitimate interest in, representing small and medium-sized enterprises may take action according to the national law concerned before courts or before competent administrative bodies on the grounds that contractual terms drawn up for general use are grossly unfair within the meaning of the Directive, so that they can apply appropriate and effective means to prevent the continued use of such terms.[98]

ePrivacy Directive

The Commission has proposed to insert into Directive 2002/58/EC on privacy and electronic communications an additional mechanism to enhance enforcement to the existing provisions against the sending of unsolicited commercial communications. The proposal reads:

> Without prejudice to any administrative remedy for which provision may be made, inter alia under Article 15a(2), Member States shall ensure that any individual or legal person having a legitimate interest in combating infringements of national provisions adopted pursuant to this Article, including an electronic communications service provider protecting its legitimate business interests or the interests of its customers, may take legal action against such infringements before the courts.[99]

In the view of the European Data Protection Supervisor (EDPS), this provision is intended to enable internet service providers to tackle spammers who abuse their networks, to sue entities counterfeiting sender addresses or hacking into servers for use as spam relays.[100] The problem identified by the EDPS is that individual subscribers 'have neither the money nor the incentives' to take action themselves, whereas internet service providers and other providers of public electronic communication services (PPECS) have the financial strength and technological capability to investigate spam

---

[97] *Ibid*, art 3.4.

[98] *Ibid*, art 3.5.

[99] Proposal for a Directive of the European Parliament and of the Council amending Directive 2002/22/EC on universal service and users' rights relating to electronic communications networks; Directive 2002/58/EC concerning the processing of personal data and the protection of privacy in the electronic communications sector; and Regulation (EC) 2006/2004 on consumer protection cooperation, COM(2007) 698, 13 November 2007, art 2(5) adding art 13.6 to Directive 2002/58/EC, at <http://op.bna.com/pl.nsf/r?Open=byul-7dqnxy> accessed 11 June 2008.

[100] Opinion of the European Data Protection Supervisor on the Proposal for a Directive of the European Parliament and of the Council amending, among others, Directive 2002/58/EC concerning the processing of personal data and the protection of privacy in the electronic communications

campaigns, to identify the perpetrators and, it is thought, to take legal action against spammers. The EDPS considers that the proposed provision would also permit consumer associations and trade unions representing the interests of spammed consumers also to take action on their behalf. It is not entirely clear whether the remedies envisaged here extend beyond injunctive relief or criminal penalties to damages claims.

Environmental Protection

Directive 2004/35/EC on environmental liability with regard to the prevention and remedying of environmental damage includes a role for natural and legal persons, including non-governmental organisations.[101] The approach under this Directive is of a different kind to that of the Directives discussed above. This Directive imposes obligations on operators of occupational activity to take preventive action and remedial action in respect of specified environmental damage. Control is exercised by national competent authorities. Specified natural or legal persons are entitled to submit to the competent authority any observations relating to instances of environmental damage or an imminent threat of such damage of which they are aware and shall be entitled to request the competent authority to take action under the Directive.[102] The natural or legal persons so specified comprise those:

a) affected or likely to be affected by environmental damage; or
b) having a sufficient interest in environmental decision making relating to the damage; or, alternatively
c) alleging the impairment of a right, where administrative procedural law of a Member State requires this as a precondition.

Category b) will include a number of civil society organisations, and it is provided that:[103]

> [T]he interest of any non-governmental organisation promoting environmental protection and meeting any requirements under national law shall be deemed sufficient for the purpose of subparagraph (b). Such organisations shall also be deemed to have rights capable of being impaired for the purpose of subparagraph (b).

It will be seen that these provisions do not give a formal enforcement role to private persons or organisations, such role remaining the responsibility

sector (Directive on privacy and electronic communications), 10 April 2008, at <http://www.edps. europa.eu/EDPSWEB/webdav/site/mySite/shared/Documents/Consultation/Opinions/2008/08-04-10_e-privacy_EN.pdf> accessed 11 June 2008.

[101] [2004] OJ L143/56.
[102] *Ibid*, art 12.
[103] *Ibid*, art 12.

of the public authorities, but the energies and cooperation of such private persons and organisations are encouraged and enlisted generally in a scrutiny role. A model of public enforcement has been continued under the proposed Directive on the protection of the environment through criminal law,[104] in which no role is stated for private individuals or bodies. General involvement of non-governmental organisations in environmental protection has actively been encouraged under official programmes.[105]

COMPENSATION FOR CRIME VICTIMS

Although this is not a collective procedure, but relates to individuals, it is worth noting the harmonisation of national schemes on provision of compensation for victims of violent intentional crime, under Directive 2004/80.[106] This procedure is relevant because it is adjacent to, but distinct from, the *partie civile* mechanisms that exist in many Member States but are not harmonised, under which individuals may 'piggy-back' as private parties on criminal procedures instituted by the state and be awarded damages. Examples have been mentioned above in relation to France, Spain and the UK, and this mechanism will prove to be of relevance to the analysis later in this book. The advantage of the *partie civile* procedure is that the individual claimant incurs no cost or cost risk, and is able to take the benefit of a public prosecutor's powers on access to evidence and prosecution. By contrast, the procedures for compensation for victims of violent crime, who may claim compensation from the Member State in whose territory the crime was committed, is of little relevance in most consumer protection redress situations because of the criteria that violent crime must have been committed.

CONCLUSIONS

The above analysis reveals that EU competence to legislate on civil justice issues is limited. Since 1999, the EU has been extending significant energy

---

[104] Adopted 22 May 2008.

[105] Council Decision of 16 December 1997 on a Community action programme promoting non-governmental organisations primarily active in the field of environmental protection, 97/872/EC, [1997] OJ L354/25; Decision No 466/2002/EC of the European Parliament and of the Council of 1 March 2002 laying down a Community action programme promoting non-governmental organisations primarily active in the field of environmental protection, [2002] OJ L75/1; Decision No 786/2004/EC and see <http://europa.eu/scadplus/leg/en/lvb/l28041.htm> accessed 5 May 2008.

[106] [2004] OJ L261/15. See summary of national provisions at <http://ec.europa.eu/civiljustice/comp_crime_victim/comp_crime_victim_gen_en.htm> accessed 11 June 2008. See also Commission Decision of 19 April 2006 establishing standard forms for the transmission of applications and decisions pursuant to Council Directive 2004/80/EC relating to compensation to crime victims (2006/337/EC), at <http://eur-lex.europa.eu/LexUriServ/LexUriServ.do?uri=OJ:L:2006:125:0025:0030:EN:PDF> accessed 11 June 2008.

into building both court-based and extra-judicial mechanisms. Much of this work has largely gone unnoticed, but it provides a useful framework on which to build further cooperation on civil justice issues, irrespective of whether formal harmonisation of voluntary national alignment may occur. An emphasis on ADR has been a strong emerging feature of European dispute resolution policy, and was recently supported by the European Parliament, which called for greater resources for European Consumer Centres, SOLVIT and ADR, plus the establishment of a European Consumer Ombudsman in the European Ombudsman's office.[107]

Some consumer protection measures have included mechanisms under which *collective protection* may be sought in the form of injunctive relief from infringing activity, but there are no provisions for collective restitution of monies paid or for compensatory damages to be paid. A significant barrier to progress has been the existence of opposed approaches towards enforcement systems in the Member States, as noted in chapter two, with some states relying strongly on public authorities and others on private bodies, at least for some consumer protection functions—notably unfair contract terms and unfair competition. This diversity was ignored for the purposes of the Injunctions Directive on cross-border issues, but the nettle was grasped in the UCP Directive, and the public authority model was preferred. Accordingly, once sufficient time has elapsed for national public consumer protection authorities to have gained internal stability and experience on mutual collaboration, the alignment provided by this model would provide a vital foundation for further evolution.

This development would provide a solution to the issues that have been noted with empowerment of private sector bodies in enforcement of public norms. Such empowerment, even if limited in scope, has been a feature of EU consumer protection policy. As an experiment, however, it has not been a particular success, either in those states where it had no prior history or on a cross-border basis. A recent development has been the involvement of trade associations in a collective capacity: it will be interesting to see whether they fare any better than consumer associations in their ability to produce effective outcomes. Many trade associations suffer from the same constraints on funding and resources as consumer associations, but there may be circumstances in which businesses may be prepared to fund particular collective action.

Despite the general limited picture of achievement revealed above, intellectual engagement with provision of collective redress, and how it might be best achieved, has occurred for some years in the consumer protection field. As will be seen in the following chapter, this issue has not, however, appeared in the competition field until the end of 2005.

---

[107] 'Report on the EU Consumer Policy Strategy 2007–2013' (2007/2189(INI)) A6-0155/2008 <http://www.europarl.europa.eu/sidesSearch/search.do?type=REPORT&language=EN&term=6&author=28263> accessed 11 June 2008.

5

Technical Issues

ANY COURT-BASED MECHANISM that aggregates a group of individual cases that appear to have some similarities so as to avoid deciding every case individually has to confront the same series of issues.[1] The key issues include: what threshold criteria apply so as to trigger the special aggregated procedure; who represents whom; who makes the decisions; at what stages generic and individual issues need to be identified and decided; what decisions are binding on whom; who has notice of what; whether the mechanism is opt-in or opt-out; who pays for what; how conflicts of interest are controlled; how much remuneration intermediaries receive; and who approves and is bound by a settlement.

The existence of a special procedure is designed so that the courts can progress multiple similar cases efficiently and expeditiously. The essential objective is that of producing judicial economy in managing cases through the court system. Bearing in mind that the foregoing analysis has identified that the focus on collective redress mechanisms needs to be wide enough to encompass both court-based and other mechanisms, what broad issues need to be considered in looking at future policy? It is not intended here to provide an exhaustive analysis of the various essentials and differing approaches to procedure that have emerged to handle class actions or aggregated claims, but to highlight selected aspects that are particularly important in relation to consideration of broader policy on collective actions.

SIMILARITY OR DIFFERENCE?

Where all individual cases are essentially the same, it can be seen that it is efficient to resolve one or a small number rather than requiring all claimants to be involved. This approach is cheaper and quicker for claimants, courts and defendants. Yet there are some circumstances in which what may appear to be a group of similar claims turns out to have significant diversity, and there is no efficiency in adopting a common approach. This situation is recognised by the US class action requirements of commonality

---

[1] This was a finding of the Globalisation Project conference in December 2007, see <http://globalclassaction.stanford.edu> accessed 11 June 2008.

(that there are questions of law or fact common to the class), predominance (that common issues must predominate over questions affecting only individual members) and superiority (that the class approach is superior to other approaches).[2]

Well-known examples in which class approaches can be inappropriate are pharmaceutical or tobacco product liability cases or mis-selling cases, in which individual issues of reliance, adoption of risk and causation are usually predominant. In such cases, single determination, or an opt-in rule, is pointless since determination of one case, even if it involves one or more common issues, is insufficiently determinative of most of the others, which still all need to be determined individually. It follows that where cases need to be determined individually, it is unjust that a previous decision would apply in any subsequent case which the court thought was the same as the first, since that approach would deny the subsequent litigants any right to be represented in the court's decision.

Thus, the principal issue in designing an aggregation system is to be able to identify the situations in which a single determination might be more appropriate than proceeding individually. In what circumstances is it reliable to assume that one or a small number of claims are similar to a larger number of others? The benzodiazepines and Vioxx case studies show that it can be an expensive mistake to allow all possible claims into a pool without verification of individual facts. This is, of course, a powerful argument against adopting an opt-out approach as a blanket rule. On the other hand, case studies such as replica football shirts and airline fuel surcharges principally involve a single common issue that could be resolved efficiently once, followed by a procedure for individuals to prove individual qualification. Before proceeding further with the analysis, it is useful to refer to the opt-in versus opt-out issue.

OPT-IN AND OPT-OUT: BINDING SOLUTIONS, AVOIDING ABUSE AND DELIVERING JUSTICE

There is considerable debate over whether a collective mechanism should be opt-in or opt-out. The opt-in versus opt-out debate has three technical aspects: the first involves the mechanistic need to produce a result that is binding on relevant individuals; the second involves observation of fundamental rights; and the third involves issues of financing a collective action. These issues will be considered in turn, but ultimately the issue is how to maximise justice. How can people who have valid claims be compensated, and defendants be made to pay up when they should, without making defendants pay when it is not justified? Solving this issue opens

---

[2] See Federal Rule of Civil Procedure 23.

up considerations of power and abuse. The decision is ultimately one for resolution as a political decision.

The difference between the opt-in and opt-out mechanisms is straightforward to understand, but selection between them is far more difficult, since the consequences that flow from both are complex and require a difficult balancing exercise to be undertaken. The model that has been adopted in most EU jurisdictions for court-based rules is that claimants must take a positive step to assert their rights and formally join a coordinated procedure (opt-in). This is the rule in England, Sweden, Germany and arguably Italy. The converse position, of which the US class action is the prime example, is that a single claimant may be approved to represent a class of claimants, on the basis that all the individual cases of all class members are substantially the same, so resolution of the single case will by definition resolve all of the other cases. This is the position for consumer claims in Portugal and, in differing defined circumstances, in Denmark, Norway and the Netherlands. In the latter circumstances, there is no requirement for anyone to opt in at the start of the class representative proceeding, but instead notice must be given to all class members so that each is entitled to opt out of the class, and have the opportunity either not to assert his or her claim or to bring it individually.

A principal objection to an opt-out methodology is that it can lead to significant abuse in practice. Evidence in the United States (see chapter six) is that an opt-out mechanism can lead to a large number of claims being asserted that have insufficient merits, but because of their size often force defendants to pay out since this is cheaper on a commercial basis.[3] It is then argued that mechanisms can be put in place to control against abuse, notably strong control over cases by judges, particularly by an initial certification stage so as to weed out unmeritorious cases. The counter argument then is that a certification stage can only impose a low threshold of merit, amounting effectively to whether there appears at that stage to be a plausibly arguable case, and the result is that certification of a large opt-out class inevitably imposes considerable pressure on defendants to reach settlements on economic grounds. Thus, justice is not served since a number of class cases involve low merits and unjustified, costly settlements result.[4] Hence, the arguments overall involve a wish to increase justice for claimants, but to avoid injustice for defendants.

One possible solution here is to ensure that the court (either alone or perhaps assisted by some third party) is required to approve a settlement and also any money paid to both the lawyers (on both sides) and any investors.

---

[3] Note DR Hensler, NM Pace, B Dombey-Moore, B Giddens, J Gross and EK Moller, *Class Action Dilemmas: Pursuing Public Goals for Private Gain* (RAND Institute for Civil Justice, 2000).

[4] See the Vioxx case study.

However, the experience in the United States and elsewhere is that settlements can be agreed by defendants irrespective of the merits of a claim, but so as to save money overall. A possible way round this problem might be for courts to be required to approve the fairness of settlements, as a matter of merits and the effect on the general economy. If courts had power to reject overly generous settlements, this might tend to equalise settlement values with justice. The court might not need to go into the merits of a case in detail, but might rely (similar to a provision in the Israeli Class Actions Law) on the written opinion of an independent third party.

Binding Effect and Inclusivity

The key technical issue is to produce a binding result that applies to all who ought to benefit from it, with minimum cost and delay. As the Leuven study identifies, a principal issue is the extent to which decisions are binding on group members, *or non-group members.*[5] However, underlying this debate are questions of justice. On the one hand, an opt-in rule may constitute a barrier to genuine claimants joining a case because of issues of lack of knowledge of the procedure and costs, and thus a barrier to justice. Conversely, an opt-out rule may inflate the number of claimants claimed to be in a class and increase the pressure on a defendant to settle (see the 'blackmail settlement' issue discussed in chapter six).

The practical objection made to the opt-in approach, however, is that individuals may not be aware of the existence of their right to claim or of the existence of the concerted arrangements.[6] This may particularly be the case for small value claims involving consumers, of which the French mobile phones case study is a clear example. Accordingly, an insufficient number of individuals opt in to a case, and therefore an insufficient number participate in any judgment.[7] The result is that justice is not served if an acceptable majority of those who have rights are not vindicated, if damage goes uncompensated or unrectified and if defendants keep illicit gains. These considerations arise, of course, in the context of addressing post facto situations through damages claims, but not in the context of preventative steps such as injunctive relief. The solution that some jurisdictions have adopted for this situation is the representative opt-out mechanism: a case will be deemed to represent all similar cases and be binding on them unless

[5] See paras 419 *ff*. It cites as examples of the test case approach the German *Munsterverfahren* and *KapMuG* procedures and the Austrian *Munsterprozessen*, but concludes that potential delay and the lack of automatic binding authority make a test case less 'able to discharge the courts' as much as a group action: para 389.

[6] RP Mulheron, *The Class Action in Common Law Legal Systems: A Comparative Perspective* (Hart Publishing, 2004).

[7] RP Mulheron, *Reform of Collective Redress in England and Wales: A Perspective of Need* (Civil Justice Council, 2008).

an individual has asserted the right to opt out of the concerted proceedings. As long as those notionally included in a group have no costs to pay to fund a collective claim and no risk of liability for adverse costs, but merely the prospect of gaining some benefit, it is both economically and psychologically rational that few would opt out.[8]

Thus, at a mechanistic level, the choice between opt in and opt out is closely linked with the choice over which basic form of mechanism is to be applied: does one case represent all others (like a US class action) or is the group composed of all individual claims (like an English GLO)? A key question is whether it can reliably be assumed that all cases are essentially the same and that some judicial economy can be gained, or that the cases contain some similarities that might be resolved in some efficient manner, but they cannot be completely resolved without dealing with significant individual issues.

It does not necessarily mean that it is always necessary to have a concerted procedure that involves everyone who may be entitled. An individual (test) case may have persuasive or binding subsequent effect. Thus, some states have found that test cases are dispositive of issues and the results are subsequently applied voluntarily or with little further mandatory cost. However, there may obviously be further costs in asserting a subsequent case in the courts, and individuals may be unaware that they are entitled. It might be argued that the significance of such a gap in justice is of variable significance depending on the amount of damages involved: the smaller the quantum of individuals' claims, the greater the argument that it is disproportionate to facilitate them. It would follow that the argument for intervention is stronger where the total illicit gain is large, although, as will be explored in subsequent chapters, the issue here increasingly changes from one of compensation to the regulatory one of rectification of markets, and other options of achieving this objective may arise.

Every opt-out rule ultimately also has to involve an opt-in procedure at the time of qualifying for individual damages or participating in a settlement.[9] Thus, an opt-out approach may be effective in covering claims that have small values at the initial certification stage and if any judgment is given (which evidence from most jurisdictions indicates is a rare event), but the JJB Sports case study clearly shows the unsurprising proposition that if the individual loss is small, many may choose not to opt in to a case in

---

[8] The evidence from the United States is that in consumer cases, fewer than 0.2% exercise the right to exclude themselves from a class case, and this may often be because they are persuaded that they may gain a higher benefit of they pursue their claim individually: see T Eisenberg and G Miller, 'The Role of Opt-Outs and Objectors in Class Action Litigation: Theoretical and Empirical Issues' (2004) 57 *Vanderbilt Law Review* 1529.

[9] RP Mulheron, *The Class Action in Common Law Legal Systems: A Comparative Perspective* (Hart Publishing, 2004).

order to collect compensation when liability has been established.[10] This would leave those who do opt in with a financial advantage over those who do not. The difference may be small, but it is an imbalance in individual restorative justice. It is not rectified if the defendant pays some money to the representative organisation or to charity on a cy près basis, since that benefit would presumably be shared by all, including those who have been paid. The US evidence points to similar unresolved problems, in that consumer class actions are often settled by making available small cheques or coupons, many of which may not be redeemed.[11]

The propensity of individuals to opt in to a settlement should rise as the sums at stake increase. This was what happened in the Dexia case, where a minority of 10 per cent (a not inconsiderable cohort of 23,000) chose to opt out of the proposed settlement, thereby prolonging overall resolution, in the belief that higher recovery was achievable in their cases. The problem here was that finality is desired whenever a settlement has been agreed, and probably after a judgment, so as to avoid relitigating cases. This is also an observation from the United States. Individuals may consider that they have a higher chance of recovering more money, or that the costs will be less, if they pursue a claim individually. A settlement should, of course, involve a compromise that is fair to the claimants, and the ability not to achieve finality may act as an incentive on a defendant to raise its offer. That is desirable if the offer is too low, but not if it is fair. Hence, the logical response would be for the court to approve a settlement. Another reason for this is to safeguard the interests of sub-groups, such as if some claimants have a genuinely higher claim than others, so that they will not be disadvantaged by a general settlement, particularly if the settlement is effectively negotiated and controlled by intermediaries.

Claimants' views can be affected by intermediaries: in the Dexia case, the views of those who opted out were significantly influenced by claims management intermediaries, whose own commercial interests were furthered if litigation continued. Hence, if a significant number of individuals choose to opt out of a settlement, the attractiveness for defendants of such a mechanism in offering binding closure diminishes. These considerations tend to support the view that the advantages of an opt-out rule are best seen for low value multiple claims, which ideally involve few sub-groups. However, as will be seen below, there may be other alternatives for achieving the desired result, which may be preferable.

It was noted in the previous section that where individual issues predominate in a class of claims, the US approach is that an opt-out class action will

---

[10] The JJB Sports case involved a follow-on claim for damages after a binding finding of illegality, involved no cost for any individual and was widely thought to involve no risk. In fact, the defence argument that was raised, that there was no liability for damages because there was no detriment, was not widely appreciated.

[11] See ch 6.

not be certified. Instead, cases must proceed individually or may be subject to some form of Multi District Litigation managerial control, as with an English GLO, which are inherently opt-in. The observation is, therefore, that there is a limit beyond which any concerted procedure will be inappropriate if the issues and cases are too diverse, but that within that limit it may be possible to *manage* a group of relatively similar cases so as to produce procedural economy (through MDL or a GLO) without pre-determining the precise procedural approach in any further detail. Management decisions may be, under such a managerial approach, therefore, left to the judge, who may exercise professional discretion over whether to decide issues or cases in some efficient order. It is obvious that an important pre-condition for adoption of a case-management approach must be that the legal system can accommodate judicial discretion[12] and the judge must be experienced.

The adoption of an opt-in collective action where there was previously none should clearly increase access to justice, including for impecunious claimants. The Irish Law Commission recognised this in recommending adoption of an opt-in rule,[13] noting the need to avoid abuse and provide a filter for spurious claims following the experience of the English product liability cases.[14] The European Commission has also expressed the view that an opt-in approach avoids windfall compensation to people not sufficiently motivated to bring an individual action, and hence provides what would now be described as a proportionality filter.[15]

Fundamental Rights

An opt-out approach raises constitutional and human rights issues, and this is a significant concern in many European states.[16] Article 6 of the European Convention on Human Rights (ECHR) provides that:

> In the determination of his civil rights and obligations ... everyone is entitled to a fair and public hearing within a reasonable time by an independent and impartial tribunal established by law.

[12] Ch 3 has noted that this may be a problem in some civil law traditions and particularly in the political circumstances of states, such as Central and Eastern Europe, which are currently uncomfortable with judicial discretion because it reminds them of the bias shown by judges under Communist control.

[13] The Law Reform Commission, 'Report: Multi-Party Litigation' (2005) LRC 76-2005, especially ch 2. In reaching this conclusion, it rejected the view of the Ontario law Reform Commission that small claims would be excluded by an opt-out rule: Ontario Law Reform Commission, 'Report on Class Actions' (1982) 480–1.

[14] See ch 6.

[15] Memorandum form the Commission: Consumer Redress COM(84) 692, 12 December 1984 XIV.

[16] H-W Micklitz 'Collective private enforcement of consumer law: the key questions' in W van Boom and M Loos (eds), *Collective Enforcement of Consumer Law* (Europa, 2007). J Stuyck, above, paras 380 and 400–6, concluded that art 6 of the ECHR and constitutional principles are widely understood to form an obstacle to the opt-out approach in Europe.

The First Protocol further provides that:

> Every natural or legal person is entitled to the peaceful enjoyment of his posses-
> sions. No one shall be deprived of his possessions except in the public interest
> and subject to the conditions provided for by law and by the general principle of
> international law.[17]

The right to a fair administration of justice holds a crucially important
position in a democratic society.[18] It has been held that the existence of
a collective system for settlement of compensation disputes is not per se
contrary to article 6 of the ECHR provided the interests of each individual
are safeguarded, albeit indirectly.[19] The Court of Human Rights held that
the limitations must not:

> ... restrict or reduce an individual's access in such a way or to such an extent that
> the very essence of the right of access [to the courts] is impaired.

Thus, national legislation was compliant where it established a scheme for
compensation of shareholders' holdings through nationalisation, in which
shareholders appointed and were represented by a single representative. It
was legitimate to avoid, in the context of a large-scale nationalisation, a
multiplicity of claims and proceedings by individuals. The Court held that
there was here 'a reasonable relationship of proportionality between the
means employed and this aim'.

The right to valid remedies has long been determined by the European
Court of Justice to be a general principle of Community law.[20] The ECHR
principle has more recently been enshrined in the Charter of Fundamental
Rights of the European Union:

> Everyone whose rights and freedoms guaranteed by the law of the Union are
> violated has the right to an effective remedy before a tribunal in compliance with
> the conditions laid down in this Article.

> Everyone is entitled to a fair and public hearing within a reasonable time by an
> independent and impartial tribunal previously established by law. Everyone shall
> have the possibility of being advised, defended and represented ...[21]

---

[17] Art 1.

[18] *Delcourt v Belgium*, judgment of 17 January 1970, Series A, No 11; (1979–80) 1 EHRR
355.

[19] *Lithgow and Others v The United Kingdom* [1986] 8 EHRR 324. Followed in Decision
as to the Admissibility of Application no 71630/01 by Albrecht Wendeburg and others against
Germany, No 71360/01, ECHR 2003-II, 36 EHRR CD 154.

[20] Case 222/84 *Johnson* [1986] ECR 1651.

[21] Art 47.

This approach is mirrored in the constitutional provisions of various Member States that guarantee access for each citizen to a judicial decision-maker, for example Germany[22] and France.[23] In France, the *Conseil constitutionnel* decided that group litigation might be commenced by labour unions on behalf of their members only provided that any employee be:

> ... afforded the opportunity to give his assent with full knowledge of the facts and that he remained free to conduct personally the defence of his interests.[24]

In addition, there are universal principles of French justice that an individual cannot be made a plaintiff without his or her knowledge (the 'due process rule'), that all those involved in a lawsuit must have their identity known (the doctrine of '*nul ne plaide par procureur*'), so members of the class have to be identified before the beginning of the action and be parties to it, and, consequently, that those who do not opt in are not bound by a decision in the case ('*autorité relative de la chose jugée*', under art 5 of the Civil Code).

In the context of a collective court procedure, the above provisions would ostensibly require all members of a class to be notified of the declaration of a class and of a settlement or judgment. Individual members may wish to take part in the case and make submissions to the court, or may wish to object to a settlement. An individual must have an opportunity to decide whether he or she wishes to take part in a procedure that affects his or her rights under substantive law and his or her right to representation in proceedings, as well as any liability for costs. These issues obviously give rise to a constitutional or due process problem in adopting an opt-out approach, as the European Parliament has recognised.[25]

The essence of the debate gives rise to a clash between traditional principles of rights and considerations of efficiency. These considerations significantly influenced the form of the German KapMuG and the Netherlands' Collective Settlement Act. In the former, the compromise was to permit the court power to select an individual model case from all cases within an opt-in group, and to permit (but not encourage) all individuals in the group to take some (limited) part in the hearing of the model case, the outcome of which would be binding on them. A settlement approved by the court under the Dutch Act will be binding on all in the group unless they opt out. Accordingly, neither of these mechanisms raise a particularly strong

---

[22] H-W Micklitz and A Stadler, 'The Development of Collective Legal Actions in Europe, Especially in German Civil Procedure' [2006] EBLR 1473–503.

[23] V Magnier, 'Report on France' (Globalisation Project), from which the following points are taken.

[24] Dec. Cons. Const. N°89-257 DC, 25 July 1989. See Appendix VII, specifically pt 24.

[25] 'Report on the EU Consumer Policy Strategy 2007–13' (2007/2189(INI)) A6-0155/2008 <http://www.europarl.europa.eu/sidesSearch/search.do?type=REPORT&language=EN&term=6&author=28263> accessed 11 June 2008 para 39.

challenge to the fundamental rights point, since they do not involve solely the selection of an individual claimant or case the result of which will bind all others.

Funding and Cost Considerations

Both opt-in and opt-out approaches can involve significant costs in order to satisfy requirements of notification, information, control and avoidance of conflicts. The requirement to notify all those whose rights may be affected may, of course, be achieved through mass media communications, such as newspapers, radio, television, email and internet, rather than post, in those circumstances where these are appropriate. Some of these means of communication may bring reduced costs, but newspaper advertisements can be expensive. Notification costs can clearly be reduced where the identity of those in the group is known. Where identity is not known, general means of communication through mass media are required. An opt-out rule may produce some economy for courts in some types of case, but may equally involve significant costs of identifying and notifying all claimants, perhaps at least twice during a case (initiation and settlement). Equally, an opt-in system will be expensive in some situations, in requiring individuals to pay for initiation of their cases[26] and also where it is necessary to fund a proportion of the generic costs.

The Leuven study notes that claimants who opt in bear up-front costs before the merits have been assessed, and this may be a significant disincentive to initiating an action,[27] whereas for opt-out, the potential members need only be notified once a settlement has been proposed. It notes that opt-in 'assists the defendant in knowing the size of the pool of potential claimants' (this is in some cases essential for reasons of insurance and requirements of sound business management). The study concludes that there are many factors (several relating to costs) that determine whether a collective action is practical and effective, but opt-out is probably a decisive factor.[28]

It is important to recognise that an opt-out rule only works in practice where claimants are not subject to a 'loser pays' rule and, usually, not required to fund the initiation and the entire running of a case. This is one aspect of the constitutional problem discussed below: it is wrong as a matter of principle for individuals to be subject to an obligation to pay legal

---

[26] Ch 3 noted that costs can be limited by adopting simplified procedures, such as mere registration, although it may be important in some types of case for individual claims to be screened to ensure that they satisfy joining criteria so as to prevent unjustified claims joining the procedure and to avoid later costs in weeding claims out.

[27] para 434.

[28] para 440.

costs in a transaction in which they have not had all relevant information and agreed to be bound. Hence, an opt-out rule may be unacceptable as a matter of principle in those jurisdictions that value a 'loser pays' rule highly. Those jurisdictions that have opt-out rules all have mechanisms that provide funding for the initiator and lawyer, such as public funding for a consumer organisation (Austria, Germany) or Consumer Ombudsman (Nordic states). The English collective competition damages procedure in the CAT assumes that individual consumers will not contribute to funding and insulates them from adverse costs liability.[29] It will be interesting to see what impact the development of legal expenses insurance and third-party investors may have on this situation.

Thus, the principal issues here relate to how systems should enable a case to be funded and how the risk of adverse costs should be dealt with—this issue does not arise in the United States. In Europe, where claimants have to fund intermediaries and bear the risk of adverse costs, the first solution is to spread both these financial obligations across all members of a group. However, the number of members in the group must be defined, so that it is clear exactly what financial liability applies to each person at every stage. Individuals may therefore be in a position to take fully informed choices about whether or not to assume the liability and risk. The overall position, therefore, resolves whether the litigation is financially viable as a whole—in other words, whether the available funds cover agents' costs and leave a suitable profit (the damages recovered) when divided amongst the members of the group. The complexity of the financial situation and calculations that are inherently involved in such a situation have, unsurprisingly, led some to call for more radical approaches to financing group claims and simplify the approach through removing the 'loser pays' rule as a last resort.[30] The position is certainly made easier in those states where, for example, consumer associations are given some exemption from liability for costs in collective cases, on the assumption that they are sufficiently responsible not to bring unjustified claims. However, the 'loser pays' principle is generally firmly entrenched in European legal culture.

DISCUSSION

The OECD recommends that all states should adopt mechanisms that enable consumers to be able to resolve disputes effectively, whether individually, collectively or through public authorities, and does not state a

---

[29] See ch 2 above.
[30] Civil Justice Council, 'Improved Access to Justice—Funding Options & Proportionate Costs' (2007).

preference between opt-in and opt-out mechanisms, but states criteria for both, including the need to inform consumers adequately.[31] The most recent experiments can be seen in Norway and Denmark, as noted in chapter two. Considerations of caution have preserved the opt-in rule in those two states, but the court may decide to apply an opt-out approach within certain parameters, such as that a case is of low value (Norway) or that the Consumer Ombudsman applies (Denmark). These cautious but innovative experiments deserve wider consideration, but may not be the last word. Further analysis of which approaches work for what particular types of case may prove fruitful. It will, however, be argued in chapters eight and nine below that the opt-in/opt-out conundrum can in fact be circumvented by other means.

At the European level, the issue seems to have been decisively resolved, at least for some years, by the 2008 policy decision of the European Commission to avoid legal and political controversy in preferring the opt-in solution in its proposal for collective redress in competition damages claims.[32] The considerations that have been most influential are, first, those of fundamental rights, which is closely linked to the absence of effective financial systems in which group members can avoid funding and costs liability, given the loser pays rule. Secondly, there is concern about the potential for abuse.

The mechanistic objective of a court-based multi-party mechanism is to ensure that the result is *binding* on all relevant people, and hence achieve economy of process. The purpose of aggregation is to ensure that all those who have claims of the defined type are included in the proceedings and bound by the result. However, this objective may be achieved by different mechanisms. One approach may be that all those who wish to assert their rights should join the concerted procedure, have an opportunity to be heard and be bound by the result. However, the problem there is whether that result should also be binding on any other individuals who have not joined in, whether from choice or ignorance of the proceedings. Considerations of rights argue that they should not be so bound, but considerations of efficiency argue that they should. To what extent is it a misuse of state resources and inefficient for defendants and claimants to permit multiple bites at the same cherry?

A second approach is that one or a small number of test cases can be heard, and the result applied in all subsequent similar cases. However, the

---

[31] OECD, 'Recommendation on Consumer Dispute Resolution and Redress' (2007) <http://www.oecd.org/dataoecd/43/50/38960101.pdf> accessed 11 June 2008.

[32] White Paper on damages actions for breach of the EC anti-trust rules, COM(2008) 165, 2 April 2008. Commission Staff Working Paper accompanying the White Paper on damages actions for breach of the EC anti-trust rules, SEC(2008) 404, 2 April 2008 ('Staff Working Paper').

problems there are that the principles of fundamental rights are clearly abused (through non-involvement in the procedure for claimants in asserting their claims, but also defendants in asserting defences) and, thus, that absent a robust rule on *res judicata*, defendants might not observe the result, thereby putting claimants to the cost and effort of re-litigating issues, if they know about them, and using this pressure to defeat justice.

The use of a test case will only be efficient in situations in which parties on either side are either legally bound by the result or willing to observe it in other similar cases. Examples of voluntary observance often arise where company defendants have reputations to lose and there is a vigilant media, as illustrated by the English FOS procedures in Appendix 2. On the other hand, if a binding court-based result is required, traditional principles of rights and *res judicata* come under pressure. The Dexia case shows that final efficient closure cannot be reached unless a result applies to all parties: this may be the case if a court delivers a judgment, but is more difficult if a significant number of claimants opt out of a settlement or of a collective procedure.

So far, European jurisdictions have paid less attention to the option of widening the binding effect of a test case, and focused instead on the more upfront mechanisms of whether binding effect is to be achieved *within* a group procedure through an opt-in or opt-out mechanism. However, it is suggested that the problems that may arise with either an opt-in or opt-out mechanism can be avoided by looking more closely at the advantages of adopting a broader approach to the binding effect of judgments that affect many parties. This is not to ignore the fact that fundamental rights for all parties may need to be observed, but it is to recognise that if efficient procedures are to be followed that deliver improvements in efficiency, thereby making justice more widely available, some traditional approaches may need to be modified. The result would be that decisions could be reached efficiently that would bring effective outcomes for the greatest number of those affected.

The problem to be overcome here would be to ensure that defendants apply results in all relevant cases and all relevant claimants have the ability to be compensated. The traditional model involves individual autonomy, with individuals choosing to assert their individual rights. This leads to a model in which anyone who wishes to assert their rights together with others, in order to take advantage of pooling of costs, expertise and negotiating power, may opt in to concerted arrangements. Hence, if a concerted procedure is established, it is efficient for the court system if everyone can be given notice of its existence and so have an opportunity to join in to this single procedure.

CONCLUSIONS

Underlying these considerations is the reality that involvement in any concerted procedure necessarily involves a partial surrender of individual rights and autonomy, in order that the concerted procedure may operate effectively and efficiently.

The debate over opt-in or opt-out is more difficult than it appears at first sight. Considerations of consumer justice and market control can favour opt-out. Considerations of fundamental rights and avoiding procedural abuse favour opt-in. On closer inspection, problems arise with both approaches. For the present, the consensus amongst European Member States is clearly in favour of staying with opt-in, although the limited Nordic experiments with permitting opt-out in tightly controlled circumstances are interesting.

In any event, the European Commission has made a policy decision in 2008 that the opt-in procedure is to be preferred and the opt-out avoided in any Community measures that may be put forward.[33] There may be further heated debate on this issue, but this political decision is likely to stick and to be influential with Member States. This gives space for the experiments in Portugal, Denmark and Norway to be observed objectively over time.

Considerations of efficiency favour test cases and a wider approach to binding effect, and this area may repay further consideration. It does not necessarily follow that deficiencies with either an opt-in or opt-out procedure would be solved by adopting the other. Consideration of the case studies, especially the JJB Sports and French Telecom cases, leave the impression that better solutions may lie outside a court-based mechanism. In chapters eight and nine, different approaches towards redress, in addition to the court-based systems discussed here, will be considered. Some of these avoid the opt-in or opt-out issue whilst resulting in solutions that involve wide coverage, involvement and binding effect in an efficient manner.

---

[33] *Ibid.*

6

The Problems that Need to be Avoided

THERE IS A widely quoted mantra in European policy documents that collective mechanisms within the litigation system in the United States operate badly, produce unacceptable results and should not be emulated in Europe. Further, it is said that European proposals will not lead to the adverse US litigation disease happening here. The EU Competition Commissioner has criticised the US system as having excessive and undesirable consequences, and said that she wished to produce a competition culture and not a litigation culture, and therefore expressly was not proposing to introduce class actions or contingency fees.[1]

The essential question to be asked in this chapter is: what undesirable consequences should a collective redress system seek to avoid? In order to answer this, it is helpful to observe some features of abuse that have been produced in other systems: the primary focus will be on the US civil litigation system, but some relevant points will be considered from Australia and England. It is beyond the scope of this book to undertake a detailed investigation into these or other civil justice systems and the reasons why they produce particular features of benefit or abuse. Those are issues on which opinion may, in any event, be divided or relevant evidence lacking. However, some pointers can at least be identified that can enlighten the European debate over what issues of abuse should be looked for, and what features of a system might produce abuse and should, therefore, be regarded with care.

UNDESIRABLE CONSEQUENCES

The prevailing European perception of the US litigation system is that it *can* produce the following undesirable consequences:

a) access to the courts that is too easily available;
b) no cost-benefit or other 'rationality check' by claimants on bringing litigation, or control over decisions made in cases;

---

[1] Amongst several similar statements, see speech by Commissioner N Kroes at the Harvard Club, 22 September 2005. Importantly, the Competition Damages Green Paper avoids references to class actions and contingency fees.

c) excessive volume of litigation, particularly unmeritorious claims;
d) capture of litigation, and especially class actions, by lawyers or other intermediaries, who regard litigation as a business investment run solely for their own profit;
e) conflicts of interest between clients and lawyers (conflicts can be especially significant in settlement decisions; and many consumer class actions produce modest benefits for consumers,[2] such as 'coupon settlements');[3]
f) litigation processes that are inherently very expensive;
g) disproportionate lawyers' fees in class actions, and hence excessive transactional costs of litigation;[4]
h) class action procedures, coupled with no 'loser pays' rule and high attorney fees, which produce huge financial pressure on defendants to settle irrespective of the merits of cases (the commercial result is 'blackmail settlements');[5]
i) the size of the financial pressure on defendants being increased by the potential for punitive damages;[6] and
j) the overall cost of the litigation system, being a function of the volume of litigation, the size of damages awarded, the size of intermediaries' costs, is too high and imposes a significant unnecessary burden on the economy.

Some of these propositions are, of course, highly contentious in relation to the US system.[7] For example, the data shows that punitive damages are in fact only awarded rarely by US juries, and that the few headline-grabbing

---

[2] M Gilles and G Friedman, 'Exploding the Class Action Agency Costs Myth: The Social Utility of Entrepreneurial Lawyers' [2006] *Univ. Pennsylvania Law Rev* 105, 102 assert that US consumer class actions are not intended to, and never do, provide compensation for consumers. Their sole purpose is deterrence, through internalising costs (whether fines or damages) by offenders. US judges and academics have been wrong to try to reduce attorneys' fees. This reduces deterrence, and larger fees should be permitted.

[3] Cases that were settled on the basis that consumer class members were given a coupon that could be redeemed on stated conditions. Various problems arose, such as that limitations in the conditions or inertia might reduce the number of coupons redeemed, and tying the value of class counsels' remuneration to the gross rather than the redeemed value.

[4] See the overview by C Silver, 'Does Civil Litigation Cost Too Much?' (2002) 80 Tex. L. Rev. 2073. It has been asserted that 19% of tort costs go to claimant lawyers and the total in the early 2000s was almost $40 billion a year, which was 50% more than Microsoft or Intel and twice that of Coca-Cola, so the combined cost would be somewhat more than that: Centre for Legal Policy, 'Trial Lawyers, Inc.' (Manhattan Institute, 2003) <http://www.triallawyersinc.com> accessed 11 June 2008.

[5] Blackmail settlements are said to occur where claims that have poor or uncertain merit are settled because it is commercially cheaper for a defendant to do so, in order to avoid the unrecoverable costs of defence, business disruption, adverse publicity and damage to shareholder value.

[6] CR Sunstein, R Hastie, JW Payne, DA Schkade and WK Viscusi, *Punitive Damages. How Juries Decide* (Chicago, 2002).

[7] A recent review of the main arguments in the US anti-trust arena is RH Lande and JP Davis, *Benefits From Private Anti-trust Enforcement: An Analysis of Forty Cases* (American Anti-trust Institute, 2007). The authors note strong criticisms of the system from scholars, judges and business, and argue that little empirical evidence is available that would prove or disprove them. Their conclusion is that the private attorney class actions model has produced 'tremendous benefits for the United States economy'. The study and its limitations are mentioned below.

large awards are usually significantly reduced or reversed on appeal.[8] Further, even if claimants have no risk, lawyers do, and would normally undertake a cost-benefit assessment before taking on a case of whatever size. Therefore, the system does provide some type of filter for unmeritorious cases.[9] A possible counter argument might be that some attorneys, being repeat players, can afford to invest in a case of low merit, either because they are extremely rich, or because they can hedge by holding a portfolio of cases or spreading risk with others, and will reap handsome rewards through a settlement in which the size of the potential legal costs and number of people in the opt-out class distorts the true value of the claim and exerts a disproportionate commercial effect.[10] It seems difficult to achieve the right balance between parties here, in the desire to assist meritorious claimants against defendants with large resources and the objective of not imposing an excessive blackmail threat.

This is not the place to give a comprehensive analysis of the US civil justice system. The true position is far more complex than is usually asserted by European commentators, and some myths are referred to below.[11] It is clear that there are certain features in the United States that are either wholly or largely absent from European traditions, notably:

a) Decisions on both liability and damages are made by juries.
b) Judges are elected in state courts, and issues of objectivity and impartiality can arise.[12]
c) A claimant typically has no financial outlay or risk of liability for costs if the case is lost. There is generally no 'loser pays' rule. The claimant's attorney's fees are either waived (on a no-win, no-fee basis) or paid by the defendant if the case is won or settled, on a contingency fee basis. Under some statutes, a defendant is required to pay the claimant's attorney's fees. In fact, some claimant attorneys are paid or indemnified on an hourly rate basis by their clients (the 'lodestar' system). The claimant's expert witnesses are usually paid by his attorney.
d) Punitive damages can be awarded in civil cases. Triple damages are awarded in anti-trust cases.

---

[8] See Sunstein and Viscisi, above.

[9] HM Kritzer, 'Contingency Fee lawyers as Gatekeepers in the Civil Justice System' (1997) 81 *Judicature* 22, 24. HM Kritzer, 'Seven Dogged Myths concerning Contingency Fees' (2002) 80 Wash. ULQ 739–94.

[10] JH Stock and DA Wise, 'Market Compensation in Class Action Suits: A Summary of Basic Ideas and Results' (1993) 16 *Class Action Rep.* 584 597–8. It has been argued that fee-shifting provisions in statutes, such as dealing with human rights and discrimination, in which there are restrictions on unsuccessful defendants paying plaintiff's attorneys' costs, can be circumvented by reaching settlements in which larger fees can be paid: M Pacold, 'Attorneys' Fees in Class Actions Governed by Fee-Shifting Statutes' (2001) 3 *The University of Chicago Law Review* 68 1007–34.

[11] See W Haltom and M McCann, *Distorting the Law: Politics, Media, and The Litigation Crisis* (University of Chicago Press, 2004).

[12] See American Tort Reform Association, 'Judicial Hellholes 2007' (2007) and previous reports at <http://www.atra.org/reports/hellholes> accessed 11 June 2008.

Continental civil law, but not common law, systems also traditionally have limited disclosure of documentary evidence and, in modern cases against corporate defendants, the extent of materials that have to be disclosed can be very substantial, and create considerable effort to produce. In civil law jurisdictions, expertise is obtained from experts appointed by the court rather than by the parties, whereas in the common law tradition expert witnesses are traditionally produced and paid by each party.[13] The risk with the latter approach is production of conflicts of interest and evidence that is insufficiently objective.

One view is that it is the entirety of the US system that produces abuse, and since Europe does not have some of the essential features of the United States, similar abuse could not happen here. That would be a naïve view. The fundamental problems of abuse relate to the role that is played by money in the system, and who gains it at whose expense. Issues such as punitive damages or higher general damages should be discarded within the debate at this point as irrelevant to the European situation, save that they increase the claimants' bargaining power and the intermediaries' financial incentives. However, it is clear that if individual claims are aggregated, that *should* (but might not) of itself increase the financial stakes involved, particularly for the intermediaries. Hence, a class action rule that may be commenced by a single individual who is 'first past the post' and claims to represent a large number of others, who must opt out if they do not wish to be bound, will clearly give rise to issues of conflict between the potentially diffuse interests of the group members and the increased incentives for intermediaries.[14]

The explosion of consumer class action litigation in the United States is recognised to have been the unintended by-product of an intention to liberalise access to the courts and create a more efficient legal system, so that individuals with meritorious claims—particularly in the context of civil rights violations—would be able to have their day in court. However, the Advisory Committee that proposed the expansion in Federal Rule 23 in the early 1960s failed to recognise that, in creating incentives for meritorious claimants to bring their claims on a group basis, they were opening the door to widespread litigation abuse, as a result of the effect of the increased financial incentives.[15] It is, however, important to realise that the US legal system includes more mechanisms for managing multiple similar claims in different courts than just the class action: other important management

---

[13] Nevertheless, there are signs of some convergence in both civil and common law jurisdictions on access to evidence and numbers of experts.

[14] S Isaacharoff, 'Governance and Legitimacy in the Law of Class Actions' (1999) S. Ct. Rev. 337.

[15] See Report of the Senate Judiciary Committee on the Class Action fairness Act of 2005, S. rep. 109-14 (28 February 2005), 6–7; AR Miller, 'Of Frankenstein Monsters and Shining Knights: Myth, reality, and the "Class Action Problem"' (1979) 92 Harv. L. Rev. 664 669–70.

techniques are the Multi District Litigation (MDL) procedure,[16] consolidated trials, bankruptcy protection and informal aggregation.[17]

In many US consumer class actions, the individual amounts claimed are modest and the most significant recovery is by class counsel, not by any class member. The size and proportionality of lawyers' fees are inevitable, given payment is based on a percentage of the common fund. Judith Resnik has described the situation as a state-created mechanism for subsidising the litigation of claims that could not otherwise be justified.[18] The answer as to how this could be justified has more to do with deterrence and private enforcement of law than with compensation, as discussed in chapter eight below.

A relevant question is whether it is possible to control against abuses. An initial filter control is that a US class action initiator must persuade a court that statutory criteria are satisfied before the court will certify a class action. However, this can result in satellite litigation at the certification stage, the outcome of which is crucial in practice for whether a case will be dismissed or settled. US attempts to control some of the undesirable features have met with limited success. The Private Securities Litigation Reform Act of 1995 included various counter-abuse provisions, such as a requirement for each representative plaintiff to serve a sworn certification that he or she had reviewed the complaint and authorised it, had not purchased the security involved in the claim at the direction of plaintiff's counsel in order to participate in the action, and would not accept any payment for serving as representative party beyond the pro rata share of any recovery save as ordered by the court.[19] The Securities Litigation Uniform Standards Act of 1998 imposed further restraints following evidence that the 1995 Act had led to securities class actions shifting from federal to state courts and involved abuses.[20] The Class Action Fairness Act of 2005 sought to limit contingency fees in 'coupon claims',[21] cap fees and restrict some class actions to federal courts, but it is limited in scope. Most class action rules in the United States are still based on an opt-out rather than opt-in mechanism, which can lead to inflated numbers in class actions.[22]

---

[16] The MDL procedure has some interesting similarities to the English GLO managerial approach. The existence of the MDL technique is little known in Europe, and the known stereotype of a class action is therefore misleading.

[17] See DR Hensler, 'Revisiting the Monster: New Myths and Realities of Class Action and Other Large Scale Litigation' (2001) 11 Duke J. Comp. & Int'l L. 179; N Pace, 'National Report for United States' (Globalisation Project).

[18] J Resnik, 'Money Matters: Judicial Market Intervention Creating Subsidies and Awarding Fees and Costs in Individual and Aggregate Litigation' (2000) 148 U. Pa. L. Rev. 2119.

[19] 15 USC 78a.

[20] 15 USC 78a.

[21] See above.

[22] SB Burbank, 'The Class Action Fairness Act of 2005 in Historical Context: A Preliminary Review' U. of Penn. Law School, Public Law Research Paper No 08-03 <http://ssrn.com/abstract=1083785> accessed 11 June 2008.

Distinguished US scholars have shown, first, that the level of contingency fees in many individual (not class) actions is often modest and proportionate,[23] and secondly, that the quantum of compensation awarded to claimant attorneys in class actions bears a strong linear relationship to the amount of money at stake in a case, so can be interpreted as being proportionate and not excessive.[24] Nevertheless, the amounts involved in class action remuneration still strike most Europeans as extremely large by comparison with European cost levels, and wholly disproportionate. A study of some 370 class action cases between 1993 and 2002 found that the mean gross recovery was $100 million (median $11.6 million, both in 2002 $ values), that the fee awards in the 59 cases in which fee shifting applied had a mean of 37.5 per cent and median of 33 per cent, and the fees in 303 non-fee-shifting cases had a mean of 21.9 per cent and median of 23.2 per cent.[25] A recent study of 40 recent, successful, large-scale private anti-trust cases[26] confirmed that the courts awarded class counsel a percentage of the recovery that was usually 30 or 33.3 per cent for (17) cases involving recoveries under $100 million (albeit only 7 per cent in one case, generating $4.55 million). For recoveries over that sum and below $500 million, the awards (eight cases) ranged between 20 and 33.3 per cent, and for recoveries over $500 million (five cases), the range was between 5.2 and 33.3 per cent. The relevance is in the amounts rather than the percentages: one-third of $50 million is $16.65 million, and 6.5 per cent of the largest recovery of $3,383 million is $219.90 million. At the extremes, US attorneys' fees can be vast[27] and a small number of law firms control large blocks of claims.[28] However, costs differ between different types of case.[29]

The issue of whether costs are proportionate and justify the benefits gained is one for social and political judgment.[30] It would be relevant, of

[23] HM Kritzer, 'Seven Dogged Myths concerning Contingency Fees' (2002) 80 Wash. U. L. Q. 739–94.

[24] T Eisenberg and GP Miller, 'Attorney Fees in Class Action Settlements: An Empirical Study' (2004) 1 *Journal of Empirical Legal Studies* 1 27–78.

[25] *Ibid*.

[26] RH Lande and JP Davis, *Benefits From Private Anti-trust Enforcement: An Analysis of Forty Cases* (American Anti-trust Institute, 2007). The study therefore does not cover all cases, nor any unsuccessful cases or ones with 'small' recoveries.

[27] Lawyers who acted for various states that sued tobacco companies were initially awarded $8.2 billion for representing three states, and settlements collectively generated between $18 and $38 billion in fees: A Tabarrok and E Helland, *Two Cheers for Contingency Fees* (The AEI Press, 2005); and K Viscusi, *Smoke-Filled Rooms: A Postmortem on the Tobacco Deal* (University of Chicago Press, 2002).

[28] DR Hensler and MA Peterson, 'Understanding Mass Personal Injury Litigation: A Socio-Legal Analysis' (1993) 59 Brook. L. Rev. 961 966.

[29] See C Silver, 'Does Civil Litigation Cost Too Much?' (2002) 80 Tex. L. Rev. 2073; and DR Hensler, 'Fashioning a National Resolution of Asbestos Personal Injury Litigation: A Reply to Professor Brickman' (1992) 13 Cardozo L. Rev. 1967 1997.

[30] See DR Hensler, 'Revisiting the Monster: New Myths and Realities of Class Action and Other Large Scale Litigation' (2001) 11 Duke J. Comp. & Int'l L. 179; and N Pace, 'National Report for United States' (Globalisation Project).

course, to evaluate the benefits gained for claimants and the economy, and costs saved in public enforcement, and to note the large sums of money at stake in commercial and governmental enterprises, plus the size of remuneration paid to corporate and governmental executives and shareholders. Lawyers have been described as portfolio managers who invest in risky cases in the hope, or expectation, of obtaining satisfactory returns.[31] Most class actions settle once certified.[32] The conclusion for Europe here is that in a system in which intermediaries operate, they will seek to maximise rent-seeking—and under the theory that they operate as 'private attorneys general' are encouraged to do so—and it can be difficult to impose effective controls under which costs remain proportionate. Some US commentators have criticised the courts for failure to impose regulatory control over fees[33] and failure of professional ethics.[34]

Whatever the true position in the United States, there is a widely held perception in Europe that the US system imposes significant costs on the national economy and can lead to abuse.[35] If true, such a result would not be consistent with what in Europe would be 'Better Regulation' or 'improving competitiveness' policies. The European perception is that the US system provides compensation for more valid claims than Europe does, but in doing so compensates too many false claims. By itself, that produces a drag on the economy, which is further increased by the inherently large and disproportionate transactional costs of the system.

It is difficult to obtain fully reliable data on the costs or benefits of the US litigation system, but the following figures have been published. Many of the data have been generated by industry and so unsurprisingly deal more with costs than benefits.

[31] HM Kritzer, 'Seven Dogged Myths concerning Contingency Fees' (2002) 80 Wash. U. L. Q. 739–94.

[32] T Eisenberg and GP Miller, 'Attorney Fees in Class Action Settlements: An Empirical Study' (2004) 1 *Journal of Empirical Legal Studies* 1 27–78. In 1961, it was asserted that fee recovery was achieved, mostly through settlements, in over 90% of cases brought on a contingency fee, so the risk of obtaining no fee was very remote, and that could hardly be considered to be a contingent risk: presiding Justice B Botein, Address at the New York State assn. of Plaintiffs' Trial lawyers Annual Luncheon (16 September 1961), printed in B Botein, *Co-operation of Bench and bar in the Regulation of Negligence Litigation* (NYLJ, 21 September 1961) 4.

[33] T Eisenberg and GP Miller, 'Attorney Fees in Class Action Settlements: An Empirical Study' 1 (2004) *Journal of Empirical Legal Studies* 1 27–78.

[34] JR Macey and GP Miller, 'The Plaintiffs' Attorney's Role in Class Action and Derivative Litigation: Economic Analysis and Recommendations for Reform' (1991) 58 *University of Chicago Law Review* 1–118; but see HM Kritzer, 'Lawyer Fees and Lawyer Behaviour in Litigation: What does the empirical Literature really say?' (2002) 80 Tex. L. Rev. 1943.

[35] Repeated statements were made by Commissioners Kroes and Kuneva in 2006–08 that they recognised the abuse and excesses of the US system and were intent on creating a competitive economy, not a compensation culture, in Europe.

a) A US federal government analysis in 2002 concluded that excessive tort litigation costs in 2000 were an $87 billion drag on the national economy.[36] The study estimated that the impact of wasteful legal expenditures equated to a 1.3 per cent tax on consumption or a 2.1 per ecnt tax on wages.

b) Over the past 50 years, direct tort costs in the United States grew more than 100-fold from less than $2 billion in 1950 to $247 billion in 2006, exceeding Gross Domestic Product (GDP) growth by an average of over two percentage points.[37] The 2006 figure equated to a 'litigation tax' of $825 per person, compared to $12 in 1950, and was equal to 1.87 per cent of the GDP of the United States. Nearly one in six jury awards are $1 million or more, and over 7 per cent of businesses experienced a liability loss of $5 million or more during the past five years.[38]

c) In 2005, the annual tort cost for small US businesses was $98 billion. This equates to $20 per £1,000 of revenue. Small businesses bear 69 per cent of US business tort liability, but take only 19 per cent of revenues. They pay $20 billion of their tort costs out of pocket, as opposed to through insurance.[39]

d) A survey of 500 US Chief Executives by the Conference Board found that lawsuits caused 36 per cent of their companies to discontinue products, 15 per cent to lay off workers and eight per cent to close plants.[40]

e) A Gallup survey of US small businesses found that 26 per cent of owners said that fear of liability kept them from releasing new products, services or operations to the market.[41]

f) US corporations paid $9.6 billion to shareholders to settle securities class actions in 2005, excluding a $7.1 billion settlement involving Enron.[42] Settlements in securities cases have grown successively over the past decade: in 735 cases between 1997 and 2005, the total settlement amount was $26 billion.[43] This would have yielded plaintiffs' lawyers' fees $7.8 billion, assuming the average 30 per cent contingency fee.

---

[36] US Council of Economic Advisers, 'An Economic Analysis of the US Tort Liability System' (2002).

[37] *2007 Update on US Tort Costs Trends* (Towers Perrin, 2007).

[38] *U.S. Tort Costs and Cross-Border Perspectives; 2005 Update* (Towers Perrin-Tillinghast, 2006).

[39] *Tort Liability Costs For Small Business* (US Chamber Institute for Legal Reform, 2007). Small businesses are defined here as those with less than £10 million annual revenues and at least one employee in addition to the owner. The tort cost increased 13% from 2002 to 2005.

[40] 'US Senate Commerce Committee Report on Product Liability Reform Act of 1997'.

[41] National Federation of Independent Businesses, 'National Small Business Poll' (2002).

[42] LE Simmons and EM Ryan, *Post-Reform Act Securities Settlements: 2005 Review and Analysis* (Cornerstone Research, 2006).

[43] *Ibid.*

g) Over 200 insurance companies failed in the United States in the past decade.[44]

h) High litigation risks and stringent regulations were the principal factors in a 2007 report that New York is in danger of losing its status as world financial centre.[45]

It is recited above that the cost of the tort system equated to 1.87 per cent of US GDP in 2006. In contrast, the same source cited European tort costs as a percentage of GDP in 2003 as 0.6 per cent in Poland and Denmark, 0.7 per cent in France and the UK, 1.1 per cent in Germany and 1.7 per cent in Italy.[46] Some sources allege that the full cost of the US system is $865.37 billion, which is equivalent to an eight per cent tax on consumption or a 13 per cent tax on wages.[47] There has been strong criticism of these figures,[48] but, whatever the true figures may be, the cost of the US civil justice system is clearly high and is argued by industry to constitute an unnecessary and debilitating tax on business and the economy, with disproportionately little benefit to competition, consumers or the economy.[49]

Data is available on US securities class actions. Settlements totalled $25.4 billion in 755 cases settled between December 1995 and August 2005.[50] In contrast, in 1994, the year before the Private Securities Litigation Reform Act of 1995 was passed, settlements from all securities class action law suits totalled $899 million.[51] Five law firms handled 70 per cent of the cohort of 755 cases, with one firm handling 43 per cent of the cohort and

---

[44] AM Best, 'Rising Number of P/C Company Impairments Continues Trend' (10 March 2003), quoted in D Deal *et al*, *Tort Excess 2005: The Necessity for Reform from a Policy, Legal and Risk Management Perspective* (US Chamber of Commerce, 2005).

[45] MR Bloomberg and CE Schumer, *Sustaining New York's and the US's Global Financial Services Leadership* (2007). Significantly, the authors are usually political opponents.

[46] *US Tort Costs and Cross-Border Perspectives; 2005 Update* (Towers Perrin-Tillinghast, 2006). The data in this analysis is obtained from the insurance industry, but the basis for these European figures is not transparent.

[47] *Jackpot Justice: The True Cost of America's Tort System* (Pacific Research Institute, 2007). The authors calculated that the excess (ie unnecessary) annual social cost in 2006 was $588.63 billion, and the excess annual accounting cost was $664.15 billion. They also asserted that the annual wealth loss to US stockholders is $684 billion; 60,000 workers have been displaced through asbestos bankrupcies, at an economic cost of $226 million in 2006 $s; each worker losing up to $50,000 over his or her career. Human capital losses total up to $3.16 billion in lost wages, and $559 million capital lost to pensions.

[48] See R Posner <http://www.becker-posner-blog.com/archives/2007/04/is_the_tort_sys. html> accessed 11 June 2008.

[49] The state of Mississippi, for example, passed reform legislation in 2003, after which levels of claims fell, industry started to reinvest, employment levels rose and doctors returned to practice in the state. See C Ross, 'Jackson Action: In Mississippi Tort Reform Works' *The Wall Street Journal* 15 September 2005.

[50] AV Thakor, JS Nielsen and DA Gulley, *The Economic Reality of Securities Class Action Litigation* (Navigant Consulting and the US Chamber Institute for Legal Reform, 2005).

[51] M Bajaj, SC Mazumadar and A Sarin, *Securities Class Action Settlements: An Empirical Analysis* (2000).

generating fees and expenses of $1.7 billion.[52] In securities class actions, large institutional shareholders generally break even from their investments in stocks impacted by fraud allegations, as a result of expert portfolio management, and receive a net benefit even before settlement proceeds are taken into account, whereas undiversified investors are at a greater risk of losing money.[53] In other words, whilst the model of private enforcement of securities fraud is intended to protect all investors, the sophisticated corporations end up better off, but the small-time individual investors end up losing and paying.

One function and consequence of the US tort system is to perpetuate provision of funding for the health and social care costs of injury, since the largely privatised healthcare system fails to cover the population adequately as many are unable to afford cover and Medicaid is limited.[54] In contrast, European states have markedly more extensive health and social security provision. It may also be relevant that the political rhetoric of class actions has historically contained a strong element of social equalisation and redistribution of wealth, such as involving human rights, overcoming racial segregation and access to education from the 1960s. Consumerism similarly had some resonance in Europe from the 1960s onwards, but at least by 2000 such associations had ameliorated and current headline European policy is more concerned with competitiveness and Better Regulation.[55]

It may obviously be selective to choose a single example from the vast US class action experience, but the Vioxx case is recent and illustrates some relevant features. On investigation, it also reveals features that may differ from popular perception.

Case Study: Vioxx

Vioxx is a medicinal product that was approved as a pain reliever and used for arthritis and other chronic pain. It was approved in the United States in 1999 and in other countries worldwide around the same time. It has been estimated that approximately 20 million people used Vioxx

(continued)

---

[52] AV Thakor, n 50 above.

[53] AV Thakor, *The Unintended Consequences of Securities Litigation* (US Chamber Institute for Legal reform, 2005).

[54] In 2004, 15.7% of the United States' population were without health insurance coverage, 59.8% were covered by employment-based health insurance and 27.2% were covered by government health insurance programmes: US Census, 2005. See also SD Sugarman, *Doing Away with Personal Injury Law: New Compensation Mechanisms for Consumers and Business* (Quorum Books, 1992); and R Avraham and M Schanzenbach, 'The Impact of Tort Reform on Private Health Insurance Coverage' (2007) *Northwestern University School of Law Public Law and Legal Theory Series* 07–16.

[55] See ch 7 below and S Weatherill (ed), *Better Regulation* (Hart Publishing, 2007).

in the United States[56] and many more prescriptions were written worldwide. The purpose of Vioxx was to provide anti-inflammatory relief comparable to traditional NSAIDs,[57] but with a reduced risk of the serious gastrointestinal problems—including potentially fatal bleeding ulcers—that NSAIDs can cause. In September 2004, the manufacturer Merck voluntarily withdrew the product after a clinical trial showed a small but statistically significant increase in the incidence of confirmed cardiovascular thrombotic events from long-term use.[58] On the day after the announcement was made, The Wall Street Journal reported that the firm's market capitalisation dropped 27 per cent.[59]

While there was some litigation related to Vioxx prior to the voluntary withdrawal, the number of cases increased significantly thereafter.[60] The plaintiffs' primary allegation in the litigation was that the company withheld information about Vioxx's cardiovascular safety. Some plaintiffs attempted to bring personal injury class proceedings in the United States, but no class was certified. The US District Judge who was in charge of the coordinated federal litigation denied certification of a nationwide personal injury and wrongful death class for multiple reasons including that the individual issues—such as each plaintiff's unique medical history—predominated over any common issues.[61] Eventually, there were over 60,000 potential individual claims in the United States.[62]

(*continued*)

---

[56] Heather Won Tesoriero *et al*, 'Merck's Tactics Largely Vindicated As It Reaches Big Vioxx Settlement' *Wall Street Journal* (10 November 2007) A1.

[57] A non-steroidal anti-inflammatory drug (NSAID).

[58] Press Release, Merck & Co, Inc, 'Merck Announces Voluntary Worldwide Withdrawal of VIOXX®' (30 September 2004) <http://www.merck.com/newsroom/vioxx/pdf/vioxx_press_release_final.pdf> accessed 11 June 2008 (announcing the voluntary withdrawal of Vioxx); PS Kim, 'Vioxx: Setting the Record Straight', Chem. & Eng's News (3 January 2005) 5 (asserting that the increased risk observed in the trial did not become statistically significant until after approximately 30 months).

[59] Editorial, 'A Vioxx Elegy' *Wall Street Journal* (1 October 2004) A14.

[60] See, eg 'US District Court for the Eastern District of Louisiana Vioxx Product Liability Litigation' <http://vioxx.laed.uscourts.gov/> accessed 11 June 2008; 'New Jersey Judiciary Vioxx Information Center' <http://www.judiciary.state.nj.us/mass-tort/vioxx/index.htm> accessed 11 June 2008; and 'The State of Texas Multidistrict Litigation—Vioxx' <http://www.justex.net/Courts/CIVIL/CourtSection.aspx?crt=12&sid=47> accessed 11 June 2008.

[61] *In re Vioxx Prods. Liab. Litig.*, 239 FRD 450 (ED La 2006).

[62] See Press Release, Merck & Co, Inc, 'Merck Progress Report on Enrolment in Program to Resolve US VIOXX® Product Liability Lawsuits' (3 March 2008), available at <http://www.merck.com/newsroom/press_releases/corporate/2008_0303.html> accessed 11 June 2008 (stating that as of 31 December 2007, in the United States, Merck & Co, Inc had been served or was aware that it had been named as a defendant in lawsuits which include approximately 47,275 plaintiff groups alleging personal injuries resulting from the use of Vioxx and that approximately 13,230 claimants had entered into tolling agreements with the multi-district litigation Plaintiffs' Steering Committee that established a procedure to halt the running of the statute of limitations for certain categories of claims allegedly arising from the use of Vioxx by non-New Jersey United States citizens).

Merck defended the individual cases by presenting evidence that the company carefully studied Vioxx both before and after approval and responsibly disclosed the results of those studies to the medical community and regulatory agencies. Merck also presented evidence in individual cases that it was the plaintiffs' pre-existing risk factors, not Vioxx, that caused the alleged injuries.[63]

Of the cases that went to trial, as at June 2008, juries decided in Merck's favour on the product liability claims 12 times and in the plaintiff's favour five times.[64] Two plaintiffs' verdicts have since been overturned on appeal, including one case in which the jury awarded over $250 million, which was first reduced under Texas law to approximately $26 million, and then overturned in the Court of Appeal, on the basis that the claimant had 'failed to show that the ingestion of Vioxx caused her husband's death'.[65] One of the previous Merck verdicts was set aside by the court and has not been retried. Another Merck verdict was set aside and retried, leading to one of the plaintiff verdicts.

The company allocated $1.9 billion to defence attorney and experts costs, and by November 2007 had spent $1.2 billion.[66] The company's litigation strategy had reduced the expectations of the value of a settlement.[67] The company agreed a settlement with US claimant lawyers totalling $4.85 billion, in which eligible claimants would be allocated payments based on an individualised evaluation of their claims.[68] The company made no admission of wrongdoing or causation.[69] The amount that would be

(continued)

---

[63] See, eg Press Release, Merck & Co, Inc, 'Merck Wins Product Liability Case in Florida Circuit Court' (5 October 2007) <http://www.merck.com/newsroom/press_releases/corporate/2007_1005.html> accessed 11 June 2008 (explaining that the evidence showed that the plaintiff's longstanding cardiovascular disease caused his heart attack); and Press Release, Merck & Co, Inc, 'Merck Wins Product Liability Case in Madison County, Ill.' (27 March 2007) <http://www.merck.com/newsroom/press_releases/corporate/2007_0327.html> accessed 11 June 2008 (explaining that the evidence showed that the plaintiff's multiple risk factors put her at increased risk for sudden cardiac death, having nothing to do with Vioxx).

[64] Various verdicts are under appeal. In May 2008, one of five plaintiffs' jury verdicts (which totalled $32 million against Merck & Co, Inc) was overturned by an appellate court as being based on '"legally insufficient" evidence': *Merck & Co, Inc v Garza*, No 04-07-00234,2008 Tex. App. LEXIS 3470 (4th Dist., 14 May 2008).

[65] *Merck & Co, Inc v Ernst* No 14-06-00835-CV (Tex. App. 29 May 2008).

[66] See *Tesoriero et al*, above.

[67] The settlement was greeted favourably by Wall Street, with comments that had a class action been certified, the settlement would have cost a great deal more.

[68] See Settlement Agreement Between Merck & Co, Inc and The Counsel Listed on the Signature Pages Hereto (9 November 2007) (amended 17 January 2008) <http://www.merck.com/newsroom/press_releases/corporate/2007_1109.html> accessed 2 July 2008.

[69] *Ibid*, § 13.1.

paid to claimants' attorneys was determined by the attorneys' individual agreements with their clients.[70]

Outside the United States, more than 70 cases have been litigated and dismissed up to February 2008, most of them in Europe.[71] The company has stated that it has not been established in any of these cases that Vioxx has caused the adverse reactions alleged and that court-appointed experts have found in a significant number of cases that plaintiffs' individual risk factors, not Vioxx, were responsible for plaintiffs' alleged injuries.[72]

Not surprisingly, the contrast between payments to US patients and the absence of payments to non-US patients has attracted adverse criticism in Europe. The public impression is that the drug and the company were at fault, and the European legal system is adversely compared to the US system in failure to deliver compensation. Yet the company continues to assert that its drug was not defective and that no legal case has yet been made out for payment of compensation because many cases involve no causation: heart attacks and strokes happen for many reasons. The only reliable way to resolve the conflict here would be to undertake an independent assessment of causation in all European and US claimants, but that is unlikely to be possible. It is relevant that the US settlement provides for the division of the total settlement sum between all claimants who register and are then assessed on a points basis, the gateways for allocation of points being more closely related to division of a sum of money amongst a pre-defined group than amongst those who qualify by providing scientific evidence of causation of injury.[73] This case achieved a pragmatic commercial settlement of asserted claims, but is some way from providing objective evidence that a defective product caused injury in any individual case.

---

[70] *Ibid*, § 9.1. The fees payable under most of the individual contracts would presumably be based on a percentage of amount recovered, perhaps 20–30%. On those percentages, the sums paid to attorneys would total $970 million and $1.45 billion. Out of that sum, the Agreement specifies that 8% of the settlement sum ($388 million) is to be paid to the class counsel.

[71] BBC Transcript, 'Face the Facts' (27 December 2007) <http://www.bbc.co.uk/print/radio4/facethefacts/transcript_20071227.shtml> accessed 11 June 2008; and Press Release, Merck & Co, Inc, 'Trifft Vereinbarung über US-amerikanische VIOXX®Klagen' (9 November 2007) <http://www.msd.de/aktuelles/ak_071112_00043.html> accessed 11 June 2008.

[72] *Ibid*.

[73] The three gates are: an injury gate requiring objective, medical proof of myocardial infarction or ischemic stroke; a duration gate based on documented receipt of at least 30 Vioxx pills; and a proximity gate requiring receipt of pills in sufficient number and proximity to the event to support a presumption of ingestion of Vioxx within 14 days before the claimed injury: see Settlement Agreement and summary <http://www.merck.com/newsroom/press_releases/corporate/2007_1109.html> accessed 11 June 2008. These criteria assume entitlement, but do not prove causation or liability.

Given the difficulty of verifying the underlying merits of individual cases, and so whether the company's assertions on widespread absence of causation and liability were correct, and the inadvisability of drawing universal conclusions from one case,[74] however large, it does appear that there is cause for concern that a class action system may deliver compensation when it is not due. In addition, this case illustrates a view that the US litigation system as a whole can produce expensive outcomes, in which the justice of individual outcomes is not a primary concern. Complaints are made that cases are run as business enterprises by lawyers, who target 'deep pocket' defendants and pressure them into settling. From a company's perspective, the considerations include the cost of defending cases, disruption of management time, the harmful effect on the corporate image of bad publicity, depression of the share price, and consequential issues for employment and ability to raise capital. These issues all crystallise if a class action is certified, and produce pressure for financial resolution between the financiers of claims and the defendants or their insurers.[75]

A system in which litigation costs are excessive will adversely impact on: economic competitiveness; the ability to produce new goods and services (innovation); employment levels; the availability of insurance; the financial viability of businesses, with a disproportionate impact on smaller enterprises; and social divisiveness. If Merck had not had to pay some $2 billion to lawyers, the money could have funded the development and making available of two major new therapeutic medicines.[76] The point similarly applies to the extent that some of the further $4.5 billion was objectively unjustified. It could not be said that litigation operated directly as enforcement of regulatory standards in this case, since the company voluntarily withdrew the product. It might be argued that the threat of damages actions was a primary factor in prompting the voluntary withdrawal, but that point cuts both ways: one view is that the litigation threat safeguards the public, but another view is that it removes useful products. A society that encourages behavioural control through litigation can anticipate increased

---

[74] Further, the Vioxx case was not, of course, a class action, but it was settlement of a class of claims.

[75] For criticism of the settlement process and whether a deal is simply between attorneys and the company irrespective of individual merits, providing insufficient information for claimants and pressuring them towards acceptance with little protection of individual rights: see A Sebok and B Zipursky, 'Getting With the Program: The Vioxx Settlement Agreement' *Findlaw* (20 November 2007) <http://writ.news.findlaw.com/scripts/printer_friendly.pl?page=/commentary/20071120_zipursky.htm> accessed 11 June 2008.

[76] The average cost of discovering and developing a new drug is now put at over $800 million, and rising at an annual rate of 7.4% above general price inflation: Boston Consulting Group, *A Revolution in R&D: How Genomics and Genetics are Transforming the Biopharmaceutical Industry*, (Boston Consulting Group, 2001); J DiMasi, RW Hanson and HG Grabowski, 'The price of innovation: new estimates of drug development costs' (2003) 22 J. Health Econ. 151–85; DW Light and RN Warburton, 'Extraordinary Claims Require Extraordinary Evidence' (2005) *Journal of Health Economics* 24(5) 1030–33.

legal and insurance costs, a cooling of innovation and practice of defensive medicine. The litigation culture in the United States also has the effect of polarising relations between consumers, the trial bar and industry. This is evident in deep political rifts and entrenched rhetoric on all sides.

What is the true nature of the US problem? It does not lie fundamentally with any of the individual features, such as the class action procedure, the opt-out rule, the contingency fee system, the general absence of a 'loser pays' rule, punitive damages, decisions by juries, or the ability of lawyers to advertise. The fundamental problem lies with the *behavioural effects* that the totality of these individual parts produces as a result of the size of the financial incentives that are generated by the system. The legal system is positively intended to encourage action by private actors, within a privatised model of behavioural enforcement in a capitalist system: this is considered further in chapter seven. However, many in Europe may conclude that the fruits of such a model are undesirable, and that the US legal and political systems have failed to impose controls on undesirable excesses. These considerations also give rise to a question over the advisability of adopting an enforcement model that primarily relies on private action.

THE AUSTRALIAN TORT CRISIS

Australia has a common law system based originally on English law and procedure. It suffered a major crisis around 2000, and strenuous legislative action was required to stabilise the economic and legal systems. The causes were multiple and included the following factors. First, successive judicial decisions from the 1960s had expanded liability under the law of negligence[77] and relaxed causation rules,[78] in part based on the assumption that liability insurance would always be available and that any misfortune deserved compensation. Secondly, a growth of specialist plaintiff law firms occurred following deregulation of legal advertising in 1993 and deregulation of legal fees. Thirdly, both contingency fees and class actions (known as representative proceedings) were introduced.[79] By June 2000, the insurance market also experienced a trough. The spiralling costs of insurance led to the collapse of a major insurer and a medical indemnity organisation, and a crisis in the continuation of medical practice because of the lack of insurance.

The government had to put in place emergency indemnity arrangements, followed by several Acts, in order to stabilise the insurance sector,

---

[77] Hon JJ Spigelman, 'Negligence: The Last Outpost of the Welfare State' (2002) 76 ALJ 432.
[78] *Lisle v Brice* [2002] 2 Qd R 168 at 173.
[79] For example, Federal Court of Australia Act 1976 (Cth) Pt IVA.

particularly in relation to ensuring ongoing medical practice. Federal and state-level reform of negligence law and practice was also undertaken.[80] Amongst a raft of proposals,[81] the law of negligence was subject to statutory restrictive restatement, causation and limitation rules were strengthened, damages were capped, punitive damages abolished in negligence cases, recoverable costs limited, and plaintiff lawyers were subject to a requirement to certify that they had investigated the merits of a case.[82]

THE ENGLAND AND WALES PRODUCT LIABILITY CASES

Prior to the reform of litigation funding systems and civil procedure in 1999, a series of product liability claims were brought in England and Wales, as collective actions under the forerunner of what became the GLO rule.[83] These mainly involved medicinal products, which are intrinsically difficult cases in which to succeed. The overwhelming number of a total of several thousand claims in around 10 different actions were unsuccessful.

The cases were nearly all funded by the legal aid system, as it then existed.[84] There was widespread criticism that the legal aid system involved inadequate controls on evaluation of the merits of cases, and that funding was made available too readily. In the cases under consideration, the result was that large sums of public money were paid to the claimants' lawyers (and paid by defendants or insurers to their counterparts), but very few claimants' cases succeeded.[85]

These cases were criticised as being lawyer-led, generating large cohorts of claimants through newly liberalised rules on advertising,[86] whose expectations of success were fuelled and then dashed.[87] The operation of the

---

[80] Commonwealth of Australia Treasury, 'Review of the Law of Negligence: Final Report' (2002) <http://revofneg.treasury.gov.au/content/reports.asp> accessed 11 June 2008.

[81] Many of which have been implemented at federal level, although the reform position throughout the states is currently patchy.

[82] See Commonwealth of Australia Treasury, 'Review of the Law of Negligence: Final Report' (2002) <http://revofneg.treasury.gov.au/content/reports.asp> accessed 11 June 2008.

[83] The story is set out in the case histories in C Hodges, *Multi-Party Actions* (Oxford, 2001).

[84] Lawyers have consistently argued that large multiple cases are too expensive to bring without significant external funding (such as is available to some successful US attorneys), so legal aid, private third-party investment or some other change in the system (such as removal of the loser pays rule) is essential.

[85] Conversations with claimant lawyers involved have revealed differing views on the underlying merits of cases.

[86] The removal of solicitors' monopoly on real estate conveyancing to competition from other providers from 1968 carried with it the sudden repeal of the statutory ban on advertising by lawyers. Inevitably, however, there have since been calls in England for regulation of some excessive adverts, for example in relation to personal injury claims or potential multi-party claims. The issue is summarised at C Hodges, *Multi-Party Actions* (Oxford, 2001) ch 6.

[87] Law Society, *Group Actions Made Easier* (1995) paras 6.6.7 *ff*.

legal system in producing this result was costly and merely resulted in rents to the intermediaries. Against that, it was argued that important issues of public safety were raised and deserved to be investigated in court, but that the opt-in system and cost rules prevented this. It is relevant that any action in relation to the marketing or labelling of the medicines involved had been taken by the companies and regulators long before the cases reached court.

Between 1995 and 2000, the legal aid system was dismantled and replaced by a privatised system of conditional fee agreements (CFAs).[88] This was followed by a rapid rise of claim-farming intermediaries. The intermediary system gave rise to major frauds on consumers, which required the government to introduce legislation to regulate intermediaries.[89] The combined effect of the CFA and CPR reforms has led to a general fall in claims generally. A number of GLO claims have been brought, but mainly only in areas on which public funding has remained, such as cases on abuse of children in care homes. Lloyd's of London estimated the annual cost of litigation to British industry in 2004 to be £10 billion a year and rising at 15 per cent annually.[90]

CONCLUSION: ABUSE COULD HAPPEN ANYWHERE

The types of excess that are particularly identified from the above analysis are: first, excessive costs of intermediaries; secondly, cases that involve a high proportion of unmeritorious cases; and, thirdly, the 'blackmail settlement' effect, in which it is cheaper for defendants to settle large cases irrespective of their merits. The main consequences fall on defendants with deep pockets, such as large businesses and governments, or their insurers, but since costs are ultimately passed on to customers and consumers, the overall effect is felt on the economy as a whole.[91] The three jurisdictions

---

[88] Access to Justice Act 1999 s 27; Conditional Fees Agreements Regulations 2000. The system is undergoing further development: see Department for Constitutional Affairs, 'New Regulation for Conditional Fee Agreements (CFAs): Response to Consultation' (2005) CP[R] 22/04; and Civil Justice Council, 'Improved Access to Justice—Funding Options & Proportionate Costs: Report & Recommendations' (2005).

[89] Compensation Act 2006. The Better Regulation Task Force, 'Better Routes to Redress' (2004) said: 'Media reports and claims management companies encourage people to "have a go" by creating a perception, quite inaccurately, that large sums of money are easily accessible.' However, there is little public understanding that the level of damages that apply to most claims is low: over 55% of county court awards in 2002 were for less than £3,000.

[90] C Fleming, 'Europe Learns Litigation Ways' *Wall Street Journal* (24 February 2004) A16.

[91] Insurers assert that compensation culture is spreading in Europe; company boards spend 13% of their time discussing liability issues, companies produce fewer innovations and prices rise: 'Directors in the Dock: Is Business facing a Liability Crisis?' (Lloyd's, 2008) <http://www.lloyds.com/NR/rdonlyres/6ADDD9EC-3145-4B38-A7A7-06BBECC161D9/0/360_Directorsinthedock_finalwithlinks.pdf> accessed 11 June 2008.

considered above are, of course, common law and not civil law traditions, but they are leading jurisdictions which offer experience of multi-party court actions. The picture that emerges from their experience highlights some serious issues of adverse consequences that can arise in multiple court litigation procedures.

It is a fundamental tenet of modern economic theory that any system can be captured by its intermediaries if the opportunities for rent-seeking are too great. There is clear evidence of this in relation to litigation systems from around the world, as indicated above. This is not to criticise lawyers. They and other financial intermediaries are behaving in normal and predictable ways in a capitalist economy, seeking to maximise their income. Indeed, some systems, such as that in the United States, positively encourage active vigilance by private actors. The issue that arises is how to control the level of activity and the rents of intermediaries so that neither becomes excessive, by which society regards profits as disproportionate and enforcement activity overbears desirable economic activity. Controlling the level of such profits and the ability to earn them may require society to intervene, usually through some form of regulation. It will be noted that the potential for abuse arises where there are private sector intermediaries, but it is more limited where a collective procedure is operated by a public authority, such as a Nordic ombudsman.

The second fundamental lesson is that a legal system does not need to have particular American features in order to enable intermediaries to earn excessive profits. The fact that a national civil justice system can produce unmerited litigation and abuse by intermediaries whenever the financial incentives for intermediaries offer significant rewards and are uncontrolled appears from the Australian and English systems, which are structurally different from that of the United States. Thus it may be irrelevant that a European legal system does not have certain features that are present in the legal system of the United States. What is important is the internal balance within a given legal system between costs and outcomes. The question for each legal system is what economic outcomes are produced by the particular balance that pertains between funding systems, rules on payment of costs and the procedures applied?

Clearly, various aspects of a civil justice system can affect the size of the financial incentives for claimants and intermediaries. The above three cases indicate that particularly important features that influence large intermediaries' costs may be whether there are effective controls, such as controls by clients or courts that would impose a proportionality requirement, and whether costs may be increased because the transaction involves multiple claims. It is not difficult, therefore, to see arguments by lawyers that they deserve significant remuneration for work on large and complex cases, or arguments by claimants' funders (who may be lawyers or financiers) that they deserve significant remuneration for their investment, especially if it involves the risk of paying further costs if the case is lost, or arguments by defendants and insurers that they are exposed to excessive bills, especially if they are forced to pay large sums to settle bad cases on a commercial basis. Litigation, especially collective litigation, is big business for the repeat players involved. The European concern is that this market may be in the process of significantly increasing and is insufficiently regulated.

ISSUES FOR EUROPE

Three questions arise for Europe out of the foregoing analysis. First, would changes to the civil justice systems significantly increase the risk of producing abuse? Secondly, if such a risk does arise, can controls be imposed effectively that would avoid or limit it to an acceptable level? Thirdly, to what extent does Europe wish to move from a public towards a privatised enforcement model? The third issue will be deferred for consideration in subsequent chapters. For the present, consideration is limited to the important points on civil justice systems.

What level of confidence can there be that European proposals that are expressly intended to increase litigation will not produce excessive adverse consequences? It has been seen above that it is incorrect to assume that individual changes could not have significant impact on any given European civil justice system. Every civil justice system must be understood as a complex system consisting of multiple inter-related parts. Change in any part may produce unforeseen consequences in another part of the system. Viewed in this light, it is irrelevant to argue that Europe is not adopting the precise procedure of a class action as it is understood in the United States,[92] or does not have certain features that are found in the United States, such as juries or a contingency fee system as such. What should be considered is the combined effect of the financial incentives that operate in a given system.

It is clear that the introduction of *any* collective or representative mechanism will reduce the cost of bringing individual claims, and that *any* mechanism for rewarding lawyers through 'no win no fee' or success fees will affect their financial incentive to seek work. *Any* increase in the transactional cost to claimants or intermediaries must be considered in context. *Any* fee system must include some element of regulation if it is to avoid producing excessively high fees in a collective claim situation—irrespective of

---

[92] Accordingly, the Leuven Report misses the point when it asserts that the current European reforms do not imitate the typical US class action, in that US disclosure is not imported, rules on 'loser pays' and cost-sharing arrangements remain strict, 'opt-out' principles are used with great reluctance, and rules on standing, evidence, formalism, the role of the judge and so on remain embedded, and that punitive damages 'are not inherent to class actions': para 427. It is true that the omission of some features will not add to a cumulative effect produced by other factors that do operate, but such omissions are not conclusive on their own if other factors exist or change.

whether the precise mechanisms involved are 'class actions' or 'contingency fees' or some other procedure.

It is suggested that the ability of the courts to control against abuses in litigation or costs is very limited. First, it would be a denial of fundamental rights for judges to stray too far in refusing cases on their merits at early stages. The argument that a robust initial certification stage by the court is sufficient to control the problem of meritless claims is unconvincing. Any initial inquiry cannot go far into merits without breaching principles of fundamental rights over access to justice, so initial scrutiny can only filter out cases with extremely low merit, although this is clearly a useful function. The class action experiences of the United States and Canada show that a certification stage usually turns into a major and expensive fight, in which defendants try to defeat or limit claims on grounds that do not in fact apply a merits test (the US criteria relate instead to commonality, superiority, adequacy of representation, etc). Similarly, a 'strike out' power can only be used in the most obviously meritless or abusive cases. Once a class is certified, the risk is that it may be cheaper for the defendant to settle irrespective of merits. The courts may not be involved in certifying the merits' settlements. They may be asked to approve attorneys' fees and to address the *comparative* fairness of settlement terms as between different sub-groups of claimants. So a certification stage does nothing for promoting justice in settlement. Secondly, several of the case studies above, such as the JJB Sports and French cases, resulted in very high legal costs for the parties, irrespective of whether they proceeded through the court process or (like JJB Sports) were settled. The parties and the courts were unable to deliver a result in which costs were proportionate.

A second incorrect assumption is that the European civil justice systems are in balance and will remain static.[93] The significance of this is that if other aspects of the system are changing, the assumptions that are made about the effect of particular changes (in this case, the impact of introduction or extension of a collective mechanism) may be inherently incorrect.

European national civil justice systems are, in fact, currently far from static and are undergoing a period of significant change, in both their procedural and financial aspects.[94] On the procedural side, there is a clear trend

---

[93] The Leuven Report, for example, does not take into account the extent to which the assumptions noted above, such as changes in funding or 'loser pays' rules, are sensitive to change and that changes would impact the position. It is now *incorrect* in stating that contingency fees are not allowed in continental civil law jurisdictions, but it notes methods of financing lawyers' initial costs in Austria, Sweden and England: para 437. It notes that some states waive the 'loser pays' rule for cases in the public interest, but merely comments that businesses are likely to spend even more on defence in order to intimidate and defeat consumers: para 438.

[94] C Hodges, 'Europeanization of Civil Justice: Trends and Issues' (2007) 1 *Civil Justice Quarterly* 96–123. M Storme (ed), *Procedural Laws in Europe: Towards Harmonisation* (MAKLU, 2003).

towards modernisation of traditional procedures in many Member States. The proliferation of collective action mechanisms within a short period has been noted in previous chapters.

Litigation funding systems are also now beginning to change considerably, and this brings considerable instability and uncertainty. There are, of course, two aspects to funding: the claimant must first have sufficient funds to finance the bringing of his or her claim (court fees and intermediaries' fees) and, secondly, must have sufficient resource to cover the risk of having to reimburse the costs of an opponent if the case is lost. Both of these features differ from the US system, in which contingency fees enable the intermediary lawyer to finance a claim at no cost to the claimant, and the claimant has no risk because of the absence of a 'loser pays' rule.

There is a strong adherence in Europe to the 'loser pays' principle, but some amelioration of the rule has been identified above in relation to claims by consumer associations. Justification for a 'loser pays' rule rests on various grounds. First, it accords with normal corrective justice principles (that he or she who causes damage should pay for it). Secondly, it encourages proportionality between the costs and benefits of claims, and so discourages less meritorious claims and defences. Thirdly, it encourages settlement. It is unlikely that the 'loser pays' rule will be abrogated in Europe as a matter of general principle or practice, but its existence does necessarily involve difficulties over funding some cases, such as those that have high costs and risk, irrespective of their merits, of which collective actions are a significant example. If the 'loser pays' rule is to remain, the essential issue is how to fund and cover the risk of meritorious cases, especially those that would otherwise not be brought, without encouraging unmeritorious cases and producing the high transactional costs and abuse seen in the United States.

Both individual resources and legal aid have limitations in collective actions. The English pharmaceutical group actions funded on legal aid illustrate the failure of legal aid in group actions. In any event, governments have shown no enthusiasm for extending legal aid in the current economic climate. Indeed, the legal aid system was recently deconstructed in Sweden and in England and Wales: in the former they were replaced by insurance and in the latter by conditional fee agreements that permit success fees in order to balance a 'no win no fee' approach.

A summary of the general position on the permissibility of speculative fees is shown in Table 6. Nearly all Member States permit success fees, and this foothold may be developed. In 2006, contingency fees were permitted in Italy and the German Constitutional Court held that it was impermissible to ban them and called for legislation.[95] Opposition to contingency fees is

---

[95] BVerfG, 12 December 2006, case no 1 BvR 2576/04.

Table 6—Speculative Fees in Europe: 2008

Country	Contingency fee
Austria	N, but a German financing company takes 30 per cent.
Belgium	Not allowed (although success fees may be allowed for part of lawyers costs).
Cyprus	N
Czech Republic	N
Denmark	Conditional fee.
Estonia	Y
Finland	Y
France	Success fee.
Germany	N (Y through intermediary).
Greece	Success fee to 20 per cent: according to Lawyers' Code, lawyers' fees may be agreed on a contingency basis (agreement in writing).
Hungary	Y
Ireland	Success fee—contingency fees illegal, but it is common for solicitors to operate on a 'no win no fee' basis.
Italy	Y 2006 (agreement must be in writing).
Lithuania	Y—contingency fees are permitted by the Law on the Bar.
Luxembourg	N
Malta	N
Netherlands	Success fee. Bar lifted ban on contingency fees 2004, but Ministry not approved.
Norway	Conditional fee.
Poland	Conditional fee (in practice).
Portugal	Success fee.
Romania	Contingency fee prohibited by bar association. Success fee allowed, only in addition to ordinary fee.
Slovakia	
Slovenia	Y to 15 per cent.
Spain	Y
Sweden	Y
Switzerland	Success fee 2005.
UK: England	CFA 1995/1999.
UK: Scotland	Success fee.

Y = contingency fee permitted: defined as a fee which includes a proportion of the sum recovered.

N = not permitted.

A conditional or success fee is payable only upon a successful conclusion of the case and may include an uplift over normal rates.

Note: third-party funders are known to be operating in Germany, Austria, the UK and probably elsewhere.

Primary Sources: National Reports in the Stanford-Oxford Global Class Actions Project <http://globalclassaction.stanford.edu> accessed 11 June 2008; and Reports in the IBA Task Force on International Procedures and Protocols for Collective Redress, 2007 (restricted copy).

strong, but showing signs of insecurity. Various proposals have been made to introduce contingency fees in collective actions.[96]

Perhaps the most significant development in relation to funding is that third-party investors have emerged during the latter 2000s in Germany, Austria,[97] and England and Wales.[98] Third-party funders pose interesting issues. They can offer access to justice for some claims, based on an inherent need only to invest in good risks and hence having undertaken a reliable risk assessment, which should identify good cases and filter out bad risks. Yet the US experience demonstrates that pressure on defendants to settle will increase if the amounts of damages and/or costs at stake are high, such as if the number of claimants is large, even if the underlying merits are less strong. The involvement of third-party investors introduces extra layers of cost: even if lawyers' fees are retained at proportionate levels, the investor will seek a return on investment in exchange for assuming the transactional funding and costs risk. The risks here are that investors may dictate outcomes based on their own commercial interests, market unfairly and demand excessive costs. A 'no win no fee' rule clearly facilitates claims, and a success fee adds to the cost of settlement for defendants. The spread of third-party investors will be a seismic shift in funding and add another layer of cost for those who pay. Governments will need to regulate both the activities and fees of investors.

Against this background, some in Europe advocate even greater change and emulation of the US precedent by enhancing financial incentives for private organisations and intermediaries to take civil action. Thus, for example, the European Commission pondered whether, in order to encourage more competition damages claims, the 'loser pays' rule should be removed and there should be double damages, contingency fees, collective actions and other changes aimed at lowering the costs of claims and increasing incentives.[99]

Advertising by lawyers is a further relevant phenomenon that is quietly spreading in Europe in any event and is also a characteristic of US litigation. This has historically been banned, either by law or professional codes,

---

[96] The proposal in the first draft of the Swedish Class Action Act has been noted above. The Dutch bar has voted to approve contingency fees, but the government has not as yet approved this. In England and Wales, the Civil Justice Council has recommended contingency fees and removal of 'loser pays' as a last resort for collective actions: Civil Justice Council, 'Improved Access to Justice—Funding Options & Proportionate Costs' (2007).

[97] The rapid spread of third-party funding for the national consumer associations' activities in those states has been mentioned in ch 2 above.

[98] The initial development was independent funding of insolvency claims, since this was legally permissible. As the rules on the acceptability of private funding have been liberalised, significant funds are now available from Australian companies, insurance companies such as Allianz, and private equity funds. Brokerage firms have emerged during 2007.

[99] Green Paper: Damages actions for breach of the EC anti-trust rules, COM(2005) 672, 19 December 2005; and Commission Staff Working Paper: Annex to the Green Paper Damages actions for breach of the EC anti-trust rules, SEC(2005) 1732 19 December 2005.

but prohibitions are gradually falling. It is, after all, a primary principle of markets that suppliers should be able (and encouraged) to provide full information on their goods or services and consumers should be entitled to full information.[100] Against this background, it is curious that the ban on lawyers' advertising should have been maintained for so long. In any event, full deregulation of advertising by any professional is contemplated by the proposed liberalisation of services within the EU.[101]

It should, of course, be noted that the principles and levels of damages are fairly stable in European jurisdictions and are usually modest. Awards are not subject to the unpredictability that occurs with the US jury system. Punitive damages essentially have no place in Europe, save in exceptional circumstances, but if private enforcement is espoused this assumption will be reconsidered.[102]

Hence, the overall conclusion is that two of the important variables in civil justice systems (procedure and funding) are changing. In the context of collective actions, the outcome is difficult to predict. The extensive evidence from the US system points towards a need to include anti-abuse mechanisms in collective systems.[103] The evidence from the British claims handlers points to a need to control the behaviour of such third-party intermediaries.

The conundrum is that any court-based private mechanism, and certainly a collective procedure, needs adequate funding to be available in order to enable it to operate (witnessed by the ineffectiveness of many national consumer association mechanisms referred to in chapter two), but if funding is freely available, this increases the risk of capture by intermediaries and can lead to excesses. No mechanism has yet been found that provides a suitably balanced outcome. A certification stage does not control post-certification activity. Even approval by the court of settlements and intermediaries' fees has not produced proportionality in the United States, and there is no reason to discount this risk in Europe. Amelioration of cost-shifting raises issues of unfairness to defendants and the risk of unmeritorious settlements. In sum, these problems raise the question of whether there may be a better solution outside a court mechanism.

---

[100] Among many authorities on this point, see AI Ogus, *Regulation: Legal Form and Economic Theory* (Oxford, 1994) ch 7. For a recent example of the importance of a right to information, see Proposal for a Directive on services in the internal market, COM(2004) 2, 21 December 2005, art 7; latest version Council Working Document 15310/1/05 21 December 2005.

[101] Following the Green Paper on Services of General Interest COM(2003) 270 21 May 2003, the Commission introduced a provisional proposed Directive which has proceeded slowly in Brussels, but has the support of the Council. See also Communication from the Commission on Professional Services—Scope for more reform: Follow-up to the Report on Competition in professional Services, COM(2004) 83 of 9 February 2004, COM(2005) 405 5 September 2005.

[102] The collective claim by Which? in the UK football T-shirt cases included a claim for exemplary damages on the basis that the fine imposed did not cover consumer detriment.

[103] Note the conclusions of the Globalisation Project.

7

Towards a European Collective Approach to Damages

THE DEVELOPING DEBATE

IT HAS BEEN seen in chapter two that mechanisms exist for obtaining injunctions in consumer protection cases on a widespread basis at national level. In contrast, the use of injunctions against competition infringements is not found in practice: authorities proceed straight to imposing financial penalties and the mere commencement of investigations has a salutary effect. It was identified in chapters two and three that some Member States are recently experimenting with innovative procedures for obtaining damages in multiple cases, either as general court mechanisms that could be applied to any type of case or in relation to specific situations, notably consumer protection or competition claims.

Debate at European level over extension of collective redress has erupted from 2005, again largely in the context of the two distinct but related areas of consumer protection and of competition law. As a precursor, there was a small flurry of interest when one of the questions included in the Green Paper on the Product Liability Directive issued by the Commission's Directorate-General on the Internal Market asked whether a class action mechanism should be included.[1] However, the issue was effectively dropped by the subsequent Commission Report, as being of insufficient relevance given the low level of product liability claims then existing within the internal market.[2]

The purpose of this chapter is briefly to recount the history of the debate at European level, so as to be able to identify the issues that arise, and hence enable subsequent analysis at greater depth. The issues that have arisen in relation to consumer protection and competition law are different (the debate largely takes place in silos), so will be traversed here individually, but since developments in one area have had some influence on the other at a macro

---

[1] The issue was also raised in the COM(1999) 396.
[2] See Third report on the application of Council Directive on the approximation of laws, regulations and administrative provisions of the Member States concerning liability for defective products (85/374/EEC of 25 July 1985, amended by Directive 1999/34/EC of the European Parliament and of the Council of 10 May 1999), COM(2006) 496, 14 September 2006.

policy level, it is necessary to jump between the two (more or less chrono-logically) before being able to adopt an overview.

CONSUMER PROTECTION

Previous chapters have set out the position that the provision of consumer redress has a long history in Community terms. A sizeable corpus of substantive consumer law, the consumer *acquis*, has been created and is undergoing revision.[3] However, it is all very well to declare that individuals have rights, but it is pointless to do so without providing the means for those rights to be enforced. Furthermore, in the internal market context, there remains concern that lack of an effective mechanism with which to enforce consumer rights, or an absence of confidence that such rights could be enforced in another Member State, is a barrier to trade and leads to an insufficient level of cross-border shopping.

Meglena Kuneva, the European Commissioner for Consumer Affairs, said in 2007:[4]

> In Roman law, if there was no legislation, the judge would say 'non liquit', I cannot help you. We cannot say this. I receive lots of letters from citizens, some as a last resort. ... Should public authorities be involved? Do we want to be a nanny state? Why not individuals? This is about having active individuals. The FIFA ticket sale case[5] is not as important as Equitable Life but is really irritating. We have failed to bring a sense of fairness to society.

> I agree we should deal with cross-border issues first. Only 1% of consumers use cross-border retail financial services. Only 26% shop cross-border. 48% wish to. 58% of the EU economy is the citizens' market. What could we give to the economy if we could [empower] and encourage competition? I wish I could have an impact on Member States but the first step could really change the picture.

---

[3] See recently Commission Report on Responses to the Green Paper on the Consumer *Acquis* at <http://ec.europa.eu/consumers/cons_int/safe_shop/acquis/acquis_working_doc.pdf> accessed 12 June 2008. The report states that 'the need for introducing collective redress mechanisms at EU level is highlighted by consumer organisations and some Member States'. It also says that many respondents ask for more ADR mechanisms and easier access for consumers to ADRs and the courts.

[4] The following comments were noted by the author at the Portuguese Presidency Conference on Collective Redress for Consumers, Lisbon, 9 and 10 November 2007.

[5] Various problems were associated with the 2006 football World Cup, including allegedly insufficient allocation of tickets to fans as opposed to sponsors, allocation to senior officials who had conflicting personal financial interests, and activities of touts selling at inflated prices; see European Commission press release, 'Competition: Commission welcomes improved access to tickets for the 2006 World Cup' (2 May 2005); and N Harris, 'Fifa executive in World Cup ticket scandal' (17 January 2006) <http://www.independent.co.uk/sport/football/internationals/fifa-executive-in-world-cup-ticket-scandal-523359.html> accessed 3 July 2008.

The issue here is not essentially one of a gap in the enforcement of consumer protection law—in contrast to the position in competition law, as will be seen below. There is no great call that the existing enforcement mechanisms in this sector are generally ineffective or that a large proportion of serious infringements are undetected. The enforcement architecture is one of national competent authorities operating together within a mutual recognition framework, and in fact increasingly closely and effectively.[6] The Commission (DG SANCO) has a coordinating role in some circumstances, but not an enforcement role, and this is in itself strong evidence of an absence of widespread or serious cross-border problems.

The real issues here are to improve existing enforcement systems in cross-border scams, to address deficits in many national civil justice systems in delivering compensation in low value mass situations, and to apply market equalisation where traders 'skim off' small individual sums from many customers which add up to large illicit profits that have a distorting effect on the market. The second and third of these situations overlap, but the arguments for market rectification are stronger than for delivery of small amounts of compensation. The real concern is to ensure that the market works effectively. However, the rhetoric of 'consumer compensation and redress' is used as a political justification.

Surveys revealed that the average percentage of EU consumers who had carried out an EU cross-border purchase in the previous 12 months had increased from 12 per cent in 2003 to 26 per cent in 2006.[7] The incidence varied significantly between Member States, ranging from 67 per cent in Luxembourg to 7 per cent in Greece, and involving over one-third of consumers in 11 of 25 Member States.

Accordingly, one of the headline policies set out in the EU's Consumer Strategy 2007–13 was the overhauling of the legislation of cross-border shopping rights and the creation of strong systems for redress and enforcement, including consideration of collective redress mechanisms.[8] However, the Commission was aware that evidence of a need for a collective redress mechanism, especially on a cross-border basis, had not been demonstrated. After a 'brainstorming event',[9] two studies were commissioned, to report in late 2008.

---

[6] The provisions on consumer protection have been described above at ch 4. See G Betlem, 'Public and Private Transnational Enforcement of EU Consumer Law' [2007] EBLR 683. Also see the consumer safety measures, Directive 2001/95/EC on general product safety, the RAPEX system, and the sectoral measures described in C Hodges, *European Regulation of Consumer Product Safety* (Oxford, 2005).

[7] European Commission, Eurobarometer Special Report 252, 'Consumer Protection in the Internal Market' (2006) QB1.

[8] COM(2007) 99 13 March 2007.

[9] Commission's 'Brainstorming Event on Collective Actions' (Leuven University, 29 June 2007) summary at <http://ec.europa.eu/consumers/redress/collect/index_en.htm> accessed 12 June 2008. Arguments were put both ways, but there was overall identification of arguments for EU action.

The views of the European Parliament were significantly influenced by its Committee of inquiry into Equitable Life. Governmental and parliamentary opinion was also influenced by the opening of leading US claimant and defence class action law firms in Europe, and their appearance of considerable wealth.[10]

Case Study: Equitable Life[11]

The Equitable Life Assurance Society, a highly regarded mutual assurance company, issued policies from the 1950s, including around 90,000 with guaranteed annuity rates (GAR). Subsequently, life expectancies increased and interest rates fell, and the society consistently underreserved sufficient funds to cover the guaranteed annuities of policy holders. After the House of Lords held that the society could not subsequently alter the GAR agreements, its asset shortfall was critical (£1.5 billion) and it closed to new business and in 2001 cancelled interim bonuses and cut all pension policy values (£4 billion) by 16 per cent (14 per cent for life policies). A scheme to alter the status of GAR and non-GAR investments was approved by shareholders and the court in 2002. In 2001, there were some 1 million with-profits policyholders, mostly in the UK, with around 15,000 in Germany, Ireland and other EU states.

A small number of policyholders issued proceedings in the courts: the outcomes are unclear, but some later policyholders were apparently repaid in full. Of around 6,000 complaints made to the Financial Ombudsman Service, by March 2007 some 2,087 had resulted in awards of compensation. The FOS processed claims by resolving a sequence of lead cases, which were illustrative of others. Since nearly all policyholders had a grievance, the FOS commented that awards merely reduced the value of the fund available to other policyholders.

An investigation by the European Parliament[12] concluded that the society had been chronically short of assets through the 1990s, that the UK had not correctly implemented the Third Life Directive, its 'light touch' to regulation had not been sufficient and there had been insufficient communication between regulators in different states. It noted that litigation was not a viable option for the average policyholder in view of the costs and risks, that, although the FOS was one of the more advanced ADR schemes in Europe, it was not an appropriate means of redress in

(Continued)

---

[10] Commission officials were taunted by some MEPs merely with the phrase 'Lear jet'! Personal communications with the author.

[11] Report on the crisis of the Equitable Life Assurance Society, 2006/2026(INI), A6-0203/2007.

[12] European Parliament Resolution on the crisis of the Equitable Life Assurance Society, 2006/2026(INI), P6_TA(2006)0293.

the circumstances, and alternative solutions were required including strengthening the EU's FIN-NET system. It concluded that the losses involved were relatively small for individuals, but nevertheless caused real hardship, and that the UK Government should assume responsibility for failures of supervision and provide compensation for all victims. It also recommended that consumers should be able to act collectively before national courts against providers or supervisory authorities.

The Equitable Life saga illustrates a number of salutary lessons. First, the amounts involved are often individually small (but may be larger and important to individuals), but add up to significant total sums. Secondly, traditional court-based remedies always involve costs that impose viability thresholds and make these mechanisms inherently less appropriate for claiming small sums. Even where collective court mechanisms are available, the size and complexity of some claims will still make them unviable (as the English medicines product liability claims found). Thirdly, in some cases, where the size of the available pot is limited, providing for some individuals or groups to succeed in claims may simply disadvantage others who have genuine grievances. On a macro scale, this may apply in relation to any diminution in the value of corporate assets which are widely held by pension or investment funds. Fourthly, there remains a need for speedy, expert, accurate, fair and cheap determinations of facts. As situations become more complex and affect more people—in the EU context some 500 million citizens—these challenges only increase. Further, there is a need for flexible and imaginative solutions. Are courts fit for purpose to deliver such solutions? The inter-linking of oversight (parliamentary, governmental, regulatory) interests with commercial and citizens' interests can pose huge challenges. Who is to provide authoritative, disinterested and effective coordination of all avenues so as to reach an effective, efficient and speedy solution? Are solutions such as ADR, the FOS and Nordic consumer ombudsmen part of the answer?

These considerations challenge what is meant by justice. Provision of justice for an individual may harm other innocent individuals. Further, by what means can we deliver justice in these new and challenging situations? Can courts deliver fair solutions at an acceptable cost? Is it necessary for private parties and/or regulators and governments to adopt more flexible and imaginative outcomes and procedures in order to achieve justice?

EVIDENCE OF NEED IN CONSUMER PROTECTION: A COMPENSATION OR MARKET RECTIFICATION ISSUE?

It is widely accepted that governments should make policy on the basis of sound empirical evidence of need and of the effectiveness of the proposed solutions. Legislative proposals by the European Commission are subject to a requirement for formal impact assessments that analyse the likely economic and social impacts, consider all alternative policy options, and compare the impacts of different options.[13] As will be seen below in considering the Impact Study for the White Paper on competition damages, the current approach does not go far enough: it evaluates benefits and risks, but has no empirical grounding.

There are two aspects to demonstration of need for new legislation. There should be evidence, first, that there is a practical problem and, secondly, that existing mechanisms are inadequate. For both of these aspects, one needs to know the size of the problem. In the absence of quantification, one cannot know whether it justifies attention, what sort of attention, or what baseline exists against which to judge whether any new approach has improved the position. In relation to collective redress, the best evidence of need of the first type would clearly be empirical data demonstrating the incidence of cases that had not been compensated.

For some years, the European debate on collective redress has been curiously hampered by an absence of empirical evidence of need. In the consumer field, empirical evidence has not been pursued of examples where multiple victims have been unable to pursue clearly valid compensation claims or where rogues have amassed and been able to keep large illicit profits 'skimmed off' from multiple individuals or customers. Examples of such situations have been identified, as can be seen from the case studies referred to above, but, despite significant effort in considering the issue, satisfactory empirical evidence has not been gathered and published that would demonstrate that the size of the gap in compensation or compliance is sufficiently large and widespread to justify particular proportionate measures.

At cross-border level, the formal evidence, referred to in chapters two and three above, is that only a single cross-border case was brought under the Injunctions Directive,[14] that there was not an overwhelming cross-border pressure under the CPC Regulation, and that there were very few national damages claims in the competition field. It is inherently difficult to identify how many private damages claims might be brought if an EU level mechanism were to be introduced, since national systems may not make such data transparent and it is well established that more than 90 per cent of court cases settle before judgment.[15]

Various survey statistics have been available in the consumer protection debate, but these are not particularly illuminating evidence. General surveys are not intrinsically strong evidence and would not be an acceptable foundation for a regulatory impact assessment: in any event, answers to survey

[13] European Commission, Impact Assessment Guidelines, SEC(2005) 791 15 June 2005.
[14] See ch 4.
[15] Eurobarometer survey, 'European Union citizens and access to justice' (October 2004) <http://ec.europa.eu/consumers/topics/facts_en.htm> accessed 12 June 2008.

questions can notoriously be influenced by the nature of the questions asked. Broadly, the survey results are that European consumers are concerned about the effectiveness of cross-border redress and would prefer safety in numbers: neither of those points is surprising. A 2002 survey of consumers' main reasons for feeling less confident in buying abroad than in their own Member State identified difficulties with the resolution of after-sales problems, such as complaints, returns, refunds and guarantees (88 per cent), and the difficulty of taking legal action through the courts (83 per cent).[16] A survey in late 2007 found considerable apprehension amongst citizens in getting involved in civil justice matters abroad and preferring EU harmonised common rules to trusting national rules.[17]

A survey in 2006 found that when European consumers were asked about the best measures to protect them, the right to take sellers or providers to court was in the lowest position (17 per cent), along with their right to join together with other consumers (13 per cent).[18] A 2004 survey found that 67 per cent of EU citizens would be more willing to defend their rights before a court if they could join with other consumers who complain about the same issue,[19] and this figure increased to 74 per cent in the 2006 survey.[20] On this basis, the European consumer organisation BEUC asserted that collective actions are particularly suitable to obtain compensation for damages where a large number of consumers are involved, and that, if handled individually, such claims would never be brought to court by the victims.[21]

On the other hand, the evidence is that when collective mechanisms are available, consumers simply do not regard their individual level of detriment to be worth joining in making a compensation claim, even when the chances of success are high (such as in 'follow on' cases) or when the costs risk is very low. The high profile cases brought by both the French

---

[16] Standard Eurobarometer 57.2, reported in 'Public Opinion in Europe: Views on Business-to-Consumer Cross-Border Trade' (14 November 2002) <http://europa.eu.int/comm/consumers/cons_int/safe_shop/fair_bus_pract/green_pap_comm/studies/gfa_report_en.pdf> accessed 12 June 2008 3, 20, 39–40.

[17] Special Eurobarometer 292, 'Civil justice in the European Union' (2008) <http://ec.europa.eu/public_opinion/archives/ebs/ebs_292_en.pdf> accessed 12 June 2008.

[18] European Commission, Eurobarometer Special Report 252, 'Consumer Protection in the Internal Market' (2006) <http://ec.europa.eu/consumers/topics/eurobarometer_09-2006_en.pdf> accessed 12 June 2008.

[19] Eurobarometer survey, 'European Union Citizens and Access to Justice' (October 2004) 36.

[20] European Commission, Eurobarometer Special Report 252, 'Consumer Protection in the Internal Market' (2006) QB28.5. The report notes that since Greeks are those who most regard resolving a consumer dispute in court as easy (51%), it is not surprising that 86% of them would be willing to assert their claims in a joint action. At the other end of the scale, 53% of Hungarians would not be more motivated to take joint court action.

[21] The European Consumers' Organisation, 'Review of the Consumer Law Acquis: Preliminary BEUC Comments' (24 October 2005).

and English consumer associations both elicited very low rates of signing up by individual consumers (0.6 per cent in the French mobile phone case and arguably 0.3 per cent in the JJB Sports case).[22] The Leuven Report concluded that small claims procedures would only be used by European consumers if the amount involved exceeds around €500.[23] In this context, it should be remembered that the European Small Claims procedure is to have an upper limit of €2,000.

Nevertheless, the 2006 survey also found that an average of 42 per cent of Europeans considered it easy to assert their claims against suppliers through some alternative means of dispute resolution such as arbitration, mediation or conciliation.[24] However, the Commission noted that a substantially higher percentage of consumers in northern Member States, Cyprus and Greece, as compared to consumers in Spain, Portugal and most new Member States including those in Central Europe, believed that resolving disputes through an arbitration, mediation or conciliation body as well as through court is easy.[25] With regard to alternative dispute resolution, only around 30 per cent of consumers in the latter group of countries considered it to be easy, against over 60 per cent of consumers in the former group.[26]

Further context is provided by the 2006 survey findings, in that a majority of EU consumers believed that providers and sellers respect their rights as consumers (the range was 41 per cent in Portugal to over 90 per cent in Finland).[27] It also found that a majority of Europeans were satisfied with their national consumer protection system (54 per cent) and that they trusted their public authorities to protect their rights as consumers (57 per cent).[28]

---

[22] See these case studies. The UK Office of Fair Trading accepts that it is difficult to determine the extent of demand for greater redress and that individual losses may be so small that it is not in an individual's interest to pursue: Office of Fair Trading Discussion Paper, 'Private actions in competition law: effective redress for consumers and business' (April 2007).

[23] J Stuyck *et al*, 'Study on alternative means of consumer redress other than redress through ordinary judicial proceedings' (Catholic University of Leuven, 17 January 2007, published April 2007).

[24] Eurobarometer Special Report 252, 'Consumer Protection in the Internal Market' (European Commission, 2006) QB28.1. This is supported by a UK survey that although 34% reported experiencing one or more problems with goods or services in the previous year, amounting to an estimated 26.5 million problems within the UK and estimated consumer detriment of £6.6 billion, 55% of these resulted in consumer detriment below £5, only 4% involved detriment over £1,000, and no less than 64% complained or took action (70% where detriment was over £5), of whom most (28%) contacted the public authority's Trading Standards services or the national Consumer Direct service: Office of Fair Trading, 'Consumer detriment: Assessing the frequency and impact of consumer problems with goods and services' (2008) OFT992.

[25] The survey found that the majority of Slovaks (66%), Czechs (57%), Slovenes (57%), Portuguese (53%), Poles (52%) and Hungarians (50%) find it harder to resolve disputes with suppliers through an arbitration, mediation or conciliation body.

[26] See Commission Staff Working Document, First Consumer Markets Scoreboard, COM(2008) 87 para 3.2.

[27] European Commission, Eurobarometer Special Report 252, 'Consumer Protection in the Internal Market' (2006) QB28.7.

[28] *Ibid*, Q28.6.

Again, trust was higher in the old Member States (around 60 per cent) than in the new ones (around 45 per cent).

Mulheron has claimed that an analysis of the types of case which are brought in common law jurisdictions that have aggregated mechanisms leads to the 'incontrovertible conclusion' that there is an unmet need for better redress of common grievances that have allegedly given rise to monetary loss and damage to a class of claimants.[29] She bases her conclusion on 19 'building blocks' of evidence, in which one of the strongest empirical observations is that the Australian and Ontario opt-out class action regimes both include types of case that are not brought in England. A significant number of these 'building blocks' in fact address the different argument that opt-out regimes include more people than opt-in regimes, granted that opt-out regimes generally, if not always, require individuals ultimately to opt in in order to claim loss or participate in a settlement.[30] The case that might be made here is that certain types of claims might arise in a jurisdiction, but there is little empirical evidence whether they do in fact arise in the jurisdiction studied, England and Wales. Interestingly, the UK Government's response to its consultation on possible extension of consumer collective mechanisms, published with knowledge of Mulheron's study, remained that although some possible cases that might benefit from representative actions had been put forward, 'further work is needed to properly establish an evidence base'.[31] If empirical need were to be established, the consequential issue that arises is what mechanism, or combination of mechanisms, would be best to provide solutions. The debate on collective redress too often revolves around the assumption that a court-based private law action is the only mechanism to be considered.

Faced with the inescapable conclusion that evidence of both cross-border and domestic need for further mechanisms would resolve otherwise unmet gaps in enforcement or compensation in consumer claims, DG SANCO commissioned two studies to investigate the issue and report in late 2008.[32] One study was to evaluate the effectiveness and efficiency of existing collective redress mechanisms, assess whether consumers suffer a detriment in those Member States where collective redress mechanisms are not available and examine the existence of negative effects for the single market and distortions of competition. The second study was to provide more information on the key problems faced by consumers in obtaining redress for mass claims, and analyse the consequences of such problems for consumers, competitors and the relevant market. It would not be surprising

---

[29] RP Mulheron, *Reform of Collective Redress in England and Wales: A Perspective of Need* (Civil Justice Council, 2008).

[30] These issues are considered at ch 5.

[31] Department for Business, Enterprise and Regulatory Reform, 'Representative Actions in Consumer Protection Legislation. Responses to the Government consultation' (2008).

[32] See Answer to Parliamentary Question by Ms Kuneva, E-2020/2008, 29 May 2008.

if the outcome of these studies were simply the conclusion that many of the existing national mechanisms give rise to a variety of unsolved problems. The European Parliament adopted a notably cautious tone in May 2008 by stating that:

> before starting any reflections about legislation at EU level, a thorough examination of existing problems, if any, and the envisaged benefits for consumers should be undertaken.[33]

Hence, the Parliament was supporting an evidence-based approach and not jumping to conclusions about whether any empirical need existed.

In the absence of empirical data, this current analysis will not make any assumption as to justification, but, given the existence of differing models, will proceed to question whether it is possible to identify methodologies that may offer the best solutions. It is notable that although Consumer Commissioner Kuneva focused on the need to encourage cross-border purchases by 'defending collective redress', Internal Market Commissioner McCreevy emphasised the need not to patronise consumers, and stressed how successful the EU's SOLVIT (ADR) network has been.[34]

There has, however, been a growing acceptance from mid-2007 that, even if empirical evidence had not by then been identified, the issue of collective redress deserved attention. It could be said that there was something of a sea-change in attitudes towards this issue,[35] which was identifiable at the Portuguese Presidency Conference in November 2007, at which speakers from many backgrounds concurred in the view that there is a need for improved formal mechanisms to provide for collective redress for consumer protection, and that the issue is not just a national issue, but a cross-border one.[36] Indeed, it was recognised that in these days of international and web-based selling, the issue is of wider significance than for the EU and is an international one.[37] It is certainly plausible that situations will arise in

---

[33] Report on the EU Consumer Policy Strategy 2007–13 (2007/2189(INI)) A6-0155/2008 <http://www.europarl.europa.eu/sidesSearch/search.do?type=REPORT&language=EN&term=6&author=28263> accessed 12 June 2008 para 38.

[34] ALDE (Alliance of Liberals and Democrats for Europe), 'Group Seminar on consumer policy' (European Parliament, 17 October 2007).

[35] H-W Micklitz and A Stadler, 'The Development of Collective Legal Actions in Europe, Especially in German Civil Procedure' [2006] EBLR 1473–503.

[36] An illustration of a common view was given by Mr Henrik Saugmandsgaard Øe, the Danish Consumer Ombudsman, who considered that there is a cross-border problem that needs solving, and that giving national competent authorities the ability to tell a foreign company to repay in their Member State under the CPC Regulation would be a workable solution, and consistent with regulation Rome I (applying the law of the home country) and the existing mutual recognition precedent of the CPC Regulation.

[37] See 'International Bar Association Task Force on International Procedures and Protocols for Collective Redress: draft Guidelines for Recognizing and Enforcing Foreign Judgments for Collective Redress'.

which mass problems may arise, and which could efficiently be addressed by appropriate collective approaches. However, what is not known is how often such situations might occur. If it was known what size and shape of problem there may be, policy makers would be able to design effective solutions to minimise the risk of engendering unintended consequences.

COMPETITION DAMAGES AND ENFORCEMENT

The issue of collective redress in relation to breaches of competition law shares with consumer protection law an aspect of regulatory enforcement, but in a different and arguably more compelling context. There is an important difference in the structure of enforcement between these two areas. In consumer protection, the system is one of mutual recognition between national competent authorities, with no Commission or other central agency having substantive enforcement powers. In contrast, the Commission's Directorate-General on Competition (DG COMP) has overarching enforcement powers, conferred in 1962,[38] and is at the centre of a system of trans-EU and national enforcement, involving national competent authorities (NCAs) and national courts.

Further, the substantive law that is enforced in the competition field is harmonised throughout the Community, being articles 81 and 82 of the EC Treaty. This has, however, only applied from 1 May 2004, when the Modernisation Regulation[39] provided for direct application of articles 81 and 82 EC by national courts and NCAs. This implemented a policy of expansion and some decentralisation in competition enforcement, empowering the national authorities and courts in a significant transfer of power, whereas previously national proceedings had to be suspended pending a Commission decision on the applicability of article 81(3).[40] A culture was thus created of diffuse competition law enforcement.[41]

The Commission has been interested in encouraging private enforcement of articles 81 and 82 EC (or their predecessors) since the 1970s.[42] The issue was given impetus when the European Court of Justice (ECJ) held that an individual has a right to damages for breach of Community competition law. Although the private enforceability of directly applicable EC law

---

[38] Council Regulation 17 of 1962.

[39] Regulation (EC) 1/2003 of 16 December 2002 on the implementation of the rules on competition laid down in arts 81 and 82 of the EC Treaty.

[40] JS Venit, 'Brave New World: The Modernisation and Decentralisation of Enforcement under Articles 81 and 82 of the EC Treaty' (2003) 40 CMLR 545 554.

[41] AP Komninos, 'Public and Private Anti-trust Enforcement in Europe: Complement? Overlap?' (2006) 3(1) Comp. L. Rev. 5.

[42] Commission, reply to Mr Vredling, Parl. Question 519/72 [1973] OJ C67/54; Commission, 'Thirteenth Report on Competition Policy' (Luxembourg, 1983) ¶¶ 2-7-18; and Commission, reply to Mr Moreland, Parl. Question 1935/83 [1984] OJ C144/14.

derives from *Van Gend en Loos* in 1963,[43] the first overt suggestion of a private right to damages emerged only in 1993 in an opinion of Advocate General Van Gerven in *Banks*.[44] Only in 2001, in *Courage and Crehan*, did the ECJ confirm that a right to damages for breach of Community competition law existed, and that it was justified as a function of assisting in Community law and policy. The ECJ stated that:

> [T]he practical effect of the prohibition laid down in article 81(1) EC would be put at risk if it were not open to any individual to claim damages for loss caused to him by a contract or by conduct liable to restrict or distort competition.[45]

In *Manfredi*, the ECJ affirmed the approach:

> It follows that any individual can claim compensation for the harm suffered where there is a causal relationship between that harm and an agreement or practice prohibited under article 81 EC.
>
> ... actions for damages before the national courts can make a significant contribution to the maintenance of effective competition within the Community.[46]

The Commission published a Green Paper in December 2005 that announced the intention to facilitate private damages claims, especially through a collective mechanism.[47] The new policy followed the finding of a study that there were very few damages claims at Member State level in relation to losses caused by infringements of competition law, and that the mechanism was 'totally underdeveloped'.[48] This was despite the finding that nearly all Member States did have civil litigation systems under which damages claims may be brought. The motivation for the new policy was twofold, and linked the separate issues of private compensation and public enforcement. The intention was to increase the number of damages claims not only so as to increase the payment of compensation to victims of competition infringements, but also, and in particular, to enhance enforcement of competition law.

---

[43] Case 26/62 *NV Algemene Transporten Expeditie Onderneming van Gend en Loos v Nederlandse Administratie der Belastingen* [1963] ECR 1.

[44] Opinion of AG Van Gerven of 27 October 1993 in Case C-128/92 *HJ Banks & Co Ltd v British Coal Corp* [1994] ECR I-1209.

[45] Case C-453/99 *Courage and Crehan* [2001] ECR I-6297 at [26] and [27].

[46] Joined Cases C-295–298/04 *Manfredi* [2006] ECR I-6619.

[47] Green Paper: Damages actions for breach of the EC anti-trust rules, COM(2005) 672 19 December 2005; Commission Staff Working Paper: Annex to the Green Paper 'Damages actions for breach of the EC anti-trust rules', SEC(2005) 1732, 19 December 2005.

[48] D Waelbroeck, D Slater and G Even-Shoshan, 'Study on the conditions of claims for damages in case of infringement of EC competition rules' (Ashurst, 2004). The Ashurst study found 60 cases in which judgment had been delivered in Member States, but it was not able to report on cases that are brought but settled, nor cases that are not brought (whether settled or not).

The Green Paper raised a large number of possible reforms that would increase the financial incentives for bringing competition damages claims, both for claimants and their lawyers. The main questions that were raised were:

a) whether there should be special rules on access to documentary evidence (eg through the introduction of discovery rules, which would be foreign to civil law traditions, and through access to evidence held by authorities);

b) whether there should be special rules on burden and standard of proof;

c) whether there should be a requirement to prove fault;

d) how expert evidence should be obtained;

e) whether the rules on causation need to be clarified to facilitate damages actions;

f) whether new rules should govern how damages should be defined and calculated;

g) whether damages should include some punitive element, such as double damages;[49]

h) whether there should be a defence that loss has or should have been, mitigated by the claimant (eg through the 'passing-on' defence or a restriction on a claimant's standing to bring a claim);

i) whether special procedures should exist for bringing collective actions;[50]

j) whether claimants should be insulated from the costs risk, both of funding claims and of liability for opponents' costs if the claimants lose;

k) how private and public enforcement systems could be integrated, so as to achieve consistency in approach;

l) what substantive law should apply; and

m) whether limitation periods should be suspended or altered.

It will be seen that many of these mechanisms relate to altering the financial incentives for bringing litigation of any kind, and not just to competition damages claims. This issue raised the question of whether the competition area deserved special treatment, distinct from any other areas of either enforcement or damages claims. If reform of such matters was undertaken in the competition area alone, interesting questions would be raised about what the knock-on effect might be on national civil justice systems, on whether the balance of civil justice systems should in any event be amended, and on the effect in relation to the principles of fairness and equality of arms.

---

[49] In the United States, triple damages may be awarded.

[50] This gives rise to difficult issues of standing (the classic debate is over opt-in versus opt-out mechanisms), quantification of damages and distribution of damages.

The Commission's views were based on a series of assumptions.[51] The first assumption was that there was an insufficient number of decided cases involving competition damages claims at national level across the EU and, therefore, a significant number of consumers and competitors that deserved compensation were going uncompensated. Given that nearly all Member States did have civil litigation systems under which damages claims could be brought, the number of cases identified was believed to be extraordinarily low.[52] The issue is, therefore, one of an insufficiency in corrective justice and access to justice. Underlying this assumption was a view that national civil justice systems are inadequate to cope with competition claims, which sometimes have certain complexities, and this deters people from bringing claims. Given the low likelihood that many Member States would undertake adequate reforms in their general civil justice systems within a reasonably foreseeable time, and given the particular complexities of competition damages claims, the Commission believed that solutions needed to be found speedily that would increase compensation when due.

The Commission's second assumption was that there was a deficit in enforcement. This was of greater importance than delivery of compensation per se. The Commission believed that infringement of competition law was widespread and serious, and that strong forces needed to be deployed that would increase compliance. It also argued that it had insufficient resources to act as an effective regulator and also that national competition regulatory agencies vary in effectiveness, so it was necessary to widen deterrence and enforcement through enlisting consumer and competitor power through the civil justice system. The inspiration came from the enforcement policy in the United States, which, as outlined in chapter six above, involves not only a dual approach between public enforcement and 'private enforcement', but also primacy of the latter, occurring through private damages claims, particularly in class actions. Hence, it was proposed to adopt a policy in Europe of 'regulation through litigation'. The evidence for an enforcement deficit will be examined below.

The third assumption by the Commission was that the correct approach towards producing compliant behaviour by commercial entities is through deterrence, and that imposing high monetary consequences on identified infringers, whether involving fines or damages, is the reliable and effective tool through which to affect deterrence and behaviour. This issue will be examined at chapter eight below.

Fourthly, the Commission assumed that there would be no adverse effects from increasing litigation in the proposed fashion. Surprisingly, the Green Paper made no mention of any risks in its discussion of options, and so omitted any attempt at a risk assessment or balanced judgment.

---

[51] C Hodges, 'Competition enforcement, regulation and civil justice: what is the case?' [2006] CMLR 43, 1381–407.

[52] D Waelbroeck, D Slater and G Even-Shoshan, 'Study on the conditions of claims for damages in case of infringement of EC competition rules' (Ashurst, 2004).

Interestingly, albeit confusingly, in subsequent speeches the Competition Commissioner criticised the US system as having excessive and undesirable consequences, and said that she wished to produce 'a competition culture and not a litigation culture' and therefore expressly was not proposing to introduce class actions or contingency fees.[53] However, a barrage of objections from business interests followed the Green Paper, arguing that excessive and costly litigation would inevitably result and would harm, rather then enhance, the European economy.[54] The arguments on the potential for abuse or capture of private litigation mechanisms have been considered in chapter six.

The expansionist approach to litigation that clearly underpinned the Green Paper of the Competition Directorate-General can be contrasted with the emphasis on maintaining a balanced liability system, which is evident from the Report on the product liability Directive issued by the Directorate-General for the internal market.[55] It is interesting to contrast the different rhetoric used by the different Directorates-General of the Commission here. The Competition Green Paper did not refer to any possible issues on producing abusive litigation or a need for balance. A question may, therefore, arise over the extent to which the Commission's policies are coordinated and aligned.

Academic opinion in the debate has ranged across a wide spectrum, from supporting European harmonisation[56] to questioning whether empirical evidence supports any need for dramatic change, and to concern over the inevitable adoption of US litigation culture.[57] Professor Sir Francis Jacobs, a former Advocate General at the European Court of Justice, has said that competition law calls for considerable specialisation (legal, economic, accountancy and public policy) and that the EU decentralisation of competition law will bring challenges of clarity and consistency through decisions

---

[53] See Speech by Commissioner N Kroes at the Harvard Club, 22 September 2005. The Green Paper avoids references to class actions and contingency fees.

[54] See the responses at <http://ec.europa.eu/comm/competition/antitrust/actionsdamages/green_paper_comments.html> accessed 3 July 2008, notably by UNICE and the European Justice Forum.

[55] Third report on the application of Council Directive on the approximation of laws, regulations and administrative provisions of the Member States concerning liability for defective products (85/374/EEC of 25 July 1985, amended by Directive 1999/34/EC of the European Parliament and of the Council of 10 May 1999), COM(2006) 496, 14 September 2006.

[56] H-W Micklitz and A Stadler, 'The Development of Collective Legal Actions in Europe, Especially in German Civil Procedure' [2006] EBLR 1473–503. T Eilmansberger, 'The Green Paper on Damages Actions for Breach of the EC Anti-trust Rules and Beyond: Reflections on the Utility and Feasibility of Stimulating Private Enforcement through Legislative Action' [2007] CMLR 44 431, argued that private enforcement is a necessary complement to administrative action, and that EU legislation is necessary.

[57] WPJ Wils, 'Should Private Anti-trust Enforcement Be Encouraged in Europe?' (2003) *World Competition* 26(3) 473–88; and C Hodges, 'Competition enforcement, regulation and civil justice: what is the case?' (2006) CMLR 43, 1381–407. N Reich, 'Horizontal Liability in EC law: hybridisation of remedies for Compensation in Case of Breaches of EC Rights' (2007) CMLR 44 705 argued that EU legislative action is not necessary on collective actions, and that the US model is foreign to the European conservative tradition.

by multiple tribunals, and he called for specialised national competition courts or, better, specialised lower courts and general higher courts.[58] Debate on collective redress in Brussels has ranged from those in favour[59] to those urging caution in view of the need to avoid abuse that would have the ironic effect of harming rather than enhancing the European economy.[60]

THE 2008 COMPETITION DAMAGES WHITE PAPER

On the competition side, the Commission published its White Paper, supporting Working Papers[61] and independent Impact Study in April 2008.[62] The proposals in the White Paper were finely calculated to tread a careful path through the morass of complex political, legal and technical issues. However, the approach of DG Competition contrasted with that of DG Consumer Protection, in that the latter progressed carefully by studying empirical need and benchmarking national systems, whereas the former asserted need and proposed actions.

DG Competition's starting point was the assertion that victims of EC anti-trust infringements only rarely obtain reparation of the harm suffered, and that the amount of compensation being foregone is several billion euros a year.[63] This asserted failure was attributed to various legal and procedural hurdles in Member States' rules governing actions for anti-trust damages before national courts. In effect, therefore, this constituted a condemnation of national civil justice systems, since there is no reason why any deficiencies are unique to competition damages claims. However, the Commission was careful to limit its comments and proposals to competition damages claims.

---

[58] Lecture at King's College (London, 31 October 2007).

[59] BEUC Conference in European Parliament, 'Group Action: Taking Europe Forward' (11 October 2007); see documents at <http://www.beuc.eu/Content/Default.asp?PageID=1513> accessed 12 June 2008; and W van Boom and M Loos, *Collective Enforcement of Consumer Law* (Europa, 2007). German Federal Bar Association Position on collective redress, October 2007, asserted that there is a practical need for a practicable and balanced collective redress instrument, since there are blockages to individual enforcement, but marginal damage cases result in high cost. It was argued that there is a problem and bundling cases can solve it.

[60] 'BUSINESSEUROPE Position on Collective Actions' (2007); BDI and Freshfields Bruckhaus Deringer, 'Private Enforcement in the European Union—Pitfalls and Opportunities' (2007); and 'Position Paper 1: Civil Justice in Europe—A Balanced System' (European Justice Forum, 2007) <http://www.europeanjusticeforum.org/documents/ejf_position_paper_i.pdf> accessed 12 June 2008.

[61] White Paper on damages actions for breach of the EC anti-trust rules, COM(2008) 165, 2 April 2008; Commission Staff Working Paper accompanying the White Paper on damages actions for breach of the EC anti-trust rules, SEC(2008) 404, 2 April 2008 ('Staff Working Paper'); and Commission Staff Working Document accompanying the White Paper on damages actions for breach of the EC anti-trust rules: Impact assessment, SEC(2008) 405, 2 April 2008 ('Impact Assessment Report').

[62] A Renda, J Peysner, A Riley, R Van den Bergh, S Keske, R Pardolesi, E Camilli and P Caprile, 'Making anti-trust damages actions more effective in the EU: welfare impact and potential scenarios', final report submitted to the Commission on 21 December 2007 ('Impact Study').

[63] Impact Assessment Report s 2.2. This assertion will be considered further below.

The Commission asserted that the 'current ineffectiveness' of anti-trust damages actions is best addressed by a combination of measures at both Community and national levels, in order to achieve effective minimum protection of victims' rights. The Commission emphasised two important policy decisions. First, it asserted that its proposals constitute *balanced* measures, which are rooted in European legal culture and traditions. This statement was made to recognise extensive concern that a European model must be found that is not open to the 'excessive and unmeritorious litigation'[64] and abuses found in the US class action system, and to avoid the facilitation of unmeritorious claims.[65] Secondly, it followed the guiding principle of preserving strong public enforcement of competition law, and that the creation of an effective system of private enforcement of competition law by means of damages actions is intended to complement, but not replace or jeopardise, public enforcement.[66] Thus, for example, no principle of 'private attorney general' is mentioned, nor is the US rule of triple damages.

The Commission proposed a series of measures aimed at facilitating damages claims for breaches of competition law. Although the proposals would apply solely as a matter of competition law, they could be argued to set precedents in other areas of substantive law or in relation to civil justice systems generally. Proposals that tended to involve a greater substantive, as opposed to procedural, element were the following:

a) A final decision on article 81 or 82 taken by a national competent authority (NCA) and a final judgment by a review court upholding an NCA decision should be accepted in every Member State as irrebuttable proof of the infringement in subsequent civil anti-trust damages cases.

b) National courts cannot take decisions in damages cases that run counter to decisions of NCAs or review courts.

c) Liability for competition damages should follow proof of breach of articles 81 or 82, unless the defendant demonstrates that the infringement was the result of a genuinely excusable error. In other words, liability would not be fault-based.

d) In order to facilitate the notoriously difficult (and therefore costly) area of calculating damages in competition cases, the Commission is to draw up a framework with pragmatic, non-binding guidance for quantification of damages in anti-trust cases, for example by means of approximate methods of calculation or simplified rules on estimating the loss.

---

[64] Staff Working Paper para 2.

[65] Staff Working Paper paras 12, 16 and 32. The Commission considered that the proposals put forward to a very large extent remove any risk of abuse of the judicial system by unmeritorious claimants: Impact Assessment Report para 141.

[66] Staff Working Paper, paras 17 and 18. This policy led directly to the proposals on protection from disclosure of corporate statements made in the context of leniency programmes, and on limitation of civil liability on the part of successful leniency applicants; see below.

e) In accordance with the principle that damages should provide full compensation,[67] indirect purchasers should be able to rely on the rebuttable presumption that the illegal overcharge was passed on to them in its entirety, but defendants should be entitled to invoke the passing-on defence, namely that the claimant's loss had been passed on to a subsequent purchaser or operator.

f) The limitation period for competition damages claims should not start to run:

   i) before the victim of the infringement can reasonably be expected to have knowledge of the infringement and of the harm it caused him or her;

   ii) in the case of a continuous or repeated infringement, before the day on which the infringement ceases;

   iii) but subject to a new limitation period of two years from the infringement decision by an authority on which a follow-on claimant relies has become final.

Certain other proposals related more closely to national civil justice systems:

a) The Commission considered that a mechanism was needed for aggregation of individual claims, and was particularly influenced by the view that individual consumers and small businesses may otherwise be unable to obtain redress since they tend to suffer scattered and relatively low-value damage. The Commission suggested a combination of two complementary mechanisms for collective redress:

   i) Representative actions, brought by qualified entities, such as consumer organisations, state bodies or trade associations, on behalf of identified or, in restricted cases, identifiable victims. The entities would be either officially designated in advance or certified on an ad hoc basis by a Member State for a particular anti-trust infringement to bring an action on behalf of some or all of their members; and

   ii) Opt-in collective actions, in which victims expressly decide to combine their individual claims for harm they suffered into one single action.

b) In order to address the problem that competition damages cases are fact-intensive and there is informational asymmetry because much of the evidence is concealed from victims, national courts would have the power, under specific conditions,[68] to order parties, or third parties, to

---

[67] Staff Working Paper ch 6. The Commission argued that the *Manfredi* decision is that punitive damages are not contrary to European public order, and permissible. However, the Impact Assessment Report para 71 stated that punitive damages raise serious issues as regards their compatibility with public policy and/or basic principles of tort law in many Member States.

[68] Staff Working Paper para 70 recognises that various unwelcome externalities are to be avoided, such as 'fishing expeditions', 'discovery blackmail', and procedural abuses and excessive costs for defendants.

disclose precise categories of relevant evidence. Conditions for disclosure would include that the claimant has presented plausible grounds for a case based on all the evidence available to him or her, that he or she is unable to produce the requested evidence, that precise categories of evidence to be disclosed have been specified, and that the court is satisfied that the disclosure is both relevant to the case and necessary and proportionate.[69] However, corporate statements submitted by an applicant for leniency would remain undisclosable.

c) States should reflect on their costs rules and:
   i) design procedural rules to foster settlements, so as to save costs;
   ii) set court fees so that they do not become a disproportionate disincentive to anti-trust damages claims;
   iii) give national courts the option of issuing costs orders derogating, in certain justified cases, from the normal cost rules, preferably upfront in the proceedings. Such cost orders would guarantee that the claimant, even if unsuccessful, would not have to bear all costs incurred by the other party.[70]

In these proposals the Commission demonstrated a significant degree of pragmatic political restraint, in tempering its previously expressed enthusiasm for a more ambitious programme. For example, the proposals on costs were merely matters of encouragement to Member States, with no binding force, given the difficulties of subsidiarity over jurisdiction in the diverse civil justice systems. The Commission rightly identified that the funding of a private action is the primary key issue,[71] but refrained from putting forward legislative proposals at this stage.

Similarly, the Commission rejected the opt-out model of a damages class action, and so avoided the risk of running into serious constitutional arguments. It accepted that opt-out actions in other jurisdictions have been perceived to lead to excesses.[72] Instead, it built on the precedent of the national models of civil society representative organisations *and* public authorities, recognising that the situation in Member States differs, encompassing what have been identified in chapter two as Models A and B. This is similar to the

---

[69] It will be seen that this proposal takes the partly revolutionary step of importation of the common law concept of discovery into civil law systems. However, national systems have been evolving in recent years, and a number of civil law systems permit disclosure of documents in particular situations, especially in commercial cases. Directive 2004/48/EC already includes a similar discovery provision in art 6.

[70] The ideas here include exemption of certain bodies from costs, because of the nature of the body, and taking into account the objective of protecting genuine claimants from a level of costs that would be too great. A precedent is the English mechanism of the court imposing a cost capping order at the start of a case, which has the effect of assisting case management through limiting the amount of work claimable by successful defendants.

[71] Staff Working Paper para 45.

[72] Staff Working Paper para 58.

approach taken in consumer protection law of the CPC Regulation,[73] but it inherently perpetuates the national diversity over whether public or private entities in practice take the lead. The theory, or hope, is that such entities, whether public or private, can be more trusted not to bring unjustified claims or produce abusive practices.[74] In the light of the findings of this book, it can be commented that it may, however, remain the case in practice that, at least in those states that adopt Model A, consumer associations take little interest in running representative actions. Further, it has been seen that the trend in relation to consumer protection enforcement may be moving away from collective redress involving private entities, from Model B towards Model A.

The representative model proposed would only apply to claimants who are *identified* or *identifiable*. Such an approach would tend to avoid the problems that have been found with classes of claimants that are of uncertain size, such as over the cost of notification, conflicts of interest, quantification of individual damages and 'blackmail settlements'.

The Commission also proposed that a second mechanism was justified. This would permit stand-alone actions, whereas the representative action model would arguably be used more for follow-on actions. However, as discussed, the mechanism would be opt-in only. If the Commission's suggestion of two mechanisms for collective claims for damages is taken forward, it will, of course, be necessary to avoid double recovery,[75] but also double jeopardy and duplicated actions.

Consideration now needs to be given to the extent to which the Commission based its proposals on reliable empirical evidence. What evidence is there that would substantiate an empirical case on the size of any unmet need for compensation, or enforcement? The position turns out to be far from established, and this raises important questions about whether policy is being based on reliable evidence. Both the Impact Study and the Impact Assessment (running together to some 800 pages) set out a series of options that, at either extreme, plausibly lead to under- or over-production of compensation (on the one hand) and deterrence (on the other hand). However, selection (which is different between the advisers and the Commission) of which of the various options is recommended at striking a happy, balanced medium surely requires empirical evidence in order to locate the suggested option as being balanced in the spectrum of what constitutes too little or too less compensation, deterrence and observance. Thus, the policy selection is not founded on empirical rationality, and the selection of any of the options is, in the absence of reliable empirical evidence, subjective guesswork. The Commission's proposal of an option from roughly the middle of the range might be right or wrong, but the policy seems to be based more on political considerations than evidence.

---

[73] See ch 4.
[74] Staff Working Paper para 32.
[75] Staff Working Paper para 61.

EVIDENCE OF NEED: A COMPETITION DEFICIT?

It has been noted above that the primary arguments made by the Commission for reform in the competition field relate to gaps in both compliance and in delivery of compensation. These issues, if true, are more serious in scale and significance than the position as it appears for consumer protection. What would be required to establish these points would be empirical evidence of the differences between the actual and ideal levels of compliance and the due and actual paid levels of compensation. Regrettably, such evidence is, once again, lacking. Some evidence is available, but on enquiry is less than robust or convincing.

Taking the points in reverse order, it may be accepted that damages were rare in competition cases until this decade, and that damages claims in competition cases give rise to fact-intensive cases that are complex and costly. As a result, corporate claimants may be expected to bring claims, but SMEs and consumers will be at a significant disadvantage because of the adverse cost-benefit ratio.[76] Although national civil justice systems had indeed long provided for damages claims based on negligence, the substantive Community law on competition infringements, on which damages claims could be directly based, only applied from 1 May 2004, when the Modernisation Regulation came into effect, as mentioned above.[77]

Since that time, as may be expected, an increasing number of damages claims have been brought, and evidence has emerged that, again as expected, settlement of private claims has occurred consistently.[78] As at April 2008, the number of national judgments forwarded to the Commission since 2003 under articles 81 and 82 EC included 41 from France, 35 from Germany, 33 from Spain, 17 from each of Belgium and the Netherlands, 10 from Austria, and three from each of the UK and Sweden, of which a not insignificant (but unidentifiable) proportion had been associated with damages claims.[79] The former President of the *Bundeskartellamt* stated that around 900 private

---

[76] R Van den Bergh and L Visscher, 'The Preventive Function of Collective Actions for Damages in Consumer Law' (2008) 1 *Erasmus Law Review* 2 5.

[77] Regulation (EC) 1/2003 of 16 December 2002 on the implementation of the rules on competition laid down in arts 81 and 82 EC of the Treaty.

[78] Bundesverband der Deutschen Industrie eV and Freshfields Bruckhaus Deringer, *Private Enforcement in the European Union—Pitfalls and Opportunities* (2007). BJ Rodger, 'Private Enforcement of Competition Law, the Hidden Story: Competition Litigation Settlements in the United Kingdom, 2000–2005' [2008] ECLR 2, 96 found 43 settlements where only one had previously been reported, and an increase in claims in 2005.

[79] <http://ec.europa.eu/comm/competition/anti-trust/national_courts/index_en.html> accessed 10 April 2008. The number of anti-trust cases notified in the network from 1 May 2004 to 31 March 2008 was 861, of which 156 involved the Commission and the remainder national authorities, and of which an envisaged decision was submitted in 255 cases: <http://ec.europa.eu/comm/competition/ecn/statistics.html> accessed 12 June 2008.

law anti-trust cases had been registered between 2002 and 2006; 68 of 240 decisions between 2002 and 2004 had been asserted offensively, of which 38 had involved damages claims.[80] Notifications of judgments also, of course, shed no light on the number of cases settled, which is usually a far higher percentage.

These figures show a picture of both more claims than was apparent from the 2004 Ashurst study on which the Green Paper was based, and an increase in claims since 2004. There are, however, indications that the incidence and increase in claims are not uniform across the Community. It may be that the incidence of damages cases will increase further, as a result of various factors that are already acting, including not only the clarity in the right to claim brought about by the ECJ, but also national reforms and the high profile that damages claims has taken as a result simply of the Green Paper. However, the real incidence of competition damages claims remains unknown, as does the normal benchmark level that may be reached as a result of the current increase. Accordingly, no reliable measurement has been made of the extent to which any real gap exists in competition damages claims. It will also be impossible to measure the increase in damages claims that would be referable to any changes brought about by future reforms.

The number of cases that would be justified should have some relationship to the number of infringements. It should in fact be below the number of infringements (absent blackmail settlements) if cases are still currently based on negligence in some Member States rather than simply infringement of articles 81 and 82, or cases are not worth pursuing because the cost-benefit ratio is unfavourable. So, what is the level of infringement? This turns out to be totally unknown.

It is widely asserted within the competition world that only between 10 and 20 per cent of cartels are detected in Europe.[81] However, these figures are estimates based on calculations made on numbers of cartels *detected*.[82] It may admittedly be difficult to measure the total number of cartels, particularly those undetected, but it would seem important to do so if major policy decisions are to be founded on the figure and there is a significant element of risk in some policy options. For example, the figure is central to the calculation that

---

[80] U Böge and K Ost, 'Up and Running, or is it? Private enforcement—the Situation in Germany and Policy perspectives' [2006] ECLR 197.

[81] These figures were taken as benchmarks for calculations and policy in the 2008 White Paper: see Impact Assessment, fn 29. See also Office of Fair Trading, 'Private actions in competition law: effective redress for consumers and business' (2007) <http://www.oft.gov.uk/shared_oft/reports/comp_policy/oft916resp.pdf> accessed 12 June 2008 para 5.7.

[82] A report by a New Zealand commission asserted that deterrence requires the *damages* awarded to be 100% of the damage to all victims adjusted for such factors as the likelihood of detection and successful punishment: Ministry of Commerce, 'Penalties, remedies and court processes under The Commerce Act 1986: A discussion document' (1998) <http://www.med.govt.nz/upload/17936/1pen.pdf> accessed 2 July 2008.

produced the Commission's assertion that the annual direct cost to consumers and other victims in the EU ranges between €13 billion and €37 billion.[83]

Only two significant attempts have been made to estimate detection rates for cartels,[84] one in the United States on data now over 17 years old, and the other recently on cases dealt with by the European Commission between 1969 and 2007. Bryant and Eckard examined cases selected from those pursued by the US Department of Justice to a successful conclusion from 1961 to 1988.[85] They calculated that the annual probability of getting caught *for the cartels in their data set that were eventually detected* was between 13 and 17 per cent.[86] The reliability of this data and relevance to contemporary European conditions, with its significantly different and evolving enforcement regime, is highly questionable. Combe and colleagues have recently reviewed the 86 cartel cases dealt with by the European Commission between 1969 and 2007.[87] Their calculations were that the probability of detection in a given year for this group, *conditional on being detected*, was between 12.9 and 13.2 per cent. However, of course, none of these estimate the number or proportion of cartels that will in fact be detected. Combe noted after 1996, when the EU introduced its leniency programme, the detection rate increased from an average of 1.64 per annum to 5 per annum (again, of those actually detected).

Thus, the reality is that the level of infringements (cartels and general competition law) and the level of damages claims that are brought and that could be brought are all unknown. This is hardly an impressive basis on which to make important policy, especially given the risk that changes would not produce the desired increase in economic competitiveness, through either insufficient or excessive damages claims and enforcement. There would seem to be a need for a far more empirical approach. Given that it is totally unknown what the incidence of cartels is in contemporary Europe, whether at national or Community levels, it may also be questioned whether it is disingenuous to quote a level of 20 per cent or any other figure, and whether any policy should be made without better information.

Given that the only hard data that are available relate to enforcement activity, it is surprising that the number of case investigations of which the

---

[83] Impact Assessment para 42 and Impact Study para 2.1.1.

[84] The Impact Study para 2.1.1 lists a series of references prior to the Combe *et al* study that derive from the Bryant and Eckard study, except for a small data set of international cases reported. See OECD, 'Report on the Nature and Impact of Hard Core Cartels and Sanctions against cartels under National Competition Laws', DAFFE/COMP(2002)7 (9 April 2002).

[85] PG Bryant and EW Eckard, 'Price Fixing: The probability of getting caught' (1991) 73 *Review of Economics & Statistics* 531–6.

[86] GJ Werdan and MJ Simon, 'Why Price Fixers Should Go to Prison' (1987) 32 *Anti-trust Bulletin*, 917–37.

[87] E Combe, C Monnier and R Legal, 'Cartels: The Probability of Getting Caught in the European Union', BEER paper no 12 <http://www.concurrences.com/article.php3?id_article=13955> accessed 12 June 2008 (registration required).

EC Network has been informed has *fallen* consistently since 2004, at both Commission and national level, as shown in Figure II. Given the increased powers and enforcement activism by the authorities generally in this period, this is counter-intuitive. It is clear that the Commission's policy in the modernisation programme is to push cases down to Member State level, so that the Commission itself can concentrate on the larger cartels.[88] However, possible further explanations for the fall might be that the authorities' investigative capacity has fallen significantly, or that the authorities are uncovering larger cartels that need increased resources, or that there may be fewer significant cartels and other infringements worthy of investigation. There is a need for further inquiry into this position. It is asserted by industry that anti-trust enforcement by European public authorities has been increasingly strong and effective.[89]

	Total Year 2004	Total Year 2005	Total Year 2006	Total year 2007	01/01– 31/03/2008
Total number of case investigations of which the Network has been informed [1]	301	203	165	150	42
—of which COM cases	101	22	21	10	2
—of which NCA cases	200	181	144	140	40
Cases in which an envisaged decision has been submitted by NCAs during the period indicated [2]	32	76	64	72	12

[1] Case investigations started whether by an NCA or by the Commission.
[2] Cases having reached the envisaged decision stage; only submissions from the NCAs under article 11(4) of Council Regulation (EC) 1/2003 of 16 December 2002 on the implementation of the rules on competition laid down in articles 81 and 82 of the Treaty.

Figure II—EU Competition Case Investigations 2004–08[90]

[88] See Report on Competition Policy 2006, COM(2007) 358 <http://ec.europa.eu/comm/competition/annual_reports/> accessed 12 June 2008.
[89] Bundesverband der Deutschen Industrie eV and Freshfields Bruckhaus Deringer, *Private Enforcement in the European Union—Pitfalls and Opportunities* (2007).
[90] <http://ec.europa.eu/comm/competition/ecn/statistics.html> accessed 12 June 2008.

THE CHALLENGES AT EU LEVEL: DIFFERENT NATIONAL MODELS

In considering the debate at EU level, it is important to bear in mind that, as mentioned above, the context in which formal collective redress mechanisms operate is that of each Member State's national civil justice system, and that each such national system is not only different but evolving. To the extent that there is an insufficient number of competition or consumer protection damages claims, the primary cause lies within national systems. However, many Member States are reviewing their civil justice—and ADR—systems, and reforming them. Hence, it would be reasonable to expect that both planned reforms and natural evolutions in procedures and funding systems for litigation and alternative dispute resolution would have an impact on the number of national damages claims, whether they are brought individually or collectively.

Further, as also noted above, considerable liberalisation of funding systems is occurring at national level, in an unplanned fashion, and the consequences are not understood. Although contingency fees are banned, ways are being found to circumvent the rules, but, in any event, there is a general trend towards liberalisation of the rules and involvement of private funding for litigation. Success fees are permitted in virtually every Member State. Of considerable significance is the fact that third-party investors are swiftly emerging, who will fund claims in return for a share of the profits. Furthermore, these developments in procedures and in funding systems are not occurring in a coordinated or controlled fashion in Member States.

What can be said at this stage of the enquiry is that, assuming evidence of need for collective redress exists and the Community possesses legislative competence, there remains a considerable challenge at the present time in proposing a workable method of harmonising the varying national systems. The finding from chapters two and three above is that Member States have adopted very different models towards collective court-based mechanisms and enforcement of regulatory law.

Chapter two found that there are in fact opposing policies on enforcement, based on whether the primary actor is a public or private body. The various models can be summarised as the following:

a) Some Member States have a tradition of strong public authorities that take enforcement action. An example is the UK, with agencies such as the OFT, FSA, HSE, MHRA, trading standards departments (TSDs), etc. The primacy of the public authority is maintained by limiting the ability of consumer organisations to institute actions: an NGO must satisfy criteria to be empowered to act in protecting consumers' legal rights. Indeed, the only consumer organisation currently empowered is somewhat uncomfortable with having an enforcement role.

b) The Nordic model has similarly empowered public officials, namely consumer ombudsmen backed by market courts. Those four states differ in how they have balanced whether the ombudsman's powers are coercive or persuasive, but they are now moving towards more mandatory models, and within 2007–08 all four states will have enacted collective damages actions. Private actions may also be permitted in some states, but might in practice not occur as long as the ombudsman is available to undertake the coordination and persuasive function.

c) In contrast, some Member States have empowered consumer organisations to take a primary role in enforcement of consumer law. The origins of this approach can be different. Germany and Austria have had no federal public enforcement agency until implementing the CPC Regulation, and have traditionally relied on consumer associations to enforce unfair competition and unfair contract terms. Italy's court system has effectively been non-operational for many years, so consumer organisations have developed bilateral negotiated settlements with business as an ADR mechanism. In post-Communist Portugal, the consumer organisation filled a gap and offers effective ADR-type solutions, on limited funding.

d) In addition to the above mechanisms for enforcement of public law, courts will increasingly recognise a need for rules to enable them to process multiple similar claims efficiently. Hence, collective claim rules have been introduced in England and Wales, Sweden, Spain, Germany and Italy. Some of these are horizontal and some are at present are only sectoral and experimental.

e) ADR is increasingly popular, both at national and Community level. Various different approaches exist, involving either courts or voluntary mechanisms, and with either binding or non-binding determinations.

The Leuven study noted that all common law jurisdictions have collective actions for damages,[91] but identifies a gap in the collective redress system of many Member States, where there are multiple consumers with a very small claim, especially where the business is not willing to solve the problem through direct negotiation. In common law jurisdictions, individual consumers have standing to commence group claims, whereas in continental jurisdictions there is a preference for consumer organisations or arms of government to bring actions rather than individuals.[92] No homogeneous criteria and thresholds exist that require the authorities to act against a business systematically harming consumers. Although some Member States are experimenting with collective actions, in many states consumers may have no means to obtain redress.

Given this complex and evolving picture at both national and Community level, the 2007 Leuven study[93] stated the important conclusion that

---

[91] J Stuyck *et al*, 'Study on alternative means of consumer redress other than redress through ordinary judicial proceedings' (Catholic University of Leuven, 17 January 2007, issued April 2007) para 384.

[92] *Ibid*, para 396.

[93] *Ibid*. This important study includes reports from every EU Member State plus the United States, Canada and Australia on the range of existing mechanisms.

alternative dispute resolution in the EU Member States is a *continuum*, encompassing the main elements of direct negotiation, mediation/arbitration, small claims procedures, collective actions for damages and actions for injunctions. Indeed, the Leuven study found that a multitude of ADR methods are used. Every Member State has put in place a unique mix of the different mechanisms, encompassing formal court procedures, direct negotiation between parties, mediation and arbitration, and the emerging collective mechanisms. From this divergence, the report concluded that it is far from self-evident to identify one 'ideal' ADR system. The ADR matrix in a state must be seen in the context of the organisation and effectiveness of its ordinary judicial proceedings, the way its business is structured and consumers are organised, the effectiveness of market surveillance, the way administration operates at local and general levels, and historic, political, socio-economic, educational and cultural factors. The report's conclusion is that no particular method or mix of ADR processes or techniques can be put forward as the best choice from a consumer perspective. It is neither possible nor appropriate to propose a ranking. The implication is that political choices must be made.

THE POLICY OPTIONS FOR EUROPE

This picture of diversity presents a challenge for European harmonisation. To the extent that there is, or will be, an internal market problem to be solved, it is difficult to identify a single model that is the best solution. Further, the existing national models seem to be almost impossible to harmonise, at least without considerable violence to national structures. In addition, the position is not static, since many Member States are engaged in ongoing evaluation and development of their mechanisms. The period is one of experimentation, with some uncertainty. This means that data on which to draw conclusions on the comparative effectiveness of different models may not be available for some years. Perhaps above all, the problem is not intrinsically a European one alone: the global economy and the internet make this an international issue, with rogue traders deliberately locating themselves outside the EU.

Thus, it is unrealistic to contemplate full harmonisation of a collective redress mechanism. There was also recognition that, because of the differing and evolving national models, any solution put forward at EU level will have to be limited to cross-border claims only.[94] Instead, an approach based on establishing minimum standards and mutual recognition would logically be an achievable way forward. However, it would

---

[94] See Speech by Diana Wallis MEP at <http://www.dianawallis.org.uk/resources/sites/82.165.40.25-416d2c46d399e8.07328850/Lisbonspeech.pdf> accessed 12 June 2008.

also be advisable to put in place mechanisms to capture data about the differing national and cross-border issues and solutions, so that a full comparative assessment can be made in time. Such data may be influential in identifying which models are more effective or appropriate than others, and so lead not only to better practice, but also to possibly closer harmonisation of national systems.

Despite evidencing some frustration at not being able to proceed more speedily, Commissioner Kuneva indicated at the Lisbon conference on 10 November 2007 a need to proceed in a careful and logical fashion on the issue of collective redress in relation to consumer protection. She announced two initiatives. First, she established a Consumer Market Scoreboard[95] to identify markets and sectors that are not functioning well, so that any future action can tackle real problems. The Commission will collect national data on small claims, ADR and other mechanisms. This initiative is of considerable significance in marking a shift in emphasis from an approach to policy-making that moves from an instrument-led approach (harmonisation of mechanisms) towards an evidence-based approach founded on measuring outcomes. The initiative requires access to data in order to be successful, and the Commission's proposal was to undertake sector-specific research, applying five main indicators, namely complaints, price levels, satisfaction, switching and safety.

Secondly, she announced consultation to agree on a set of benchmark criteria that should be used to evaluate the various different models. Such a comparative exercise was designed to lead to the development of consensus on which national models do or do not work best, and hence ought to lead to greater alignment of national systems through appropriate internal reforms.

There was a general realisation at the Lisbon conference that enough examples of problems have been put forward that a case can be made that damages are not being delivered in mass situation, either at all or effectively enough. On the other hand, the Commission accepted that it will need to assemble proper data so as to satisfy its internal requirements to undertake an impact assessment and careful cost-benefit analysis. This means that formal proposal from the Commission will not emerge before at least late 2008. So the approach will be incremental, with a limited first step, and will be intended to develop further over time, after all the Member States have adopted at least a minimum benchmark standard (half have no internal mechanism at present).

---

[95] Communication from the Commission: Monitoring consumer outcomes in the single market: the Consumer Markets Scoreboard, COM(2008) 31, 29 January 2008 <http://ec.europa.eu/consumers/strategy/com2008_31_final_en.pdf> accessed 12 June 2008.

The benchmarks suggested by Commissioner Kuneva at Lisbon, on which public consultation followed, were as follows:[96]

a) The mechanism should enable consumers to obtain satisfactory redress in cases which they could not otherwise adequately pursue on an individual basis.

b) It should be possible to finance the actions in a way that allows either the consumers themselves to proceed with a collective action, or to be effectively represented by a third party. Plaintiffs' costs for bringing an action should not be disproportionate to the amount in dispute.

c) The costs of proceedings for defendants should not be disproportionate to the amount in dispute. On the one hand, this would ensure that defendants will not be unreasonably burdened. On the other hand, defendants should not for instance artificially and unreasonably increase their legal costs. Consumers would therefore not be deterred from bringing an action in Member States which apply the 'loser pays' principle.

d) The compensation to be provided by traders/service providers against whom actions have been successfully brought should be at least equal to the harm caused by the incriminated conduct, but should not be excessive as for instance to amount to punitive damages.

e) One outcome should be the reduction of future harm to all consumers. Therefore, a preventive effect for potential future wrongful conduct by traders or service providers concerned is desirable—for instance by skimming off the profit gained from the incriminated conduct.

f) The introduction of unmeritorious claims should be discouraged.

g) Sufficient opportunity for adequate out-of-court settlement should be foreseen.

h) The information networking preparing and managing possible collective redress actions should allow for effective 'bundling' of individual actions.

i) The length of proceedings leading to the solution of the problem in question should be reasonable for the parties.

j) Collective redress actions should aim at distributing the proceeds in an appropriate manner amongst plaintiffs, their representatives and possibly other related entities.

These draft benchmarks, whilst constituting a useful first attempt, suffer from a number of drawbacks. The most significant issue is that, as drafted, they are insufficiently wide to encompass and allow evaluation of all possible models, and read as if the model in contemplation is a court-based representative damages claim. It is not proposed critically to examine the benchmarks at this point. The issue will be returned to in chapter nine in the context of wider policy issues. However, the general direction of travel is moderately clear, and there is a hint that there may be significant common ground between stakeholders.

---

[96] <http://ec.europa.eu/consumers/redress_cons/collective_redress_en.htm> accessed 12 June 2008.

CONCLUSION: SUMMARY OF THE ISSUES

It will be seen that the question of collective redress arose in both the consumer protection and competition fields. However, collective redress was not otherwise on the Commission's agenda for civil justice systems or dispute resolution mechanisms generally at EU level. DG Justice was only brought into the debate during 2007 after DG COMP and DG SANCO had made considerable progress in developing their own policy. Although the issue of collective redress has previously been mooted in other sectors, such as product liability, employment or environmental protection, the intensity of debate in those sectors on whether a need for reform exists has been comparatively low. All the political running and debate relates to competition enforcement and consumer protection, and usually takes place within each of those areas without much reference to the other.

These two areas, competition and consumer protection, have various features in common, even if such features are not exclusive to those areas. First, both relate to the effective functioning of the internal market. Secondly, both involve challenges of overcoming adverse economic effects for consumers, although economic effects also arise in the competition sector for SMEs and perhaps any size of competitor or customer. Thirdly, they both raise issues of access to justice for potential claimants who may not have much resource nor be able to take the risk of litigation. Fourthly, such matters in turn raise issues over the effectiveness and efficiency of national civil justice systems. Indeed, the White Paper on competition damages constitutes a strong implicit criticism of the state of many national civil justice systems.

Fifthly, significant issues arise of the effectiveness of enforcement of regulatory provisions. An important difference here is that the competition sector has enforcement authorities at both Commission and national levels, whereas enforcement in the consumer protection sector effectively exists only at national level, and cross-border mechanisms are based on the principle of mutual recognition between the Member States, with the Commission having a somewhat limited coordinating function.[97] Thus, the Commission acts as a regulatory enforcement authority in competition, but not in consumer protection, and experiences considerable frustration in the former role at a growing workload, perceived insufficient resources, ongoing serious infringements of competition law and sensitivity to criticism by comparison with the largely privatised enforcement position in the United States.

Sixthly, questions arise in both areas of the extent of any need for enhanced enforcement or compensation, and hence for new approaches to collective redress. Overall, some big questions arise about the effectiveness

---

[97] Regulation (EC) 2006/2004 on cooperation between national authorities responsible for the enforcement of consumer protection laws, [2004] OJ L364/1.

of enforcement mechanisms and of civil justice systems, both individually and in how they might inter-relate. These issues will be examined in greater detail in the following chapters.

Notwithstanding various issues in common between consumer protection and competition law, there are some important differences, particularly on enforcement structure and policy. Cafaggi and Micklitz observe that, unlike the United States, there is no preparedness to establish European regulatory agencies akin to the US federal enforcement agencies, which have pan-EU enforcement powers. Constitutional and political restrictions constrain any such federal-like development, and Member States remain seized of enforcement powers.[98] This is true as a general political matter and applies in the consumer protection field, but the Commission does have an overriding enforcement role for competition. It has, perhaps surprisingly, taken major steps to devolve enforcement to Member States.

On enforcement policy, no unified or harmonised approach has been identified in consumer protection at Member State level. Many Member States may have no published enforcement policy. However, the Commission's policy on competition infringements is clear, and strongly influences national approaches, being explicitly based on general deterrence through large fines based on some effectively arbitrary view of turnover, and taking little if any regard of the level of detriment actually caused.

Finally, it is curious that, despite wide-ranging debate, no convincing empirical evidence of need, or the scale of need, of problems that would be solved by collective mechanisms has yet been produced in the consumer protection field. The argument for need in relation to competition damages is somewhat confused: whilst there were historically few damages cases, there is clear evidence of a recent increase in cases, which may continue to rise, although it may be that the position is highly variable across Member States. The proposals in the Commission's 2008 damages White Paper are intended to produce a rise in the number of cases across the Community through a minimum harmonisation approach to reform of various procedural rules, and these can be expected to increase litigation generally. So, there is insufficient evidence that would objectively satisfy the Commission's requirement under impact assessment rules for evidence of cross-border need and evaluation of the costs and benefits of the relevant policy options.[99] However, there is no body of evidence that would establish the baseline incidence of cases that are not currently brought, from which the effectiveness of any reforms could be measured.

---

[98] F Cafaggi and H-W Micklitz, 'Administrative and Judicial Collective Enforcement of Consumer Law in the US and the European Community', European University Institute Working papers, Law 2007/22.

[99] See the latest draft Impact Assessment Guidelines 2008 <http://ec.europa.eu/governance/impact/consultation/docs/ia_guidelines_draft_text_final_en.pdf> accessed 2 July 2008.

This reveals a serious flaw in European policy-making. The White Paper's Impact Assessment Report and Impact Study both seek to satisfy the requirement of an impact assessment by identifying options and then assessing, at great length, the benefits and risks of each option. The options can logically be ranked into a sequence, with those at one end having the greatest benefits and risks (increased compensation and increased deterrence, but increased abuse) and those at the other end with least benefits (minimal increased compensation and deterrence, but no abuse). At the first end, it is then claimed that there may be *over*-deterrence or the like. The flaw in this is that there is no empirical quantitative matrix against which to fix what in fact constitutes *over* or *under* compensation, compliance, deterrence, abuse or any other parameter. The options may reveal qualitative comparisons between them, but there is no empirical evidence that would identify where on the sliding scale we are now, where we want to be, or whether any changes introduced have moved us to. Governmental institutions make policy on the back of large studies, but this is an example, which may be far from rare, of where a more thorough investigation is called for. Such an investigation may be more difficult and take longer, but given its inherent importance is worth doing. Meanwhile, policy is made in a vacuum, without any useful risk assessment.

8

The Policy Rationales for and Goals of Collective Redress

G IVEN THE FINDING that there is a divergence and proliferation of collective redress mechanisms, it is instructive to take a step back and ask the fundamental question: what are we trying to achieve by using these mechanisms? Each different mechanism seems to have its own different origins and policy rationales. The fundamental questions are: what are the basic policy objectives, are they justifiable, and can they be improved on or rationalised? This chapter examines the following principal issues: improving access to justice, enhancing the economy, litigation as enforcement, deterrence, enforcement theory and restorative justice.

ACCESS TO JUSTICE

The basic claim is that collective actions are perceived as tools for increasing access to justice.[1] The argument is that consumers or small businesses with small-value claims cannot afford to bring them, and may not even know that they have suffered loss or how to claim compensation. The result would be that loss is uncompensated and those who cause it have had an unjust windfall. The classic position is illustrated in the JJB Sports and French mobile phones case studies, in which the premise is that a large

---

[1] For the US situation, see S Issacharoff, 'Governance and legitimacy in the law of class actions' [1999] S. Ct. Rev. 337; and D Rosenberg, 'The regulatory advantage of class action' in K Viscusi (ed), *Regulation through litigation* (Brookings Institution Press, 2002) 244 *ff*. For Europe, see J Stuyck *et al*, 'Study on alternative means of consumer redress other than redress through ordinary judicial proceedings' (Catholic University of Leuven, 17 January 2007, issued April 2007). This statement of the aim and rationale of collective actions in the consumer field is important since, unlike the position in the competition field, the rationale for collective mechanisms is not primarily presented on 'regulatory enforcement deficit' grounds, but on basic access to justice grounds, on the premise that there is a gap in access to justice resulting from the high cost of resolving many consumer claims, and particularly multiple claims which have low value. The role of collective actions in deterring infringements of competition law, of 'private enforcement' and the German 'skimming off of excess profits' in unfair competition law, are noted later but not so strongly emphasised: para 381.

number of consumers suffered loss, but very few opted in to collective proceedings brought on their behalf by consumer organisations.[2]

Underlying this situation is the fact that there is a cost to bringing a legal claim, so if similar claims can be pooled then the total costs can be shared. This produces the result that the cost-benefit ratio increases for any claim which can be aggregated with others. Accordingly, some claims that would have been too expensive to pursue in relation to the risk and potential return would become economically viable if included in a cost-sharing group. This would be so irrespective of the size of the claim, but may be particularly relevant for small claims. Every legal system produces an inevitable cost-benefit threshold for any case, below which it is uneconomic to pursue a claim. The cost-benefit ratio is also affected by the relative strength of a case or a defence and its complexity.

In addition to the cost-benefit ratios for each participant is the achievement of judicial economy, or an efficient use of the state's resources within its civil justice budget. This issue influenced the development of the court-based collective mechanisms analysed in chapter three.

Since most consumer claims involve small amounts, the argument for extending access to justice for multiple similar consumer claims is readily understood. In essence, it is that consumer claims would not otherwise be pursued. Increasing access to justice in smaller value claims through adoption of an aggregation technique has been a constant theme of the discussions at national level. However, the argument becomes more complex and less clear cut. Since the value of some claims is not worth pursuing, it is a feature of European civil justice systems that the pursuit of such claims should not be encouraged. Accordingly, mechanisms such as the 'loser pays costs' rule encourage proportionality of both individual and state resources by encouraging individuals to take account of cost-benefit criteria in disputes. Thus, justice is not regarded as an absolute and unlimited good, and access to justice is made subject to proportionality criteria.

A tendency to rigorousness in such an approach is, however, rightly tempered where multiple similar claims arise, such that a concept of collective justice is seen to rise above that of individual justice. Hence, society may wish to intervene to facilitate access to justice in cases where large numbers of individuals or companies have suffered damage, even though the individual quanta may be small. Again, however, such intervention requires a balance to be struck between justice and proportionality. In addition, the existence of multiple similar situations raises a separate issue of the economic effect of the activity in question: if a small sum has been 'skimmed off' from many people, then the combined effect may be significant and may

---

[2] However, as the JJB Sports and several other case studies show, the popular perception of the merits of a claim can, on further inquiry, turn out to be illusory.

justify taking remedial action. The economic argument here is, of course, a different issue from that of providing individual access to justice, and it is discussed further below. It may well be that the argument for maintaining a balanced market is stronger than that of providing individual redress, in which case issues arise of what type of mechanism is appropriate to produce the desired and proportionate effect.

However, the Leuven study concluded that economic literature in fact reveals no consensus about the cost-benefit justification of collective actions.[3] It noted that potential advantages can be put forward, but so can risks and disadvantages,[4] as is particularly shown in the literature on the US class actions. It also noted that, in 2004, 31.7 per cent of federal class actions were civil rights cases and 20.3 per cent were securities actions. These data highlight the point that it is misleading to generalise about 'class actions', 'collective actions' or 'access to justice' since it is relevant to consider what types of case are intended to be facilitated, and what other types of case might also be facilitated by any changes. In this respect, the issue is a wider one of considering the complete range of formal and informal dispute resolution options that exist within a jurisdiction, and how the overall balance might be affected by change in one aspect.

The balance between costs and benefits in any civil justice system will be affected by many internal factors. In some European states it is recognised that the civil justice system is inefficient, the costs of litigating may be too high and disproportionate, and full access is not provided for some people. In these circumstances not only may a collective mechanism be a means of filling the gap, but it may be seized on by a government, sometimes with loud political fanfares, as a solution to 'access to justice for consumers' whilst in reality masking failure to address the underlying problem with the national civil justice or wider dispute resolution systems. It remains the general current perception in Europe that the threshold balance point of

---

[3] J Stuyck *et al*, above n 1. This is obviously an important statement, although the study did not review the literature, but cited the precedent of the French consumer organisation UFC Que Choisir? investing €500,000 on a damages case against mobile phone operators for overcharging, but only 12,500 consumers (0.6%) opted to join and bring claims (see the French mobile phones case study).

[4] The report identifies a significant concern for consumers of the potential for one interested party to achieve additional gains at the cost of another, notably in the case of legal counsel: para 377. For business, there is the concern about unmeritorious claims, pressure on businesses to settle even bad claims and the risk of bankruptcy. The report claims that mechanisms can be provided to prevent unmeritorious claims, such as having judges assess the claim at an early stage. (It later notes that in Sweden a judge applies a cost-efficiency test at an early stage, and in Australia there is a requirement that the award should exceed the costs: para 393.) It dismisses the bankruptcy risk, stating that it is businesses' failure to adhere to proper standards of conduct that drives bankruptcy, and no bankruptcies have occurred in Canada: para 378. For the legal system, the report dismisses the risk that courts would be overwhelmed, as this has not happened in Sweden, Canada or Australia. (The report does not note the fundamental influence of local funding systems and cost rules on the incidence of claims.)

cost-effectiveness viability is too high in many European civil justice systems in relation to small claims of certain types that arise for many people at the same time because legal costs are too high.

Access to justice is often used as a political slogan. It is quoted in policy papers, but is arguably not a real driver to the changes under consideration in this book. If improving access to justice were really important, Member States would all be modernising their national civil justice systems, such as rules of civil procedure and funding mechanisms.[5] Some Member States have taken some steps to address this issue,[6] but the position is seriously inadequate in others.[7] Perhaps governments regard modernisation of civil justice systems as too complex, expensive and uncertain, so look instead for alternative approaches that may offer quicker fixes, which might attract votes. The slogan of 'increased access to justice' will also be supported by intermediaries in dispute resolution as part of their maximisation of commercial rent-seeking.

Politics has also played another significant part. The involvement of consumer organisations in mechanisms to enhance the enforcement of consumer protection legislation can be seen as a political move to encourage the European consumer movement, and for European institutions to try to create closer links with citizens and voters and make Europe seem to have greater relevance to them.[8]

It is usually thought desirable to encourage private parties to settle disputes between them. The settlement will involve both parties discounting their expectations, depending on the relative strength of each case. The ideal should be equality of arms between the parties, such that the negotiation is not distorted by unequal bargaining power. The bargaining position of individual claimants with small claims against large companies or a government is obviously limited. The position can, however, be reversed in a class action situation. Achieving the right balance here can be a major challenge. One the one hand, genuine claims may not be pursued, and potential defendants may reap large illicit gains. On the other hand, unmerited claims may result in 'blackmail' settlements based on the commercial evaluation of risk.

---

[5] A very significant part of the whole thrust behind the European Commission's attempts to encourage more competition damages claims rests on a serious criticism of the inadequacy of national civil justice systems in providing effective mechanisms.

[6] See a summary at C Hodges, 'Europeanization of Civil Justice: Trends and Issues' (2007) *Civil Justice Quarterly* 1 96–123. 'Cost-effective measures taken by States to increase the Efficiency of Justice: Report prepared by the European Committee on Legal Co-operation (CDCJ) in consultation with the European Committee on Crime Problems (CDPC)', 23rd Conference of European Ministers of Justice, 8–9 June 2000.

[7] Green Paper: Access of consumers to justice and the settlement of consumer disputes in the single market, COM(93) 576, 16 November 1993 57.

[8] Green Paper on European Union Consumer Protection COM(2001) 531, 2 October 2001 9. See also Communication from the Commission to the Council, the European Parliament, the European Economic and Social Committee and the Committee of the Regions: Updating and simplifying the Community acquis, COM(2003) 71, 11 February 2003.

These observations apply to private law claims. The position is made more complex when the private claims process is also intended to cover enforcement of public standards. The traditional approach to public law is that of an all-or-nothing divide between observance and infringement. It is difficult to see how concepts of relative merits (or relative bargaining power) should apply here.

ENHANCING THE ECONOMY

Of great relevance to understanding the current development of the origins and goals of collective redress in Europe is the part that it is perceived to play in regulation of the internal market. This is another example of law as an economic tool, in contra-distinction to as a social tool, such as in following redistributive political policy.[9]

Maintaining the healthy functioning of the market is, of course, the fundamental rationale of EC law. High level EU economic policy[10] is to boost EU productivity, which is some way behind that of the United States, despite the fact that there has been favourable growth in EU employment. The policy is to promote innovation, enhance investment in human, information and communications technology-related capital, foster competition and streamline the regulation of product, labour and financial markets. If research and development (R&D) intensity were to increase from 1.8 per cent of GDP in 2005 to the expected EU level of 2.6 per cent of GDP by 2010, growth in both GDP and productivity would be raised by 0.2 of a percentage point per annum. This effect might be twice as high if favourable cross-border effects are taken into account. Competition is viewed as crucial for both the level and growth rate of productivity.

Improving European competitiveness is currently the primary political priority of the Community, at both European and national level.[11] It is held that competitive markets generate innovation, employment, wealth and peace. Accordingly, maximising competition within the internal market is a major policy. Enlisting consumer power is also invoked in the pursuit of

---

[9] U Mattei and FG Nicola, 'A "Social Dimension" in European Private Law? The Call for Setting a Progressive Agenda' (2007) 7 *Global Jurist* 1 (Frontiers) art 2.

[10] Communication from the Commission to the Council, the European Parliament, the European Economic and Social Committee, the Committee of the Regions and the European Central Bank, The EU Economy: 2007 Review. Moving Europe's Productivity Frontier, SEC(2007) 1507.

[11] Communication from the Commission, Working Together for Growth and Jobs: a New Start for the Lisbon Strategy COM(2005) 24. Communication from the Commission, Common Actions for Growth and Employment: the Community Lisbon Programme COM(2005) 330. Communication from the Commission, Implementing the Community Lisbon Programme: A policy framework to strengthen EU manufacturing—towards a more integrated approach for industrial policy COM(2005) 474, 5 October 2005.

enhancing competition.[12] However, consumer protection per se is a less important policy than pursuit of economic health. This subsidiarity is, indeed, built into the EC Treaty, which treats consumers as economic actors and, therefore, at a fundamental level, places less emphasis on human, social or consumer values than on economic values.

A consequence of this ranking of economic and social policies reveals an insight into why competition law is of greater importance in the Community than consumer protection and access to justice. As discussed above, the amount of detriment suffered by consumers individually as a result of infringements of consumer law is typically small—and it is, of course, their small size that gives rise to the access to justice issue. However, viewed overall, the amount of illicit gain for an infringer may be large, and this may have a significantly distorting effect on the market. The larger the illicit gain, the greater the arguments for intervention, for reasons of both injustice and distortion of the market. Further, a market distortion effect may be greater as a result of infringement of competition law (which is by definition a horizontal control across all market sectors) than as a result of infringement of consumer protection law, because SMEs in addition to consumers may be harmed. SMEs are of considerable market importance to governments, since they are viewed as essential engines of innovation and enhanced competitiveness. These considerations explain why breach of competition law may be of greater economic importance than breach of consumer protection law.

The enhancement of competitiveness has given rise to another important policy, which raises some degree of conflict with the policy that has been indicated for enhancement of competition through collective actions. The 'better regulation' policy seeks to reduce burdens on business through various means.[13] However, the potential for conflict between the policies arises because the competition, access to justice and possibly consumer protection policies are positively aimed at increasing the volume of civil litigation, whereas the 'better regulation' policy would oppose that result. Thus, if collective redress is pursued through court-based collective actions involving private law damages claims brought by lawyers, the risk, following the American precedent of the class actions experience outlined in chapter six above, is that of producing excessive litigation and legal transactional costs, blackmail settlements and punitively high costs for business that would impose significant unnecessary drag on the economy and innovation.[14]

---

[12] Communication from the Commission, Consumer Policy Strategy 200–06. EU Consumer Policy strategy 2007–13, COM(2007) 99, 13 March 2007.

[13] Communication from the Commission, A Strategic Review of Better Regulation in the EU, COM(2006) 689, 14 November 2006. See C Hodges, 'Encouraging Enterprise and Rebalancing Risk: Implications of Economic Policy for Regulation, Enforcement and Compensation' [2007] *European Business Law Review* 1231.

[14] BusinessEurope, Response to the Commission's Green Paper on the Review of the Consumer *acquis* COM(2006) 744 FINAL, 27 May 2007 <http://ec.europa.eu/consumers/

A significant number of the case studies gives rise to concern that the costs of collective claims in Europe are high and disproportionate to the benefit they produce. If this observation holds true on a general basis, it is of considerable concern for Europe in considering what models are appropriate for delivering redress and collective redress.[15] Political statements have been made that the goal is a 'competition culture', not a 'compensation or litigation' culture. Industry and insurers argue that compensation culture is spreading across Europe, that the cost of handling cases has already reached an unacceptable level, and that unnecessary price increases are being passed on to consumers.[16] It will be argued further in chapter nine that the issues boil down to which mechanisms for pursuit of collective redress present what risks.

There is also a market-function issue that is closely related to the access to justice issue mentioned above: construction of a market based on an extensive corpus of harmonised substantive rights and obligations will simply be ineffective if the substantive provisions are unenforceable, and the proper functioning of the market may be seriously undermined if the result is significant non-compliance.[17] It is for this reason that the Commission has turned its attention since around 2000 to improving enforcement and redress mechanisms, as discussed at chapter four.

Whether there is a quantitative difference between the levels of infringement in competition and consumer protection legislation is unknown.

---

rights/responses_green_paper_acquis_en.htm> accessed 3 July 2008. Response to the European Commission's Green Paper 'Damages actions for breach of the EC anti-trust rules' COM(2005) 672, European Justice Forum, (2006) <http://ec.europa.eu/comm/competition/anti-trust/actionsdamages/files_green_paper_comments/european_justice_forum.pdf> accessed 12 June 2008.

[15] The author estimates the following costs payable by companies in the following damages cases, excluding any regulatory proceedings: JJB Sports (£2 million for a settlement of some £18,000 whilst it appears that no consumer suffered detriment); airline fuel surcharge ($70 million with repayments to customers of $200 million); benzodiazepine tranquillisers (£40 million paid by public funds and say £80 million paid between two companies, with no money paid to any claimants); MMR vaccines (£100 million, again split between public funds and companies, with no money paid to any patient); Shell ($30 million for $90 million paid to shareholders); Deutsch Telecom (100 million, the outcome remaining unclear for several years); and Vioxx ($1.2 billion, with $4.85 billion to be shared between some 60,000 Americans). See Table 7 below.

[16] Lloyd's, 'Directors in the Dock: Is Business facing a Liability Crisis?' (2008) <http://www.lloyds.com/NR/rdonlyres/6ADDD9EC-3145-4B38-A7A7-06BBECC161D9/0/360_Directorsinthedock_finalwithlinks.pdf> accessed 12 June 2008. This asserts that in 2004–07, 38% of companies have seen some increase in the number of cases brought against them, 34% have experienced growth in the size of claims, 58% have increased their use of lawyers to manage litigation-related issues, 34% have increased prices to cover the increase in litigation-related spending—and 39% expect to have to do so in the next three years, and over 50% believe that demand for products and services will fall as a result of the economic situation and instability of financial markets.

[17] 'The Internal Market after 1992: meeting the challenge, 1992' (the Sutherland Report) 5 and 35; Green Paper: Access of consumers to Justice and the settlement of consumer disputes in the single market, COM(93) 576, 16 November 1993.

However, there is an important structural difference in the European enforcement mechanisms in these two fields: the Commission's Directorate-General for Competition has a central regulatory and enforcement function, notwithstanding significant recent delegation to national competent authorities, whereas the Consumer Directorate does not. Enforcement of consumer protection law, as with most regulatory law generally, is a matter for Member States. Community case law establishes that Member States that enforce Community law must impose penalties that are effective, proportionate and persuasive.[18] Although consumer protection enforcement is currently coordinated on a mutual recognition basis,[19] there has been an absence of notable evidence of a major deficit in performance.[20] It has certainly been the case in the past few years that the Commission's Directorate-General for Competition has pursued the issue of collective redress with greater zeal than the Directorate-General for Consumer Protection.[21]

The above economic considerations provide the basis for the argument that there is an economic case for taking action to provide collective redress as an important feature of market control and economic policy. Proof that the benefit/cost ratio is favourable is, nonetheless, a necessary requirement for legislative action at European level, and this ought to (but curiously might not be formally required) involve proof of empirical need for action.[22] The current evidence on the extent of any need was referred to above in chapter seven. However, the counter argument is that aggregate litigation involves inherent and large transactional costs and produces over-compensation, both of which would chill rather than enhance economic competitiveness.

REGULATION THROUGH LITIGATION

A further driver has been the argument that litigation can be enlisted as a regulatory instrument. The argument for 'private enforcement' would

---

[18] Case 68/88 *Commission v Greece* [1989] ECR 2965 at [22]–[7]; Case C-326/88 *Anklagemyndighedem v Hansen & Sons I/S* [1990] ECR I-2911; Case C-36/94 *Siesse v Director da Alfandega de Alcantara* [1995] ECR I-3573 at [19]–[21]; Case C-83/94 *Leifer* [1995] ECR I-3231 at [32]–[41]; Case C-341/94 *Allain* [1996] ECR I-4631 at [24]; and Case C-29/95 *Pastoors v Belgium* [1997] ECR I-285 at [24]–[6].

[19] See Regulation 2006/2004 on consumer protection cooperation, discussed in ch 4.

[20] It was for this reason that the Commission began studies in 2007 on the extent of any need in both the competition and consumer areas.

[21] Nevertheless, the more measured approach taken by DG SANCO may prove to be solidly productive in the long term.

[22] Communication from the Commission on Impact Assessment, COM(2002) 276, 5 June 2002; European Commission, 'Impact Assessment Guidelines', SEC(2005) 791, 15 June 2005; and Communication from the Commission on an EU common methodology for assessing administrative costs imposed by legislation, COM(2005) 518, 21 October 2005. An Impact Assessment is to be undertaken before introducing new legislation, which is to assess the costs of a proposed measure and ensure that the benefit/cost ratio is favourable. An influential analysis was OECD, *Regulatory Impact Analysis: Best Practice in OECD Nations* (1997). See S Weatherill (ed), *Better Regulation* (Hart Publishing, 2007).

rest on a conclusion, if it is reliable, that public (regulatory) enforcement is either inadequate to control behaviour on its own or is an inefficient means of doing so. Therefore, the issues that need examination are as follows. First, what is the best way to produce compliance or to control non-compliance, and to rectify non-compliance and its consequences? Secondly, given that both public and private mechanisms are available that may influence behaviour and deliver compensation, what are their relative benefits, costs and risks? Thirdly, is there a gap between the ideal and actual levels of observance of regulatory norms (and of delivery of compensation)? Fourthly, could the gap be significantly closed by enlisting further techniques, such as private litigation? These are questions that involve issues of behaviour and efficiency: there is a mass of economic theory available on this topic, but little application of behavioural science. The economic approach, which seeks to assess costs and benefits, has considerable influence in the competition world, but is vulnerable to an absence of reliable empirical data and to its theory being dislocated from reality.

In the American context, Stephenson has compared the advantages of private enforcement (ie compensation claims) and its disadvantages.[23] He listed the advantages as: more enforcement resources; a check against agencies shirking their responsibilities; and fostering innovative strategies and settlement techniques. He considered the disadvantages to be: inefficiently high levels of enforcement leading to waste of judicial resources and excessive deterrence; direct interference with public enforcement; and diminished democratic accountability of private enforcers.

The argument made in the Green Paper on competition damages was motivated less by concern about delivery of compensation than by rectifying a perceived gap in compliance, which produced a deleterious effect on the market and competitiveness.[24] The argument was that the enforcement resources of the Commission were overstretched and those of national authorities were very variable and in many cases totally inadequate to exercise the powers that had been delegated to them under the 2004 modernisation programme, and that public enforcement is an inefficient mechanism and subject to resource constraints and prioritisation. Hence, the Commission took inspiration from US colleagues in proposing to enlist private resources as at least an adjunct to public enforcement. An increase

---

[23] MC Stephenson, 'Public Regulation of Private Enforcement: The Case for Expanding the Role of Administrative Agencies' (2005) 1 *Virginia Law Review* 91 93. His conclusion was that agencies themselves should make, or at least be involved in, the decision on whether to permit private enforcement, rather than legislators.

[24] Green Paper: Damages actions for breach of the EC anti-trust rules, COM(2005) 672, 19 December 2005 <http://eur-lex.europa.eu/LexUriServ/LexUriServ.do?uri=COM:2005:0672:FIN:EN:PDF> accessed 12 June 2008; and Commission Staff Working Paper: Annex to the Green Paper 'Damages actions for breach of the EC anti-trust rules', SEC(2005) 1732, 19 December 2005 <http://ec.europa.eu/comm/competition/anti-trust/actionsdamages/sp_en.pdf> accessed 12 June 2008.

in damages claims brought on the basis of infringement of regulatory norms would, it was argued, increase pressure for compliance through deterrence. This extra private deterrence would also relieve pressure on public finances. From the economic perspective, the pressure for commercial operators to internalise the costs on non-compliance can equally well be produced by fines imposed by public authorities (whether enforcement authorities or courts) as by damages and costs imposed by private actions. Both mechanisms involve the same medium, money, and pressure is therefore both equal and transferable between the two mechanisms.

The US enforcement system is almost the mirror image of the European approach. In the United States, the norm is 'private enforcement', which exceeds public enforcement by a ratio of nine to one in competition cases.[25] In contrast, competition enforcement in Europe has always been through public entities, as has consumer protection. Private enforcement will only be produced to any significant extent if there are significant financial incentives for private actors, or more often intermediaries. However, the counter argument is that such a system produces significant abuse through conflicts of interest (especially between nominal losers and intermediaries), very large transactional costs, disproportionate reward for actors (high damages and windfall amounts inflated by the possibility of punitive damages and high costs of defending) and intermediaries (fees that are excessive by European standards), and excessive deterrence and compensation (blackmail settlements).

There is a profound distinction between the US and European approaches to the balance that is struck between public and private law remedies and procedures. In the United States, the Constitution and individuals have, from the origins of the country, placed enormous emphasis on the ability for individuals to assert their individual rights, and have distrusted distant powers. Kagan has vividly charted these as leading to a system of 'adversarial legalism', with free access to civil courts and unimpeded right to challenge the powers and actions of federal government and big corporations.[26] Scholars have also referred to the confusion which can result when private litigation is used as a substitute for regulatory or enforcement action by public authorities.[27]

---

[25] Anti-trust cases filed in US District Courts 1975–2007, Table 5.41.2007 shows that the percentage of private to public cases has only fallen below 90% in 9 of the 32 years (mainly around 1990, lowest 83.4%) and since 2000 the trend has risen to 96.6% in 2007 (*Sourcebook of Criminal Justice Statistics Online* <http://www.albany.edu/sourcebook/pdf/t5412007.pdf> accessed 12 June 2008). See ch 6 above.

[26] RA Kagan, *Adversarial Legalism* (Harvard University Press, 2001); and RD Kelemen, 'Suing for Europe. Adsversarial Legalism and European Governance' (2006) 39 *Comparative Political Studies* 1 101–27.

[27] The chaotic situation in the United States is illustrated by various contributions to WK Viscusi, *Regulation through Litigation* (AEI-Brookings Joint Centre for Regulatory Studies, 2002).

Allegations are made of inconsistent decisions between public agencies in enforcement of regulatory law and decisions of courts in liability cases.

Private actions, of course, pre-dated public enforcement. The right to assert claims in the courts is a Constitutional and deeply cultural phenomenon in the United States, and this individualism and respect for the authority of the courts, coupled with mistrust of federal authority and of large corporations, has led to a socio-political system in which adversarial legalism plays a fundamental role.[28] When US federal agencies emerged in the twentieth century,[29] they adopted a policy of only taking enforcement action in a small minority of cases, and this was able to avoid significant expense. Although extensive regulation exists in the United States, the vast majority of 'enforcement' is left to private actors enforcing private law rights through the civil justice system. Indeed, the system is widely referred to as 'private enforcement' through 'private attorneys general'. Accordingly, private anti-trust enforcement[30] and tort law have far greater significance and lead to a far greater volume of litigation in the United States than in Europe. This policy explains the extensive financial incentives that are in place to encourage private action (acting as traditional 'bounty hunters') and to impose 'public sanctions' such as punitive damages.[31] Hence, the relationship between public and private law is quite different in the United States to the position in Europe. In short, the US model relies primarily on *private* enforcement, whereas the European on model relies primarily on *public* enforcement. The US legal system therefore provides a number of causes of action that can be pursued by private actions in relation to what might be public law provisions in other systems.

Regulatory theory postulates that a risk with any regulatory system is that the regulator may be captured by those it regulates, and become biased and ineffective. There is a widely articulated view in the United States that the federal agencies are ineffective and not to be trusted because they are politicised and captured. This view, whether true or not, reinforces

---

[28] RA Kagan, *Adversarial Legalism. The American Way of Law* (Harvard, 2001).

[29] The first significant anti-trust legislation was the Federal Sherman Act of 1890, and the Food and Drug legislation emerged from the 1930s. There are various powerful US federal regulatory agencies, such as the Department of Justice, the Securities and Exchange Commission, the Federal Trade Commission, the Food and Drug Administration, and the Office of Safety and Health Administration. All of these agencies are largely mirrored in European states. The extent of regulatory requirements and the agencies' powers of market surveillance, inspection, enforcement and sanctioning are also extensive and largely similar in both the United States and the EU (whether at state or EU levels).

[30] CA Jones, *Private Enforcement of Anti-trust Law in the EU, UK and USA* (Oxford, 1999).

[31] A recent example is a class action filed in January 2008 against The Dannon Company, Inc over allegedly falsely claiming hat certain yoghurts had 'clinically' or 'scientifically proven' health benefits. See <http://www.csgrr.com/dannon> accessed 12 June 2008.

reliance on the civil courts as a safety valve against abuse.[32] However, capture by business is hardly a realistic contemporary description of the leading European competition or consumer protection agencies.

Further insights relate to the role and enforcement of competition law. The tradition of US anti-trust law is based on *encouraging* competition, and a claimant has the burden of showing that a restraint of trade is *unreasonable*.[33] Private actions, predating public enforcement, have consistently been encouraged as the primary mode of controlling monopolies. Whilst court judgments require evidence of wrongdoing, claims that are settled on commercial grounds may not. In contrast, the EU tradition emphasises public enforcement seeking to control dominant firms from *infringing* controls, as an integral part of the overriding policy of market integration.[34] Thus, the models are structurally profoundly different.

In introducing the illegality of anti-trust behaviour into the United States in 1890, the Sherman Act[35] and its successor the Clayton Act[36] expressly provided for private rights of action for damages by any injured person in addition to criminal penalties, and that private claims would recover triple damages.[37] The Clayton Act also gave private parties the right to seek injunctive relief,[38] and any finding of violation in civil or criminal proceedings would be prima facie evidence of violation in private civil cases.[39] The US Government has throughout maintained a restricted policy on taking enforcement action.[40] Recent enforcement policy by the US Department of Justice has been to concentrate on cases involving larger amounts of commerce and seeking increased fines and longer terms

---

[32] The film 'Erin Brokovich' is based on the premise that the environmental authorities failed to control dumping of toxic materials and that 'justice' was only available through a damages class claim in the civil courts.

[33] K Bernard, 'Private Damages Actions: A US Perspective on Importing US Damages Actions to the EU' (eCCP, October 2007) <http://www.globalcompetitionpolicy.org/index. php?&id=579&action=907> accessed 12 June 2008. The Supreme Court's invention of the 'Rule of Reason' was significant, under which only unreasonable restraints of trade were forbidden under the statute: *Standard Oil Co of New Jersey v United States*, 221 US 1 (1911).

[34] CA Jones, *Private Enforcement of Anti-trust Law in the EU, UK and USA* (Oxford, 1999).

[35] Act of 2 July 1890, c 617, 25 Stat. 209, 15 USC §§1–7.

[36] Act of 15 Oct.1914, c 323, 38 Stat. 730, 15 USC §§12–27.

[37] Clayton Anti-trust Act s 7 as amended. Ironically, the triple damages rule was inspired by the English Statute of Monopolies, 21 Jac. I, c 3 (1623). There has been criticism that triple damages are objectionable in principle as constituting unfair windfalls to claimants of penalties that should be paid to the state: *Conference of Studio Unions v Loew's, Inc*, 193 F 2d 51, 55 (9th Cir. 1951). It is widely considered that the US rule on recovery of triple damages and the EU rule on interest on judgments being backdated to dates of infringement effectively equate to similar sums of money: see CA Jones, n 34 above, ch 19.

[38] Sect. 26, 15 USC §16.

[39] Sect. 5(a), 15 USC §16(a).

[40] The Justice Department received no funds at all for enforcement for the first 13 years: HB Thorelli, *The Federal Anti-trust Policy: Origination of an American Tradition* (Baltimore, 1954) 588 and 590.

of imprisonment.[41] As a result, it is said that in the United States 'private enforcement' represents the vast majority of all anti-trust court actions: a ratio of private to public cases ranging from 10 to 1 to 20 to 1,[42] at least 90 per cent in the 1980s[43] and arguably over 95 per cent recently.[44]

Thus, it can be understood why European civil justice systems do not contain features such as 'loser pays' rules, contingency fees, juries (trial by peers) or punitive damages. All of these features have some logic as parts of a legal system, such as that of the United States, which emphasises unrestricted access to courts, private enforcement and mistrust of public or large power. Statements by US trial lawyers consistently emphasise their intended dual role as both providers of compensation to those injured and as rooters out of corporate and governmental wrongdoing.[45] Private enforcement is argued to provide both compensation and deterrence,[46] to save scarce public funds on enforcement, to maintain enforcement from the vagaries of fluctuations in the attitude of public enforcers or public budgetary processes, and to help ensure the stability of legal norms by preventing abrupt transitions in enforcement policy.[47] Against this, there have been arguments on the relative efficiency of public versus private enforcement.[48] The important 'Georgetown Study' of 1985,[49] which examined some 1,900 cases filed in five US District Courts in 1973–83, found that the system included both bad cases and meritorious cases that

---

[41] AK Bingham, 'The Clinton Administration: Trends in Criminal Anti-trust Enforcement', Address to Corporate Counsel Institute (San Francisco, California, 30 November 1995).

[42] CA Jones, n 34 above, 85.

[43] S Salop and L White, 'Private Anti-trust Litigation: An Introduction and Framework' in L White (ed), *Private Anti-trust Litigation: New Evidence, New Learning* (Cambridge, Mass., 1988) 3.

[44] K Bernard, 'Private Damages Actions: A US Perspective on Importing US Damages Actions to the EU' (eCCP, October 2007) <http://www.globalcompetitionpolicy.org/index. php?&id=579&action=907> accessed 12 June 2008. CA Jones, n 34 above, states that the number of private actions between 1985 and 1999 was in the range of 600 and 1,000 annually.

[45] See MD Hausfeld and AL Hertzfeld, 'A Victim's Culture' [2007] EBLR 1209.

[46] See Supreme Court judgments in *Perma-Life Mufflers, Inc v International Parts Co*, 392 US 134, 139 (1968); *Brunswick Corp v Pueblo Bowl-O-Mat, Inc*, 429 US 477 (1977); and *Illinois Brick v State of Illinois*, 431 US 720, 748 (1977) (Brennan J dissenting).

[47] JC Coffee, Jr, 'Rescuing the Private Attorney General: Why the Model of the Lawyer as Bounty Hunter is not Working' (1983) 42 Md. L. Rev. 215, 217.

[48] See, arguing that there has been too much litigation at too high a cost, resulting in 'over-deterrence', K Elzinga and W Breit, *The Anti-trust Penalties: A Study in Law and Economics* (New Haven, Conn., 1976); W Schwartz, *Private Enforcement of the Anti-trust Laws: An Economic Critique* (Washington, DC, 1981); and arguing for a dual public and private approach, V Sarris, *The Efficiency of Private Anti-trust Enforcement: The 'Illinois Brick' Decision* (New York, 1984) 53–4 and 63.

[49] 'Georgetown Study of Private Anti-trust Litigation: Papers from the Georgetown Conference on Private Anti-trust Litigation' (Airlie House, Virginia, 8–9 November 1985). Later versions of some papers are in L White (ed), *Private Anti-trust Litigation: New Evidence, New Learning* (Cambridge, Mass., 1988) 3.

would not have been brought by the government, whilst around 80 per cent of cases settled after two years, and of those that proceeded to trial the plaintiffs won less than 30 per cent.

A further consequence of empowering private enforcement is that the scope for conflicting decisions between courts that make decisions on damages (exacerbated by the reliance of juries in the United States) and regulatory decisions made by public authorities. This tension has, for example, given rise to an ongoing dispute over whether decisions by the Food and Drug Agency on the approval of medicines as being safe, and the mandating of advertising and scientific information given out, may be ignored in a private damages action. After many years of uncertainty in decisions involving medicines, only recently has the US Supreme Court held in *Riegel v Medtronic, Inc* that an express provision in a 1976 federal enactment that no state should impose any requirement relating to the safety of effectiveness of devices that differed from any of the new federal regulatory provisions meant that state tort claims were pre-empted.[50] The court noted that since the tort law system was shown by 1970 to be unable to manage the risks associated with dangerous devices, Congress stepped in and made medical devices subject to regulatory control by the Food and Drug Agency.

Given that the European approach to enforcement is based primarily on public authorities, any argument that such a mechanism is ineffective and should be replaced or significantly enhanced by private litigation would need strong empirical justification. A fundamental issue is what level of enforcement deficit exists in Europe at present. There is currently little evidence of much of a gap in the consumer protection field (but there is concern over the effects of increasingly global trading and need for jurisdictional silos to be overcome so as to address cross-border issues). In the competition field, there may be increased enforcement activity at national level in some Member States through the modernisation programme and an increasing number of damages claims, and these trends may not yet have stabilised to reach a plateau, but the position may be patchy across Member States. However, the evidence for the level of undiscovered competition law infringements, wrongly claimed to be 15 to 20 per cent, is in fact entirely lacking.

Law and economics scholars have traditionally held that regulation and litigation are substitutes in the task of deterring potentially harmful conduct.[51] Prevailing normative models suggested that as public regulation increases, private litigation should decline, and vice versa. However, recent

---

[50] *Riegel v Medtronic, Inc*, Supreme Court of the United States, judgment of 20 February 2008.

[51] D Wittman, 'Prior Regulation Versus Post Liability: The Choice Between Input and Output Monitoring' (1977) 6 J. Legal Stud. 193; S Shavell, 'A Model of the Optimal Use of Liability and Safety Regulation' (1984) 15 RAND J. Econ. 271; and S Shavell, 'Liability for Harm Versus Regulation of Safety' (1984) 13 J. Legal Stud. 357.

analysis of US data by Helland and Klick found no evidence to support the proposition that public regulation and private regulation function as substitute channels to deter harmful behaviour.[52] Instead, their analysis of an extensive data set, from 130 insurance companies and describing 748 cases filed between 1992 and 2002, revealed that litigation and regulation tend to piggy-back on each other. The general likelihood of facing a suit appeared to be predicted by general factors of a suit's success. There was a positive and statistically significant relationship between the likelihood that an insurer would face a class action and the fraction of class actions in a given state that led to a plaintiff recovery at trial. The authors commented that the piggy-back effect makes sense in a world in which decisions on litigation and regulation are not made by a selfless social planner, but rather by self-interested individuals.

Accordingly, these findings indicated levels of care and response that exceed the socially optimal level.[53] They also undermine the theory that private damages actions will identify infringements that are not identified by public authorities and hence fill any enforcement deficit. The desire would be that private actions would be of the 'stand alone' type, whereas the empirical evidence indicates that the profit motive that drives private action dictates that a significant number of cases pursued will merely be parasitic on the easy 'follow on' situations and so duplicate public enforcement, producing clustering of cases and duplicative financial consequences and costs.

As seen above, much of the debate about collective redress in Europe has taken place in the separate but related contexts of competition law and consumer protection law. Recent research has compared the US and UK positions on corporate law. In a thorough and wide-ranging examination, Armour, Black, Cheffins and Nolan noted that private enforcement of shareholder rights is, contrary to popular belief, not necessary to safeguard strong securities markets.[54] They contrasted the existence over many years of extensive private litigation and class actions in this sector in the United States, compared with virtually no private litigation in the UK. They also noted that the vibrant UK capital and corporate market was far from being bereft of effective controls, which comprised a matrix of public formal and informal mechanisms and private informal and self-regulatory mechanisms.[55]

---

[52] E Helland and J Klick, 'The Tradeoffs between Regulation and Litigation: Evidence from Insurance Class Actions' (2007) 1 *Journal of Tort Law* 3 art 2.

[53] *Ibid.*

[54] J Armour, B Black, B Cheffins and R Nolan, 'Private Enforcement of Corporate Law: An Empirical Comparison of the US and UK', Working Paper (Universities of Cambridge, Oxford and Texas, 2008).

[55] See also J Armour, 'Enforcement Strategies in UK Corporate Governance: A Roadmap and Empirical Assessment', European Corporate Governance Institute, Law Working Paper No 106/2008 (2008). The principal methods of public enforcement are the Financial Services Authority, the Financial and Reporting Review Panel, the Takeover Panel and the Department

Whatever the state of the argument on the extent to which private damages may be a surrogate for public enforcement, the European Commission clearly signalled in 2008 that its internal debate was resolved as a matter of policy in favour of regarding enforcement as achieved through public authorities, and that the primary role of private mechanisms was the delivery of compensation rather than deterrence. The White Paper adopted the guiding principle of preserving strong public enforcement of competition law, and the creation of an effective system of private enforcement of competition law by means of damages actions would be intended to complement, but not replace or jeopardise, public enforcement.[56] It followed that the adoption in Europe of financial mechanisms that would enable private mechanisms to be a primary enforcement mechanism, such as punitive damages and minimal risk private funding of litigation (contingency fees, no loser pays), would not be relevant under the European approach.

DETERRENCE AND BEHAVIOUR MODIFICATION

Deterrence is claimed to be the primary purpose of enforcement of competition law.[57] All of the recent European policy papers on collective redress in competition law invoke the primary justification that private actions are necessary to provide enhanced deterrence (given the supposed enforcement deficit referred to above).[58] The underlying assumption is one of economic theory, namely that forcing companies to internalise the costs of non-compliance produces deterrence, which produces compliant behaviour. On this theory, the response to a compliance deficit is to increase the size of the financial penalties on those who are identified and/or to identify more infringers than are identified by the authorities.

---

for Business Enterprise and Regulatory Reform. Armour details informal private enforcement methods including the Combined Code on Corporate Governance, and pressure arising from shareholder removal of directors, from the possibility of takeovers, from shareholder decision rights, and from share ownership and voting patterns.

[56] Staff Working Paper paras 17 and 18. See ch 7 above.

[57] OECD, 'Report on the Nature and Impact of Hard Core Cartels and Sanctions against cartels under National Competition Laws' DAFFE/COMP(2002)7 (9 April 2002).

[58] Notably Green Paper: Damages actions for breach of the EC anti-trust rules, COM(2005) 672, 19 December 2005; and Commission Staff Working Paper: Annex to the Green Paper 'Damages actions for breach of the EC anti-trust rules', SEC(2005) 1732, 19 December 2005. In the UK, see recently Department of Trade and Industry, 'Consultation Paper: Representative Actions for Damages' (2006); and Office of Fair Trading Discussion Paper, 'Private actions in competition law: effective redress for consumers and business' (April 2007). The UK authority has published a survey of companies and private advisers, who viewed private actions as the least effective aspect of the competitive regime in achieving compliance, and gave the encouragement of private damages actions as amongst one of the most frequent response for encouraging compliance: Office of Fair Trading, 'The deterrent effect of competition enforcement by the OFT' (2007) <http://www.oft.gov.uk/advice_and_resources/resource_base/consultations/deterrent> (registration required) OFT962 and OFT963.

The Commission is under an express requirement to 'ensure that its action has the necessary deterrent effect':[59]

> Fines should have a sufficiently deterrent effect, not only in order to sanction the undertakings concerned (specific deterrence) but also in order to deter other undertakings from engaging in, or continuing, behaviour that is contrary to articles 81 and 82 of the EC Treaty (general deterrence).

Accordingly:

> The Commission will pay particular attention to the need to ensure that fines have a sufficiently deterrent effect; to that end, it may increase the fine to be imposed on undertakings which have a particularly large turnover beyond the sales of goods or services to which the infringement relates.[60]

As discussed above, enforcement of public law measures is normally a matter for individual Member States, and this is the case in relation to EU consumer protection measures. However, the Commission has an enforcement role in some limited situations, possibly the most extensive and significant of these being competition law.

The Commission's enforcement policy in relation to articles 81 and 82 EC is substantially founded on the imposition of fines.[61] The Commission's fines are based on a supposedly arithmetic approach to the level of economic effect that the illegal activity had on the market: the basic amount is related to a proportion of the value of sales of the entity (usually up to 30 per cent), depending on the degree of gravity of the infringement, multiplied by the number of years of infringement.[62] The basic amount may be increased or decreased where there are aggravating or mitigating circumstances, the latter including instances such as where the undertaking terminated the conduct on being found out, or owned up voluntarily.[63] It will be seen that such an approach is inherently imprecise, and it is acknowledged to involve a wide margin of discretion,[64] subject to the final sum not exceeding 10 per cent of the undertaking's turnover.[65]

---

[59] Guidelines para 4, citing Joined Cases 100–103/80 *Musique Diffusion française and others v Commission* [1983] ECR 1825 at [106].

[60] Guidelines para 30. Analysis of the 39 cartels listed by the Commission between 1999 and 2006 reveals that once the gravity of the offence is set, the basic fine increases most as a result of the application of the 'sufficient deterrence' uplift an duration: C Veljanovski, 'Cartel Fines in Europe: Law, Practice and Deterrence' (2007) 30 *World Competition* 65–86.

[61] Guidelines on the method of setting fines pursuant to art 2392)(a) of regulation 1/2003, 2006/C 210/02: hereafter 'Guidelines'. Undertakings can also be accepted.

[62] Guidelines paras 19 and 21.

[63] Guidelines paras 27–34. Commission Notice on Immunity from fines and reduction of fines in cartel cases, 2006/C 298/11.

[64] Guidelines para 2.

[65] Guidelines para 32.

Thus, the approach of the Commission, which is mirrored by many national authorities,[66] is that, in basing the fine on an undertaking's turnover, competition enforcement is aimed at maximising *general* deterrence. Fines for an individual who has been caught are multiples of the risk that an individual who has been caught will be caught. Since the approach is founded on the undertaking's financial data and performance, as affecting the value of commerce affected, it does not directly take into account the level of damage actually suffered by other undertakings, customers or the market, nor the gain actually made by the undertaking.[67] It does not take into account the undertaking's actual behaviour in the past and future, such as the extent to which the undertaking could have influenced the activity, or intended not to commit the offence,[68] or has taken remedial steps to avoid repetition. In short, the fine has been described as an arbitrary administrative figure.[69] Fines are approached solely as economic levers, and whilst the behavioural consequence of deterrence plays a strong part in the official process, it is curious that deterrence is not approached in behavioural terms (individual deterrence), but on the basis of economic theory (general deterrence).

Further, imposing financial penalties on the basis of the effect on the market as a whole (inflated by a general deterrence factor) *and* providing for individuals to claim damages (where it appears few previously did so) would seem to impose a high overall financial consequence on infringers. The consequence may be arbitrary as between those who suffer either public and/or private penalties, and introduce an individual deterrent effect that would seem very high indeed and a general deterrent effect that is also high. Such a system appears both unjust to individuals and to provide unquantified consequences. The immediate issue is that there would be no coordination between the public penalty and private damages. This would continue for as long as the public system is focused on macro economic effects (the notional effect on the market and the level of undetected infringements) without taking account of amounts paid on private compensation.

---

[66] But not all: it is unnecessary to undertake a comprehensive analysis for the purposes of this inquiry into collective redress. However, it was said the 'calculation of gain is crucial for sanctioning policy' in 'Sanctioning pursuant to the Norwegian Competition Act', English translation of a report by the committee of the Norwegian Competition Authority (25 March 2001) <http://www.konkurransetilsynet.no/iKnowBase/Content/415989/SANCTIONING%20PURSUANT%20TO%20THE%20NORWEGIAN%20COMPETITION%20ACT.PDF> accessed 12 June 2008. The reasons given were that gain should be a starting point for estimation of optimal sanctions, being more effective, and furthering deterrence.

[67] As can be seen from the JJB Sports Plc case study, in some cases there may be no gain for the undertaking, which highlights issues of justice and proportionality.

[68] Save that evidence of negligence is a mitigating factor; Guidelines para 29, third indent.

[69] C Veljanovski, 'Cartel Fines in Europe: Law, Practice and Deterrence' (2007) 30 *World Competition* 65–86.

The fines imposed by the Commission since 1990 have consistently increased very significantly, and exponentially since the 2004 Guidelines, in pursuit of increased deterrence: see Figures III and IV.

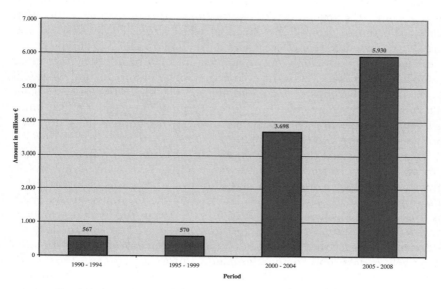

Figure III—Fines Imposed by the EU Commission 1990–2008[70]

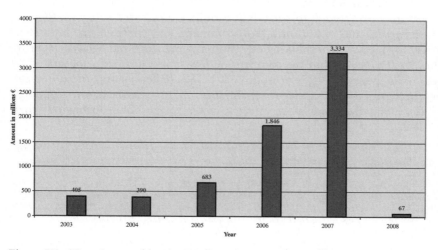

Figure IV—Fines Imposed by the EU Commission 2003–08[71]

[70] <http://ec.europa.eu/comm/competition/cartels/statistics/statistics.pdf> accessed 12 June 2008, not corrected for subsequent court judgments.
[71] *Ibid.*

As a general rule, it may be argued that deterrence will be effective in modifying behaviour if the measure imposed is sufficiently large. This view underlies the Commission's power to increase fines above a level that would otherwise be justified as a response to an individual wrongdoer, so as to enhance the general deterrent effect.[72] Further, it may be argued that fines are a simple penalty, the effects of which are easily understood and may have some deterrent effect, again depending on the level at which they are imposed. Yet how high must a financial penalty be in order to produce compliance that is universal, or even acceptably widespread, and what will be the undesirable consequences of doing so? The imposition of ever higher financial penalties may indeed produce an enhanced deterrent effect, but it is a blunt and uncalibrated instrument that may not address the source of a problem and may also impose higher detriment than is necessary.

It has been argued that the arbitrary 10 per cent cap on fines is far too low to provide deterrence at the margin and introduces an asymmetry in punishment between diversified and non-diversified firms.[73] Industry has also argued that the level of fines imposed by the Commission is so high as to be stifling business and innovation, rather than encouraging competition.[74] Wils has argued that competition law must impose sanctions on individuals because the level of fines imposed on employers that is required effectively to deter anti-competitive conduct by their employees far exceeds the employers' ability to pay,[75] and because an employer may not in reality be capable of adequately controlling the behaviour of its agents (see an illustration of this below).[76]

The above approach to behaviour modification, based solely on theories of economics and of authoritarian 'command and control', has been challenged by more recent thinking on criminal sentencing and behavioural psychology. Debate within the competition law world has been dominated by economic theory and this orthodoxy is being challenged by criminological, psychological and socio-legal scholarship.[77] The essence of the argument is: first, that there are more effective ways of modifying behaviour than

---

[72] It is interesting to consider the effect of potential breach of individual rights and the principle of proportionality if an individual is subject to an excessive punishment *pour encourager les autres*.

[73] I Bos and MP Schinkel, 'On the Scope for the European Commission's 2006 Fining Guidelines under the Legal Maximum Fine' *Journal of Competition Law and Economics* 2(4) 673.

[74] N Tait, 'Brussels urged to cut cartel fines' *Financial Times* (24 January 2008).

[75] It has been argued that the level of fines imposed would need to increase significantly in order to achieve deterrence of price-fixing: C Veljanovski, 'Cartel Fines in Europe: Law, Practice and Deterrence' (2007) 30 *World Competition* 65–86.

[76] WJ Wils, 'Is criminalisation of EU competition law the answer?' in KJ Cseres, MP Schinkel and FOW Vogelaar (eds), *Criminalisation of Competition Law Enforcement: Economic and Legal Implications* (Edward Elgar, 2006) 81.

[77] AP Reindl, 'How strong is the case for criminal sanctions in cartel cases?' in KJ Cseres, MP Schinkel and FOW Vogelaar (eds), *Criminalisation of Competition Law Enforcement: Economic and Legal Implications* (Edward Elgar, 2006) 116.

solely relying on financial penalties; secondly, that if fines are set at a level that is intended to have deterrent effect, whatever that may be thought to be, they may exceed what is just and impose excessive costs on the undertaking that chill economic competitiveness rather than enhance it; and, thirdly, that the current Guidelines take little or no account of the infringer's actual behaviour and the extent to which it may be more efficiently modified in future by imposition of another penalty. In short, there may be a better way of achieving the desired result. This issue will now be considered further.

REGULATORY AND ENFORCEMENT THEORY

There has been a considerable flowering of scholarship on regulation and enforcement over the past 20 years. Regrettably, its fruits have not been effectively applied in some areas of law-making or in debates on the use of compensation mechanisms as surrogate mechanisms for public enforcement. The following account is a brief overview of some of the most significant findings of regulatory research in the English-speaking world. The purpose of examining this literature is to enable an informed approach to be taken to the role that compensation systems may play, if any, in affecting behavioural compliance, deterrence or enforcement. Quite a few widely held views are challenged by this line of inquiry.

Scholarly research has established a number of theories of regulation and enforcement, and more may yet be propounded. It is clear that a public authority should adopt a judicious mixture of the individual enforcement policies and techniques that have been identified, depending on the circumstances of the industrial sector and situation that it has to control and other factors such as its budget.[78] It is unlikely that any single enforcement technique will be the optimal solution on its own. In particular, reliance on traditional theories of punishment, which stress retribution and deterrence, are by themselves unlikely to be either effective or efficient. This finding alone has significant implications in raising questions over the supposed benefits of collective compensation mechanisms.

The following are some of the leading theories on enforcement policy. First, as discussed above, a traditional authoritarian policy would be to impose penalties at a high level on every infringer in order to increase deterrence on the individual and others. Baldwin argues that a punitive approach:

> ... assumes a model of corporate behaviour that is unrealistic and, as a result, brings a number of dangers. It may fail to make best use of self-regulatory capacities,

---

[78] A rational and economic basis for the exercise of discretion by enforcement authorities was set out by P Fenn and CG Veljanovski, 'A Positive Economic Theory of Regulatory Enforcement' (1988) *The Economic Journal* 98 1055. For the problem of 'creative compliance' by those regulated, see D McBarnet, *Crime, Compliance and Control* (Ashgate, 2004).

it may chill healthy risk-taking and it may make successful regulation more, rather than less, difficult to achieve.[79]

Regulatory strategies should, therefore, seek to involve pro-active regulatory strategies based on persuasion, negotiation and cooperation:

> ... that seek to link legal sanctioning to broader corporate incentive regimes, and involve demands that companies themselves generate explicit assurances on how they will proceed towards compliance.[80]

Secondly, 'responsive regulation' defines an 'enforcement pyramid', with a peak sanction of removal from society (removal of liberty or licence to operate) and a broad base of simple, low-key discussions, which regulators would progress depending on the extent of non-compliance by the regulated business.[81] The theory advocates that a regulator should have strong powers (a big stick), which would rarely be used in relation to genuine businesses, which would usually prefer to comply with clear requirements, guidance and persuasion. Instead, rogues could be targeted by enforcement resources, involving increasingly serious penalties. Ayers and Braithwaite argued that regulatory compliance was best secured by persuasion in the first instance, with inspection, enforcement notices and penalties being used for more risky businesses further up the pyramid. The essence of the enforcement approach depends on a 'tit for tat' response to regulatees' behaviour.

Thirdly, 'smart regulation' places more emphasis on *ex ante* controls such as screening or considering whether resort to non-state controls, such as trade associations, professions or corporations themselves, will work better than state sanctioning.[82]

Fourthly, 'risk based' regulation seeks to target public resources on enforcement to areas where the evidence base indicates there is greatest risk. This is UK Government policy:[83]

> Globalisation increases competition and places a premium on a strong business environment. As markets become more competitive, it is important to do more to ensure the right conditions are in place to enable businesses and individuals to respond to new opportunities and incentives ...

> It is no longer true that most businesses, if unregulated, will act irresponsibly. Well-informed consumers, corporate social responsibility, organised labour, pressure and interest groups have all encouraged businesses to take measures to

---

[79] R Baldwin, 'The New Punitive Regulation' (2004) 67(3) MLR 351–83.

[80] *Ibid*, 382.

[81] I Ayers and J Braithwaite, *Responsive Regulation* (Oxford, 1992); and J Braithwaite, *Restorative Justice and Responsive Regulation* (Oxford, 2002).

[82] R Johnstone, 'Putting the Regulated Back into Regulation' (1999) 26 JLS 378.

[83] HM Treasury, Better Regulation Executive, and Cabinet Office, 'Implementing Hampton: from enforcement to compliance' (November 2006).

reduce risk to society. For example, the number of reported non-fatal injuries at work has fallen by 68 per cent between 1974 and 2006.

In this context it is clear that regulatory regimes need to adapt to the changing world of the 21st century. The Hampton principles[84] outline a risk-based approach to regulation which sits in line with a world where competition is fierce, consumers are better informed, and resources are scarce.

The UK Treasury Review of 2006 also stated:

> Underpinning the review's recommendations on advice was the principle that regulators should also support economic progress by only intervening where there was a clear case for protection, as well as taking action to encourage economic growth where possible. Therefore it is important that regulators take responsibility for any costs that they bring to businesses and work to minimise them. Regulators should also be held accountable for their effectiveness.[85]

This approach also accords with European policy on 'better regulation', which is based on improving competitiveness through reducing unnecessary burdens on business, and increasing efficiency in public services including enforcement.[86] Thus, the UK's 'Hampton' approach seeks to reduce the administrative burden of regulation on business, while maintaining or improving regulatory outcomes. An important finding by Hampton was that regulators lack effective tools to punish persistent offenders and reward compliant behaviour by business.[87]

Similarly, the UK Consumer Strategy[88] included a strong recapitulation of the responsive regulation and risk-based enforcement approaches:

> We have rejected the old-fashioned idea that businesses need to be routinely regulated and inspected to keep them in line. The vast majority of businesses want to act responsibly. The pressure to attract and retain customers is a far more powerful and effective incentive on business to act with integrity and responsibility than anything Central or Local Government can do.[89]

---

[84] The Hampton Report proposed that the regime should be simplified and enforcement be made subject to a risk assessment approach. P Hampton, 'Reducing administrative burdens: effective inspection and enforcement' (HM Treasury, 2005).

[85] HM Treasury, Better Regulation Executive, and Cabinet Office, 'Implementing Hampton: from enforcement to compliance' (November 2006) 32.

[86] S Weatherill, *Better Regulation* (Hart Publishing, 2007); and C Hodges, 'Encouraging Enterprise and Rebalancing Risk: Implications of Economic Policy for Regulation, Enforcement and Compensation' [2007] EBLR 1231.

[87] Hampton, above, para 7.

[88] Department of Trade and Industry, 'A Fair Deal for All. Extending Competitive Markets: Empowered Consumers, Successful Business' (2005). See also Department of Trade and Industry, 'Extending Competitive Markets: Empowered Consumers, Successful Business', Consultation Document (2004); and Department of Trade and Industry, 'Empowering Consumers in the Enterprise economy: The Enterprise Bill Consumer Measures' (2002).

[89] Department of Trade and Industry, 'A Fair Deal for All. Extending Competitive Markets: Empowered Consumers, Successful Business' (2005) para 1.2. A 2008 survey of 180 lawyers in

Our consumer regime will be based on the principle of proportionate, risk-assessed and evidence-based intervention. Instead of regulating and inspecting on a routine all-inclusive basis, we want to see more effort targeted on rogue traders, and a lighter touch for mainstream responsible businesses.[90]

More recently, Baldwin and Black have expounded a fifth approach, namely that to be 'really responsive' regulators have to be responsive not only to the compliance performance of the regulate, but also in five further ways: to the undertakings' own operating and cognitive frameworks (their 'attitudinal settings'); to the broader institutional environment of the regulatory regime; to the different logics of regulatory tools and strategies; to the regime's own performance; and finally to changes in each of these elements.[91] Baldwin and Black assert that a 'really responsive' approach is holistic in combining the other approaches within a rational framework in differing ways depending on the circumstances, so as to deliver the five functions of enforcement (namely *detecting* undesirable or non-compliant behaviour, developing tools for *responding* to that behaviour, *enforcing* those tolls and strategies on the ground, *assessing* their success or failure and *modifying* approaches accordingly).[92] This approach highlights the need to assess performance not only on a continuing basis, but also in a manner that responds to shifts in objectives and regulatory environments, if the regime is to cover previously uncontrolled behaviour and respond to changing circumstances.

Many official documents not only fail to take these enforcement policy issues into account, but also to identify which infringers are being targeted on the spectrum of rogues to responsible operators. Whichever theory or combination of theories on enforcement may be preferred, it is clear, first, that compensatory mechanisms in private law fall a long way short of complying with the requirements of an effective or efficient enforcement regime and, secondly, that the competition authorities' enforcement policy adopts exclusively the traditional 'command and control', deterrence-based approach.

The scholarly literature on regulation also stresses the importance of performance assessment in evaluating enforcement practice. It may be difficult

---

multinational companies in five large EU states found that the most important considerations when considering whether to contest or settle a dispute are: impact on corporate reputation; financial cost of losing; and impact on relationships and customers (Lovells, 'The Shrinking World: Research Report: how European in-house counsel are managing multinational disputes' (2008)).

[90] *Ibid*, para 1.9.

[91] R Baldwin and J Black, 'Really Responsive Regulation' (2008) 71(1) *Modern Law Review* 59–94. This article includes an overview of the arguments and literature on the four theories outlined above.

[92] See R Baldwin and J Black, *A Review of Enforcement Measures* (Defra, 2005).

enough for some public authorities to develop robust systems of performance assessment, but it will be far more difficult to achieve through a system of diffuse private litigation. These findings are, of course, directly relevant to the issues of compliance with competition and consumer protection law that are at the core of the collective redress debate. They indicate that the current absence of reliable empirical evidence of non-compliance in areas such as competition and consumer protection law is highly unsatisfactory.

Regulatory policy requires there to be consistency over time in the identity and policies of a regulator. Such consistency cannot be achieved where regulatory functions are split between multiple regulators, especially if they are infrequent repeat players. Thus, 'private enforcement' (regulation through litigation, where regulatory consistency is threatened by multiple claimants and court decisions) and the empowerment of both consumer organisations (if they duplicate public agencies, or if the exist as multiples) is simply inconsistent with the 'better regulation' policy, since they would lead to proliferation of both enforcement authorities and decisions. One might save the direct costs of a public regulator, but at the expense of increasing costs to the general economy through increased litigation.[93] Private litigation could not comply with a policy of being 'risk-based enforcement': it would not have its flexibility, and, indeed, it may be arbitrary. However, the use of ombudsmen would be consistent with the policy.

The implication of regulatory theory is that a punitive approach towards every infringement is ineffective, either as a rational use of state resources or as in influencing compliant behaviour. Indeed, an enforcement policy that relies simply on imposing financial penalties is thoroughly unsophisticated. This conclusion clearly undermines the case for relying on damages as a quasi-punitive means of 'private enforcement'. Responsive regulation is based on a sociological approach to controlling behaviour and challenges orthodox economic theory head on. The claim to 'deterrence' by use of an economic lever alone is open to attack as insufficiently flexible and imprecise. It is entirely plausible that a sufficiently large financial penalty may deter and produce behavioural change, but are there other ways of achieving the same effect? Might alternatives be cheaper or more effective? Is the economic penalty aimed at the correct target?

As an illustration of the last question, one might take the case of a cartel. Imposing a financial penalty on a corporation or individual that does not wish to comply (eg a rogue) will not bring about behavioural change. Imposing a financial penalty on a corporation or individual who does wish to comply (eg a public company with a reputation and shareholder value to protect) may produce behavioural compliance, especially if the fine is

---

[93] C Hodges, 'Competition enforcement, regulation and civil justice: what is the case?' (2006) CMLR 43 1381–407.

large enough. However, it ultimately hurts the shareholders, employees and customers of the company, who end up paying in some form. Imposing any penalty on a corporation should produce the effect of encouraging it to have and operate internal compliance systems, if these are not too expensive. Imposing a penalty on the managers responsible for overseeing the operation of a system should lead to correct oversight and operation of the system, but does not guarantee compliance by those who are subject to the system and work within it. In order to achieve total compliance, it is necessary to cover all of these aspects, not forgetting imposing a penalty on those who work within a system. Several of these steps are not covered when DG Competition merely imposes a fine on a corporation. Although the existence of a compliance programme is a mitigating factor under the Guidelines, it can be argued that a corporation's ability or efforts to produce internal compliance, and hence likelihood of reoffending, should play a more central role in setting a penalty.

There is considerable behavioural psychological evidence of the impact of deterrence in relation to influencing the behaviour of *individual* offenders,[94] but little in more complex groupings,[95] such as *companies*.[96] There is in fact little evidence on what levers in a corporate context modify the behaviour of most human instigators of law-breaking. If large fines are imposed on the company, its share price and brand reputation may fall, and hence its senior management may lose their jobs and its shareholders (eg public pension funds) may lose value, and this may encourage the company to have and operate internal compliance systems, but this lever does nothing to deter or modify the behaviour of the perpetrating salesmen directly.

The above analysis should illustrate that penalties that are intended to produce behavioural compliance should be targeted at the right individuals. Really responsive regulation indicates how best to influence behaviour in the most effective manner, depending on the circumstances. There may be no need to waste resources on enforcement of a responsive company—a tap on the shoulder may suffice. The person who taps should ideally have a big

---

[94] J Darley, S Fulero, C Haney and T Tyler, 'Taking Psychology and Law into the Twenty-First Century' in JRP Ogloff (ed), *Psychological Jurisprudence* (2002) 35–59; and P Robinson and JM Darley, 'The Role of Deterrence in the Formulation of Criminal Law Rules' (2003) *Georgetown Law Journal*.

[95] JM Darley, AL Teger and LD Lewis, 'Do Groups Always Inhibit Individuals Responses to Potential Emergencies' (1973) *Journal of Personality and Social Psychology* 26 395–9; and AG Greenwald and MR Banaji, 'Implicit Social Cognition: Attitudes, Self esteem, and Stereotypes' (1995) *Psychological Review* 102 4–27.

[96] C Davis, 'Making Companies Safe: What Works', presentation at Health and Safety Executive Conference on 'Director Responsibility for Health and Safety: What the evidence shows' (London, 6 October 2005). This study notes that members of senior management in responsible companies are significantly influenced by the twin goals of regulating positive company credibility and preventing the loss of that credibility, and employees who may have directly caused the offending behaviour may not be singled out as the cause.

stick, but need not use it. In contrast, a recidivist or perpetrator of serious infringements should, as a matter of responsive regulation, be subject to a more serious penalty, perhaps involving deprivation of licence or liberty.

Whether one accepts really responsive regulation or not, what is clear from this analysis is that relying on arguments that a civil justice system may be a flexible or effective tool in achieving behavioural compliance is no longer a sophisticated or reliable policy. It may be true that fines or damages produce some level of 'deterrence', but there are other or better policies. The implication is that those states and agencies that rely on financial forces (whether fines or damages) as mechanisms for influencing behaviour may be pursuing ineffective policies in promoting deterrence and compliance. If true, this argument would significantly undermine the argument for 'private enforcement'. Further empirical research is needed on this issue. Meanwhile, a new approach to enforcement policy needs to be considered, since it may offer a transformational solution to issues of collective redress.

PENALTIES AND SANCTIONS THEORY: RESTORATIVE JUSTICE

It is not proposed here to embark on an exhaustive analysis of criminal sentencing policy. The focus is on the potential for linkage between sanctions for breaches of regulatory law and provision of compensation. If no such linkage is appropriate, then certain options for developing collective redress will not be fruitful. However, the example of the Nordic consumer ombudsmen and others suggests that the activities of public authorities may include provision of compensation as well imposition of appropriate public sanctions. The introduction of some linkage into competition enforcement policy may prove transformational.

A new theoretical approach towards linkage between public and private consequences of illicit behaviour has recently emerged in the UK. The UK has mandated that the purposes of all criminal sentencing are as follows:[97]

a) the punishment of offenders;
b) the reduction of crime (including its reduction by deterrence);
c) the reform and rehabilitation of offenders;
d) the protection of the public; and
e) the making of reparation by offenders to persons affected by their offences.

These purposes have been developed further by Professor Richard Macrory in his review of penalties,[98] which is being adopted as binding on public

---

[97] Criminal Justice Act 2003 s 142.
[98] R Macrory, *Regulatory Justice: Making Sanctions Effective* (HM Treasury, 2006).

enforcement agencies.[99] Macrory's initial aim was to ensure a level playing field for all businesses through removing any financial gain from failure to comply. Most breaches would face penalties that are quicker and easier to apply while there would be tougher penalties for rogue businesses that persistently break the rules. Greater flexibility would be introduced so as to provide regulators with better deterrence options and therefore encourage compliance from business.[100]

Macrory identified Six Penalties Principles:

1. Aim to change the behaviour of the offender;
2. Aim to eliminate any financial gain or benefit from non-compliance;
3. Be responsive and consider what is appropriate for the particular offender and regulatory issue, which can include punishment and the public stigma that should be associated with a criminal conviction;
4. Be proportionate to the nature of the offence and the harm caused;
5. Aim to restore the harm caused by regulatory non-compliance, where appropriate;[101] and
6. Aim to deter future non-compliance.

It will be seen that Principles 1, 2, 5 and 6 are also claimed to be functions of private collective actions. Accordingly, what is the inter-relation between the purposes and functions of public penalties and private compensation systems? Is there undue duplication here? Should not the two systems be harmonised in some way?

If removal of illicit profit is a function of public penalties and can adequately be achieved by that system, there is little justification for duplicating resources on private restitution. Macrory recommends that courts

---

[99] The Macrory Principles are included in Department for Business Enterprise and Regulatory Reform, 'Regulators' Compliance Code' (2007) <http://www.berr.gov.uk/files/file45019.pdf> accessed 12 June 2008 para 8.3. The Code is made under s 22 of the Legislative and Regulatory Reform Act 2007. The Regulatory Enforcement and Sanctions Bill will also give public enforcement officers an extended armoury of powers, in part implementing the Macrory Report, including compensation orders. However, the OFT has yet to modify its deterrence-based approach to competition enforcement. A review in 2008 of the extent to which the OFT had adopted the Hampton and Macrory approaches contained no evaluation of compliance with the Macrory Penalties Principles: Better Regulation Executive, 'Effective inspection and enforcement: implementing the Hampton vision in the Office of fair Trading' (2008). This is curious in view of the formal target that the OFT delivers direct financial benefits to consumers of at least five times that of its cost to the taxpayer: OFT, 'Approach to calculating direct benefits to consumers' (2008) OFT955. Adoption of a restorative justice approach as suggested here could deliver considerably in excess of a multiple of five.

[100] Surprisingly, the OFT does not mention the Macrory Review or its conclusions, but repeats an old-fashioned approach to deterrence and removal of illicit profit as being a justification for private collective actions: OFT Discussion Paper, 'Private actions in competition law: effective redress for consumers and business' (April 2007).

[101] This is the 'restorative justice' approach: referred to by Macrory at 69. See also J Braithwaite, *Restorative Justice and Responsive Regulation* (Oxford, 2002).

should take explicit actions, separately from imposing fines or other penal-ties, to address the level of illicit gain by an offender.[102] Indeed, a sentenc-ing court or enforcing authority would not, in fact, be able to apply the principles in any circumstances in which loss or damage had been caused to individuals or companies without taking into account, in the required calculation on eliminating any financial gain, the extent to which any private law compensation had been paid or was achievable. In addition to a question of logic in the calculation, to approach public penalties and private reparation separately might, ironically, not be fair to defendants (since 'double or excessive recovery' might apply). However, it might also fail to take advantage of opportunities to maximise effective and cost-efficient enforcement.

A Macrory approach to enforcement would start with a decision by a regulator that an infringement had occurred. If no infringement had occurred, the public authority would not take the matter further and some other mechanism would be required to cover provision of compensation. It may be that the regulator might have more important priorities, or limited resources, or have been captured by its regulatees, or made bad decisions on priorities. A regulator should always have discretion on which cases to take and on how to approach them. Accordingly, a regulator might not cover every case in which individuals might seek redress and some other option would be required.

On the other hand, if an infringement had occurred, a regulator would continue to take the usual enforcement steps. In this case, an important question in relation to establishing what level of sanction might be appro-priate is 'how bad' the infringer had been. In other words, it should be an essential step in the sentencing process, and hence a function of a regulator, to identify the value of the illicit gain obtained by an infringer. Identification of how much a company has benefited from illegal activity provides the opportunity for overseeing restitution of that sum.

These considerations point towards a new understanding of the bal-ance between private and public action in this field. In order to fulfil their sentencing function, courts would not only take account of the extent of illicit gains, but also make appropriate orders for restitution.[103] Penalties would then be able to be fixed as a separate item, adopting an appropri-ate policy, such as restorative justice or risk-based sentencing (likelihood of repetition). If the compensatory amounts involved were too low, or

---

[102] In the UK context this would involve profit orders and confiscation orders. See Better Regulation Executive, 'A Code of Practice for Regulators—A Consultation: Consultation on the Regulators' Compliance Code and the scope of the Code and the Principles of Good Regulation' (Cabinet Office, May 2007). See also A Ogus, 'Better Regulation—Better Enforcement' in S Weatherill (ed), *Better Regulation* (Hart Publishing, 2007).

[103] See ch 2 for the public enforcement powers in the UK.

presented complex issues in identifying claimants or achieving returns, or costs would be too high, the restitutionary function would be dispensed with and the state would keep any illicit gains. Punitive penalties could be imposed where relevant, but would accrue to the state and not be windfalls to individuals.

It may be objected that it is not the function of public authorities to arrange private law damages, and to do so would cost too much and delay resolution of the public enforcement process. One possible response to the cost issue is that the public authority could recover the costs involved in its work in arranging for compensation, in the same way that any successful private party would be entitled to costs in litigation. Some public administrations may be uncomfortable with cost recovery, on the basis that it is the function of public authorities to pass any fines on to public treasuries rather than keep them, in order to avoid allegations that their activities might be motivated by income-generation as opposed to disinterested priorities.

However, there are various approaches to how public authorities might play an effective role in achieving restitution of losses by citizens. In addition to having express powers to order that compensation be paid, or to ask a court for an order to that effect (as in the developing Nordic system), a public authority could merely make available its evidence or use its persuasive power.

PRACTICAL EXAMPLES

Various examples are available in the case studies in which a restorative justice response towards payment of compensation could have been adopted. One long-established method is the continental *partie civile* procedure, in which a private individual may 'piggy back' as a private party on a public prosecution, and gain compensation without incurring the costs of taking independent private action.[104] The recent Nordic approach of empowering consumer ombudsmen to combine enforcement and restitutionary compensation is an extension of such an approach, providing further fusion. The approach was also adopted, even if unintentionally, by the UK's Ofcom in its response to a GMTV consumer overcharge 'skimming off'.[105]

---

[104] M Chiavario, 'Private Parties: The Rights of the Defendant and the Victim' in M Delmas-Marty *et al* (eds), *European Criminal Procedures* (Cambridge University Press, 2005) ch 10.

[105] A similar approach was adopted in a number of subsequent similar cases against other companies; see Sanctions Committee Adjudications dated 8 May 2008 at <http://www.ofcom.org.uk/tv/obb/ocsc_adjud> accessed 12 June 2008.

Case Study: GMTV Competitions

The television channel GMTV Ltd included viewer competitions in its programmes between August 2003 and February 2007. The communications regulator, Ofcom, found GMTV to be in breach of various provisions of the Broadcasting Code (not conducting competitions fairly, not describing prizes accurately, and making rules clear and appropriately made known) and the ITC Programme Code (not retaining control of and responsibility for the service arrangements, including all matters relating to their content). Ofcom imposed a fine of £2 million and required GMTV to broadcast a statement of Ofcom's findings on three occasions.

In its decision,[106] Ofcom stated that the financial penalty would have been higher had GMTV not put in place such an extensive programme of reparations and remedies. These included that GMTV did not intend its competitions to be conducted in a way that was not compliant with the relevant codes. GMTV cooperated willingly and fully with Ofcom's investigation and had taken extensive steps to remedy the consequences of the breaches. These included:

a) the decision by its managing director to take full responsibility for GMTV's failures and therefore to resign from his post, along with the Head of Competitions;

b) offering refunds on a potential 25 million entries, a number which it believed was 'certainly far higher than the number of people who would have actually been disenfranchised';

c) setting up a free-phone number for viewers to request a claim form, which could also be downloaded from its website;

d) promoting the refunds every day on GMTV for a five-week period and taking out advertising for the refunds in national and regional newspapers;

e) holding 250 new free prize draws, each with a £10,000 prize, for all entrants on the refund database, at a total cost of £2.5 million; and

f) making a £250,000 donation to the children's charity ChildLine, to take account of the data it had not been able to retrieve.

In addition to the reparations and remedies, GMTV had introduced improved internal codes of conduct and compliance for any future premium rate activities.

---

[106] Decision of Ofcom Content Sanctions Committee, 26 September 2007 at <http://www.ofcom.org.uk> accessed 12 June 2008.

The result in this case should have produced,[107] as a result of voluntary action by the company: restitution of loss to consumers; an improved system to guard against future non-compliance; retribution for those held responsible; and imposition of a public penalty. The public penalty was based on both responsive and restorative approaches: if the risk of future infringement was low, there was a low need for individual deterrence. General deterrence was provided by swift publication of these actions. However, this methodology would not be possible under an approach in which general deterrence is deemed to be the paramount enforcement goal, as it is in competition policy. This begs the question of which approach is more just and effective in controlling behaviour. The individual approach is clearly more just. The behavioural outcome could only be answered by lengthy empirical observation, not by assertion.

Various issues arise in applying a responsive and restorative approach. In some cases, the task of an authority that is investigating an infringement is simple, and involves minimal effort or expense in producing the desired outcomes. Thus, where it is possible to identify all those who have suffered loss and quantify how much loss each person has suffered, there is no difficulty in arranging for repayment to each individual. This was the situation in the airline fuel surcharges and GMTV case studies. The companies involved had computerised lists of their customers and could identify how much each had been overcharged. There was no need to expend effort in calculation of damages. In effect, of course, this is an opt-out solution, in that it delivers restitution to everyone involved without their needing to affirm any claim, unless they wish not to participate. It should be possible for individuals to opt out of such solutions and pursue claims in court, but some courts might impose costs penalties on wasteful litigation.

There are other cases, of course, in which it is not possible easily to identify either all the individual victims or the amounts involved. An example is the milk cartel: the companies would not know which consumers had overpaid what amounts at what times. How should one deliver justice in such circumstances? The traditional approach might be that every consumer could bring a court claim. If a collective mechanism with an opt-in rule applied, each individual would have to prove their claim and their damage. The process might be shortened by deciding any common aspects first, followed by individual issues. It is possible that some overall settlement might be agreed, as anticipated by the Dutch or Italian laws, but those mechanisms would require agreement by all parties and do not provide for compulsion. Alternatively, individual consumers might not bother to pursue their claims. The small amounts involved and difficulties of proof even exceeded the costs and risk threshold of a collective damages action.

---

[107] At the time of writing, it appears that GMTV may not have repaid consumers in full: see R Taylor <http://www.ofcomwatch.co.uk> accessed 12 June 2008. The lesson to be drawn would be that the regulator should have the power to accept enforceable undertakings or some other power so as to oversee the repayment.

> ### Case Study: Milk Price Cartel
>
> On 20 September 2007, the OFT issued a provisional finding of collusion between five large supermarkets and five dairy processors over the retail prices of milk and certain dairy products between 2002 and 2003. On 7 December 2007, it announced agreement with six companies, which admitted involvement and paid penalties totaling £116 million, including significant reductions for cooperation. One company received complete immunity after applying for leniency disclosure.[108] The companies denied wrongdoing and asserted that their action in raising prices had been under pressure from the government in order to assist dairy farmers.[109]
>
> The small amounts of individual compensation and difficulties over proof led law firms to conclude that a case under the existing opt-in procedures would not be viable. This meant that consumers received no redress in relation to an estimated total cost of £270 million.[110]

If, on the other hand, an opt-out rule were to apply, there would have to be some *cy près* approach towards quantification and distribution of damages in such a case.[111] Alternatively, the lawyers or a consumer association involved might negotiate a settlement involving a similar 'rough and ready' basis. A precedent of such a 'rough and ready' settlement is the agreement reached by the Portuguese consumer association DECO with Portugal Telecom that the latter would provide free calls for all subscribers for a weekend. This may have been a windfall for some, but all consumers were treated equally, and there would have been restorative justice if the cost to the company at least roughly equalled its gain from the relevant infringement. Thus, a voluntary solution such as this equates to the universal coverage objective of an opt-out rule and applies the approximation of a *cy près* solution, but avoids delay and the transactional cost. How could restorative justice be produced in such a situation? Would there be a simple big stick that could encourage voluntary repayment by the infringers? The public authorities could have exerted pressure to deliver restorative justice with minimal extra cost as part of their enforcement activities in the milk case, but missed the opportunity.

A methodology in which public and private law approaches operate synergistically in a fused manner might run as follows. An authority would

---

[108] OFT Press Release <http://www.oft.gov.uk/news/press/2007/170-07> accessed 12 June 2008.

[109] J Moore, 'OFT pays Morrisons £100,000 damages over price-fixing claims' *The Independent* (24 April 2008).

[110] N Rose, 'Class actions will make claims easier' *Gazette* (21 February 2008).

[111] Although initially attracted to a *cy près* approach, the English Civil Justice Council has in 2008 cooled towards such an approach after hearing of problems with the approach in Canada: comments by His Honour Judge G Jones in May 2008.

notify an entity that it is commencing an investigation, and may later give notification that it proposes to make a finding of infringement to impose or seek penalties. It would be open to a company voluntarily to announce that it undertook to effect a repayment plan.[112] In recognition of such action, the penalty imposed on the company would be reduced, as in the GMTV case.

The authority's policy on penalties would need to include a clear commitment that credit would be given if sums were repaid: the logic is the same as the principles on which the competition leniency programme is based, namely the promotion of disclosure, but also the moral good of reparation. Such a policy would give an authority the opportunity during an investigation to ask what a prospective defendant's proposals were in relation to restitution. This approach seemingly presents fewer difficulties of adoption in relation to consumer protection cases than it does in competition cases, given the orthodoxy that competition fines are based on general deterrence rather than on individual deterrence. Questions arise as to the extent to which such an approach accords with concepts of individual justice and discrimination as well as whether it is the most effective approach.

A repayment plan would either involve restitution of the exact amount due to each identified customer or a reasonable just alternative solution. On a Nordic approach, if a defendant did not make an acceptable compensation offer, it would be open to the authority to apply to the court for compensation arrangements to be ordered. The result might simply cost the company more in court costs. A defendant might be able to ask for the court's approval of a proposed repayment plan. It would be necessary that the illicit gain be removed. Hence, the value of the free telecom calls or reduced-price milk would need to be roughly equivalent to the amount of the illicit gain.

Case Study: Private Schools Cartel

Many of the private schools in the UK were found to have fixed prices. If the OFT were to have imposed its normal level of fine, it would have had to have been funded by parents who had not paid the inflated prices, and many schools might have been forced into bankruptcy. The negotiated solution was that the schools would pay comparatively modest amounts into a scholarship fund for the further education of those pupils whose parents had paid inflated fees.

---

[112] In the JJB Sports case, the company made a voluntary offer at an early stage in order to protect its commercial reputation, and the offer was taken up by 16,000 consumers, whereas a maximum of 900 people signed up to the subsequent costly litigation by the consumer association (the number would have been less, since 900 was the number of shorts involved, and some consumers may have been in both cohorts). Thus, the voluntary action reached more people at a far lower cost. The objective of achieving redress would be to reach an optimal number and avoid unnecessary cost.

Some flexibility might be required in identifying what a reasonable just solution would be in given circumstances. In this respect, the UK schools cartel case affords a contrast to the milk and telecom situations: it involved an ad hoc solution founded on restorative justice and in which, unusually, the normal high fines based on the theory of deterrent punishment were ignored. It would be important that a defendant should make an offer that is just and not have opportunities to avoid due compensation. The incentives that should achieve justice in this respect might involve the giving of a formal, disinterested opinion on the reasonableness of a proposal by the public authority involved, or a court, or an independent panel. Governments, trade associations or individual companies might consider it worthwhile convening independent panels of 'the great and good' which would be able to give their opinion that a proposal to pay specified amounts to individuals who qualified under certain criteria or to named charities was acceptable.

Which of the above options delivers a result that is just, fast, cheap and effective: a court-based system or a system in which regulators use their powers to achieve a voluntary or mediated result? The position will be examined further in chapter nine. For the present, some significant challenges can be recognised for civil justice systems in being able to deliver effective and efficient solutions for these situations. Under the 'fused' approach, the promotion of voluntary settlement behaviour accords with responsive regulation. The 'big stick' comprises the combined effect of the threat of more costly consequences involving both public penalties and private litigation, and of prolonged damage to reputation. These levers encourage desirable voluntary action by regulatees. For those traders who are less responsive to the pressure on reputation, a more coercive approach would be needed, such as effective public powers or coordinated private action.

It can be seen that under the 'fused' approach, the concept of 'justice' that results is more flexible and responsive than a traditional approach to payment of damages. It may involve tailor-made solutions. It ought to afford speedier and cheaper solutions than a precise, detailed and laborious legal analysis of traditional rights. Such a solution has certain pre-requisites. Thus, it could operate only when a public authority is involved, where the authority proposes to take action in respect of an infringement, and where there is an alignment between penalties policy and compensation paid.

The above discussion assumes that an infringement of regulatory law, such as competition or consumer protection law, has occurred. Many compensation claims are settled on the basis of the risk involved to the parties, which principally involves the strength of the underlying case. However, it must be recognised that empowerment of public authorities is itself not without risk. Theory predicts excessive zeal and abuse wherever there is a concentration of power.[113] If a fused approach is to be operated regularly, it may be necessary to impose some checks and balances, such as court review and political oversight and accountability. Ombudsmen may play an effective role here. The European Ombudsman's 2007 Report notes a real change in attitude towards placing citizens at the centre of concerns and producing concrete results.[114] An unprecedented 35 per cent of enquiries were closed after the relevant institution agreed to settle the matter, although he criticised standards in 15 per cent of cases. The ombudsman has power to open own-initiative enquiries as well as handle complaints.

CONCLUSIONS

It is axiomatic that two essential public policy goals are valid. First, states should seek means to maximise compliance with norms by private individuals and economic operators. Secondly, when actionable harm is caused by illegal activity, the damage caused should be compensated. Further, it is the responsibility of governments to pursue the economic health of their citizens, and to seek to resolve disputes through means that are effective, speedy and proportionate. The challenge is how to achieve all of these goals in the best way.

Academic research challenges some existing methodologies and policies. Restorative justice offers a way of producing restitution and compensation through public enforcement coupled with encouragement of voluntary behaviour. New approaches to regulation and enforcement indicate that responsive approaches may produce better and cheaper outcomes than punitive sanctions. Considerations of fairness and proportionality challenge a sanctioning policy that emphasises general deterrence and marginalises individual justice and behavioural risk.

Taken together, these insights indicate that the traditional separation between public and private enforcement may effectively be combined. However, the American approach of relying on private compensation claims as the primary mechanism of public enforcement is not only foreign to European traditions, but, if imported, would bring a number of problems, notably issues of consistency, duplication and excess. The European approach may lie in the converse of the US model: maintaining the primacy of public enforcement, but delivering increased compensation through subsuming that goal into a fused system. The next step would be to examine the public and private models as means of delivering compensation.

---

[113] Americans would cite the zealous prosecution activities of New York Attorney Spitzer. In *Morrisons v OFT*, the regulator was sued for libel over allegations of involvement in the milk cartel case and was forced to make a public apology and pay substantial damages and costs: J Moore, 'OFT pays Morrisons £100,000 damages over price-fixing claims' *The Independent* (24 April 2008).

[114] PN Diamandouros, 'The European Ombudsman: Annual Report 2007' (10 March 2008).

9

Evaluating the Options

ESTABLISHING CRITERIA

W ITH THE ABOVE background in mind, the task now is to examine the potential models that can be put forward for furthering collective redress, and to measure these against benchmark criteria. Such evaluation should involve consideration of empirical data on the extent of any gaps in mechanisms and the operation of national systems, so as to supply a clear and transparent assessment of the costs and benefits of gaps and any proposed solutions. Very little data currently exists that would satisfy impact assessment requirements, both because of the amount of change identified above and because governments do not systematically collect the relevant data. Any future legislative proposals would, of course, require proper impact assessments. However, it is possible to draw some conclusions for future policy based on exiting evidence and logic. Given the current diversity in national models and the currently insuperable challenges in relation to potential harmonisation, the most effective approach is to establish criteria by which any future systems and mechanisms can be evaluated.

What criteria should be selected against which to measure the various models that might deliver collective redress? The criteria that are selected must be capable of horizontal application to each of the available models. They must take into account fundamental norms such as justice (substantively and procedurally in terms of fairness) and deliver efficiency requirements such as speed and proportionate cost. Since they operate in a particular socio-political system, they must deliver political objectives such as enhancing economic competitiveness, providing acceptable access to justice and promoting conformity with desired behaviour. Learning from available experience, the models should also be measured against their ability to give rise to unacceptable effects, so that appropriate comparative risk assessments can be made.

The criteria that are suggested here are as follows:

a) To what extent does the model deliver justice?
b) Does the model further the health and competitiveness of the European (or national) economy overall?
c) Does the model remove illicit gains from infringers?
d) Does the model restore the position of those who have been harmed by illegal activity?

e) Does the model promote compliance in future behaviour by the infringer and others?
f) Is the model accessible and simple to operate?
g) Does the model operate acceptably speedily?
h) Are the costs of the model low and proportionate to the amount involved? and
i) Does the model give rise to a risk of abuse?

These criteria will now be applied to the main models that have been identified above, namely the private litigation model, the public oversight model and the voluntary or ADR model. Some assistance may be gained here by reviewing the case studies noted above, a summary of which is at Table 7. Whilst recognising that these may give an incomplete picture, the main purpose is to illustrate techniques, outcomes and costs.

Table 7—Summary Of Case Study Outcomes

Case Study	Methodology	Outcome	Likely Overall Cost of Compensation, Including Defence Costs
Replica football shirts	Public enforcement then NGO damages claim.	Fine £6.7 million. Voluntary offer £400,000. Damages claim settlement £18,000; low opt-in. Argued no consumer detriment.	£2 million.
Airline fuel surcharges	Public enforcement then law-firm-led US class action.	Settlement of £73.5 repaid to UK passengers.	$30 million.
Austrian cases	Public prosecution then NGO damages claim.	Settlement of €19.7 million including costs.	See left.
Portugal Telecom charges	NGO actions.	Settlement: those with receipts were reimbursed; all consumers entitled to make some free calls.	?
Spanish colza oil	Prosecution then NGO damages claim.	Court awarded €3,000 million damages.	High?
Benzodiazepine tranquillisers	Private claim.	Failed.	£60 million?
MMR vaccine	Private claim.	Failed.	£30 million?

(Continued)

Table 7—(Continued)

Case Study	Methodology	Outcome	Likely Overall Cost of Compensation, Including Defence Costs
Bank charges	Claims to ombudsman and to courts.	1. Many claims via Ombudsman settled. 2. Court test case likely to last several years.	1. Low. 2. High.
DES	Private claims.	Settlement €35 million.	High?
Dexia Bank	Private claims.	Settlement.	?
Shell hydrocarbon reserves	US public enforcement then US class action plus Dutch settlement.	Fine $120 million. Settlements in the United States ($90 million) and EU ($352 million including some of the fine).	$100 million?
Deutsche Telekom	1. US class action. 2. German private action.	1. Settlement $120 million. 2. Ongoing—several years.	1. $60 million? 2. ?
French mobile phones	Public enforcement then NGO claim.	Fine €534 million. Under 1 per cent opted in, to claim €800,000. Case ongoing.	?
Duchesne SA	Public enforcement.	Fine up to € 1 million. No compensation claim.	?
Vioxx	US class action.	Settled for $4.85 billion; liability disputed.	$1.45 billion.
Equitable Life	Multiple ombudsman and court claims.	Varied results; cross-border result unsatisfactory.	High.
GMTV competitions	Public enforcement.	Fine £2 million and voluntary offer to pay compensation (unclear whether paid).	Low.
Milk price cartel	Public enforcement.	Fines totalling £116 million; private cases not viable.	?
Private schools cartel	Public enforcement.	Fines and fund for restitutionary support.	?

1. THE PRIVATE LITIGATION MODEL

The first model that would occur to many people is that of resolving collective redress through private collective actions in the courts. Yet, as will be seen below, it is neither the only possible model nor necessarily the best.

From the perspective of a legal system and of the provision of individual fundamental rights, it is arguable that a jurisdiction is required to provide a court-based system that may resolve damages claims. Yet does this necessarily imply provision of a collective mechanism in addition to individual pathways? There may ultimately be an argument that a civil justice system that is incapable of processing multiple individual claims within a reasonable time and at proportionate cost infringes individual rights under article 6 of the ECHR.

Yet that argument collides with the inevitability of a cost-benefit threshold, below which claims must be processed through a 'small claims' procedure or, rationally, abandoned. Above that threshold, cost-benefit assessments are inherent in all litigation, especially in systems that impose barriers designed to promote rational and efficient behaviour such as a 'loser pays' rule. The threshold will, in any event, vary from case to case, depending on the particular costs and benefits of any case, whether individual or collective. It has been noted above that court-based systems give rise to difficulties in balancing individual rights with procedural efficiency (notably evident in the opt-in versus opt-out debate).

Aggregation of individual claims is specifically intended to reduce costs and duration of proceedings, and should often do so significantly. A collective mechanism will therefore both lower the cost-benefit viability threshold for litigation and give the claimants increased power in negotiation (not only through strength in numbers and pooled economic resources, but also through heightened potential for media pressure) compared to the limited or even minimal power that each might possess individually (absent the power of adverse publicity on a defendant).

The private model gives rise to a conundrum over whether to adopt an opt-in or opt-out approach. Both have advantages and disadvantages, and might be preferable in particular situations. The opt-in approach preserves individual rights and gives rise to less abuse, but can restrict access to justice. In contrast, the opt-out approach initially covers more people, but still requires individuals to opt in at some stage. The latter often ends up covering more people, but can give rise to injustice through encouraging blackmail settlements. Both approaches involve some costs.

The drawbacks with court-based collective private damages claims are cost,[1] delay,[2] possible inflexibility of procedure and of outcomes, and the risk of abuse that is associated with the inevitable involvement of intermediaries

---

[1] The high cost of the court-based tort compensation scheme compared to other alternatives was established some decades ago; see P Cane, *Atiyah's Accidents, Compensation and the Law* (7th edn, Cambridge, 2006) ch 16.

[2] For examples of delay of several years in resolution of mass court claims, see in particular the case studies on benzodiazepines, MMR vaccines, bank charges, DES, Deutsche Telekom and Equitable Life.

in mass claims. In relation to behaviour, the problem arises from the fact that damages claims operate ex post facto. Incentives for compliance could be increased through raising levels of damages or introducing punitive damages, but European tradition separates punitive sanctions from compensation systems. The size of the penalty incentive in a post facto system may need to be so large in order to produce compliance in all or many situations as to be grossly disproportionate in the majority of situations. It is worrying, moreover, that the above arguments are theoretical and unsupported by empirical evidence of what levers in fact affect behaviour, and do so best. Also, as noted, private actions raise inconsistencies with a 'responsive regulation' approach to modifying behaviour.

The involvement of intermediaries will inherently increase costs, and representation of multiple parties founds a claim to enhanced costs. However, there is currently a significant degree of uncertainty over the level of costs and intermediaries' profits that will be generated within national civil justice systems as a result of inevitable changes in litigation funding systems. Success fees are now widely permissible; there are signs that contingency fees may be spreading; and third-party investors are clearly going to make significant impact on the national litigation scene. Whilst lawyers' fees and behaviour may be regulated, and hence their ability to seek disproportionate fees may be controlled, the addition of a profit element for independent third-party investors brings a new situation that has not been confronted before, even in the United States. Economic reality ought, of course, to mean that it will be in third-party funders' interests to undertake careful risk assessments before investing in any claim. Nevertheless, an investor would also take into account not just the legal merits of a case, but also the extent to which the claimants' side's negotiating power in settlement negotiations is enhanced because of the collective strength. It is not easy to predict how close this might come to a 'blackmail settlement' situation, but the risk exists.

A rational response to the abuse risk is to seek to devise controls, such as are evident from the recent laws in a number of states discussed in chapter three. A principal mechanism relies on strong judicial control over gate-keeping, conduct, settlement and costs (predictability and resulting quantum). Such mechanisms are new and untried, yet the US experience is not encouraging.

If private damages actions are to have a significant (as opposed to incidental) function in 'private enforcement' of regulatory law, especially in substantial substitution for extension of public enforcement mechanisms, it is inevitably necessary to provide adequate encouragement for private actors in the form of financial incentives. This is inherent in the US approach, with no financial risk for nominal claimants, but significant financial incentives for intermediaries to act as 'bounty hunters'. In the European context, the only viable option for funding an extension of litigation, given the economic reality that further public funds will not be made available, is through extension of private funding mechanisms—one or more of removal of the 'loser pays' rule, increased success fees for intermediaries, higher damages, the ability for intermediaries to be paid out of monies recovered, an opt-out approach that maximises the group and hence the size of recovery, and punitive damages. Several of these aspects have traditionally been anathema. To what extent are they acceptable reforms now?

Overall, then, countries may need court-based private law systems for collective damages claims, but there are significant drawbacks and only a low score against the criteria. This prompts the question of whether there may be better alternatives.

2. A PUBLIC BODY APPROACH

It may at first sight appear surprising that a public authority, whose primary function is to enforce regulation, may be effective also in delivering private compensation, but there is growing evidence that this can be the case. After all, the concept that a public entity may deliver private remedies is merely the converse of the thesis that private bodies may deliver public enforcement. In a situation in which the overall objective contains mixed elements of both public and private redress, both alternatives deserve consideration. Furthermore, the evidence is that the public route can score highly against the criteria.

The most developed public system to date is that of the Nordic consumer ombudsmen considered in chapter two. They exercise the normal regulatory enforcement functions for consumer protection law in both individual and collective situations, and now have the added power to apply to the court for damages to be paid, again in both individual and collective situations. Although the powers are new, initial signs are very encouraging. Various other examples are available from the UK and Ireland. In the UK, the FSA has statutory powers to apply for a compensation order, although existing experience is limited and many compensation claims are resolved by the FOS. This approach to compensation is fully consistent with a Macrory approach to sentencing: the first step in setting a penalty should be to identify the size of the illicit gain and remove it. (In the competition field, the OFT is responsible for regulation but not compensation, which is privatised in a collective situation to the consumers' association, but the initial experience of this has been mixed.[3]) This model is close to the continental *partie civile* mechanism in which a private party 'piggy backs' on a criminal action, without extra cost, but with the ability to benefit from the evidence and conclusions in a follow-on damages award.

---

[3] See the replica football shirt case study.

However, the GMTV case study shows that it is not in fact necessary for a public authority to possess powers to apply to a court for collective damages in order to achieve speedy payment. The inherent authority of a public body coupled with the threat of damage to a trader's reputation after the announcement of the imposition of a public penalty and risk of private collective damages claims can lead to a responsible trader volunteering, or being persuaded to volunteer, payment of compensation. This situation is a classic example of the 'responsive regulation' theory of influencing behaviour. If the incentives are aligned and there is a sufficiently 'big stick', then normal entities will act in accordance with the desired behaviour. The implication here is that public pressure can be most effectively combined with a self-regulatory model. This is discussed further below.

As the GMTV example shows, what is necessary for a fused responsive approach to enforcement and compensation is that public policy on penalties should take account of compensation aspects. The incentive for an infringer to make a compensation payment within the context of a public body's investigation will be low if there is no relief from the severity of the public penalty. This is consistent with policy in the competition field on applying leniency in return for voluntary disclosure. What made the GMTV case study work was that the trader's speedy adoption of a full programme of voluntary restorative actions was responded to by imposition of a significantly lower fine, as well as closure of both public enforcement and private compensation aspects. The trader bought closure of all aspects by paying back the money, disciplining the staff responsible, putting in place improved systems, paying a fine and permitting future scrutiny of compliance with the required standards and improved systems. Unlike any financial lever (whether damages or fine), such a solution is not only far more flexible and responsive, but inherently designed to affect future behaviour.

The public model ought to give universal coverage of those entitled to compensation. In the situation where payment is voluntary or agreed, it should operate akin to an opt-out model. The Danish Ombudsman has power to order a company to divulge its customer list along with all other evidence, so can identify what should be paid to whom. If it is necessary for the authority to take the matter to court, the authority has power to apply that the normal opt-in rule can be disapplied and an opt-out rule applied in appropriate circumstances. This provides a flexible approach that can be adapted to the circumstances.

It can readily be seen that a public approach along the above lines scores very highly against the criteria. This is so irrespective of whether the model involves a Nordic-style coercive power to take a damages case to court or merely empowers a regulator or court to operate a fused approach to penalties and damages by giving credit for compensation paid. The former approach may deliver a greater incentive, but the latter can clearly work provided the regulator/court has sufficient flexibility and influence.

To be specific, the public oversight model can be quick (depending on the resources and efficiency of the public body). It can clearly be quicker than many private law court-based systems. Both public and private systems will be slowed down when confronted by more complex cases.

The public model can deliver a cheaper outcome overall, by fusing public and private redress. (This is the counterpart of the argument for collective private redress that can include some enforcement element.) A public authority can have powers and resource to overcome barriers of investigating potential infringements,[4] gaining access to evidence, ability to understand complex evidence, and access to expertise (all of which will be necessary for a public enquiry). It can maintain the confidentiality of proprietary and commercially sensitive evidence, but can produce appropriate evidence, sometimes before a specialist tribunal (eg the CAT in the UK or the Market Court in the Nordic states).

The public model offers universal access to all citizens and businesses without cost to them. It will involve a public body at effectively no extra cost if it adopts the UK's fused 'giving credit for repayment' approach. If it is necessary for the public body to calculate damages and apply to a court, there will be some increased cost for the body. Against that cost increase, it might be argued that there may be benefits to the general economy through restoration of illicit gains, arguably greater compliance, and possibly more fines accruing to the public purse. Whether the level of fines might decrease as a result of the introduction of this system is debatable, and depends at what level fines are set, either initially or as a result of a reduction for payment of compensation. However, the argument on what the net effect might be on public finances is more affected by consideration of whether adoption of a 'responsive regulation' approach to penalties as a whole is justified, in relation to producing greater compliance overall and being more just than a policy based solely on imposition of fines.

It might be argued that a public body could recover the costs of the compensation restoration exercise, in the same way that a successful claimant would be entitled to recover costs from a paying defendant. Such recovery may be acceptable in some systems, but not all. In some states, all moneys paid to public bodies, whether fines or costs, are passed on to the government treasury and not retained. To retain fines and costs would expose the public body to the perception of temptation that its enforcement actions were more motivated by selfish commercial considerations that by impartiality and the prioritisation that is necessary in order to operate within a budget.

A particular attraction of a public oversight approach is that it involves no intermediaries, and hence no risk of the abuse that private investors

---

[4] Dawn raid powers are in Regulation (EC) 1/2003.

and intermediaries can produce. There are fewer conflicts of interest: a public body should be impartial and only interested in the monetary aspects in relation to ensuring just restitution and compensation.

The possible disadvantages of involvement of any public body are well known, such as limited resources, inefficiency or capture by regulatees.[5] There is some irony in the position that many in the United States distrust their federal agencies and this view drives them towards emphasising a privatised enforcement system, whereas the European approach is almost a mirror image. Regulators might argue that it would be inconsistent for them to assume a private compensation role alongside their public functions. However, as Macrory shows, in some cases a significant part of enforcement work positively involves important aspects of the compensation function, namely in identifying and quantifying the size of the illicit gains, how many people were involved and what has happened to the assets. Further, the role of a public body is whatever is mandated by parliament, and if the advantages of assumption of some compensation oversight role are persuasive and duly mandated, that is final.

A further objection might be the undesirability of giving too much power to authorities. The response to this issue would be that the ultimate responsibility for decisions on compensation and penalties would remain with the courts. An entity which felt that the proposals of a public authority in relation to compensation were unfair should remain entitled to have the issue decided by an independent tribunal, such as a court (or, as proposed below, some other ADR-style body).

Overall, therefore, the public oversight model is very attractive and deserves to be adopted more widely across European states, following the developing precedents available from the Nordic states, the UK and Ireland. At the theoretical level, the public oversight model is attractive because it offers the opportunity to set in place a principled, fused approach in relation to the functions of evaluation of the scale of wrongdoing, removal of the illicit gain by effecting repayment, and the superimposing a suitable penalty, hence complying with the Macrory Sentencing Principles,[6] and retributive and also 'restorative justice'.[7]

However, a public oversight approach may not cover every situation. An obvious gap would be a vertical area in which there is no regulator, or no effective regulator, or where the function of the regulator does not align with compensation goals. The model would clearly work in the areas of

---

[5] See AI Ogus, *Regulation: Legal Form and Economic Theory* (Oxford, 1994).

[6] R Macrory, *Regulatory Justice: making sanctions effective* (2007). He recommends the wider use of confiscation orders under the Proceeds of Crime Act 2002.

[7] The classic text is I Ayres and J Braithwaite, *Responsive Regulation: Transcending the Deregulation Debate* (Oxford University Press, 1992).

consumer protection law and competition law. The UK experience shows that it can be operated by the many sectoral regulators that exist there.[8]

One would not expect the approach to work, say, in product safety and liability cases—for example, where a medicines authority makes a regulatory decision on a product's safety[9] and there are also liability claims. The distinction between these two legal procedures is that the regulatory requirements and private causes of action involve different objectives and are not aligned. The fact that some regulatory action may be taken, such as approving revised labelling or a product withdrawal or even a prosecution (which is rare in Europe in this sector) would not necessarily imply that any liability for damages would arise out of the same circumstances. In short, breach of contract, negligence or strict product liability are different in nature from the product regulatory offences. The *mandatory* 'linkage' solution found in the Nordic states can operate where conduct gives rise to a regulatory infringement as well as to a damages claim: the point about a cartel offence or breach of consumer protection provisions is that a damages claim does not arise in the absence of an infringement.

What response might cover collective redress in any areas in which a public body cannot be effective? Is it necessary to have a liberalised private court-based collective system in order to cover any individual areas where an absence of public or other incentives, and an absence of a collective court-based system, is insufficient to generate adequate voluntary behaviour? It would clearly involve considerable risk to introduce a horizontal private collective system *just* in order to address a gap in one or a small number of vertical sectors. The risks of unbalancing all the other sectors that operate well on a voluntary basis would be considerable. For example, generic changes such as removal of loser pays, introduction of opt-out or of punitive damages would pose significant risks to existing progress towards balanced systems. Thus, the solution would seem to address individual problem sectors individually, by looking at which new combinations of public, private and voluntary levers might produce the best results.

3. THE VOLUNTARY AND ADR APPROACH

Reaching solutions through direct negotiation, with or without an intermediary, is well recognised to be able to satisfy criteria of accessibility, simplicity, speed, low and proportionate cost, and effective results. Indeed, this approach underpins all of the developments on the mediation and 'small claims' measures. It works for businesses that value their reputation and share prices. Voluntary

---

[8] See ch 2.

[9] Typical regulatory decisions would be that labelling should be changed or, in rare cases, a product should be withdrawn from the market. Many decisions on product withdrawals are in fact made spontaneously by companies.

restitution can be enhanced by public policy that encourages responsiveness, and by the existence of appropriate ADR mechanisms. A range of ADR mechanisms can be found, often on sectoral bases, sometimes underpinned by schemes or codes of business practice. The Nordic no-fault compensation schemes for medical or pharmaceutical injuries are outstandingly successful examples, as is the UK's FOS. The low cost, impartiality and speed of these schemes make them extremely attractive. Consumers overwhelmingly prefer them to court actions (as long as they are aware of the schemes' existence) and can accept lower compensation than might be available from the courts.

A strong advantage of a voluntary model is that it provides flexibility. This is well illustrated by the Portugal Telecom and Schools Cartel case studies and the Dutch Settlement Law. Instead of an enquiry into what individual damages are attributable to which claimants, which would be the traditional approach under the court system (absent a *cy près* power), lengthy, almost impossible to conclude and certainly involve huge and disproportionate costs given the very limited individual damages, the solutions can be free telecom calls for all consumers, a scholarship fund for the benefit of those pupils whose parents were potentially overcharged, or some other imaginative scheme of compensation. This approach illustrates the points that have been made above about a more flexible and responsive approach to the concept of justice, and to the procedures that produce just but cost-effective solutions.

The major drawback of an ADR model is that it requires the consent of all involved. Hence it is ineffective against rogues, for whom a coercive model is needed. Similarly, the risk of capture of the process by rent-seeking intermediaries is inherently limited.

The effectiveness of a voluntary model will be enhanced where encouraged by effective external pressures, such as a serious and/or ongoing loss of reputation, threat of regulatory action, court action risk of damage to reputation, cost, delay, even business interference and so on. It is regrettably not possible to adopt an empirical approach that would define which of these levers, or combination of them, will be effective or sufficient in any given situation to deliver behavioural compliance and due compensation.

In the previous section, it was said that a responsible trader may, if the levers and incentives are sufficient, make a voluntary offer of compensation within the context of public oversight. How can it be ensured that any voluntary offer is adequate? The best solution seems to provide for an independent assessment of the adequacy of an offer. This might be done by a court (Dutch model), some intermediary (consumer association model), or other independent and respected individual or panel.[10]

---

[10] It is suggested that business organisations may see advantages in creating standing or ad hoc panels consisting of 'the great and the good', whose members could give swift disinterested approval of the fairness and adequacy of proposed compensation payments or schemes. The advantage would be to deliver a speedy solution so as to avoid the costs, delay and other disadvantages of court proceedings.

4. THE NGO APPROACH

Before proceeding further, an evaluation should be made of the NGO (consumer organisation, but sometimes trade association) model, not least because it is adopted in a number of states. This model is an attempt to privatise and fuse the functions of enforcement and compensation, within a court-based system. Accordingly, it suffers from the normal disadvantages of a court-based system identified above.

Empowerment of consumer organisations is politically attractive since it can be presented as consumer empowerment through self-help and direct intervention in the market. However, it carries various disadvantages in delegating public enforcement powers: democratic accountability of the organisation to stakeholders and to the public generally; guarantee of disinterested and rational behaviour; independence from pressure groups and potential for hijack; avoidance of conflicts of interest between financial and public incentives and between sub-groups whose interests it has to balance; confusion of functions between consumer advocacy, public enforcement, litigation and damages collection and distribution roles; ability to distribute funds fairly and economically; and proliferation and diversity of regulatory/legal standards leading to confusion amongst business and government defendants.[11] Some, perhaps most, of these issues can be addressed by setting criteria for organisations to satisfy in order to be empowered, and only accepting those that have reputations that should underpin quality behaviour. Several Member States establish such gate-keeping criteria.

The other major issue for NGOs is that of funding. Without funding, no private litigation—or public enforcement—system will be operative. The German and Austrian associations have public funding and are noticeably active. DECO of Portugal operates with primarily private funding, but its record of only three collective actions over some 12 years is unconvincing. The 'loser pays' rule, which is inherent in operating in the private claims environment, requires adequate funding for the cost of bringing a case and to cover the costs risk of significant litigation, and requires a level of funding that many would find challenging. Absent public grants, permitting the funding of litigation through contingency fees or suspension of 'loser pays' rules is essentially unprincipled and unsatisfactory. Insulating the NGO to a greater or lesser extent from the 'loser pays' rule is a theoretical option, but again unprincipled. DECO argues that the Portuguese rule that they may be liable for between one-tenth and one-half of normal costs if they totally lose is a strong disincentive to bringing

---

[11] C Hodges, 'Collectivism: Evaluating the effectiveness of public and private models for regulating consumer protection' in W van Boom and M Loos (eds), *Collective Enforcement of Consumer Law* (Europa, 2007).

meritless claims. There is pragmatic force in that as a matter of behaviour. However, the argument is less strong on the basis that the rule can be used to force a settlement on some mass issue of lesser merit and hence qualify for costs. Perhaps more importantly, the position is also unclear, and possibly unstable, over what may happen across Europe as commercial third-party funders spread around national civil justice systems, as now seems strongly likely. The risk is that the changed dynamic may import commercial conflicts and capture. Therefore, this model cannot avoid the potential for abuse.

On the other hand, the NGO model can import the advantages noted above of flexibility, of which the Portugal Telecom case study is a prime example. An NGO may offer the ability to negotiate an imaginative settlement, and may offer some assurance of independence that the deal is fair and that it does not itself benefit from it. However, overall, the NGO model to collective redress does not seem to be the best model given that other more attractive ones are available.

EVALUATING THE OPTIONS—AND A HOLISTIC APPROACH

How do the above options score against the criteria? The ADR solution is attractive, but it needs to operate within a context of adequate incentives. The public model is also attractive, but does not work in every situation. The NGO model is less attractive. The private litigation model is the least attractive, in view of its cost, the risk of capture and the difficulty of balancing incentives against abuses. Thus, the four main models for collective redress can therefore clearly be ranked in that order.[12]

Having looked at the above options individually, they should also be evaluated for how they might be made to work as elements of an integrated system. In the 'real world' of European Member States, every system contains some elements of most of these models, albeit in differing combinations. There is in each state a mixture of public and private bodies that deal with regulatory enforcement and delivery of compensation as an integrated national system.[13] The OECD's 2007 'Recommendation on Consumer Dispute Resolution and Redress', in advising that all states should adopt mechanisms that enable consumers to be able to resolve disputes effectively, whether individually, collectively or through public authorities, stresses a need for a *combination* of mechanisms and for direct negotiation as the first

---

[12] This accords with evaluation against 'better regulation' principles: C Hodges, 'Encouraging Enterprise and Rebalancing Risk: Implications of Economic Policy for Regulation, Enforcement and Compensation' [2007] EBLR 1231.

[13] J Stuyck *et al*, 'Commission Study on alternative means of consumer redress other than redress through ordinary judicial proceedings' (Catholic University of Leuven, 17 January 2007, issued April 2007).

option.[14] It also states that collective measures should include procedures to discourage abusive collective actions.

All Member States do, of course, currently provide for individual private redress, both through the courts (above a viability threshold), through small claims mechanisms (theoretically below that threshold), and increasingly through ADR or schemes, sometimes sectoral schemes. In addition, there are all of the collective mechanisms provided under EU consumer legislation, and the national and Commission public enforcement mechanisms under competition law. The existence of this rich amalgam of systems might indicate that any further need that is established might only call for revolutionary reform if there were to be clear empirical evidence of widespread need unmet by other mechanisms.

The findings of Armour, Black, Cheffins and Nolan in relation to corporate law noted in chapter eight are again pertinent here: effective regulation of large and sophisticated markets can be produced through a combination of public formal and informal mechanisms and private informal and self-regulatory mechanisms, without recourse to formal private enforcement.[15] If that is so, such mechanisms may simply provide appropriate redress, including compensation, by themselves or with simple extension. It would follow that where such systems are effective, the addition of an option of private formal claims may have a significant destabilising effect on the existing mechanisms and market: in other words, the addition of an aggregate litigation model to a stable model that involves a combination of other mechanisms may involve significant risk.[16] These considerations point to the importance of considering the matrix of public, private, formal and informal mechanisms that apply, and could be developed, on a vertical, sectoral basis, rather than assuming that introduction of a horizontal aggregate mechanism, whether public or private, is appropriate.

At this point, it is relevant to contemplate what the nature is of the relevant liabilities for which remedies need to be considered. Are the liabilities regulatory in nature or susceptible to regulatory oversight, or do they arise under civil law, such as contract or tort? For competition law, breach of articles 81 and 82 EC give rise to *both* regulatory and civil liability. The availability of damages for breach of certain provisions of consumer

---

[14] OECD Recommendation on Consumer Dispute Resolution and Redress 2007 <http://www.oecd.org/dataoecd/43/50/38960101.pdf> accessed 12 June 2008.

[15] J Armour, B Black, B Cheffins and R Nolan, 'Private Enforcement of Corporate Law: An Empirical Comparison of the US and UK', Working Paper (Universities of Cambridge, Oxford and Texas, 2008).

[16] For this reason, business interests have voiced concerns over the effect that extension of group claims on a horizontal basis may have on the attractiveness of, eg the City of London as a financial market: see Department for Business, Enterprise and Regulatory Reform, 'Representative Actions in Consumer Protection Legislation. Responses to the Government consultation' (2008).

law is also established where relevant. Given the conclusion above that regulatory oversight and remedies can be the most efficient and effective, it would follow that legislators should give strong consideration to framing remedies for rights of action that give rise to damages claims so that public authorities can be at least one of the options for enforcement or collection.

Can any conclusions be drawn about how national systems should develop? It is suggested that there are strong indicators for future action. Building on the findings of the above scoring exercise, it is clear that emphasis should be on public oversight of restitution where this is realistically achievable. This has implications for enforcement policy, public budgets and substantive law provisions. The implications for budgets may, however, be modest. This follows from realisation that the existence and judicious use of adequate powers and incentives for compliance should produce increased compliance, and, where redress is necessary, also promote voluntary and ADR solutions that reduce the need for either expensive public or private enforcement.[17] Systems that assist ADR and encourage voluntary virtuous behaviour and settlement will certainly need to be emphasised. The availability of ombudsmen or authoritative independent mediators, whether formal or informal, will facilitate speedy, low-cost settlement. It is also necessary to align public penalties so as to take account of (indeed, prioritise) private restitution and compensation. However, it should not be necessary to promote private collective actions as a primary mechanism. On the other hand, private mechanisms might have a role in some situations as a long stop, depending on the extent and sophistication of other mechanisms.[18] In fixing public penalties, credit must be given for compensation paid.

It also follows that those states that have placed reliance on NGOs as a primary enforcement mechanism should evolve towards adoption of increasing reliance on public authorities, as has occurred in the Nordic states and the Netherlands. NGOs will only be effective if they are funded. Those

---

[17] AI Ogus, 'Rethinking Self-Regulation' (1995) 15 Oxford J. Legal Stud. 97–108; J Black, 'Constitutionalising Self-regulation' (1996) 59 Mod. L. Rev. 24–55; and I Bartle and P Vass, 'Self-Regulation and the Regulatory State—A Survey of Policy and Practice' (Centre for the Study of Regulated Industries, University of Bath School of Management, 2005).

[18] In the United States, a case has been made that the decision on whether a private enforcement (ie a compensation mechanism) should be available to supplement public enforcement is better taken by involving (and even delegating to) individual enforcement agencies rather than solely by Congress: see MC Stephenson, 'Public Regulation of Private Enforcement: The Case for Expanding the Role of Administrative Agencies' (2005) 1 *Virginia Law Review* 91 93. This notes the advantages of private enforcement (more enforcement resources, a check against agencies shirking their responsibilities and fostering innovative strategies and settlement techniques) and its disadvantages (inefficiently high levels of enforcement leading to waste of judicial resources and excessive deterrence, direct interference with public enforcement and diminished democratic accountability of private enforcers).

few states such as Germany and Austria, which provide public funding for NGOs, may achieve better overall results for enforcement and compensation if they funded public authorities instead.

There will still be a need for court-based mechanisms for managing private multiple damages claims, as shown by courts' demand for new procedures in Spain, England, Germany and the Netherlands, discussed in chapter three. However, if such mechanisms are not intended to be primary mechanisms in dealing with market rectification or enforcement, and other mechanisms are available and effective for delivering compensation, various policy decisions follow. First, there is no rationale at present for altering well-established rules on the loser paying costs, punitive damages or opt-in. Secondly, if, as the OECD recommends, a combination of optional public and private mechanisms are available, the incentives and controls must be such that there is no 'race to court' so that funders or lawyers can promote procedures in which can claim rents, thereby preventing cheaper solutions to operate.[19] Denying individuals access to courts is, of course, contrary to fundamental rights, but a possible approach is that of England and Wales, where the party who incurs the costs of a court claim where the alternative of an ADR approach was available may be denied recovery of his or her costs by the court, or even be ordered to pay the opponents' unnecessary costs.

---

[19] Note the activities of funders in the Dexia settlement in attracting consumers to opt out from the settlement, with the consequence that the cases took longer to settle and cost more. Similar behaviour occurred in the bank charges case study.

10

Summarising the Findings and Challenges for Europe

WHAT ARE THE findings of this enquiry? The picture on collective redress in Europe is a kaleidoscope that can confuse those who do not perceive the full picture, even though some parts of the picture are as yet impressionistic and not in focus. It is possible, however, to take an overview of the position and the developing trends, and to suggest the direction for future policy. The major areas in which policy has been developing are consumer protection and competition law. Each area needs to be considered separately. Policy on access to justice runs a poor third in relevance within the current policy debate.

CONSUMER PROTECTION

Collective actions to protect consumers have been in existence in some European states for almost 50 years. Their prime function was to provide a mechanism to enforce some types of the emerging consumer protection law, especially on unfair contract terms and unfair competition. The methodology was in all cases limited to seeking injunctive relief from the courts to stop and prevent further infringements.

Member States have, however, adopted and developed different models of enforcement mechanisms. One group, notably Denmark, Finland, Ireland, the Netherlands, Norway, Sweden and the UK, have retained public authorities as their primary enforcement mechanisms, and have only empowered consumer associations in a secondary and, indeed, restricted, capacity. The CEE states likewise have a history based on public enforcement, which is now evolving. Another group, notably Germany, Austria, Italy and Portugal, have privatised enforcement of consumer protection to significant extents, albeit in different ways, involving empowerment of newly emerging consumer associations.

This enlistment of consumer associations in exercise of what would otherwise be a public regulatory enforcement function is a unique feature of the European approach and in contrast to the development of class actions in the United States. Interestingly, the developments of the US class action mechanism and of the European consumer association-based representative mechanism occurred contemporaneously from the early 1960s. In the United States, of course, the (long pre-existing) model was also that of 'private enforcement', but by means of permitting a single private individual to begin an action on the basis that that person's case was substantially similar to many others and that they could all be resolved by resolving the single case.

The European involvement of consumer associations arose from a desire to encourage these newly created institutions by enhancing their representative role of consumer rights through practical enforcement of 'general consumer interests' in the courts, with the right to apply for injunctive remedies. In some Member States, this enforcement role was expanded significantly, whereas it remained merely nominal in those states that had effective public enforcement bodies.

The involvement of any private body in enforcement of public laws raises some thorny issues. Notable amongst these are the extent to which such a policy falls short in satisfying requirements on democratic accountability, consistency of policy and of decisions, extent of coherent market coverage, expertise, and access to funding. Involvement of consumer associations has been encouraged as part of political policy on increasing involvement of consumers in European and market affairs: the rhetoric of 'bringing consumers closer to the market' disguises a desire on the part of European policymakers to make themselves more relevant to national voters. However, the Achilles heel of an enforcement policy that relies on consumer associations is the (un)availability of funding. The associations in Germany and Austria are effective in their scope of operations because they have governmental funding, and operate functionally almost as arms of government. In contrast, an absence of funding for consumer associations severely limits their effectiveness as an enforcement tool.

On top of these differing national models, European legislation on consumer protection has imposed some harmonising provisions on consumer protection law. In particular, the Injunctions Directive requires Member States to have one or more 'qualified entities' and the states have effectively continued their previous national models of enforcement along either public or private lines. It can appear from looking at the European legislation that there is considerable reliance on the model of using private associations as representative enforcement agencies. However, on closer inspection this appearance is misleading, for the same two reasons as mentioned above: although all Member States may now grant powers to private organisations to have representative enforcement powers, these can be rarely invoked in many states because of the pre-existing primacy of public enforcement and a lack of funding to embark on litigation.

The Injunctions Directive and the Consumer Protection Cooperation Regulation have brought about important sea-changes, not only in relation to the obvious intended issue of provision of cross-border enforcement of the consumer protection *acquis*, but in requiring all Member States to put in place single national authorities for consumer protection. Hence, Germany and Austria, amongst others, have had to create federal authorities for this purpose. This is significant since it opens up possibilities for further developments to be built on these foundations in relation to cross-border enforcement of single or collective redress, and provides a possible extension of the 'Nordic and common law' states' model.

It may therefore be that the model of private enforcement through private organisations continues to have only a limited role in collective redress, whether regulatory enforcement or delivery of compensation. It might occur that Member States would solve the funding barrier, through removal of 'loser pays' for representative actions or provision of extra funding. However, the chances of this happening are not high, given widespread reliance on 'loser pays' as a general principle and the unavailability of public funding. The arrival of third-party investors in litigation in Europe is a recent and important development, which may transform the landscape. Overall, however, more effective mechanisms for redress need to be sought elsewhere.

The EU has limited competence to legislate in relation to national civil justice systems and procedures, although vertical measures taken or proposed in some vertical areas, such as intellectual property and competition law, appear to be stealthily producing an EU-level approach towards civil procedure. The national civil justice systems differ significantly, to a far greater extent than just through the 'common law versus civil law' fault line. However, a number of Member States and the European authorities have been modernising their systems in order to produce greater efficiency (quicker outcomes and proportionate costs), and have also been developing extra-judicial alternative dispute resolution systems (again aimed at quicker and cheaper solutions). This modernisation process again produces a period of experimentation that is possibly (and even hopefully) far from complete.

Widespread debate on *collective* redress has emerged in Europe in the decade from 2000. In the previous decade, some Member States started to realise and address the fact that their civil litigations systems were inherently inefficient, slow and costly, and that justice 'delayed is justice denied'. The entire tradition of European jurisprudence is based on vindication and enforcement of individual rights, so it is not surprising that questions of how to deal with collective or aggregated issues pose considerable challenges.

The existence of differing national models for both civil litigation and regulatory enforcement means that any attempt to propose a single model, convergence or legislative harmonisation between the Member States on any basis other than mutual recognition of national models is currently all but impossible. Furthermore, there is considerable innovation and experimentation in some Member States, such that the picture is not static and it is clearly premature to draw conclusions on which models are best. Between 2003 and 2008, the four Nordic states have extended the powers of their consumer ombudsmen to seek orders for (re)payment of compensation for losses to injured consumers.

Given the current situation of diversity of national approaches, as found in this work, it is logical to proceed, as the Commission is doing, by agreeing benchmark criteria against which all available models for collective redress can be measured, and by investigating the extent to which there are problems or gaps in the market, whether horizontal or vertical.

COMPETITION LAW

In contrast to enforcement in the consumer protection field, in the competition field public enforcement has always been the model. National competent authorities provide enforcement (with almost no functions delegated to private bodies) and (unlike the situation that exists with consumer protection law) the Commission's Directorate-General on Competition has an over-arching and powerful enforcement role, albeit having devolved significant powers to national authorities since the Modernisation Directive came into force in 2004. Special collective procedures for competition damages claims are only just beginning to emerge, such as the UK's representative procedure in the CAT, and this may be reformed further.

At European level, serious consideration is currently being given to collective redress for breaches of competition law, in parallel with the debate of consumer protection law. In the competition field, the specific issue is whether private damages claims, already allowed in all Member States, should be encouraged both singly and collectively. In the consumer protection field, the use of the term collective *redress* indicates consideration of wider mechanisms than just private damages actions, although many people think only of such private mechanisms. In response, business interests have reacted in horror at the spectre of a potentially huge increase in 'class action' litigation in Europe that would extend to other fields of law.

There is, however, widespread consensus in Europe that the US class action system produces abuses and that such features are not desirable for Europe. The challenge is to increase access to justice and redress in justifiable cases, and to produce competitive markets, without also producing excessive or costly litigation that leads to unjustified settlements and imposes an unacceptable cost on the economy. Lessons can be learned from the experience of multi-party litigation in the United States, Australia, England and elsewhere. The challenge of developing a European model of collective redress is an exciting one.

CONFLICTING MODELS OF INFLUENCING BEHAVIOUR

A fundamental choice needs to be made in relation to the extent to which enforcement of public law is pursued by public or private techniques. The US choice is to emphasise private enforcement, and this can produce economies for public budgets and encourage widespread vigilance, but give rise to potentially inconsistent decisions between regulators and courts.

In relying primarily on private actors to enforce public and private standards, the US model adopts a theory based on economics: imbalances in the market can be rectified by post facto re-imposing the costs caused by non-compliance on economic operators. The theory runs that this will force non-compliers to internalise these costs, and hence bring about compliant behaviour in future through deterrence caused by economic effects. From this perspective there is some logic in removing barriers to the ability of private actors to initiate corrective action and in imposing high economic penalties on wrongdoers. From the economic perspective, such rectificational financial levers may be fines or damages, or legal transactional costs or penalties (punitive damages), or any combination of the above, since they all have the same economic effect.

The 'private enforcement' model will only be effective if initiators have sufficient financial incentives to operate it, but if those incentives are too great, intermediaries will capture the system and use it to their own rent-seeking advantage. Abuses to be avoided include excessive transactional costs, settlements agreed by intermediaries that undervalue the benefits due to consumers, targeting of 'deep pocket' businesses with good reputations so as to force blackmail settlements irrespective of merits, disproportion between sums paid to consumers and intermediaries' costs, absence of transparent control over strategic decisions—especially settlement, and exploitation of minority groups of claimants.

In contrast, the above authoritarian and economic approaches to behaviour and justice have recently been challenged by scholars. First, reliance on public and private enforcement, thus on regulation and compensation, as mutually substitutable means of behaviour control, in which one factor increases as another decreases, is questionable. Instead, these two mechanisms appear to piggy-back on each other, producing clusters. Such a result would lead to over-optimal enforcement in identified cases and a dearth of redress in other unidentified cases.

Secondly, the newer approaches start from a wider perspective of the forces that affect corporate behaviour, encompassing pressure from shareholders, stakeholders and the media, some of which operate on a continuing and therefore ex ante basis, in addition to the ex post financial penalties noted above. A wider view of what influences behaviour is also taken from that which emerges solely from consideration of economic theory. Hence, it is realised that maximisation of financial penalties is not only unnecessary to control the behaviour of individual responsible businesses, but a more responsive approach also saves enforcement resources. This is not to say that strong norms and incentives are not required: they are. However, an enforcement system that incorporates discretion and a responsive approach can be both effective and economical. The 'big stick' that is necessary to produce desired behaviour may instead comprise a sophisticated and judicious combination of other levers, both legal and non-legal, and both public and private.

Thirdly, enforcement on the basis of general deterrence alone raises issues of unfairness and disproportionality. The justification for imposing very large fines comes under attack from various directions. Is it just, such as where infringers make no actual gains or impose no actual losses? Where is the evidence that it is effective in controlling behaviour? The justification on economic theory (which stresses solely deterrence) is as yet unsupported by behavioural studies, and runs counter to the responsive regulation and Hampton policies. The policy clearly imposes huge costs on those who are caught—is this in fact contrary to EU policy on improving competitiveness? For all of these reasons, the case for a fundamental review of sanctions policy in competition law appears strong.

POLICY OBJECTIVES

At the level of fundamental policy, there are various objectives. The most important policy for European governments and the Commission is currently to enhance economic performance and global competitiveness. It is asserted that there are deficits in compliance by business with competition law and, seemingly to a lesser extent, consumer protection law, although the empirical evidence for this assertion is curiously illusory. There is evidence that some cases can arise in which infringements of competition and consumer protection law can arise, and result also in financial loss for competitors and consumers. In such circumstances, the people harmed may be a small number of competitors who have significant resources and can assert their rights and recover compensation through the existing legal system or settlement. Situations can also arise in which the people harmed have limited resources, expertise or knowledge, and in which groups can suffer identical or similar losses. It is this last situation that is the core of the current challenge.

The challenge arises because every legal system will give rise to a threshold point at which the cost of pursuing a case is uneconomic, or its complexity unsurmountable, for those with limited resources. There is currently dissatisfaction that a number of European legal systems are slow and costly, and therefore give rise to a cost-benefit threshold that is unacceptably high.[1] However, whatever the cost-benefit fulcrum point is in each national system, it is inescapable in any system. This is precisely the reason why small claims procedures have been introduced, designed to operate informally and with no or minimal costs or delay. Much of the current debate on collective redress arises because of the conundrum of how to devise a collective procedure for small claims, since this would inevitably involve significantly increased formality, cost and delay.

Overall, the policy of increasing access to justice is of lesser importance than that of producing a vibrant and competitive market. This is because individual losses may be small and below the cost-benefit threshold to be worth pursuing (both for individuals and as a matter of allocation by the state of resources to deliver compensation through the courts), but the effects on the market as a whole (and on SMEs) produce significant distortion and are worth addressing. These considerations indicate that the arguments for intervention to maintain a balanced market and to remove illicit gains, since the effects are more widespread and the illicit gains may be great, are stronger than for delivering small sums in compensation to many individuals or in expending excessive cost in doing so. They also, therefore, support the argument that the mechanisms that would appear to be most appropriate in order to deliver such objectives would primarily be in public law rather than private law, and involve public authorities rather than private actors.

Various national systems, led by England and Wales, Sweden, Germany and the Netherlands, with others following, have acted to improve the internal efficiencies in their court systems when faced with processing multiple similar claims for damages. Three points are striking about the revolutionary rules that have been introduced in each of these states.

First, their approaches are all different (again raising a harmonisation problem). Secondly, they have all rejected the US class action model and its opt-out approach. It is recognised that a model in which a single representative can—in some but not all cases—be dispositive of a group of similar claims, but the associated opt-out and lawyer-led mechanistic features necessarily involve risks of excessive costs and abuse that are regarded in Europe as unacceptable. The United States may have greater 'access to justice', but it involves a level of transactional costs and litigation that Europeans view as unacceptable.

Thirdly, every court-based collective litigation model (including the different approaches of the United States and many other jurisdictions around

---

[1] CDPC, 'Cost-effective measures taken by States to increase the Efficiency of Justice: Report prepared by the European Committee on Legal Co-operation (CDCJ) in consultation with the European Committee on Crime Problems', 23rd Conference of European Ministers of Justice (8–9 June 2000); and Green Paper: Access of consumers to justice and the settlement of consumer disputes in the single market, COM(93) 576, 16 November 1993 57.

the world) needs to balance requirements of due process, selection of one or a small number of cases for decision that will be binding on or influence resolution of all or a significant number of similar cases, and provide for settlements to be binding on as large a number of those with similar cases as possible. The due process issue raises constitutional concerns that manifest themselves in the opt-in versus opt-out debate. Europe is taking a cautious approach to these issues, and this leads to maintaining an opt-in approach, as accepted by the Commission in 2008 in its competition damages proposals.

However, despite experimentation with various approaches, no national model has yet emerged as a blueprint for the future. Furthermore, the diversity is such that scope for harmonising individual mechanisms is limited: any national mechanism must in fact be seen in the context of the matrix of legal and alternative dispute resolution procedures of which it forms part.

Experimentation with collective procedures should not, however, be permitted to obscure the underlying problem of inefficiencies in national civil justice systems. Collective procedures may be new and diverting, but do not solve the ongoing problems of access to justice. Indeed, collective procedures operate within national civil justice systems and may only serve to expose the latters' inefficiencies. Will it be acceptable if, for example, multiple claims like the Deutshe Telekom shareholders case, the ongoing French mobile phone cases, or any future Italian mass case take 10 years to resolve and involve enormous cost? Hence, governments and courts still need to address the efficiency and outputs of their national civil justice systems, onto which collective procedures are grafted. The experience to date seems to point towards seeking solutions for the court systems in case management, flexibility, control of funding and costs, and multi-tracking cases. Solutions outside courts, such as mediation, compensation schemes like the Nordic Medical and Drug Insurance schemes, ombudsmen, industry schemes within codes of conduct, or public oversight of dispute resolution, all seem to offer opportunities to be developed.

REDRESS AND JUSTICE

These developments in national legal systems highlight a growing tension between, on the one hand, traditional principles of law and legal systems as being based on *rights*, individual assertion of rights, and courts that declare and deliver *justice* and, on the other hand, considerations that 'justice delayed is justice denied' and a market-inspired requirement that court systems need to operate *efficiently*, speedily and involve low and proportionate cost. A stable accommodation between these two approaches has yet be worked out in many European civil justice systems, not least in relation to 'normal' rules or procedure for individual claims. However, it is clear that acute difficulties are raised in accommodating requirements of due process and individual fundamental rights with court-based collective mechanisms.

It has also been seen above that these considerations challenge what is meant by justice and what means are appropriate to deliver justice in contemporary civil society. Can courts deliver fair solutions at an acceptable cost? Is it necessary for private parties and/or regulators and governments to adopt more flexible and imaginative outcomes and procedures in order to achieve justice?

Many of the case studies show the huge legal costs of any court-based mass system. This is clearly a US phenomenon that Europe wishes to avoid, but the benzodiazepines, football shirts, DES, Dexia, Deutsche Telekom and French telecom cases all involved large lawyers' fees.

In any event, significant modernisation needs to take place in several states' civil justice systems so as to improve their efficiency. Introducing certain reforms can be expected to cut at least some costs from the litigation process. Any cut in cost will tend to increase the number of claims that can enter the system and affect settlement leverage. The whole point of any collective mechanism is to be more efficient by pooling issues and costs, and hence make claims cheaper and more claims viable.

The debate on collective *redress* has transcended that of collective *actions*. The first step is to understand that redress can encompass both market behaviour and compensatory aspects, and systems can be designed to achieve efficient fusion of these goals. Many people in the debate think solely in terms of the US class action model, which essentially puts damages first, but is claimed to have deterrent and regulatory functions, whilst operating at huge cost and raising serious issues of abuse and (lack of) democratic accountability, consistency and subtlety. If, instead, one thinks about how to ensure effective and efficient functioning of markets, encouraging virtuous behaviour in normal activities and responding to mistakes and damage, Europe has the opportunity to adopt a different but potentially far more effective model. In the United States, the approach is that private actions take the lead and are complemented by limited public action. The opportunity for Europe arises through reversing that approach on a more integrated basis.

There have been two starting points, compensation and compliance, but the question is whether and how they can both be accommodated. Detailed consideration of how to deliver compensation in worthy cases has lead to rejection of the US class action model, but also realisation that the US model claims justification primarily as an enforcement model, mistrusting and limiting public enforcement. Detailed consideration of enforcement in Europe seeks to expand the capacity of public enforcement as a means of providing effective cross-border regulation of the internal market. Consideration of the excess of US private enforcement leads to rejection of that approach.

Delegation of enforcement to the private sector leads to many disadvantages. Although procedures for claiming damages in aggregate litigation are being introduced by some European states, this does not mean that a US private enforcement policy has been adopted: it has not.

The US legal system reflects the nature and values of the society in which it operates, namely, individual enterprise within a capitalist market. Federal or other public control is limited and huge public enforcement costs are saved by permitting individual private enforcement utilising private law remedies and class action techniques. The result produces damages in some types of case (notably for investors) and not others (consumer claims), but has questionable success in performing effective and consistent regulatory functions and imposes large costs on business.

Europe, in contrast, is only now confronting the implications of enforcement and mass compensation within a single market. The mechanisms are still routed in the primacy of public enforcement and of private individual damages claims. Existing systems seem to reveal deficits in provision of mass damages and in some regulatory enforcement aspects (in competition possibly more than in consumer protection), but the empirical evidence for this is pretty thin.

The real issues are: first and by far the most important, to deliver rectification of market imbalances; secondly, to deliver compensation when due; thirdly, to adopt effective but proportionate controls on behaviour (both before and after undesirable behaviour); and fourthly to enhance the economy, but not harm it.

Europe has a unique opportunity to do something about mass redress that is both effective and innovative, learning from the evidence. Emerging theory of regulation and enforcement shows a way forward. If public oversight of enforcement imports the policy of restorative justice, both compensation and enforcement goals can be combined. If the public authority has a big enough stick, but adopts an enlightened responsive or risk-based policy on enforcement, it should not need to wield the stick as much as it would under a 'command and control' policy. That should save resources. Further, classic regulatory theory postulates that the existence of the big stick in public hands will tend to encourage voluntary self-regulatory behaviour—redress through owning up, rectification, compensation and future individual compliance. The US model is that both public and private systems wield big sticks. A simple analogy for Europe is that one only needs one, and putting it in public hands is preferable. The analysis of risks and benefits between public and private mechanisms in chapter nine shows that the optimal model, which can deliver both compensation and enforcement (ie redress), is a system that empowers public oversight of redress, encourages voluntary compliance and utilises private mechanisms as a tertiary long stop.

Wielding of a big stick to encourage appropriate behaviour is more acceptable (and more European) if undertaken by democratically accountable public officials and wielded responsively, in proportion to the risk and need, thereby tending towards efficiency. Public bodies have significant opportunity to encourage virtuous behaviour and redress, but only if they operate along particular lines to encourage voluntary action and provide effective oversight. Private collective actions through the courts would still have a place, but need to be kept under control to avoid usurping the effectiveness of the public and voluntary models. Very significant developments in the funding of private litigation are currently occurring across Europe, which can be expected to have a profound effect on altering the dynamics and economics of litigation: governments need to review developments very seriously and regulate all funding and representative behaviour, particularly where large numbers of people and amounts of money are involved.

The point was made above that a dispute resolution system should reflect the nature and values of its society. Discussions of European society frequently stress social solidarity and cohesion. It is no accident that Europe is considered to be less litigious than the United States. This does not mean that rights or injuries should be ignored, but it does imply that approaches to rectifying problems may prefer to be responsive and informal.

Overall, therefore, reforms are called for in both civil justice systems and in policies on enforcement. The risk of producing ineffective, inappropriate and expensive systems is considerable if Europe gets the balance wrong. However, if Europe gets the balance right, it could produce a greater degree of virtuous behaviour in commerce and redress, more redress and overall lower cost, thereby enhancing both competitiveness and social and moral cohesion. Does this all sound too idealistic? Time may tell.

Appendix 1

Select Articles from France

ACTION TAKEN IN THE COLLECTIVE INTEREST OF CONSUMERS
(ARTICLES L. 421-1 TO L. 421-8 OF THE CONSUMER CODE)

Civil Action

Article L. 421-1

Properly declared associations whose expressed aim is the protection of consumer interests may, if they are approved for this purpose, exercise the rights of a party to the prosecution[1] in respect of events directly or indirectly harming the collective interest of consumers.

The organisations defined in Article L. 211-2 of the French family and social welfare code are exempt from the need for approval to go to law under the terms of this Article.

Article L.421-2

Consumer associations referred to in Article L. 421-1, when acting under the terms thereof, may ask the civil court, ruling on civil actions, or the criminal court, ruling on civil actions, to order the defendant or the accused, if necessary under pain of a fine,[2] to take any action to stop illegal behaviour or to remove illegal clauses from a particular contract or a standard contract offered to consumers.

Article L. 421-3

The criminal court to which the case is referred under Article L. 421-1 may, after finding the accused guilty, postpone sentencing and order the guilty party, if necessary under pain of a fine, to comply within a given time limit with its instructions to stop illegal behaviour or to remove illegal clauses from a particular contract or a standard contract offered to consumers.

---

[1] 'Partie civile': these rights include notice of hearings, the right to be heard, rights of appeal, and the right to demand damages.
[2] 'Astreinte': a financial penalty, often increasing with time until a court order is obeyed.

Should the criminal court combine the postponement with a fine, it must specify the rate of the fine and the date from which it shall run. Postponement can occur only once and may be decided even if the accused does not appear in person. The judge may order the provisional enforcement of the injunction.

Article L. 421-4

At the postponed hearing, which must take place within one year of the decision to postpone, the court shall pronounce the sentence and order payment of the fine, if there is one. It may, where appropriate, cancel the fine completely or reduce its amount. The fine is collected by the Treasury in the same way as a criminal fine. It cannot result in arrest and detention.

Article L. 421-5

The fine is automatically cancelled whenever it is established that the person concerned has complied with an order made by another criminal judge to stop, under pain of a fine, an offence identical to the one giving rise to the proceedings.

Action to Stop Illegal Behaviour

Article L. 421-6

Associations referred to in Article L. 421-1 and entities able to provide proof of their inclusion on the list published in the Official Journal of the European Communities under Article 4 of Directive 98/27/CE of the European Parliament and Council relating to actions to obtain an injunction to protect the collective interests of consumers may bring an action before the civil court to stop or prohibit any illegal behaviour in the light of the provisions transposing the Directives referred to in Article 1 of the aforementioned Directive.

The judge may order, on these grounds, if necessary under pain of a fine, the deletion of an illegal or abusive clause from any contract or standard contract offered to or intended for the consumer.

Legal Intervention

Article L. 421-7

Associations referred to in Article L. 421-1 may join proceedings in civil courts and, in particular, request the application of the measures provided for in Article L. 421-2, where the initial proceeding aims to repair a wrong suffered by one or more consumers due to events that do not constitute a criminal offence.

JOINT REPRESENTATIVE ACTION (ARTICLES L. 422-1 TO L. 422-3 OF THE CONSUMER CODE)

Article L. 422-1

Where several individual, identified consumers have suffered personal prejudice having a common origin through the actions of the same person, any approved association recognised as being a nationwide representative within the meaning of Title I may, if instructed to do so by at least two of the consumers concerned, sue for damages before any court on behalf of those consumers.

The instruction cannot be solicited via a public appeal on television or radio, nor via a poster campaign, tracts, or personalized letters. It must be given in writing by each consumer.

Article L. 422-2

Any consumer who has agreed, under the terms of Article L. 422-1, to the institution of proceedings before a criminal court is, in this event, deemed to be exercising the rights of a party to the prosecution as defined by the Code of Criminal Procedure. Nevertheless, all notifications concerning the consumer shall be sent to the association.

Article L. 422-3

Associations instituting legal proceedings under Articles L. 422-1 and L. 422-2 may sue for damages before the examining judge or the relevant court having jurisdiction over the registered office of the company against whom the proceedings are brought or, failing that, over the place where the first offence was committed.

ACTION TAKEN BY AUTHORISED ASSOCIATIONS FOR THE PROTECTION OF HEALTH

Article 1114-2 of the Public Health Code

When a public action has been instituted by the national Ministry or the injured party, and subject to the victim's agreement, approved nationwide associations within the meaning of Article L. 1114-1 may exercise the rights of a party to the prosecution in respect of infringements covered by Articles 221-6, 222-19 and 22-20 of the Penal Code and infringements covered by the Public Health Code which harm the collective interests of health system users.

ACTION TAKEN BY AUTHORISED ASSOCIATIONS FOR THE PROTECTION OF THE ENVIRONMENT

Article L. 142-2 of the Environment Code

Approved associations within the meaning of Article L. 141-2 may exercise the rights of a party to the prosecution in respect of acts which directly or indirectly harm the collective interests that they defend and which constitute an infringement of laws governing the protection of nature and the environment, the improvement of living conditions, the protection of water, air, soils, sites and landscapes, town planning, or laws aimed at combating pollution and nuisances, and infringements of the texts used in implementing these laws.

This right is also granted, under the same conditions, to associations which have been properly declared for at least five years at the date of the events and whose articles of association specify the aim of safeguarding all or part of the interests described in Article L. 211-1, in respect of events constituting an infringement of the provisions relating to water, or the interests described in Article L. 511-1, in respect of events constituting an infringement of the provisions relating to legally preserved buildings.

ACTION TAKEN BY ASSOCIATIONS FOR THE DEFENCE OF INVESTORS (ARTICLES L. 452-2 TO L. 452-3 OF THE MONETARY AND FINANCIAL CODE)

Article L. 452-2

If several individual persons identified in their capacity as investors have suffered personal prejudice having a common origin through the actions of the same person, any association referred to in Article L. 452-1 may, if instructed to do so by at least two of the investors concerned, sue for damages before any court on behalf of those investors.

The instruction cannot be solicited via a public appeal on television or radio, nor via a poster campaign, tracts or personalised letters. It must be given in writing by each investor.

However, if an approved association brings an action for damages before the civil or commercial courts under the third paragraph of Article L. 452-1, the presiding judge of the Tribunal de Grande Instance[3] or the Commercial Court, as applicable, may issue a summary order authorising it to solicit a power of attorney from the shareholders empowering it, at its own expense, to act on their behalf and have recourse to the advertising channels referred to in the previous paragraph.

Without prejudice to the provisions of Articles L. 612-1 to L. 612-5 of the Commercial Code, the associations referred to in the previous paragraph draw up a balance sheet, a profit and loss account and an appendix each year, the scope and presentation of which are determined by decree, which are approved by the meeting of members. When the association brings an action in accordance with the previous paragraph, it sends those documents to the presiding judge.

Article L. 452-3

Any investor having given his agreement, as provided for in Article L. 452-2, for the bringing of an action before a criminal court is deemed in those circumstances to be exercising the rights of a party to the prosecution as defined by the Code of Criminal Procedure. Nevertheless, all notifications concerning the investor shall be sent to the association.

Article L. 452-4

An association bringing a legal action under Articles L. 452-2 and L. 452-3 may sue for damages before the examining judge or the relevant court having jurisdiction over the registered office or domicile of the person against whom the proceedings are brought, or, failing that, over the place where the first offence was committed.

PRODUCTION OF EVIDENCE IN CIVIL COURT CASES

Production of Evidence Held by the Parties or Third Parties (articles 11 and 138 to 142 of the New Code of Civil Procedure)

The parties are required to cooperate in the investigative measures and the judge may draw conclusions from any failure or refusal to do so.

If a party holds evidence material, the judge may, at the other party's request, order him to produce it, if necessary under pain of a fine. He may, if requested by one of the parties, request or order, if necessary under pain of the same fine, the production of all documents held by third parties where there is no legitimate impediment to doing so.

---

[3] District Court.

Article 138

If, during the proceeding, a party wishes to rely on an authentic instrument or an instrument under private signature to which he was not a party, or a document held by a third party, he may request the judge hearing the case to order that a certified copy be sent to the court or the instrument or document itself be produced.

Article 139

The request may be made without any formality.

If the judge considers that the request is fully justified, he will order that the original or copy or extract of the instrument be sent or produced, as the case may be, under the conditions and guarantees that he determines, if necessary under pain of a fine.

Article 140

The decision of the judge will be enforceable on a provisional basis.

Article 141

If a difficulty arises or a legitimate impediment is put forward, the judge who ordered the sending or the production in court may, upon a simple request, withdraw or amend his decision. The third party may appeal against the new decision within fifteen days of its pronouncement.

Article 142

Requests for the production of evidence held by the parties must be made, and evidence must be produced, in accordance with Articles 138 and 139.

Summary Procedure—Preparatory Inquiries (article 145 of the New Code of Civil Procedure)

Article 145

If there is a legitimate reason to preserve or to establish, before any legal process, the evidence of the facts upon which the resolution of the dispute depends, legally permissible preparatory inquiries may be ordered at the request of any interested party, by way of a petition or by way of a summary procedure.

Appendix 2

UK Financial Ombudsman Service[1]

HISTORY

The technique of using an ombudsman for disputes with private-sector bodies was invented with the Insurance Ombudsman Scheme of 1981. It was based on two principles that still apply: decisions would be based on what was 'fair and reasonable' and companies would be bound by decisions but consumers would not, but would be free to take their cases to court if they wished. The second aspect was so as to encourage people to use the ombudsman scheme.

The Banking Ombudsman was created in 1985, operating from 1986. Building societies did not initially join until their 1986 Act required them to join a scheme. The Financial Services Act 1986 (operational 1988) for investments led to schemes such as the PIA Ombudsman (established by the Personal Investment Authority) and the Investment Ombudsman (established by the Investment Management Regulation Organisation).

All previous schemes were rolled into the Financial Ombudsman Service (FOS) on 1 December 2001 under the statutory requirements of the Financial Services and Markets Act 2000 (FS&MA), which also created the Financial Services Authority (FSA). The staff was then a complement of 300. Work expanded rapidly, with a yearly increase of 10 to 14 per cent, with was overlaid by complaints over mortgage endowments, and staff rose to 1,000. After the mortgage endowments issue subsided, staff fell to the current 705, achieved through natural turnover and a voluntary redundancy programme.

JURISDICTION

The FOS covers the following three areas:

1. Compulsory: all 21,000 firms regulated by the FSA and which deal with retail customers, including wider financial transactions, eg loans and credit cards.

---

[1] This information was kindly provided by David Thomas, Principal Ombudsman, at a meeting on 23 January 2008. For further information see <http://www.financial-ombudsman. org.uk/> accessed 2 July 2008.

2. Consumer credit: 100,000 businesses compulsory since 7 April 2007— anyone with a standard OFT consumer credit licence (not solicitors or accountants).
3. Voluntary: National Savings & Investments; some cross-border business originating elsewhere in the EEA directed at UK consumers; PayPal (was based in the UK, relocated to Luxembourg, but continues to accept FOS jurisdiction).

Areas 1 and 2 relate to services provided from establishments in the UK only (but their customers covered worldwide).

ARRANGEMENTS

The FOS has restructured itself on consideration of what is the fair, efficient and timely way to resolve cases. This has led to putting an intelligent enquiry-handler at the front end. The FOS receives around 600,000 enquiries, which turn into some 94,000 cases. This exceeds the number of contested cases in county courts, excluding family cases. Hence, over one in six enquiries can be resolved swiftly at the front end.

If a case proceeds, an adjudicator is assigned (from a pool of 400), who screens cases and decides if they are not worth more than any amount that has been offered. This may lead to a mediated result, reached through talking to both sides about the value of the case. If the case is not settled, the adjudicator will make a finding. Either party may then refer the case to one of the 31 ombudsmen for *de novo* review: only eight per cent of cases are so referred.

If the consumer accepts an ombudsman decision, it is legally binding on both parties. If a consumer rejects an ombudsman decision, neither party is bound, but the consumer can refer the case to court, although this is more a theoretical option than real in view of court costs. The ombudsman can award up to £100,000.

COST AND SOURCE OF FINANCE

The FOS costs £54 million annually. Two-thirds of this comes from fees: a defendant would pay £400 win or lose. Fee rates for smaller businesses are mitigated: they have two free cases per year, and the number is to be increased. The result is that only 5.5 per cent of firms ever pay this fee. The other one-third comes from a levy on all firms, based on the justification that the existence of the FOS and its ability to deal with and defuse many enquiries underpins public confidence in the industry. The rates paid are aligned to the volume of work undertaken per sector each year: number of accounts held for banks and volume of investment income for insurance.

TRENDS IN CLAIMS

The experience is that surges of specific types of cases have tended to arise at different times. These have often been driven by consumer champions, such as leading consumer advocates or claims management companies (which would be seeking fees through furthering issues). Two examples of case types are:

1. TESSAs—tax exempt special savings accounts. After an article in a Sunday newspaper, the FOS received 1,200 calls on the Monday relating to TESSAs and ultimately around 2,000 cases. The FOS issued a guidance note on the issues, which indicated that they it was thought unlikely that they would uphold claims in certain specified circumstances. The implication was that claims in other circumstances would be upheld, and that message was correctly read by all the banks, who promptly settled their cases that fell within the risky parameters. Accordingly, the FOS upheld no single claim against a bank. However, the building societies refused to settle and the FOS upheld a significant number of claims against them. One company unsuccessfully judicially reviewed the FOS.
2. Dual variable mortgage rates. Lenders advertised some mortgages on the basis of this new description, which was claimed to be an advantageous rate compared with the standard rate. However, it was not their standard rate, but a specially invented one. There were 10,000 cases mainly against four providers.

MODE OF OPERATION

The FOS has no specific collective claim mechanisms, such as the equivalent of a GLO. However, it has developed procedures that can effectively deal with multiple horizontal issues. The principal tools are as follows:

1. Lead case process. The FOS identifies if a common principle exists in a group of cases. This is usually the case only involving claims against an individual provider, in view of the fact that contractual terms vary between different providers. If complaints relate to investments made/sold, there will be individual issues for each investor, so there is unlikely to be a dispositive common issue. If complaints refer to contractual terms, then there will be a common issue.

   In the latter case, the FOS can group cases, identify an individual 'clean case' for each group (ie one in which the common issue arises without other complications) and proceed to decide that. The other group cases would be parked pending resolution of the lead case. The FOS would write to individuals to inform them what was going on. After the lead case has been decided, the FOS could lean on the provider, who would usually settle the rest of the group cases. If the consumer lost the lead case, the FOS would send an anonymised copy of the decision to all group consumers, and say that if they thought that the circumstances in their case were different, they should tell the FOS. Only around 10 per cent of people revert in those circumstances, usually on the basis that they disagree with the lead case finding on principle, rather than claiming that their cases are different.

The risk with this procedure is that a party will come up with a new argument that the FOS has not considered during resolution of the lead case. This has not so far happened—it is an inherent risk in any court decision—but the FOS has addressed the point through the 'wider implications' procedure—see below.

2. Test case procedure. If one or more cases turn purely on a point of law and the provider agrees to pay the consumer's costs, a case can be referred to the High Court for determination. This avoids the risk that a determination by the FOS will be taken to judicial review. The procedure has not yet been used, although the House of Lords decision in Equitable Life was a similar procedure, on referral from the former PIA Ombudsman. The current case on interest rates for unauthorised bank overdrafts has reached court by another route.

3. Wider Implications procedure. See <http://www.wider-implications.info> accessed 12 June 2008.

This may be invoked if wider implications relate to the FSA, FOS or OFT. There have been about 10 case studies, and 12 refused. It arose from the two-year review of the Financial Services and Markets Act 2000 and the OFT joined in. It applies where there are significant implications for consumers in general, or for industry, or even for one business: there must be a new issue. Most issues have been identified by the FSA or FOS; the consumers' association has raised one, and industry has raised none.

The first step is for the FOS and the relevant regulator to agree whether the issue is wider implications and whether the procedure should be used.

The second step is for the regulator to decide whether it is going to do anything. They intervene less often than might be imagined. The first case study (precipice bonds) is on the website. Precipice bonds involve a lump sum with a guaranteed high income level, but the small print says that if the stock market falls below a certain level, the investor's 'guaranteed' income would come out of capital. There were a number of cases against one bank, mostly involving older customers located right across the country, who were targeted through a phone call, hence indicating a formal policy rather than local practice. The FOS informed the FSA, the bank was fined £1.7 million and the FSA also indicated that consumers in a defined group should automatically be compensated, with others being entitled to go to the FOS.

If the regulator decides not to take action, for example deciding that cases need to be dealt with individually, the third step is for the FOS to decide whether to adopt a procedure which has been designed to parallel how issues would be dealt with in court, involving briefs. Thus, both the Financial Services Consumer Panel and industry liaison bodies would be asked to appoint an expert, who would act as amicus in a lead case. There would be an open due process. An example relates to s 75 of the Consumer Credit Act, under which a provider of credit is equally liable as the provider of the contract. The case involved eBay purchases on a credit cards: the arrangement is in fact that the customer's debit card would credit Paypal, which would pay the supplier. The finding was that s 75 does not apply.

The FSA has a statutory power to seek or make a restitution order (FS&MA ss 383 and 384). When deciding whether or not to use restitutionary powers, a regulator might be affected by other statutory responsibilities—such as maintaining confidence in the system or the financial viability of regulated institutions.

OTHER EU MEMBER STATES

The position is very different across the EU over which states have a financial ADR system. Financial ADRs which comply with EU standards can join a cooperative network called FIN-NET. Details of those that have registered are available at <http://www.fin-net.eu> accessed 12 June 2008. A brief summary is as follows:

a) Ireland—similar to the UK, but decisions bind the consumer;
b) the Netherlands—a single FSO, with voluntary schemes;
c) Belgium—Banking Ombudsman and Investments, not insurance;
d) France—a confused situation—there are mediations for different sectors, eg insurance; banks can appoint their own mediators;
e) Spain—other than a central bank scheme, little exists;
f) Portugal—consumer redress is based on regional chambers of commerce;
g) Italy—a mediation scheme for investment, which is moving from voluntary to a compulsory banking scheme; and
h) Germany—highly complex situation: three kinds of bank scheme (two federal, one *länder*) plus through the regulator, making some 16 schemes in all.

SOME CONCLUSIONS

The FOS scheme keeps a considerable number of claims out of court, but also provides a mechanism for resolution of many claims that would be uneconomic for consumers to take into court, or for which they would be deterred by lack of knowledge, expertise, access to evidence or time.

Appendix 3

Sweden: Group Proceedings Act 2002

<http://www.sweden.gov.se/content/1/c6/02/77/67/bcbe1f4f.pdf> accessed 12 June 2008.

SWEDISH CODE OF STATUTES

SFS 2002:599
issued by the printers in June 2002

Group Proceedings Act

issued on 30 May 2002.
The following is enacted in accordance with a decision[1] by the Swedish Riksdag.

Introductory Provisions

Group Action

Section 1 In this Act, group action means an action that a plaintiff brings as the representative of several persons with legal effects for them, although they are not parties to the case. A group action may be instituted as a private group action, an organisation action or a public group action.

Group means the persons for whom the plaintiff brings the action.

Group Proceedings

Section 2 Proceedings where a group action is brought are referred to as group proceedings. Group proceedings can relate to claims that can be dealt

---

[1] Government Bill 2001/02:107, Commissioners Report 2001/02:02:JuU16, Riksdag Communication 2001/02:246.

with by a general court in accordance with the rules contained in the Code of Judicial Procedure on civil cases.

The provisions of the Code of Judicial Procedure on civil cases apply to group proceedings, except for Chapter 1, Section 3 d, unless otherwise stated in this Act.

Group proceedings may also be brought in accordance with special provisions contained in the Environmental Code.

How a Group Action is Instituted, etc

Competent Courts

Section 3 The district courts designated by the Government shall be competent to process cases under this Act. There shall be at least one competent district court in each county.

Right to Bring an Action

Section 4 A private group action may be instituted by a natural person who, or legal entity that, himself, herself or itself has a claim that is subject to the action.

Section 5 An organisation action may be instituted by a not-for-profit association that, in accordance with its rules, protects consumer or wage-earner interests in disputes between consumers and a business operator regarding any goods, services or other utility that the business operator offers to consumers.

In the first paragraph

consumers: means natural persons who acted primarily for purposes outside business operations,
business operator: a natural person or legal entity that acted for purposes that are connected with their own business operation.

An organisation action referred to in the first paragraph may also include a dispute of another kind, provided there are significant advantages with the disputes being jointly adjudicated taking into consideration the investigation and other circumstances.

Section 6 A public group action may be instituted by an authority that, taking into consideration the subject of dispute, is suitable to represent the members of the group. The Government decides which authorities are allowed to institute public group actions.

Section 7 The right to represent the group does not end if there is a change to the circumstances on which the right to institute the action in accordance with Sections 4–6 has been founded.

Special Preconditions for Proceedings

Section 8 A group action may only be considered if

1. the action is founded on circumstances that are common or of a similar nature for the claims of the members of the group,
2. group proceedings do not appear to be inappropriate owing to some claims of the members of the group, as regards grounds, differing substantially from other claims,
3. the larger part of the claims to which the action relates cannot equally well be pursued by personal actions by the members of the group,
4. the group, taking into consideration its size, ambit and otherwise is appropriately defined, and
5. the plaintiff, taking into consideration the plaintiff's interest in the substantive matter, the plaintiff's financial capacity to bring a group action and the circumstances generally, is appropriate to represent the members of the group in the case.

Content of the Application

Section 9 An application for a summons shall, in addition to the provisions of Chapter 42, Section 2 of the Code of Judicial Procedure, contain details concerning

1. the group to which the action relates,
2. the circumstances that are common or similar for the claims of the members of the group,
3. the circumstances known to the plaintiff that are important for the consideration of only some of the claims of the members of the group, and
4. other circumstances that are important for the issue of whether the claims should be processed as group proceedings.

The plaintiff shall state in the application the names and addresses of all members of the group. Such details may be omitted if they are not necessary for processing the case. The plaintiff shall also provide details of circumstances that are otherwise important for notifications to the members of the group.

Change of Form of Action

Section 10 A person who is the plaintiff in proceedings can, by written application to the district court, request that the case should be transformed into group proceedings. In that event, the provisions of Section 9 and Chapter 42, Sections 2–4 of the Code of Judicial Procedure shall apply. An application may only be granted if the defendant consents to this or if it is manifest that the advantages with group proceedings outweigh the inconvenience that such proceedings may be deemed to entail for the defendant.

The application shall be served on the defendant for views. If the application is unfounded, the court may dismiss it immediately.

If the district court where a case is pending is not competent to deal with the group action, the application shall be transferred to a competent court. If the application is manifestly unfounded, the court may immediately reject the application instead of transferring it.

Attorneys

Section 11 A private group action and an organisation action shall be brought through an attorney who is an advocate. If there are special reasons, the court may allow the action to be brought without an attorney or through an attorney who is not an advocate.

Section 12 A power of attorney that relates to proceedings generally does not empower the attorney to institute a group action or to receive a summons in group proceedings.

Notifications to the Members that Group Proceedings have been Instituted

Section 13 If the plaintiff's application to commence group proceedings is not dismissed, the members of the group shall be notified of the proceedings.

The notification shall, to the extent considered appropriate by the court, contain

1. a brief description of the application
2. information about
   a) group proceedings as a form for processing,
   b) the opportunity for the members to personally participate in the proceedings,
   c) the legal effect of a judgment in group proceedings, and
   d) the rules applicable to litigation costs,
3. details of the names and addresses of the plaintiff and attorney,
4. notice of the date determined by the court for notices in accordance with Section 14, and
5. information about other circumstances that are important for the rights of the members of the group.

Definition of the Group

Section 14 A member of the group who does not give notice to the court in writing, within the period determined by the court, that he or she wishes to be included in the group action shall be deemed to have withdrawn from the group.

Status of the Member of the Group

Section 15 A member of the group shall be equated with a party when applying the rules of the Code of Judicial Procedure on disqualification situations, pending proceedings, joinder of cases, examination during the proceedings and other issues relating to evidence.

Disqualification

Section 16 A member of the group who is not a party may, even if he or she has not entered into the proceedings as an invervenor, present an objection regarding disqualification of a judge within two weeks from the date when he or she became aware that the judge is participating in the processing of the case. If the circumstance on which the disqualification is founded was not then known to the member, the objection may be presented within two weeks from the date when the member became aware of the circumstance.

Subsequent Processing

Obligations of the Plaintiff

Section 17 When conducting the action, the plaintiff shall protect the interests of the members of the group.

On important issues, the plaintiff shall afford the members of the group an opportunity to express their views, if this can be done without great inconvenience. If a member of the group so requests, the plaintiff shall provide such information as is of importance for the rights of the member.

Extension of Action

Section 18 The court may allow the plaintiff to extend a group action to comprise other claims on the part of the members of the group or new members of the group, provided this can be done without it causing any significant delay to the determination of the case and without other substantial inconvenience for the defendant. An application for an extension of an action shall be given in writing and contain such details as are referred to in Section 9.

Transfer of the Subject to which the Dispute Relates

Section 19 If the plaintiff or a member of the group transfers the subject to which the dispute relates to someone else, the provisions of Chapter 13, Section 7 of the Code of Judicial Procedure shall apply as regard the right and obligation of such person to enter as a member of the group.

Sub-groups

Section 20 The court may assign someone, besides the plaintiff or instead of the plaintiff, to conduct the action on a particular issue or a part of the substantive matter that only applies to the rights of particular members of the group, if this promotes an appropriate processing. Such an assignment may be given to a member of the group or, if this is not possible, someone else.

The parties and members of the group affected shall be given an opportunity to express their views before the court makes a decision, provided this is not manifestly unnecessary. The court shall specify in the decision what part of the group and the issue or part of the substantive matter that the appointment relates to.

The provisions of this Act concerning plaintiffs also apply in relevant respects to a person that has been appointed to conduct an action in accordance with the first paragraph.

Substitution of Plaintiff

Section 21 If the plaintiff is no longer considered to be appropriate to represent the members of the group in the case, the court shall appoint someone else who is entitled to bring action in accordance with Sections 4–6 to conduct the group's action as plaintiff.

If no new plaintiff can be appointed in accordance with the first paragraph, the group action shall be dismissed. If the plaintiff is the appellant's counterparty in a superior court, the court may appoint someone else who is considered appropriate to conduct the group's action as plaintiff.

Section 22 In cases other than those referred to in Section 21, another person may only take over the plaintiff's action if the plaintiff has transferred their part of the subject of dispute or if there are other special reasons.

Discontinuation of Group Proceedings or Part of Them

Section 23 If the plaintiff withdraws the group action within the time period for notice, in accordance with Section 14, the case shall be written off in its entirety. If the plaintiff, within the period, withdraws the case regarding a part that refers to a claim of a particular member of the group, that claim shall be written off.

Should, at the expiry of the period for notice, an issue arise concerning the writing off of the case in its entirety or dismissal of the group action, the court shall afford the parties and the members of the group an opportunity to express their views, unless this is manifestly unnecessary.

The second paragraph also applies if an issue arises concerning the writing off of the case or dismissal of an action in a part referable to a particular claim of a member of the group.

Section 24 The court may decide a period within which a member of the group shall give notice to the court in writing that they, if the group proceedings as regards their claim are discontinued, wishes to enter as a party and bring the action concerning their rights.

If a notice concerning entry is made in accordance with the first paragraph, the court shall separate the plaintiff's case to which the notice applies and decide on the future processing. The court may, subject to the preconditions referred to in Chapter 1, Section 3 d of the Code of Judicial Procedure, decide that the case should be dealt with applying that section.

The court can transfer a separated case to another competent court, if this is best taking into consideration the investigation and the other circumstances.

Section 25 If an appeal is withdrawn or shall be dismissed for reasons other than it having been delivered too late, the provisions contained in Section 23, second and third paragraphs and Section 24, first and second paragraphs shall apply.

If an appeal has lapsed owing to the plaintiff failing to attend a session for a main hearing, the case shall be reinstated in accordance with Chapter 50, Section 22 of the Code of Judicial Procedure upon the application of a member of the group, even if the plaintiff does not have legal excuse for their absence. The application of the member of the group may be limited to a particular claim.

Settlement

Section 26 A settlement that the plaintiff concludes on behalf of a group is valid, provided the court confirms it by judgment. The settlement shall at the request of the parties be confirmed, provided it is not discriminatory against particular members of the group or in another way manifestly unfair.

Postponement of Consideration of a Particular Issue

Section 27 If it is appropriate taking into consideration the investigation and it can be done without significant inconvenience for the defendant, the court may issue a judgment that for particular members of the group constitutes a final determination of the substantive matter and which for other members of the group involves the postponement of the consideration of a particular issue.

The court shall order each member of the group for whom the case has not finally been determined to request, within a particular period, that the remaining issue is considered. On issues concerning the members of the group who have submitted such a request, the court shall decide in accordance with Section 24, second and third paragraphs, on separation and concerning the future processing. If a member of the group does not submit a request for consideration of the remaining issue, the action of the member shall be rejected, unless the defendant has consented to the request or it is manifest that the action is founded.

Content of the Determination

Section 28 The court shall specify in a judgment the members of the group to which the judgment refers. This also applies to a decision, if this is necessary having regard to the nature of the issue.

Legal Force

Section 29 The determination of the court in group proceedings has legal force in relation to all members of the group who are subject to the determination.

Special Rules on Litigation Costs, etc

Right to Compensation and Liability for Costs

Section 30 A person who has been appointed in accordance with Section 21, second paragraph, to conduct the action of a group as plaintiff, is entitled to compensation from public funds corresponding to the costs for the preparation of the proceedings and the conduct of the action and also fees for attorney or counsel, provided the costs were reasonably incurred to protect the rights of the members of the group. Compensation shall also be paid for the plaintiff's own work and time consumed owing to the proceedings. A hearing for the presentation of an issue in a dispute that is directly relevant to the action brought shall be deemed to be a measure for the preparation of the proceedings.

The court may decide on advance payment of compensation with a reasonable amount if this is reasonable considering the amount of the costs or the work that the assignment has involved, the time that the proceedings can be estimated to continue and the other circumstances.

Section 31 A person who has been appointed in accordance with Section 21, second paragraph, to conduct the action of a group as plaintiff is not liable to pay compensation for the other party's litigation costs in cases other than those referred to in Chapter 18, Section 6 of the Code of Judicial Procedure. Instead, the person who was previously the plaintiff in the case shall, as a party, be liable for these litigation costs. He or she shall also compensate the State for that which has been paid from public funds in accordance with Section 30, to the extent the appellant or someone else is not liable to pay such compensation.

If someone has in connection with an appeal or thereafter taken over the plaintiff's action in cases other than those referred to in the first paragraph, he or she is liable as a party only for litigation costs that have arisen in the superior court. For litigation costs in the lower court, the person who was previously the plaintiff in the case shall instead be liable.

Section 32 The provisions contained in the Code of Judicial Procedure concerning liability for litigation costs shall also be applied on issues concerning compensation from public funds that are paid to a plaintiff in accordance with Section 30. Compensation for such costs shall be paid for by the State. The court shall consider the issue of compensation without being requested to do so.

Liability for Costs of a Member of the Group

Section 33 A member of the group who is not a party to the proceedings is only liable for the litigation costs regarding such cases as referred to in Sections 34 and 35.

Section 34 If the defendant has been ordered to compensate the plaintiff for litigation costs or pay such costs to the State as referred to in Section 32 and if the defendant cannot pay, the members of the group affected are liable to pay these costs. The same applies to additional costs in connection with risk agreements that the defendant has, in accordance with Section 41, not been ordered to pay. Each member of the group is liable for their share of the costs and is not liable to pay more than he or she has gained through the proceedings.

Section 35 A member of the group who is not a party to the proceedings should indemnify the costs that the member has caused by any measure referred to in Chapter 18, Section 3, first paragraph of the Code of Judicial Procedure or by such carelessness or oversight as referred to in Section 6 of the same chapter.

Section 36 If a member has entered as a party in the group proceedings in conjunction with an appeal or thereafter, the member is only liable as a party for the costs that have arisen in the superior court.

Separation of Plaintiff's Case

Section 37 If a plaintiff's case has been separated in accordance with Section 24, the plaintiff and the member of the group are jointly liable for the litigation costs that have arisen prior to the separation.

The member of the group is solely liable for costs that have arisen thereafter.

If the plaintiff or the member of the group has caused the litigation costs by carelessness or oversight, he or she shall be solely liable for the costs.

Risk Agreement

Section 38 If the plaintiff has concluded an agreement with an attorney that the fees for the attorney shall be determined having regard to the extent to which the claims of the members of the group is successful (risk agreement), the agreement may only be asserted against the members of the group if it has been approved by a court.

Section 39 A risk agreement may only be approved if the agreement is reasonable having regard to the nature of the substantive matter. The agreement shall be concluded in writing. The agreement shall indicate the way in which it is intended that the fees will deviate from normal fees if the claims of the members of the group were to be granted or rejected completely. The agreement may not be approved if the fees are based solely on the value of the subject of dispute.

Section 40 The issue of the approval of a risk agreement shall be considered in pending group proceedings by the court upon the application of the plaintiff. If the legal matter covered by the risk agreement has not been instituted at court, the person who wishes to bring the group action shall request that the issue of the approval is considered by a court that is competent to consider the dispute.

If it is not possible to determine which court is competent, the issue of approval shall be considered by Stockholm City Court.

An approval in accordance with the first paragraph ceases to apply, if group proceedings have not been commenced within six months from the approval. If there are reasons to do so, the court may extend this period.

Section 41 When considering what litigation costs are indemnifiable according to Chapter 18, Section 8 of the Code of Judicial Procedure, regard shall not be taken to such additional costs that have arisen owing to a risk agreement.

Appeals

Section 42 When consideration of a particular issue has been postponed in accordance with Section 27, the court shall decide if the judgment may be appealed against separately regarding the part where the determination is not final. However, such part of the judgment may in every case be appealed against separately if an appeal, for or against a group, is made regarding the part of the judgment that is final.

If a judgment is appealed against separately in accordance with the first paragraph, the court may order a stay of proceedings pending the judgment entering into final legal force.

Section 43 The decision of the district court as a result of the withdrawal of the action may not be appealed against, if the withdrawal has been made within the period for notices in accordance with Section 14. However, a decision on issues concerning litigation costs that has been issued in conjunction with the writing off may be appealed against.

Section 44 A decision by a district court to appoint a new plaintiff may be appealed against by the former plaintiff and by a member of the group who has proposed another plaintiff. A decision by a district court to reject a request for the exchange of plaintiff may be appealed against by a member of the group who has proposed such a change. The provisions contained in Chapter 49, Sections 4 and 11, first paragraph of the Code of Judicial Procedure shall apply to issues of appeal.

Section 45 A decision by a district court during the proceedings may, in addition to the provisions of the Code of Judicial Procedure and Section 44, be appealed against separately, if the district court has in the decision

1. rejected the plaintiff's request to be allowed to bring a private group action or organization action without an attorney or through an attorney who is not an advocate,
2. considered an issue in accordance with Section 19 concerning entry as a member of the group, or
3. considered an issue of approval of a risk agreement in accordance with Section 39.

A person who wishes to appeal against a decision referred to in the first paragraph shall first give notice of dissatisfaction. The notice shall be given immediately, if the decision has been issued at a session and otherwise within one week of the date when the appellant received the decision. A person who fails to do so is no longer entitled to appeal against the decision. If someone gives notice of dissatisfaction, the court may declare a stay of the proceedings pending consideration of the appeal, if there are special reasons.

Section 46 The provisions contained in Sections 44 and 45 also apply in connection with appeals against the decision of a court of appeal that is not final on issues referred to in those sections and which arose in the court of appeal or which have been appealed against to the court of appeal.

Section 47 A member of the group may appeal against a judgment or final decision on behalf of a group and also a decision on approval of a risk agreement in accordance with Section 39.

A member of the group is also competent to appeal, on their own behalf, against a judgment or a decision that concerns their rights.

Section 48 A notice of dissatisfaction by a member of the group who is not a party to the proceedings may be made within one week of the date for the decision provided the decision has been pronounced at a session to which the member has not been summoned nor has attended nevertheless. The same applies if the decision has not been pronounced at a session and not served on the member.

Notifications to the Members of the Group

Section 49 The court shall, in addition to what is prescribed by other provisions, notify a member of the group affected of a judgment or a final decision and also of a settlement that is subject to a request for confirmation in accordance with Section 26.

If it is necessary taking into consideration the importance the information may be deemed to have for the rights of the member, the court shall also notify a member of the group affected if

1. the plaintiff has been substituted with a new plaintiff,
2. the plaintiff has appointed a new attorney,
3. the plaintiff has waived the action,
4. that an issue has arisen concerning the approval of a risk agreement,
5. that a judgment or decision has been appealed against, and
6. other decisions, measures and overall situation.

Section 50 Notifications to members of the group in accordance with this Act shall be made in the manner considered appropriate by the court and observing the provisions contained in Chapter 33, Section 2, first paragraph of the Code of Judicial Procedure.

The court may order a party to attend to a notification, provided this has significant advantages for the processing. The party is in such a case entitled to compensation from public funds for expenses.

The provisions contained in the second paragraph also apply when notification is given by service.

This Act enters into force on 1 January 2003.
On behalf of the Government
GÖRAN PERSSON
THOMAS BODSTRÖM
(Ministry of Justice)

Appendix 4

Norway: Dispute Act 2005, Part VIII

Act of 17 June 2005 no. 90 relating to mediation and procedure in civil disputes (The Dispute Act)
Extracts

Part VIII—Special types of procedure Chapter 35. Class actions

Section 35-1 Scope. Definitions

(1) This Chapter contains special rules for dealing with class actions before the district court and for appeals against rulings in class actions.
(2) A class action is an action that is brought by or directed against a class on an identical or substantially similar factual and legal basis, and which is approved by the court as a class action.
(3) Class procedure is the set of special procedural rules for class actions.
(4) The class comprises the legal persons who have claims or obligations that fall within the scope of the class action as defined by the court and who are included in the action pursuant to sections 35-6 or 35-7.
(5) Class members are the individual legal persons in the class.
(6) The class register is the register of class members maintained pursuant to section 35-6.
(7) The class representative is the person who acts on behalf of the class in the action pursuant to section 35-9(1) to (3).

Section 35-2 Conditions for class actions

(1) A class action can only be brought if
  a) several legal persons have claims or obligations whose factual or legal basis is identical or substantially similar,
  b) the claims can be heard by a court with the same composition and in the main pursuant to the same procedural rules,
  c) class procedure is the most appropriate way of dealing with the claims, and
  d) it is possible to nominate a class representative pursuant to section 35-9.
(2) Only persons who could have brought or joined an ordinary legal action before the Norwegian courts may be class members.

Section 35-3 Bringing the action

(1) A class action may be brought by
   a) any person who fulfils the conditions for class membership if approval to bring the action is granted, or
   b) an organisation, an association or a public body charged with promoting specific interests, provided that the action falls within its purpose and normal scope pursuant to section 1-4.
(2) The action shall be brought by submission of a writ of summons to a district court before which a person who qualifies for class membership could have brought an ordinary legal action.
(3) The writ of summons shall contain the information that is necessary for the court to assess whether the conditions for a class action are fulfilled and to rule on the issues in section 35-4(2). The writ of summons shall state whether the class action is brought pursuant to section 35-6 or section 35-7.

Section 35-4 Approval of class actions

(1) The court shall as soon as possible decide whether to approve or reject the class action.
(2) If the class action is approved, the court shall in its ruling
   a) describe the scope of the claims that may be included in the class action,
   b) decide whether the class action shall proceed pursuant to section 35-6 or pursuant to section 35-7,
   c) in class actions pursuant to section 35-6, fix a time limit for registration on the class register,
   d) where appropriate, fix a maximum liability and an advance on costs pursuant to section 35-6(3), and
   e) nominate a class representative.
(3) If, in the further hearing of the case, it transpires that it is clearly inappropriate to hear the case pursuant to the class procedure or that the scope of the claims in the class action ought to be redefined, the court may on its own motion reverse or amend its ruling. Parties who are then no longer included in the class action may, within one month after the ruling for reversal or amendment becomes final and enforceable, require the court to continue to hear their claims as individual actions.
(4) Rulings pursuant to subsections (1) to (3) shall be made by interlocutory order. Section 29-3(2) does not apply to appeals.

Section 35-5 Notice of approved class action

(1) After a class action has been approved, the court shall by notice, announcement or other method ensure that the class action is made

known to those who may join it or who are class members pursuant to section 35-7.

(2) The notice or announcement shall clearly state what the class action and the class procedure implies, including the consequences of registering or deregistering as a class member, the potential liability for costs that may be incurred and the authority of the class representative to settle the action. The notice shall state the time limit for registering on the class register.

(3) The court shall decide the contents of the notice, how notice shall be given etc., including whether the class representative shall take charge of issuing the notice or announcement and paying the expenses thereof.

Section 35-6 Class actions that require registration of class members

(1) The class action shall only include those persons who are registered as class members, unless the action is brought pursuant to section 35-7. Persons who have claims that fall within the scope of the class action can register as class members.

(2) An application for registration shall be submitted within the time limit. At any time before the main hearing, the court may in special cases approve delayed registration unless regard for the other parties strongly suggests otherwise.

(3) On application from the person who has brought the class action or the class representative, the court can decide that registration shall be subject to the class members accepting liability for a specified maximum amount of costs pursuant to section 35-14. The court may also on application decide that all or part of the amount shall be paid to counsel for the class before registration.

(4) The class register shall be maintained by the court. The Courts Administration can issue more detailed regulations on the class register.

Section 35-7 Class actions that do not require registration of class members

(1) The court can decide that persons who have claims within the scope of the class action shall be class members without registration on the class register, if the claims
   a) on their own involve amounts or interests that are so small that it must be assumed that a considerable majority of them would not be brought as individual actions, and
   b) are not deemed to raise issues that need to be heard individually.

(2) Persons who do not wish to participate in the class action may withdraw pursuant to section 35-8. The court shall maintain a register of withdrawals. The rules in section 35-6(4) apply correspondingly.

Section 35-8 Withdrawal of class membership

(1) Anyone may withdraw as a class member. Withdrawal is effected by deregistration from the class register or by record in the withdrawal register. Withdrawal shall take effect when notification of withdrawal is received by the court. A class member cannot withdraw after his claim has been determined by a final and enforceable ruling.

(2) Before the case is determined on its merits by a judgement that is binding on the class members pursuant to section 35-11, a class member may withdraw without waiving his substantive claim.

(3) If a class member withdraws after the case has been determined on its merits by a judgement that is binding on the class members pursuant to section 35-11(2), the further hearing of the case, if any, shall continue before the court pursuant to the rules on general procedure or small claims procedure. If the claim of a class member who has withdrawn has been determined by the court, any application for review must be made by way of individual notice of appeal. The time limit for appeal is one month after the expiry of the time limit for appeal for the class. However, if the class has appealed, an individual appeal may be filed after the time limit has expired. In that case, the notice of appeal must be filed at the same time as the notice of withdrawal from the class, and the appeal must fall within the scope of the appeal brought by the class.

(4) Unless otherwise stated in the appeal, an appeal from the opposite party of the class shall include all persons who were members of the class when judgement that was binding on the class members pursuant to section 35-11 was pronounced.

(5) A person who has brought a claim by way of individual action shall for the purpose of the above provisions be deemed to have withdrawn from the class action. In actions pursuant to section 35-7, this effect shall lapse if the individual action is quashed.

Section 35-9 Rights and obligations in the class action. Representation

(1) The class representative shall safeguard the rights and obligations of the class in the class action. The class representative shall ensure that the class members are kept properly informed about the class action. This applies in particular to procedural steps and rulings that may have consequences for the class members' claims.

(2) Any person who can bring a class action pursuant to section 35-3(1), and who is willing, may serve as class representative.

(3) The class representative shall be appointed by the court. The representative must be able to safeguard the interests of the class in a satisfactory manner and to account to the opposite party for the class's potential liability for costs. If necessary, the court may revoke the appointment

of a class representative and appoint a new one. Section 35-4(4) applies correspondingly to rulings on revocation and new appointment of class representatives.

(4) The class shall be legally represented by counsel who shall be an advocate. In special cases, the court may grant exemptions from this requirement.

Section 35-10 Issues in dispute that only relate to one or a limited number or class members. Subgroups

(1) The court can decide that the provisions on class actions shall not apply to the hearing of issues in the dispute that only relate to a limited number of class members. In that case, the class members themselves shall have control over the issues. The court shall determine the order in which the various issues shall be heard. The court should normally hear the issues that relate to the class as a whole before it deals with specific issues that relate to one or a limited number of parties.

(2) The court can decide that subgroups shall be established if the class consists of a large number of class members and the same or substantially similar legal or factual issues apply to several of them but differ from the issues that apply to the class as a whole. The provisions of this Chapter apply correspondingly to the establishment of subgroups and to the hearing of the issues for which they are established.

Section 35-11 Rulings on claims raised in the class action. Settlement

(1) Rulings on claims raised in the class action shall be binding on persons who are class members at the time of the ruling.

(2) The court may split the adjudication and rule first on the claims of one or some of the class members if it would be impractical to rule on the merits in respect of the claims of all of the class member at the same time because of the objections and contentions that are made. In subsequent proceedings, the court shall follow the first judgement without reviewing it in so far as it is not contended that there are special reasons for deviating from the ruling. This does not apply to the determination of factual and legal circumstances against which the class members cannot apply for review by way of appeal.

(3) A settlement in a class action pursuant to section 35-7 requires the approval of the court. Section 35-4(4) apply correspondingly to rulings on approval.

Section 35-12 Costs

(1) The class representative has a right and a duty in respect of the costs of the class action.

(2) If there is a change of class representative, the court shall decide how the right and duty in respect of costs shall be allocated between them.

(3) Subsections (1) and (2) do not apply to costs in respect of issues in dispute pursuant to section 35-10(1).

Section 35-13 Remuneration

(1) The class representative is entitled to remuneration for his work and to a refund of his disbursements, including the fees and disbursements of legal counsel. The remuneration and refund of expenses shall be determined by the court. Section 20-9 applies.

(2) A claim for the class representative's costs can be made against the opposite party to the extent that the opposite party is ordered to pay costs, or against the class members within the limitations of section 35-14.

Section 35-14 The financial liability of the class members etc.

(1) Class members in actions pursuant to section 35-6 are liable towards the class representative for costs imposed on him pursuant to section 35-12 and for remuneration and refund of disbursements determined by the court pursuant to section 35-13 in so far as such liability is a condition for registration. Any amount that is not prepaid shall be paid to legal counsel for the class.

(2) Former class members who are excluded from the class pursuant to section 35-4(3) are not liable for costs pursuant to subsection (1). Amounts that are prepaid pursuant to section 35-6(3) shall be refunded. Former class members who have withdrawn from the class by deregistration are liable pursuant to subsection (1) unless the court determines otherwise. In making its decision, the court shall have regard to the consequences that exemption from liability will have for the class representative, and whether liability would be unreasonably onerous for the class member who has withdrawn, having regard amongst other things to the time of withdrawal.

(3) After he has settled his own fees and disbursements, counsel for the class shall transfer any amounts paid pursuant to subsection (1) to settle any costs awarded to the opposite party of the class before payment is made to cover the class representative's costs.

Section 35-15 A class as respondent

Where the class comprises parties who are defendants in an action, sections 35-1 to 35-14, except section 35-7, apply correspondingly to the extent they are appropriate.

...

Part IX Entry into force and amendments in other statutes Chapter 37. Entry into force and amendments in other statutes

Section 37-1 Entry into force

The Act shall enter into force from such time as the King decides. The King may decide that different provisions of the Act shall enter into force at different times.

Appendix 5

Finland: Act on Class Actions 444/2007

<http://www.finlex.fi/fi/laki/kaannokset/2007/en20070444.pdf> accessed 12 June 2008

[UNOFFICIAL TRANSLATION — Ministry of Justice, Finland, 2007]

ACT ON CLASS ACTIONS

Ryhmäkannelaki
(444/2007)

Section 1—Scope of application

(1) This Act applies, within the limits of the competence of the Consumer Ombudsman, to the hearing of a civil case between a consumer and a business as a class action. However, this Act does not apply to a civil case concerning the conduct of an issuer of securities or the offeror in a takeover bid or mandatory bid, as referred to in the Securities Markets Act (495/1989; *arvopaperimarkkinalaki*).

(2) For the purposes of this Act, *class action* is defined as an action brought by the plaintiff on the behalf of the class defined in the action, with the objective that the judgment to be delivered in the case become binding also on the class members.

(3) In addition to the provisions of this Act, the hearing of a class action shall in other respects be governed by the provisions on civil procedure, in so far as appropriate.

Section 2—Preconditions for a class action

A case may be heard as a class action, if:

(1) several persons have claims against the same defendant, based on the same or similar circumstances;

(2) the hearing of the case as a class action is expedient in view of the size of the class, the subject-matter of the claims presented in it and the proof offered in it; and

(3) the class has been defined with adequate precision.

Section 3—Competent court

Class actions shall be heard by the District Courts of Turku, Vaasa, Kuopio, Helsinki, Lahti and Oulu. Among these courts, competence shall lie with the District Court located in the same Court of Appeal jurisdiction as the District Court where the defendant would be liable to respond were a claim covered by the class action presented as a separate case.

Section 4—Standing

The Consumer Ombudsman, as the plaintiff, shall have exclusive standing to bring a class action and to exercise the right of a party to the case to be heard in court.

Section 5—Filing of a class action

(1) The application for a summons in a class action shall contain the following information:

(1) the class to which the action pertains;

(2) the known claims;

(3) the circumstances on which the claims are based;

(4) the basis on which the case should be heard as a class action;

(5) the circumstances, as known to the plaintiff, that are relevant to the hearing of the claims of given class members only;

(6) in so far as possible, the evidence that the plaintiff intends to offer in support of the action, as well as the facts that the plaintiff intends to prove with each item of evidence;

(7) a claim for the compensation of legal costs, if the plaintiff deems this necessary; and

(8) the basis for the competence of the court.

Section 6—Notice of the commencement of a class action

(1) Unless the action is ruled inadmissible or dismissed in accordance with chapter 5, section 6, of the Code of Judicial Procedure (*oikeudenkäymiskaari*), the court shall without delay and before issuing a summons give the parties a postal or electronic notice of the commencement of the class action and of the judge in charge of the preparation of the case. In addition, the court shall set a time limit for class accessions. For a special reason, the court may grant an extension to this time limit.

(2) The plaintiff shall without delay give the known class members a notice of the filing of the case. The notice may be postal or electronic. If the notice cannot be given in either manner to all class members as defined, an announcement of the class action may be published in one or several newspapers or in some other appropriate manner. The plaintiff shall give the notice also to the defendant.

Section 7—Contents of the notice

(1) The notice given by the plaintiff shall contain the following information:
    (1) a brief description of the case and the claims to be presented;
    (2) a description of the class on behalf of which the action has been brought;
    (3) the contact information of the plaintiff; and
    (4) information about how to accede to the class and about the time limit set for class accessions.
(2) In addition, the notice shall contain basic information on the class action as a form of procedure, the status of class members in the proceedings, settlement, the legal effects of a judgment delivered on the basis of a class action, the right of appeal, and the liability for legal costs.

Section 8—Class membership

(1) A class member as defined, who has delivered, within the time limit, a written and signed letter of accession to the class shall belong to the class.
(2) If a class member, as defined, delivers a letter of accession after the expiry of the time limit, but before the supplemented application for a summons has been submitted to the court, the plaintiff may for a special reason accept him or her as a class member.

Section 9—Supplemented application for a summons

The plaintiff shall prepare a supplemented application for a summons, indicating the names and addresses of the class members, the particulars of their claims and, if necessary, supplemented grounds for the claims. The application for a summons shall be submitted to the court within one month of the time limit set for class accessions. For a special reason, the court may grant an extension to this time limit.

Section 10—Summons

(1) The court shall without delay issue the summons once it receives the supplemented application for a summons.
(2) In the summons, the defendant shall be exhorted to respond to the action in writing. In other respects, the issue of the summons and the

response shall be governed by the provisions in chapter 5, sections 10–12, of the Code of Judicial Procedure, in so far as appropriate.

Section 11—Status of class members

A class member shall be held equivalent to a party to the case in the application of provisions in the Code of Judicial Procedure on the relinquishment of the subjectmatter of the dispute, the disqualification of judges, the effects of the pendency of proceedings, the joinder of actions and the hearing of parties. A class member shall enter his or her plea of disqualification of a judge as soon as possible after having been informed of the judges participating in the hearing of the case. A class member shall not participate in the proceedings as an intervener.

Section 12—Expansion of the action

(1) During the preparation of the case, the plaintiff may expand the action to cover also new class members by amending the definition of the class, if this does not cause significant delay in the hearing of the case or unreasonable inconvenience to the defendant. The information referred to in section 5 shall be provided in respect of the new class members, in so far as appropriate.

(2) The provisions in chapter 14, section 2, of the Code of Judicial Procedure apply to the alteration of the claims of the plaintiff.

Section 13—Restriction of the action

(1) If the plaintiff withdraws the action in respect of the claims of a given class member before the supplemented application for a summons has been submitted to the District Court, the court shall strike the case from its docket for the respective part.

(2) If, after the submission of the supplemented application for a summons to the District Court, the plaintiff restricts the action so that it no longer covers the claim of a given class member, the court shall set a time limit within which the class member may notify the court that he or she wishes to pursue his or her case as a party in separate proceedings.

(3) If a class member notifies that he or she wishes to pursue the case as a party, the court shall sever his or her claims in order for them to be heard in separate proceedings and decide how the proceedings are to continue. At the request of the class member, the court may transfer a severed case to be heard by another competent court, if this is expedient in view of the hearing of the case. If the proceedings are not to be continued in respect of a claim referred to above, the court shall strike the case from its docket for the respective part.

Section 14—Hearing by sub-class

The court may order that the claims pertaining to given class members or to given issues only be heard separately by sub-class, if this is conducive to the expedient hearing of the case.

Section 15—Resignation from the class

(1) Before the case is moved on to the main hearing, a class member may resign from the class by notifying the court of the same in writing or in person at the court registry. In this event, the case shall be struck from the docket in respect of the resigning class member.
(2) Once the case has been moved on to the main hearing, a class member may resign from the class as referred to in paragraph (1) only with the consent of the defendant. Also in this event, the case shall be struck from the docket in respect of the resigning class member. Once the case rests for a decision, resignation from the class shall no longer be permitted.

Section 16—Legal effects of the judgment

The decision of the court shall be binding on the class members whom the court has in the decision designated as such.

Section 17—Legal costs

(1) The provisions of chapter 21 of the Code of Judicial Procedure apply to legal costs.
(2) A class member shall not be liable for legal costs. However, a class member shall be liable to the defendant for the costs arising from his or her conduct referred to in chapter 21, section 5, of the Code of Judicial Procedure.
(3) If the claim of a class member has been severed to be heard in separate proceedings, he or she shall be liable as a party for the legal costs arising after the severance.

Section 18—Appeal

(1) The parties have the right to appeal against a decision issued on the basis of a class action, as provided in the Code of Judicial Procedure.
(2) A decision dismissing a procedural plea concerning the preconditions for a class action shall be separately subject to appeal, unless the court, in order to avoid undue delay or for some other special reason, orders that the decision be subject to appeal only in conjunction with the judgment or other final order on the main issue.
(3) If the plaintiff does not appeal a decision issued on the basis of a class action, a class member shall have the right to appeal in respect of his or

her claim within 14 days of the end of the appeal period or the respective counter-appeal period. A class member need not declare an intent to appeal. In other respects, appeal shall be governed by the provisions of the Code of Judicial Procedure.

Section 19—Entry into force

This Act shall enter into force on 1 October 2007.

Appendix 6

Spain: Extracts from Legislation

6/1985, July 1, Judicial Power Organic Act:
Article 7.3:

> Courts and Tribunals will protect legitimate rights and interests, both individual and collective, and prevent defenselessness in either case. For the defense of the later, legitimization will be recognized to corporations, associations and groups that turn out to be affected or that are legally empowered to promote and defend them.

26/1984, July 19, Consumers and Users Defense General Act:
Article 20:

> Consumers and users' associations will be incorporated pursuant to the Associations Act, and its legal purpose will be the defense of the interests, including the information and education, of consumers and users, either in general, or in connection with specific consumer goods or services, and will be able to be declared of public utility, consolidate into associations or federations defending the same rights and interests, receive public subsidies, represent its members and to file the appropriate actions to defend them, the association, or the general interest of consumers and users; and they will benefit from the legal aid advantages in those cases set forth in Article 2.2. of this Act. Its organization and functioning will be democratic.

1/2000, January 7, Civil Procedure Act:
Article 6:

> Capacity to be a party:

> Can be a party in the proceedings before Civil Courts:... 7° The groups of consumers or users affected by a damaging fact, when the individuals that are part of the group, are determined or easy to determine. In order to file a claim, it is necessary that the group is formed by a majority of the affected people.

Article 11:

> Procedural standing for the defense of rights and interests of consumers and users:
> 1. Without prejudice of the individual procedural standing of the affected people, the consumers and users associations that have been legally incorporated, are

acknowledged procedural standing to defend in Court the rights and interests of their members and those of the association, as well as the general interests of the consumers and users" (reproduces art. 20 of the Consumers and Users Defense General Act).

2. When the people that have been affected by a damaging fact are a group of consumers or users the members of which are perfectly determined or are easy to determinate, the procedural standing to undertake the defense of the collective interests corresponds to the associations of consumers and users, to the entities legally incorporated whose social purpose is the defense or protection of those, as well as to the groups of affected people themselves.

3. When the people that have been affected by a damaging fact are a plurality of consumers or users non-determined or difficult to determine, the procedural standing to defend in Court those diffused interests will correspond exclusively to the associations of consumers and users that, pursuant to the law, are representative.

Article 15:

1. Publicity and participation in proceedings for the protection of the collective and diffuse rights and interests of consumers and users. 1.—In the proceedings filed by associations or entities created to protect the rights and interests of consumers and users, or in those proceedings filed by groups of affected people, all the people that could be considered harmed because they were consumers of the product or users of the service that originated the proceedings, will be summoned to the proceedings, so that they can claim their personal or individual interests. Said summoning will be carried out by publishing the filing of the claim in media which reaches all the territorial areas where the damage of said rights or interests has taken place.

2. In those proceedings where the people affected by the harmful event are determined or are easy to determine, the claimant or claimants will have had previously to notify the filing of the claim to all the interested people. In this case, after the summoning, the consumer or user will be able to participate in the proceedings at any stage, but will only be able to carry out those judicial acts which, at that particular stage of the proceedings, can still be carried out.

3. In those proceedings where the people affected by the harmful event are not specified or are hard to identify, the summoning will suspend the proceedings up to a maximum of a two-months period, the length of which will be determined taking into account the circumstances or the complexity of the fact, and the difficulties to identify and find out the affected people. The proceedings will we continued with the participation of all those consumers that have answered to the summoning. The individual participation of consumers or users at a later stage will not be allowed. Nevertheless, they can defend their rights or interests pursuant to articles 221 and 519 of this Act.

Article 221:

Judgements awarded in proceedings initiated by associations of consumers and users: Judgments entered in connection with claims filed by associations of consumers and users having the procedural standing referred to in section 11, shall comply with the following rules:

1st Where the claim is for monetary compensation, or in order to require the defendant to do, abstain to do, or give a specific or generic thing, the judgment shall determine which consumers and users must benefit from it according to law. Where such determination is impossible the judgment shall specify the details, characteristics and requirements necessary to demand payment and, where appropriate, to apply for or take part in the enforcement of the judgment if requested by the claimant association.

2nd If, as a consequence of the judgment, or resolution, an activity or conduct was declared illicit or contrary to the law, the judgment will determine whether, pursuant to the legislation regarding the protection of consumers and users, the declaration has to have procedural effects not limited to those who have been a party in the proceedings.

3rd If specific consumers or users have been a party in the proceedings, the judgment will have to solve, specifically, their requests.

Article 222.3:

Res iudicata effect of judgments shall affect all the parties to the proceedings, including their heirs, as well as non-litigants whose rights underpin the procedural standing of the parties under section 11 of this Act.

Article 256:

Types of preliminary proceedings and how to apply for them.—1. Any judicial proceeding can be prepared: [...] 6th—Pursuant to a request by that who intends to initiate a proceeding for the defense of the interests of consumers and users, in order to specify the members of the group of affected people, in those cases in which, while the affected people is not identified, it could easily be. To that effect, the Court will adopt the necessary steps to find out the identity of the members of the group, taking into account the circumstances of the case as well as the data provided by the applicant. These might include the requirement to the defendant to collaborate in such identification.

Article 519:

Execution by consumers or users of judgments which do not identify the individuals that are to be beneficiary of the condemn: Where the judgments referred to in rule one section 221 do not determine the consumers or users benefited with the award, the enforcement court, on the application of one or several interested parties and upon hearing the defendant, shall render an order determining whether, according to the information, characteristics, and requirements set out in the judgment the applicant's recognized as being benefited by the award. The beneficiaries may then apply for enforcement by providing a copy of the award.

Appendix 7

England and Wales: Civil Procedure Rules, Part 19 III: Group Litigation Orders

DEFINITION

19.10 A Group Litigation Order ('GLO') means an order made under rule 19.11 to provide for the case management of claims which give rise to common or related issues of fact or law (the 'GLO issues').

GROUP LITIGATION ORDER

19.11

(1) The court may make a GLO where there are or are likely to be a number of claims giving rise to the GLO issues. (The practice direction provides the procedure for applying for a GLO)
(2) A GLO must—
  (a) contain directions about the establishment of a register (the 'group register') on which the claims managed under the GLO will be entered;
  (b) specify the GLO issues which will identify the claims to be managed as a group under the GLO; and
  (c) specify the court (the 'management court') which will manage the claims on the group register.
(3) A GLO may—
  (a) in relation to claims which raise one or more of the GLO issues—
    (i) direct their transfer to the management court;
    (ii) order their stay until further order; and
    (iii) direct their entry on the group register;

EFFECT OF THE GLO

19.12

(1) Where a judgment or order is given or made in a claim on the group register in relation to one or more GLO issues—
    (a) that judgment or order is binding on the parties to all other claims that are on the group register at the time the judgment is given or the order is made unless the court orders otherwise; and
    (b) the court may give directions as to the extent to which that judgment or order is binding on the parties to any claim which is subsequently entered on the group register.
(2) Unless paragraph (3) applies, any party who is adversely affected by a judgment or order which is binding on him may seek permission to appeal the order.
(3) A party to a claim which was entered on the group register after a judgment or order which is binding on him was given or made may not—
    (a) apply for the judgment or order to be set aside, varied or stayed; or
    (b) appeal the judgment or order,
    but may apply to the court for an order that the judgment or order is not binding on him.
(4) Unless the court orders otherwise, disclosure of any document relating to the GLO issues by a party to a claim on the group register is disclosure of that document to all parties to claims—
    (a) on the group register; and
    (b) which are subsequently entered on the group register.

CASE MANAGEMENT

19.13

Directions given by the management court may include directions—

(a) varying the GLO issues;
(b) providing for one or more claims on the group register to proceed as test claims;
(c) appointing the solicitor of one or more parties to be the lead solicitor for the claimants or defendants;
(d) specifying the details to be included in a statement of case in order to show that the criteria for entry of the claim on the group register have been met;
(e) specifying a date after which no claim may be added to the group register unless the court gives permission; and
(f) for the entry of any particular claim which meets one or more of the GLO issues on the group register.

(Part 3 contains general provisions about the case management powers of the court)

REMOVAL FROM THE REGISTER

19.14

(1) A party to a claim entered on the group register may apply to the management court for the claim to be removed from the register.
(2) If the management court orders the claim to be removed from the register it may give directions about the future management of the claim.

TEST CLAIMS

19.15

(1) Where a direction has been given for a claim on the group register to proceed as a test claim and that claim is settled, the management court may order that another claim on the group register be substituted as the test claim.
(2) Where an order is made under paragraph (1), any order made in the test claim before the date of substitution is binding on the substituted claim unless the court orders otherwise.

See also the Practice Direction—Group Litigation, at <http://www.justice. gov.uk/civil/procrules_fin/contents/practice_directions/pd_part19b.htm>

Appendix 8

Germany: Act on the Initiation of Model Case Proceedings in respect of Investors in the Capital Markets

The Bundestag passed the following law:

ARTICLE 1

Act on Model Case Proceedings in Disputes under Capital Markets Law (Capital Markets Model Case Act — KapMuG)

Table of Contents

Part 1
Application for Establishment of a Model Case; Reference Procedures

Section 1
Application for Establishment of a Model Case

(1) By application for the establishment of a model case, in a proceeding at first instance, in which

1. a claim for compensation of damages due to false, misleading or omitted public capital markets information or
2. a claim to fulfilment of contract, which is based on an offer under the Securities Acquisition and Takeover Act,

is asserted, the establishment of the existence or non-existence of conditions justifying or ruling out entitlement or the clarification of legal questions may be sought (establishment objective), provided the decision in the legal dispute is contingent thereupon. Application for the establishment of a model case may be made by the plaintiff and the defendant. Public capital

markets information means information directed at a great number of investors regarding facts, circumstances and statistical as well as other company data which relate to an issuer of securities or an offeror of other investments. These shall include, in particular, information contained in

1. prospectuses under the Securities Prospectus Act,
2. sales prospectuses under the Sales Prospectus Act and the Investment Act,
3. communications of insider information within the meaning of section 15 of the Securities Trading Act,
4. presentations, overviews, lectures and information in the main collection on the state of the company, including its relationships with associated enterprises within the meaning of section 400 (1) no. 1 of the Stock Corporation Act,
5. annual financial statements, annual reports, group financial statements, group annual reports and interim reports of the issuer, and in
6. offering documents within the meaning of section 11 (1), first sentence, of the Securities Acquisition and Takeover Act.

(2) Application for the establishment of a model case shall be made with the court trying the matter and shall include indication of the establishment objective and the public capital markets information. Such application must contain information on all factual and legal circumstances (points of dispute) which serve to

justify the establishment objective, and a description of the evidence the applicant intends to use to substantiate or refute factual claims. The applicant shall substantiate that the decision on the application for the establishment of a model case may have significance for other similar cases beyond the individual dispute concerned. The respondent shall be granted opportunity to submit a written pleading on the matter.

(3) An application for the establishment of a model case pursuant to subsection (1), first sentence, shall be inadmissible if

1. a decision on the dispute which the application for the establishment of a model case is based upon is already forthcoming,
2. application for the establishment of a model case is made for the purpose of delaying proceedings,
3. the evidence described is unsuitable,
4. the applicant's reasons do not justify the filing of an application for the establishment of a model case or
5. a legal question which has been exclusively raised does not appear to need clarification.

Inadmissible applications for the establishment of a model case shall be denied by order of the court trying the matter.

Section 2
Public Announcement in the Complaint Registry

(1) The court trying the matter shall announce publicly an admissible application for the establishment of a model case in the electronic Federal Gazette under the title "Complaint Registry pursuant to the Capital Markets Model Case Act" (Complaint Registry). A decision on public announcement shall be given by order of the court trying the matter. There shall be no possibility to appeal such order. The public announcement shall contain only the following information:

1. The complete name of the accused party and its legal representative,
2. The name of the issuer of securities or offeror of other investments to which the application for the establishment of a model case refers,
3. The name of the court trying the matter,
4. The case number at the court trying the matter,
5. The establishment objective of the application for the establishment of a model case and
6. the exact date of the public announcement in the Complaint Registry.

Applications for the establishment of a model case whose establishment objectives refer to the same subject matter (related applications), shall be listed in the Complaint Registry chronologically according to the date of their announcement. Applications for the establishment of a model case must however no longer be announced publicly in the Complaint Registry, if the conditions for the introduction of a model case pursuant to Section 4 (1), first sentence, have already been met.

(2) Access to the Complaint Registry shall be open to everyone free of charge.

(3) The court trying the matter carries the responsibility in respect of data protection for the data made public by him in the Complaint Registry, in particular for the legality of the collection of the data, the reliability of their announcement and their accuracy.

(4) The operator of the electronic Federal Gazette shall prepare in cooperation with the Federal Office Information Security a security plan for public announcements in the Complaint Registry, which shall include, in particular, the necessary technical and organizational measures pursuant to section 9 of the Federal Data Protection Act. The effectiveness of the measures shall be assessed at regular intervals in view of current technological developments.

(5) Data stored in the Complaint Registry shall be deleted in the event of denial of an application for the establishment of a model case pursuant to Section 4 (4), otherwise upon final and binding conclusion of the model case proceeding.

(6) The Federal Ministry of Justice shall be empowered to stipulate by order more precise provisions on the content and structure of the Complaint Registry, in particular with regard to entries, amendments, deletions, rights of access, data security and data protection. This shall include the formulation of provisions on the setting of dates for deletion and provisions which ensure that the public announcements

1. remain intact, complete and current,
2. can be traced to their origins at any time.

Section 3
Interruption of Proceedings

Proceedings shall be interrupted upon public announcement of the application for the establishment of a model case in the Complaint Registry.

Section 4
Reference to the Higher Regional Court

(1) The court trying the matter shall effect by order a decision of the next highest court of instance, the Higher Regional Court, on the establishment objective of related applications for the establishment of a model case (model case ruling), if

1. the first application according to date for establishment of a model case was submitted in the proceeding before the court trying the matter and
2. in at least nine other proceedings related applications for the establishment of a model case were submitted before the same or other courts within four months subsequent to its public announcement.

The order referring the matter to a higher court of instance shall be without appeal and binding for the Higher Regional Court. The order according to date of the applications for the establishment of a model case submitted to the courts trying the matters is determined according to the date of the public announcement in the Complaint Registry.

(2) The order referring the matter to a higher court of instance shall contain:

1. The establishment objective,
2. All points of dispute being raised, to the extent that they are relevant to the decision,
3. The evidence described and
4. A brief summary of the essential content of the rights being claimed and the measures availed of in contesting or defending the matter.

(3) The court trying the matter shall publicize the issuance and the date of the order referring the matter to the higher court of instance in the Complaint Registry.

(4) If within four months after the public announcement of the respective application for the establishment of a model case the number of similar applications required for reference of the matter to the Higher Regional Court has not been submitted to the court trying the matter, such court shall deny the application and resume proceedings.

(5) If more than one Higher Regional Court has been instituted in any given Land, rulings on model cases for which the Higher Regional Courts are competent pursuant to subsection (1) may be assigned by order of the Land governments to one of the Higher Regional Courts, provided that

this serves in the interest of ensuring the consistency of the rulings. The Land governments may transfer this authority to the Land administrations of Justice. The competency of a Higher Regional Court may be established for specific districts or an entire region of several Länder by way of treaty between Länder.

Section 5
Precluding Effects of the Order Referring the Matter to a Higher Court of Instance

Upon issuance of the order referring the matter to a higher court of instance, the initiation of a further model case proceeding for the proceeding which is to be suspended pursuant to subsection (7) shall be inadmissible.

Part 2
Conducting Model Case Proceedings

Section 6
Public Announcement of Model Case Proceedings

Upon receipt of the order referring the matter to a higher court of instance, the Higher Regional Court shall publicly announce the following in the Complaint Registry:

1. The name of the model case plaintiff and his legal representative (Section 8 (1) no. 1),
2. The complete name of the model case defendant and his legal representative (§ 8 (1) no. 2),

3. The establishment objective of the model case,
4. The case number of the Higher Regional Court and
5. The content of the order referring the matter to a higher court of instance.

The Higher Regional Court shall bear the responsibility in respect of data protection pursuant to Section 2 (3).

Section 7
Suspension

(1) After the Higher Regional Court has made public announcement of the model case in the Complaint Registry, the court trying the matter shall suspend ex officio all pending proceedings or any proceedings brought prior to the handing down of a model case ruling whose decision is contingent upon the establishment to be made on the model case or the legal question to be resolved in the model case proceeding. This shall apply irrespective of whether application was made in the proceeding for the establishment of a model case. The parties shall be heard, unless they have waived their right to do so. There shall be no possibility to appeal the suspension order. The court trying the matter shall inform the Higher Regional Court conducting the proceedings without delay of the suspension of proceedings, to include the amount of the claim, if this is the subject matter of the proceedings.

Section 8
Parties to the Model Case
Proceedings

(1) Parties to the model case proceedings shall include:

1. The model case plaintiff,
2. The model case defendant,
3. Interested parties summoned.

(2) The Higher Regional Court shall designate at its equitable discretion by order the model case plaintiff from among the plaintiffs at the court obtaining the model case ruling. Consideration shall be given to the following:

1. The amount of the claim, if it is the subject matter of the model case, and
2. Agreement among several plaintiffs designating a single model case plaintiff.

There shall be no contestation of such order.

(3) The plaintiffs and defendants of the remaining suspended proceedings shall be summoned to the model case proceeding. The suspension order shall serve as a summons in the model case proceeding. On the basis of the suspension order, the case trying the matter shall inform the interested parties summoned

1. that the pro rata costs of the model case shall make up part of the costs of the trial proceedings, and
2. that this shall not apply pursuant to Section 17, fourth sentence, if the complaint is withdrawn

within two weeks of the service of the order of suspension of the main proceeding.

Section 9
General Procedural Rules

(1) The applicable provisions stipulated under the Code of Civil Procedure for proceedings at the first instance before the Regional Courts shall apply mutatis mutandis, provided no other derogating stipulations have been agreed on. Sections 278, 348 to 350 and 379 of the Code of Civil Procedure shall not apply. Interested parties summoned must not be named in orders.

(2) Public announcement may be made in lieu of service of summonses to court hearings on interested parties. Public announcement shall be effected by entry into the Complaint Registry. There must be a span of at least four weeks between public announcement and the date of the hearing.

(3) The Federal Government and the Land governments may determine by order for their area of competency the point in time as of which electronic files are to be kept in the model case proceeding and the applicable organisational/ technical basis necessary for the creation, maintenance and storage of such electronic files. The Land governments may transfer this authority by order to the Land administrations of Justice.

(4) The Federal Government and the Land governments may determine by order for their area of competency that in model case proceedings statements are to be submitted to the court in electronic form, confirmations of receipt are to be sent in response electronically and that the parties shall be required to ensure that electronic documents may be served on them by the court. The suitable form necessary for the processing of the documents shall be stipulated by order. The Land governments may transfer this authority by order to the Land administrations of Justice.

Section 10
Preparation of the Hearing

In preparation of the hearing, the presiding judge or a member of the bench designated by him may instruct the interested parties summoned to the hearing to submit additions to the written pleadings provided by the model case plaintiff or the model case defendant, and may in particular set a deadline for the clarification of certain disputes which require further elucidation. Additions submitted in the preparatory written pleadings by the interested parties summoned shall be made available to the model case plaintiff and the model case defendant. Written pleadings of the interested parties summoned shall not be made available to any remaining interested parties. Written pleadings of the model case plaintiff and the model case defendant shall only be made available to the interested parties summoned if they have requested this of the court in writing.

Section 11
Effects of Withdrawal

(1) Withdrawal of an application for establishment of a model case shall have no influence on the status of a model case plaintiff or a model case defendant per se.

(2) If the model case plaintiff withdraws his complaint in the course of the main model case proceedings, the court shall designate a new model case plaintiff. The same shall apply in the event of the initiation of insolvency proceedings in respect of the model case plaintiff's assets, and in the event of his death, loss of capacity to sue or to be sued, loss of legal representative, a court order subjecting estate to administration or reversionary succession, provided that the legal counsel representing the model case plaintiff has applied for the suspension of the model case proceedings. Withdrawal of the complaint by the interested parties summoned shall have no effect on the progress of the model case proceedings.

Section 12
Legal Position of Interested Parties Summoned

An interested party must engage in the model case proceeding at the stage it is in at the time he is summoned; he is entitled to avail himself of means of contestation or defense and to effectively undertake all relevant procedural acts, as long as his statements and actions are not contrary to the statements and actions of his main party (model case plaintiff or model case defendant).

Section 13
Expansion of the Subject Matter of the Model Case Proceedings

(1) Within the framework of the establishment objective of the model case, model case plaintiffs, model case defendants and interested parties summoned may seek the establishment of additional points of dispute up to the conclusion of the model case proceedings, provided that the decision on their legal dispute is contingent thereupon and the court trying the matter considers them relevant.

(2) The expansion of the order referring the matter to a higher court of instance by the court trying the matter shall be without appeal and binding for the Higher Regional Court.

(3) The Higher Regional Court shall publicize the expanded order referring the matter to a higher court of instance in the Complaint Registry. Section 6, second sentence, shall apply mutatis mutandis.

Section 14
Model Case Ruling

(1) Based on an oral hearing, the Higher Regional Court shall hand down by order a model case ruling. The interested parties summoned must not be named in the heading of a model case ruling. The model case ruling shall be served on the model case

plaintiff and on the model case defendant; the interested parties summoned shall be informed thereof by informal notification. Public announcement may be made in lieu of such notification, to include the service thereof on the model case plaintiff and the model case defendant. Section 9 (2), second sentence, shall apply mutatis mutandis.

(2) The decision on the costs ensued as a result of conduct of model case proceedings shall remain a matter for the courts trying the matter at which proceedings were suspended.

(3) Sections 91a and 306 of the Code of Civil Procedure shall not apply to model case proceedings. If all interested parties (§ 8 (1)) do not consent to the settlement, conclusion of model case proceedings by way of settlement shall be inadmissible.

Section 15
Appeal on Points of Law

(1) The model case ruling may be appealed on points of law. The legal matter shall constantly have fundamental importance within the meaning of section 574 (2) no. 1 of the Code of Civil Procedure. The fact that the court trying the matter pursuant to Section 4 (1) has erroneously obtained a model case ruling may not serve as the basis for a complaint. All parties to the proceedings (Section 8 (1)) shall be entitled to file a complaint.

(2) The court of appeals shall notify the interested parties sum-

moned to the model case proceedings of the receipt of a complaint, provided that such complaint is admissible per se and was filed in the prescribed form and within the time allowed. These parties may intervene in complaint proceedings within a strict statutory period of one month as of service of such notification. Public announcement may be made in lieu of service of such notification; Section 9 (2), second sentence shall apply mutatis mutandis. The parties shall substantiate the intervening pleading within a period of one month. The time period shall begin running upon service of the notification of receipt of the complaint pursuant to the first sentence; section 551 (2), fifth and sixth sentences, of the Code of Civil Procedure shall apply mutatis mutandis. If an interested party summoned waives intervention or does not provide reasons for seeking intervention within the time period stipulated in the second sentence, then the model case proceeding before the court of appeals shall be continued without regard to him. Section 12 shall apply mutatis mutandis to the legal position of interested parties intervening in the complaint proceedings.

(3) If a model case plaintiff appeals the model case ruling on points of law, he shall then continue the model case proceedings at the appellate instance as the model case appellant. If the model case plaintiff withdraws his appeal on points of law, then the court of appeals shall designate pursuant

to Section 11 (2), first sentence, in conjunction with Section 8 (2a) a new model case appellant from among the interested parties summoned who have intervened in the appeal on points of law proceedings, unless these parties also waive continuance of the appeal.

(4) If appeal on points of law in respect of the model case ruling is not made by the model case plaintiff, but instead by one or more of the interested parties summoned, then that interested party summoned who is first to enter an appeal shall be designated the model case appellant by the appeals court. Subsection (2), first sentence, shall apply mutatis mutandis in regard to the model case plaintiff and the model case defendant.

(5) If a model case defendant enters an appeal in respect of the model case ruling, then the model case opponent to the appeal shall be the model case plaintiff determined by the Higher Regional Court. Section 574 (4), first sentence, of the Code of Civil Procedure shall apply mutatis mutandis to the interested parties summoned.

Part 3
Effect of the Model Case Ruling; Costs

Section 16
Effect of the Model Case Ruling

(1) The model case ruling shall be binding on the courts trying the matter, whose decisions depend on the establishment made on the model case or the legal question to be resolved in the model case proceedings. The order shall be defined as taking final and binding effect to the extent that a ruling has been handed down in regard to the subject matter of the model case. Without prejudice to subsection (2), the model case ruling shall have effect for and against all interested parties summoned, irrespective of whether the interested party itself has expressly complained of all the points of dispute. This shall also apply if the interested party has withdrawn its complaint in the main proceedings. Main proceedings shall be recommenced upon submission of the final and binding model case ruling by a party to the model case proceedings.

(2) Upon final and binding conclusion of the model case proceeding, the interested parties summoned shall only be heard in legal disputes brought against the opposing party which assert that the main party's presentation of the case was inadequate, provided that, on account of the stage the model case proceeding was in at the time they were summoned or on account of statements and actions of the main party, the interested parties summoned were hindered from availing themselves of means of contestation or defense, or such means of contestation or defense of which they were not aware were not availed of by the main party, either intentionally or due to gross negligence.

(3) The model case ruling shall also have effect for and against the interested parties summoned, who did not intervene in the appeal on points of law proceeding.

Section 17
Subject Matter of the Decision on Costs in Trial Proceedings

The costs ensued by the model case plaintiff and the interested parties summoned on his side for model case proceedings at first instance shall comprise part of the costs of the respective trial proceeding at first instance. The costs ensued by the model case defendant and the interested parties summoned on his side for model case proceedings at first instance shall comprise part of the costs of the respective trial proceeding at first instance. The respective share in the costs shall be determined according to the ratio of the amount of the claim made by the respective plaintiff, in so far as this is the subject matter of the model case proceeding, to the total amount of the claims made in the trial proceedings by the model case plaintiff and the interested parties summoned on his side for the model case proceeding, in so far as such claims are the subject matter of the model case proceeding. A claim shall not be considered, if the complaint in the main proceeding has been withdrawn within two weeks of service of the suspension order pursuant to Section 7. Section 96 of the Code of Civil Procedure shall apply mutatis mutandis.

Section 18
Violation of the Requirements to Reference of the Matter to the Higher Regional Court

The judgment of one of the courts trying the matter on the merits may not be contested on the basis of the allegation that the Higher Regional Court was not the court competent for handing down a ruling on a model case or that the requirements for reference to a higher court of instance in a model case proceeding have not been met.

Section 19
Decision concerning Costs in Appeal on Points of Law Proceedings

(1) The costs ensued in the filing of an appeal on points of law by the model case plaintiff or one of the interested parties summoned on his side which was unsuccessful shall be carried, depending on the degree of their intervention, by the model case appellant and those interested parties summoned who intervened in the appeal on points of law proceedings.

(2) If the appeals court itself gives the decision on the matter, the costs ensued in bringing an appeal on points of law by one of the model case defendants or one of the interested parties summoned on his side which was successful shall be carried, depending on the degree of their intervention in the model case proceedings at first instance, by the model case plaintiff and all interested parties summoned on his side.

(3) In the event of partially successful outcomes and loss, section 92 of the Code of Civil Procedure shall apply mutatis mutandis.

(4) In the event that the court of appeals sets aside the model case ruling by the Higher Regional Court and remits the matter for a new decision, the Higher Regional Court shall rule at its equitable discretion on the carrying of costs in appellate proceedings simultaneously with the handing down of its ruling on the model case proceeding. In doing so, the outcome of the model case proceeding shall be taken as its basis. Section 99 (1) shall apply mutatis mutandis.

(5) If the model case plaintiff and the interested parties summoned on his side are ordered to pay costs ensued in the appellate proceedings, they shall reimburse court fees advanced by the model case defendant or the interested parties summoned on his side and the attorney's fees of the model case defendant or the interested parties summoned on his side according to the respective value arising from the claims made by them in the trial proceedings which are the subject matter of the model case proceeding.

Section 20
Transitional Provisions

In respect of proceedings in which prior to 1 November 2010 an application for the establishment of a model case was submitted, this law and those provisions amended by Articles 2 to 8 of the Act on the Initiation of Model Case Proceedings in respect of Investors in the Capital Markets in the version in force prior to 1 November 2010 shall continue to apply.

Index